COUNSELING PARENTS OF THE MENTALLY RETARDED

A Sourcebook

COUNSELING PARENTS OF THE MENTALLY RETARDED

A Sourcebook

Compiled and Edited by

ROBERT L. NOLAND

Professor of Psychology
University of Dayton
Dayton, Ohio

CHARLES C THOMAS • PUBLISHER

Springfield • Illinois • U.S.A.

Published and Distributed Throughout the World by

CHARLES C THOMAS • PUBLISHER

Bannerstone House

301-327 East Lawrence Avenue, Springfield, Illinois, U.S.A.

Natchez Plantation House

735 North Atlantic Boulevard, Fort Lauderdale, Florida, U.S.A.

*With THOMAS BOOKS careful attention is given to all details of
manufacturing and design. It is the Publisher's desire to present books that are
satisfactory as to their physical qualities and artistic possibilities and
appropriate for their particular use. THOMAS BOOKS will be true to those
laws of quality that assure a good name and good will.*

Dedicated to parents of retarded children, whose courage, initiative, and perseverance have finally marshalled the forces of social understanding and professional assistance they have long deserved.

Introduction

ON the very day this introduction is being written, approximately 300 more infants destined to be mentally retarded are being born in the United States. They will join, at the estimated rate of 100,000 new cases a year, the six to seven *million* mentally retarded individuals in our country. The comparatively high incidence and the tragic implications of this condition may be better appreciated by comparison with other representative disabilities of a severe nature. For example, of each 100,000 persons in our population, an estimated 200 are blind, 350 have cerebral palsy, and 700 are afflicted by rheumatic heart conditions, while *3,000 are mentally retarded.* Only four significant disabling conditions − mental illness, cardiac disease, arthritis, and cancer − have a higher prevalence, but they tend to come later in life, whereas mental retardation comes early.

It has been almost two decades since the writer was invited to address a newly formed group of parents of retarded children. As a part of that evening's workshop, a fifty-item test of knowledge and attitudes regarding mental deficiency was administered to the entire group and the results then used as a basis for later discussion. I can still remember how appalled I was upon seeing their test scores. Misinformation, misbelief, misinterpretation, denial, and selective perception characterized the reactions of parents in this audience. In later meetings − both with groups and individuals − these perceptions and impressions were validated. These parents − representative we think − were confused and guilt ridden, frantically searching for help which should have been openly available to them. There are six million retarded, twelve million parents, and, with other siblings in the family, perhaps twenty-five million individuals in need of varying amounts of professional assistance, understanding, and counseling.

While little had been done to assist parents of the mentally retarded prior to the second half of our century, the professional helping specialties have since then become increasingly conscious of the need to deal not just with the retarded child but with his entire family, especially his parents.

To further this professional activity, the writer has attempted to collect for this book information specifically directed at the counseling of parents of mentally retarded individuals. The articles chosen do not deal with problems such as classification, diagnosis, or care of the mentally retarded, except in a peripheral manner. The interested reader will find ample and excellent material on these other aspects of mental retardation in the literature. Each article was chosen in terms of pertinence to the topic of "counseling parents." The several exceptions to this focus are the initial articles, intended to reveal to the reader the feelings and attitudes of parents, and several articles on genetic counseling, found in the last section.

For whom is such a book intended? The broad and diverse nature of mental retardation is such that it cuts across medical, legal, psychological, social, educational, religious, and economic lines. While there are, of course, pediatricians, child psychiatrists, and child psychologists whose specialties include this series of disorders, there are many other professional and paraprofessional workers who find themselves in the position of being asked to aid the parents of a mentally retarded child. The family physician, the psychologist, the social worker, the pastor or rabbi, and the educator are examples of individuals who may well today play a role in parental counseling or therapy. While these people are presumed to be proficient and self-confident in the performance of their professional activities, they are often at a great loss when called upon to counsel parents of retarded children, especially if the condition of retardation has just been discovered. That many parents have come away from professional interviews with feelings of hurt, bewilderment, frustration, and disbelief is readily seen in a perusal of literature reporting on parental reactions. Certain of these reactions result from parental use of ego-defensive mechanisms such as denial and selective perception. But it is also patently obvious that some unfortunate parental reactions are the result of incorrect diagnosis, evasion and distortion, callousness, and seemingly brutal frankness, with no attempt at the all-important, follow-up counseling procedures. It is hoped that a perusal of the articles in this collection will aid the reader — regardless of his or her level of competence and experience — in better understanding parental attitudes and feelings and in better preparing for effective counseling relationships.

It is also believed that this book will be useful in a number of college courses in the fields of clinical psychology and special education. It is of course well suited for specific courses in counseling exceptional children and in counseling parents of the mentally retarded child, courses which are at last finding their place in the college curriculum.

Part I of this sourcebook contains articles designed to provide an overall orientation to this topic. Included are articles designed to show parental feelings and general theory papers on parental attitudes. This section is followed in Part II by a series of papers dealing with the crucial issue of counseling parents at the time they are first told of their child's deficiency. Following these articles are others dealing with individual counseling sessions with parents. Part III contains a number of articles dealing with the group-counseling process when used for both orientation and parent therapeutic purposes. Part IV contains several articles revealing the role of casework activities and the problems involved in the parental decision to place the retarded child in an institution. Represented in the earlier sections of the book are psychiatrists, psychologists, and social workers. Part V contains a series of articles dealing with the pastoral counseling of parents, an area only now being fully recognized for its potential help and responsibility to the family of the retarded. Part VI deals with genetic counseling, an area not too often considered by the nonspecialist. However, these articles not only present excellent explanations of the genetic basis of certain types of deficiency but also provide excellent advice for the individual who must — or should — deal with the hereditable nature and consequences of mental deficiency.

The articles in this collection come from a great variety of journals and cover a twenty-year time span. The writer is less concerned with the publication date than with the quality of the contribution. The reader should realize, however, that in some ways information from rapidly changing fields — such as molecular genetics — may have changed in certain factual details; this was considered unavoidable and an insufficient reason not to include such articles. In the area of genetic counseling, for example, one would hope that more widespread use of this service will reduce the reproduction rate in high-risk cases. Also, the practical application of the literally fantastic advances in this field, (e.g. single-gene photography, gene isolation, and chemical replication) may someday allow the replacement of defective or impotent genes through enzyme-carried artificial genes, thus preventing certain types of hereditable deficiency.

The Appendix contains information for both the parents of retarded and the person serving them in a counseling capacity. The major state and national associations listed are both public and private clinics, schools, residential facilities, and day care sheltered workshops which are available nationally.

Also in the Appendix is an extensive listing of audiovisual aids — mainly films — produced to provide greater awareness and understanding of the mentally retarded child's problems and prospects.

Acknowledgments

T HE editor wishes to express his appreciation to the authors who so graciously consented to the inclusion of their articles in this sourcebook. To the extent that there is merit in collections such as this, it is obviously due to the scholarly, creative, and empathic efforts of the authors whose works are represented in this volume.

Thanks are also due to the editors and publishers of the following journals for permission to reprint articles from their periodicals: *American Journal of Human Genetics, American Journal of Mental Deficiency, Clinical Pediatrics, Exceptional Children, Eugenics Quarterly, Journal of Pediatrics, Manitoba Medical Review, Mental Retardation, Pastoral Psychology, Rehabilitation Literature,* and *Today's Health.*

R.L.N.

Contents

PART III

Group Counseling with Parents of Retarded Children

PART IV

Family Casework and Child Placement

PART V

Pastoral Counseling

COUNSELING PARENTS OF THE MENTALLY RETARDED

A Sourcebook

PART I

PARENTS' FEELINGS ABOUT
THEIR MENTALLY RETARDED CHILDREN

Chapter 1

Don't Speak to Us of Living Death

As told to ROBERTA ROBINSON

W E have a happy home life — my wife and I. A simple statement, that, but we never make it to our friends. They can't believe it. In those days before we learned, I knew that at least once during an evening out I could expect to hear Joyce, almost hysterical, say above the conversation to some earnest neighbor, "But we have a *very* happy home life, a normal one!"

Her protest always created a nervous little flurry of cleared throats, shuffling feet, or — much worse — silence.

The uselessness of trying to convince acquaintances that our home is as happy as any of theirs became clear just before our third child, Jeff, was born. Joyce and I had been out for her evening walk and had dropped in at the Burnses'. The practical nurse who lives with us was at home with Eddie and Nancy.

Across the room I heard Mrs. Burns adopt the maternal tone of our maybe well-intentioned but certainly tactless neighbors, which meant she was thinking of our boy Eddie.

"Oh, I know you're happy, my dear. I'm sure of it," she said to Joyce. "You and your husband are so *brave*, having another one. With *living death* right in your home that way . . . "

Three or four years previously such a piece of nonsense would have sent Joyce crying from the room. But with those years behind her, Joyce merely looked at Mrs. Burns, smiled and said, "Living death? What is that?"

Mrs. Burns flushed, swallowed, and looked away. She said

Note: Reprinted by permission of *Today's Health,* published by the American Medical Association, June, 1951.

nothing. Joyce and I left as soon as we could.

"What is there about people that makes them want to dig inside another person and try to hurt her?" Joyce asked as we walked home. "They look on us almost as animals. We're set apart from everyone else. They sit there, smugly training their microscopes on us to see how we react when they stick us with a pin."

"Let's quit trying to make them understand," I said. "It's no use."

We have never explained our home life since. Instead, we've made our home a mysterious island, immune to the probing, pity, and curiosity of friends and relatives. We inhabitants of that island are happy with it. We think that holds true for Eddie, our first child, now nine years old, the real object of this misplaced sympathy.

You see, Eddie is one of the million children born in every generation whose brain never develops. Our oldest boy is no more than an idiot. We accept that fact. But until that day four years ago when both of us faced it, we had no family life, we were on the brink of divorce, and Joyce teetered dangerously on the terrifying edge of insanity.

If Eddie had been born with the domed forehead and slanted eyes that characterize the mongoloid, or had been afflicted with seizures, perhaps it would not have taken us five years to resign ourselves to being parents of feeble-mindedness. But he was a beautifully formed baby, and he weighed an adequate seven pounds.

At times, because of his refusal to take nourishment, we feared he would surely starve. But today he looks for all the world like a normal nine-year-old, though his arm and leg muscles are slightly flabby from disuse. A hundred loose, brown curls twist over his head. His sole outward sign of idiocy is the vague shadow of a smile that flickers continually across his face. Joyce and I have made up a story about that smile. We say he gazes out on some rich greenness that exists only in that other world where he lived before the accident.

We always speak of what must have happened as the accident.

Dr. Green introduced us to the word. He had delivered Joyce. It was her last evening in the hospital. I sat beside her bed, warmed by the sight of her fingers lightly playing across the pink skin of the baby's face. The door opened softly. I looked up to see Dr. Green standing at the foot of the bed. His face was tight. His lips looked thin and pinched. It wasn't till he began speaking that I noticed his hands gripping the footboard of the hospital bed.

"Don't take my word as final," he said. "Yet I would be less than honest if I didn't give you my frank opinion." The words seemed to come in tiny puffs and spurts, as though he pushed them out with great effort. "Eddie is the victim of one of nature's accidents. I'm afraid his brain will never develop. He has all the signs of feeble-mindedness."

Through the closed door I heard the voices of other visitors. Somewhere a small boy cried that he wouldn't go home without his mother.

"How can you tell?" Joyce's voice, reedy, fearful, yet incisive, cut through the welter of hospital sounds and my half-formed hopes that this wasn't happening to us. Her voice was too aggressive. She drew the baby closer in a protective gesture. "He's only five days old. How can you tell?"

Joyce had expected this, then. She had already sensed something was wrong.

Instinctively I moved to the bed to stare with my wife at this man we had come to trust — our doctor. He couldn't meet our eyes. His knuckles showed white against the iron rung. His words, broken and harsh, came haltingly as he tried to explain.

"There are thousands of exceptional children born every year," he said. "You must not let it frighten you or affect your normal life."

As he talked, I reached for Joyce's hand and felt the gentle moistness of the baby's breath against my fingers. The very robustness of his young life seemed refutation enough of the doctor's theory. Feeble-mindedness went with deformed and misshapen bodies.

"It would be criminal to hold out false hope," Green was saying. "But for your own sake you should consult other doctors."

For just a split second he looked into our faces. Suddenly I was overcome with dislike for this man. I wanted to hit him. Then he turned, and without looking back he left the room.

"Don't worry," I was saying to myself, and then to Joyce as I held her hand. "We'll see other doctors. Even Green admits he may be wrong . . ."

On that note we set sail on a five-year voyage. Our ultimate goal: peace of mind. We could not know, we could not be told, that our route had been previously charted for us. We were explorers of a great unknown — we thought.

Years later, when we could face facts, we learned that we had followed a pattern so undeviating from the usual one as to be tragic. Parents, when they learn of a child's affliction, pass through three well-defined stages. Each of the first two stages is punctuated by a short intermission marked by despair of ever curing the child's idiocy. But once rested, the couple invariably sets out again on the long journey.

We went through all three stages.

Denial

Stage I is a period of frantic searching for proof that the child is not subnormal. It consists of (1) repudiation of the family physician, (2) correspondence with authorities in the field of abnormal child psychology, and (3) visits to psychiatrists and specialists all over the land. This period lasts as long as family finances allow.

Search

Stage II is a crusade to prove the specialists wrong. During this time the husband senses a gradual change in his wife. She (1) loses all interest in sex, (2) refuses to mix in society, (3) neglects her ordinary work, and (4) devotes every waking hour to frenzied training of her child. She often convinces herself that the child is actually a misunderstood genius.

This is the most dangerous stage. If it persists too long, it leads to a broken home, and sometimes to the mother's complete insanity. Birth of an afflicted child leads to divorce in 50 percent of the cases.

Acceptance

Stage III takes place only when both parents accept their child as subnormal and arrange their lives accordingly. If a separation has already taken place, the mother often devotes her days to the child's care. Sometimes a semblance of home life remains, but the parents, through fear, resolve never again to have children. The most stable people place their child in an environment specially created to care for him. These parents have two alternatives. First, they can keep the child at home, have other children, and build as nearly normal a home life as possible. Second, they can put him in an institution, have other children, build a happy life without him.

The first stage began for us on the day Joyce left the hospital, and we resolved never to call Dr. Green again. A month later I took a six weeks' leave from the engineering consultant firm where I worked, checked out all our money from the bank, and set out with Joyce and Eddie for Baltimore.

We had three conferences with the Baltimore specialist. The day we waited for our final meeting, the man in the gray suit entered the reception room and sat beside me. Twice I'd passed him on the stairs during Eddie's examinations. Once he nodded as though he would like to talk. I hurried on. For some reason I felt a shame at even being there, at this stranger's sensing that we had something in common.

"This is your first trip with your boy, isn't it?" he said softly.

I stared at the opposite wall and tried to recall by what telltale sign I had given away our secret. Eddie had been in the nursery from the moment we arrived. How could this man know why Joyce and I were here?

"This is our fourth visit," he said. "Twice we've carried our boy to Chicago. Once we went to Boston."

"Your son is . . . ," I hesitated over the right word.

"Mongoloid," he said. "A dozen different doctors have said so. But my wife won't believe it."

He hunched his shoulders and scuffed his foot on the rubber floor mat. The nurse called for Joyce and me to come into the office.

Hurriedly, I stood up. "My son isn't mongoloid." I heard my own voice, sharp and crackling. "Eddie isn't like a mongoloid at all." I walked rapidly after Joyce into the doctor's office.

The specialist gave the verdict quickly and simply. For some reason Eddie's brain was not growing. Briefly he told us what we already knew: all babies are born idiots, because the cortex is the last portion of the brain to develop. Normally, once the child is born, the cortex cells multiply and mature faster than any other part of the body. By the time the child is three, its ability to learn is formed for life. Sometimes, however, the stimulus required to start cell growth is lacking. When this happens, you must adjust yourselves to the fact that nature made a mistake.

Such arrested development can be due to birth injury, prenatal fever or virus disease in the mother, the unexplainable loss of genes when the chromosomes split up in the embryo stage, certain congenital diseases, or (after birth) to a disease affecting the meninges, or membranes surrounding the brain.

The specialist finished and smoothed the rattling papers on his glass-topped desk. It seemed useless to question the diagnosis. Dr. Green at least had left a suggestion of doubt; this man did not.

"What can we do?" Joyce said.

The specialist removed his glasses and rubbed his eyes.

"Get rid of the idea that you're responsible," he said. "I find no clue in your medical history that logically explains why this happened. Nature made a mistake. You must adjust yourselves just as you would if Eddie had been born blind."

For some time after we left the office, Joyce and I sat on a bench in a little park across from the hospital. Neither of us spoke of the diagnosis. As we waited, I saw the man in gray emerge from the hospital. He trailed behind a woman leading a small boy. After they were lost in the traffic, I wondered if I should tell Joyce about their travels. I didn't.

At the end of five weeks we had seen psychiatrists and been to hospitals in Baltimore, New York, Chicago, and Philadelphia. The result was always the same: no hope. The expensive tests and consultation fees, plus hotel and travel expenses, had exhausted our savings. I knew I should return to the office. Still I held back. I was convinced the doctors were right. But I couldn't say that to Joyce.

Then one night I awoke to hear her sobbing.

"Don't cry," I said. "Please, please, don't cry. We'll try the one in Kansas. He's supposed to be doing something new."

With her head on my shoulder, her sobs gradually died away. "I just want to go home," she said. "I can't bear to hear another doctor say it's hopeless. It's time we made the best of it. We've nothing to be ashamed of. Our family and friends will understand."

That ended Stage I. We were safely through it in less than three months. I thought it was the end of the journey; Joyce must have thought so, too . . . for a time.

It was almost as if we had come home with our son for the first time. Before we started on the round of hospitals, we had treated furtively all inquiries about Eddie. We didn't want anyone to suspect. Now we welcomed questions and paraded our newly acquired medical knowledge before all comers. We explained Eddie's lack of brains as simply as if we had been telling why his eyes were blue instead of brown. This frankness produced a curious result.

Bickering broke out between Joyce's folks and mine. Her mother and aunts, particularly, were shocked that we discussed the matter so openly. Over and over they searched the family tree to find some reason for this awful scandal. It did no good to tell them that feeble-mindedness could be traced to heredity in only 15 percent of the cases.

"I've checked every member on *our* side of the family back through Great-Great-Grandfather Justin Whiteside," Joyce's Aunt Myrtle told me. "I've decided it must come from your folks."

Naturally my mother felt she must uphold my side of the family. Joyce and I stayed busy keeping Aunt Myrtle and Mother from meeting on Main street and engaging in their grand debate.

We assumed the young married crowd we ran with would understand and be interested in our experience. But the light-hearted way in which we joked about the "guilt complex" of our families never struck our friends as amusing. We sensed in their insinuating questions an intolerable smugness. When I said such accidents might happen to anybody, a silence always fell on the room. The hostess usually changed the subject.

"I'll be darned if I go back to Grace's house ever again," Joyce said one evening as we drove home from a bridge party. She had gone to the kitchen to help with the refreshments and overheard Grace and another guest whispering about Eddie.

Not knowing we were the victims of pattern behavior as surely as if a script had given us stage directions and lines, we launched ourselves into Stage II.

We dropped all social contacts: the bridge group, the Sunday school class, Saturday nights at the country club, Sunday evenings with relatives. When we received an invitation, it always seemed easier to beg off. We had a ready-made excuse. We had to take care of Eddie.

Taking care of Eddie was a major job. From birth, he lacked the instinct to take nourishment. They fed him intravenously at the hospital. At home we frantically forced milk and baby food down his throat to keep him from starving. Eddie weighed seven pounds at birth; six months later he weighed seven and one-quarter.

Since Eddie never cried, Joyce developed extrasensory powers to discover his illnesses. She thought of nothing but his care. I prepared my own meals and spent every free minute from the office helping her. Slowly we came to understand that Eddie lived in another world. If he was to survive, we had to bridge the gap between his world and ours.

After two years, we were proud of our accomplishments. He still could not walk. He made no attempt to talk. But he was eating. The day he doubled his weight, Joyce could not have been more proud if he had graduated from college magna cum laude.

"Eddie's going to be all right," she said. "Everyone's going to see that Eddie's all right."

When his fourth birthday came around, Eddie had learned to walk. He knew to tug at his mother's dress when he wanted to go to the bathroom. He still did not talk. The three of us had a birthday party for him. The highlight came when Joyce placed a cake with four lighted candles before him. We waited, hardly daring to breathe, until he leaned forward and solemnly blew out the candles.

"Darling, he did it," Joyce fairly screamed. "He blew out the candles!"

The tears rolled down her cheeks. I could only guess at the hours she had spent with him, practicing this simple act. That she succeeded spoke volumes for Joyce's patience and courage. I smiled to show my pleasure, and Eddie watched us with his vacant, other-world expression.

But even patience and courage must be limited by human endurance. Joyce was fast approaching the breaking point. She was twenty pounds underweight and actually looked older than her mother.

I made my first visit to Dr. Green since the night he had told us of Eddie's condition. When I told him about Joyce, he shared my alarm.

He advised placing Eddie in a special training school for exceptional children. He named several, and I filed the idea for future use.

Meanwhile, I suggested to Joyce that we hire a part-time nurse to spell her a few hours each day and allow her to get away from the house. Joyce flared up at me. "How could you even think such a thing?" she said. "I'm never going to leave Eddie with a stranger."

A few days later Eddie slipped out of the house while Joyce napped. It took her an hour to find him sitting on a curb three blocks away.

"He might have been killed," she said to me over and over. "He might have been hit by a truck and killed."

What better chance could I have to mention Dr. Green's idea about the school; I stroked her tangled hair, its shine lost long ago in her preoccupation with Eddie, and Joyce gradually relaxed.

"Darling, you must get some rest," I said. "Your health will break down. It won't be for long, but let's place Eddie in a special school where they build an environment designed to . . . "

Joyce sprang from my arms like some wild animal.

"No," she cried. "You'll never take Eddie from me!"

She ran to his room and locked the door from the inside. For hours I begged her to listen to reason. Only the singsong of a lullaby reached me. I knew she was holding Eddie on her lap, rocking him. I lay awake all night, realizing Joyce no longer lived in my world. She was in that other one with Eddie.

In my desperation, Joyce's siege with pneumonia seemed a blessing. She had a cold, but again refused to let me hire a nurse to help with Eddie. Two days later she had pneumonia, and Dr. Green rushed her to the hospital.

"I'm going to keep her there for a two months' convalescence," he said to me. "You get Eddie in one of those schools I told you about."

That was how Eddie was placed in the school for exceptional children. He was with several hundred small children. Like Eddie, each lived in a special world of his own. But instead of attempting to train the children for our world, the teachers had created an environment in which the exceptional child was the norm.

Under the influence of sedatives, Joyce seemed only mildly interested. Once she asked to see Eddie, and I took him to the hospital for a visit. The fact that he was clean and his cheeks were pink and full seemed to dissipate whatever fears she felt. Most of the time I talked of other things. Dr. Green felt it was important that Joyce's interest in everyday life be reawakened.

As she grew stronger I carried popular books and magazines to her. I urged old friends to call on her. One afternoon three of them played several rubbers of bridge across the hospital bed. Rest and care worked their curative powers. After two months, we brought her home.

Perhaps Joyce's apparent progress made me overconfident. I had engaged a practical nurse to relieve Joyce of routine housework and keep her company during the readjustment period. And those first weeks after my wife came home were in many ways like the first months of our marriage. We went to church, to the theater, to ball games, to parties. Once a week we visited Eddie at the school. I believed Joyce had now accepted Eddie's idiocy. Only one worry remained.

"I want you two to have more children," Dr. Green had said. "The only way Joyce can be happy is by lavishing her love on other children."

When I considered my own desire for a large family, I knew nothing could please me more. Joyce once had shared these desires, but with Eddie's birth she changed. Even in those early days when she argued passionately that what had happened to Eddie was an accident, I found her afraid in the intimacy of our bedroom. At first she argued she was too busy with Eddie to have more children. Later I sensed in her frigidity the determination never to have another child.

In all outward respects, Joyce seemed fully recovered. But this fixation against more children remained. Then Eddie's fifth birthday came. It fell on a Sunday. Joyce asked me to bring him home for the weekend. "I'll take him back Monday morning," she said.

It seemed a harmless enough request and I agreed.

When I came in from work Monday evening, I found the house dark, the kitchen empty. The companion-nurse, Mrs. Jordan, was not there. Reassuring myself that Joyce must be visiting her mother, I went upstairs. The door to Eddie's room was locked. There wasn't a sound.

"Joyce, are you in there?" I called.

I heard footsteps in the room, then the click of the lock. In the dim light I saw her standing in the nursery door holding him in her arms.

"Didn't you take him back?" I asked. "Where's Mrs. Jordan?"

"Eddie isn't going back," she said quietly. "He wants to stay with me." She held the door open only a few inches. When I moved toward her, she slammed it and locked it in my face.

"Don't lock me out, Joyce," I cried. "What happened to Mrs. Jordan?"

"We don't need her now," she said. "I told her she could go."

Nothing I did could persuade her to open the door. When I phoned Dr. Green, he advised me to let her alone. "Joyce's mind may be permanently injured if you take Eddie from her now," he said.

For the next few weeks, Joyce acted as if the period of her illness and recovery were blanked from her memory. The routine she followed before the pneumonia attack returned, the all its confining frustration. Once again, I saw her fade. Her hair hung straight and unkempt. Sometimes at night I heard her coughing long after she went to bed in Eddie's nursery where she had set up a cot.

Knowing Joyce's breakdown would inevitably repeat itself, I brooded over my frustrated ambitions for a family. These worries showed up in my work. I made several blunders in figuring a construction job. If they had not been caught, the firm would have lost heavily. My boss ordered me to take a month's vacation. I spent hours wandering the streets.

Once I found myself in front of a bookstore. A pyramid of a hundred or more books filled the window. All had red and yellow dust jackets; all had the title, *Is Divorce the Way?*

Aimlessly I drifted along the sidewalk among the afternoon shoppers. I loved Joyce with all my heart, but Joyce was no longer the same woman I had married. In this state of mind I entered Dr. Green's office. I had reached a conclusion. If there was no hope for Joyce, then I must attempt to build a new life without her. I didn't know it, but Stage II was drawing to a close. The receptionist seemed surprised.

"Dr. Green is at your house now," she said. "Your wife phoned several hours ago that Eddie was sick."

In ten minutes I was home. Dr. Green and Joyce sat in the living room.

"I'm so glad you've come, darling," Joyce said. "The doctor and I have been having a long talk."

She told me how Eddie began running a fever that morning. She was not alarmed at first. But when he refused lunch, she called Dr. Green. I noticed a change in Joyce as she talked. A calmness had replaced the restive quality in her eyes. That baffling other-world attitude seemed to be gone. I watched her come to the divan where I sat and shyly take hold of my hand.

"Dr. Green says Eddie is sick because he misses his playmates at the school," she said. "He says Eddie will be happier if we give him some brothers and sisters.

Dr. Green was sitting across the room. My impulse was to stare at him, to demand to know what tricks he was playing on the sick mind of my wife. But some deeper sense warned me to keep silent. Trick or science, the doctor had produced a remarkable change in Joyce. She was telling me we must have other children.

Partly to make sure I wasn't dreaming and partly to hide the tears in my eyes, I pulled Joyce to me and kissed her. Gone were the inner tensions I'd felt at every previous gesture of intimacy.

"Are you sure you want to keep him, Joyce?" Dr. Green asked.

"Oh, yes," she said. "I know you're right. I've known all along there was no hope, but I couldn't help trying. I love him. I want to keep him."

"Then you've got to understand the job you have before you," he said. "You've got to restrain yourself. You cannot smother him with affection as you have in the past. You've got to limit your time with him. You must not permit his life to destroy your own."

I felt Joyce tighten in my arms; then, once again, the tautness disappeared. She sat relaxed.

Before he left, Dr. Green gave us the name of a responsible practical nurse. Mrs. Coates came the same evening. She has been with us ever since. That night we set up a schedule. As far as I know, Joyce has never violated it. She sees Eddie twice a day: thirty minutes in the morning, an hour in the afternoon. One night a week we care for Eddie while Mrs. Coates goes out.

It was hard for Joyce. During those first months I awoke several nights to find her crying beside me. But through her own determination, and with Dr. Green's kindly but firm hand to guide us, she gradually completed the journey back to our world.

We have now been in Stage III for four years. We have created a special environment in Eddie's room. It cannot last forever. Someday we'll put him in an institution. Joyce is willing. But for the time being we think his presence in our home is healthy.

Recently we celebrated his ninth birthday. This time it was no exclusive family affair. Nancy, now three, invited half-a-dozen neighborhood playmates to the party. While the other kids played rough and tumble on the nursery floor, Eddie sat quietly in his chair by the window, the wind tousling his hair.

We've told Nancy about Eddie. She treats him sympathetically. She loves him. He loves her. When the birthday cake was cut, she stood beside Eddie's chair and fed him the first piece. It was a matter of pride with Nancy. Before the party ended, each of the guests wanted a chance to feed Eddie.

Our Nancy is learning a lesson that will be with her all her life. In a home that is sunny and happy she comes in daily contact with the underprivileged — her brother. She has developed tenderness and sympathy toward him. We think it must carry over to later life.

There will be a stage when she must endure the taunts of playmates. Her own greater understanding and love will carry her through. She will be stronger than the jeers and whispers because she will pity the ignorance and superstition behind them. And what better quality could a parent want in his child than the capacity and strength to defend the mentally and physically handicapped?

As Jeff, the baby, grows older, he will share the job of bridging

Eddie's world and ours. Dr. Green agrees that as an experiment in life, our children couldn't have a better school than our home.

Living death? Don't speak to us of living death. We have a happy home and three children of whom we're proud. We feel no shame because of Eddie. He has his niche as much as any of us. Lacking in brains, doomed by an accident, he has made the greatest contribution of all: every day he teaches us anew the wisdom of courage, patience, and sympathy.

Chapter 2

The Parents of Retarded
Children Speak for Themselves*

CHARLOTTE H. WASKOWITZ

WITHIN the last decade there has been vast
development and rapid progress in the total area of mental
retardation — more and better resources; specialized clinical and
counseling services; training, educational, and recreational facilities; medical research; and financial aid. Concomitantly, there has
been widespread interest in professional circles as well as in the
community, increased understanding, acceptance, and tolerance of
the mentally retarded child and his family. Much of the credit for
the impetus to this important movement belongs to the parents of
retarded children who, because of their persistence, perserverance,
and courage, have shown the way. It is the parents themselves who
have given us clues about their own capacity and strength to find
the solutions and resolutions to their problems.

Although much has been accomplished, one area that is a
constant source of difficulty is that of communication between
parents and professional personnel. Frequently the parents of a
retarded child go away from a contact with a physician,
psychologist, or social worker with a good deal of justifiable
dissatisfaction. This is not an isolated occurrence but tends to be
rather widespread, and as professional persons we must assume the
responsibility and blame for these difficulties. The services that are
offered can and should be improved. As a means of improving

Note: Reprinted with permission from the author and *Journal of Pediatrics, 54*:319-329,
1959. Copyrighted by The C.V. Mosby Co., St. Louis, Mo.
*From the Children's Psychiatric Clinic, The Johns Hopkins Hospital, Baltimore,
Maryland.

these services, the author enlisted the participation of the Maryland Society for Mentally Retarded Children and interviewed the parents in the following exploratory study.

With the approval of the officers and members of the Society, a letter was sent to every fourth member stating the purpose of the study. A questionnaire was developed as a general guide, with the full knowledge that this study would produce qualitative material of importance although not statistically impressive. In general, the guide fell into the following categories: (1) identifying data, (2) when retardation was first suspected by parents, (3) consultations by specialists, (4) counseling by professional persons and parents' reactions to counseling, and (5) value of group organization to the parents. Interviews were held by the author in the Harriet Lane Psychiatric Clinic; the average length of interview time was approximately one hour and, with few exceptions, it was the mother who came for the interview. Of a group of fifty to whom letters were sent and follow-up contacts made, forty were seen; of the ten remaining, the majority could not be reached and only three refused to participate. It should be noted that the group was carefully selected one, and the material is based on recall; therefore, the study does not lend itself to usual statistical methods.

In general, the parents can be described as an intelligent group of young and middle-aged people, with small families of two and three children, of the white race, and the middle socioeconomic class. Diagnostically, the children could be placed into the following categories: nineteen mongoloid, fifteen brain damaged, one epileptic, one seriously emotionally disturbed, and four of unexplained etiology. There was one instance of a family with two retarded children.

Answers to the questions "When did you first suspect something was wrong?" "Was someone professionally consulted at that time?" and "Who really told you your child was retarded?" were inconclusive. One explanation is the time lapse and the problem of recall, since this material was gathered from several months to many years after the patient was diagnosed as retarded. However, other factors that bear consideration are (1) problems in diagnosing, and (2) the parents' reactions to the seriousness of the problem of retardation, to their feeling of difference from other parents, and the resultant feelings of fear and anxiety.

Often there is much uncertainty in diagnosis because many different factors must be weighed and evaluated, such as (1) physical, (2) emotional, and (3) limitations in the tests themselves and the difficulties surrounding the testing, particularly of young children. The process of considering physical factors that complicate accurate evaluation frequently involves referral to many different specialists with their variety of opinions and, certainly, their uniquely different ways of handling the parents. It is not unusual to hear such expressions as "My doctor did not know whether his slowness was due to his mental condition or to his physical sickness." "The doctor was confused as to whether the child could hear." "The doctor's first impression was muscular dystrophy and then in another examination he thought he was just retarded." Occasionally the influence of emotional factors must be considered, which necessitates intensive involvement of the parents in recapitulation of bitter life experiences. The limitations of the tests themselves, just in terms of evaluating intelligence, lend another element of doubt. Certainly the innumerable difficulties in having the child perform at his best and in obtaining as much as possible from him create questions and doubts. In other words, are the test results representative of the child's intelligence? And, lastly, the adequacy and skill of the tester add another problem to the welter of confusion.

First mention of retardation has a serious impact on parents, which is understandable in view of the attitude of society and the problems of the intellectually limited child in achieving a safe, secure place in our culture. The very practical aspects of everyday living, training, schooling, recreation and, lastly, occupation and self-support have been almost insurmountable. It is no wonder then that usual responses were "It's like someone came to you and told you your child was dead." "When we were told, it was a terrible shock — you stop living." "I was on the verge of a nervous breakdown." It is not surprising, therefore, that these reactions are followed by acute feelings of aloneness, difference, being set apart from the rest of the world, rejection, and lack of interest in the children and their problems. This is vividly illustrated by such comments as "None of the doctors said anything to me; I couldn't even get any schooling for him." "We got so nervous – everywhere we went nobody would help us." "We then thought it was God's will and we did not go anywhere." "I feel the doctors brushed me off." "I feel that the medical profession did not want to be bothered, were impatient and annoyed." "We did not find anyone who sat down and told us what the problem was." "They just push you from one person to another." Is it any wonder then that there are expressions of anxiety, embarrassment, and guilt? As one parent said, "The doctor did not want to be bothered. I was embarrassed to go to his office. I had to sit with other people's children. I was always treated with the attitude: 'Here comes this woman with this child.' The doctor did not like him and did not mince any words about it." Another said, "The majority of professional people we dealt with left us with the feeling that if you had a child who wasn't normal, you should be ashamed of it."

Of the total group of forty, in thirty of the cases studied, the parents suspected or were aware of retardation in the first year of life. Of the mongoloid group of nineteen, in thirteen instances the parents were aware of and/or were told of the serious deficiency within the first month. The brain-damaged and the etiologically unspecified cases of mental retardation took longer to diagnose. In the brain-damaged group, twelve were suspected of retardation under one year of age (3 of whom were known under the age of 1 month) and the remaining three took up to three years to diagnose. In the cases where no specific cause of retardation was known, one was diagnosed at age twenty days, one at eight months, one at one year, and one at eighteen months. In the two remaining cases, the epileptic was diagnosed at ten months, and the other was diagnosed as questionable retardation due to emotional factors. Therefore, we must conclude that mental retardation was serious enough to be detected reasonably early in this group of children.

As one would expect, it was the pediatrician who was most frequently consulted first (in 25 instances). This was followed, in order of frequency, by the family doctor in seven instances, the obstetrician in three, the neurologist in one, and the child guidance clinic in one. In three instances the parents "just knew" and did not consult anyone at the time. "Were others consulted and at what ages?" prompted mention of a succession of medical specialists too numerous to record. Illustrative is one parent's comment, "I must have had Billy to over one hundred different doctors." Another replied, "I must have spent over eight thousand dollars for various consultations, to no avail." Unfortunately, parents did not seem to obtain the help they needed early enough to prevent the trauma of endless pursuit of answers to their problems. Perhaps significant is the fact that the "end of the road" seems to be the child guidance clinic, psychologist, or psychiatrist whom the parents finally seek in desperation, usually after the child is two years of age. Also significant is the fact that one half of these patients finally reached these specialists.

"Who really told you?" produced only one significant point, namely, many parents "just knew" or suspected serious pathology long before affirmation by specialists. The author has found that it is not an unusual occurrence in clinical work for a parent to be able to state fairly accurately the intellectual level at which his child is functioning at the time he is seen. What the parents are really asking for is not just a diagnosis but total handling of the problem.

The question "How were you told your child was retarded?" evoked the most intense responses, indicative of the traumatic experiences suffered by so many of these parents. The striking thing that permeated this section was that the different reactions to what parents considered good and poor handling varied according to their own individual needs, so that one is forced to conclude that the most important consideration is the ability of the counselor to individualize and to be sensitive to where the parents are emotionally at a particular time — in other words, to empathize with the parents. Some parents wanted to be told directly as soon as retardation was suspected. A typical comment was, "The doctor was very frank about it. It was very positive and in no way abrupt. We were aware of what the situation was, and we appreciated knowing this." Another commented, "I was told right at the beginning. We were always thankful to the doctor who did tell us." On the other hand, many parents indicated their wish to be prepared gradually, as follows: "The doctor was very tactful.

He implied things right along. At first he said she was not holding her head up, not sitting up, etc. Not until two or three years later did he really tell me the child was seriously defective and had to be in an institution. He prepared me well." Another parent reported, "A pediatrician told us the child was retarded. He told us in the nicest way it could be explained. He told us it was far too early to say how much he would progress. We returned for visits frequently. As the child grew older, we were told what the future held." Apropos of this discussion, it should be pointed out that frequently parents inadvertently mentioned the names of the doctors they had consulted (in spite of the request that no names be mentioned). It is of interest to note that one parent would condemn a doctor while another would highly praise the same doctor. This obviously casts no reflection on the doctor, but emphasizes the need to individualize each situation. Another observation is that in almost every record there is an admixture of good as well as poor handling, which again emphasizes the need to handle each situation individually.

Important to note is that, when questioned specifically, only 25 percent of the parents indicated that their contact with professional people was satisfactory. The most important factor in this regard was that not only were these parents counseled sensitively and directly, but also their questions were answered, particularly those relating to implications for the future. A typical expression was, "Our family doctor was wonderful. He talked to us for about an hour. He said our child was a dull boy and to give him regular care, but to give him a little bit of extra love. He answered all my questions and told me just what to do. He prepared me well for the future." Another stated, "A psychiatrist told me for the first time my child was retarded. It was a shock, a bitter disappointment, but it was accepted. He told us what to expect and gave us wonderful advice." Another eight also indicated they were told directly, frankly, tactfully, sensitively, or slowly, but in most instances, questions pertaining to implications for the future were not answered. In three cases parents were not informed by anyone, "they just knew."

In sixteen instances parents clearly described how poorly they were told with such adjectives as cruel, abrupt, confused, blunt, upsetting, contradictory. The adjectives the parents used are graphically illustrative of descriptions of their experiences, and they reacted to them with such comments as, "They tell you your child is an idiot and everything else. There should be a nice way to tell parents. When they told us roughly, we stopped going." "The doctor said he will never be any good to you or to himself. I told him I was raised with the feeling where there's life, there's hope." "I was told my child was mongoloid without any preparation for it. I thought he was perfectly normal, and it came as a complete surprise. We had just stopped in for a checkup. The doctor said I should have him in an institution because it would be better for the child and everybody else. All I wanted was to get out, I was stunned. My husband was overseas at the time, which certainly did not help. When you think back, you can't believe anyone could be so blunt." Two parents commented that they were told over the telephone: "My husband was told over the telephone that the child was a mongoloid when the child was four days of age." "The doctor said our child was a mongolian idiot over the telephone. He acted as though it was your problem, buddy."

Numerous references were made to examinations which were considered too hasty and careless: "It was an assembly-line fashion." "The interview was not at all satisfactory. He saw us very quickly and did not even give us the results of the electroencephalogram. He sent us a note and suggested we buy a book he wrote. Good God, we still don't know whether he is epileptic or not." "I didn't have the feeling, wherever we took her, that they thoroughly examined the child." "The doctor gave her a three-minute examination and said she was brain injured and threw her out." "The mother knows first of all what the child is. She's around the child all the time. She knows him thoroughly. How can a doctor, who sees a child for one-half an hour, know about the child?"

One other complaint that was frequent in the study was a tendency on the part of professional persons to evade the issue. As one parent said, "The doctors gave me no clue that anything was amiss. In fact, they assured me everything was going to be all right."

Other complaints pertained to complicated medical terminology.

As indicated in the preceding section, there are certain generalities that can be stated, namely, that parents would want to be handled gently and warmly at all times, in language that they can understand, without evasiveness, after thorough examination, and with enough time to digest the significance of such important material. This belief was reinforced by the parents in reply to the question: "What type of service would you advice for people who are faced with this problem and are just beginning?" The response indicates that they need gentler, more sensitive handling than the usual patient. This is supported quite vividly, as they expressed intense feelings and reactions. Particularly they stressed that their children be treated as individuals, and that the counselor be interested in their problems. What they seem to be expressing is the need for more responsible, integrated services in this field. Professional people are becoming aware of this, as special diagnostic centers are developing in various parts of the country. Parents are able and willing to accept the uncertainty involved in diagnosis in an area which is not clear-cut if they can depend on a centralized resource rather than be left to shift for themselves in an endless search for answers which are not possible.

In the instances where parents indicated the wish for frank, direct diagnosis as early as possible, they felt they could accept the worst if the counselor was compassionate and respected them as parents with strength and dignity. They needed time to take in the extent of their problem, and they needed to work out solutions step by step. Questions did not arise in an organized, crystallized fashion, but formed gradually as the child grew. As one parent put it, "This is a lifetime thing."

Some of the comments of the parents are indicative of their keen feelings of anxiety and guilt, and it is important to emphasize that this is not resolved simply by articulating it for the parent. One parent said, "I got angry at people who told me not to feel guilty. It only made me feel guiltier." There seems little question that for many parents the highest degree of specialized skill is indicated in the area of counseling. If we as professional persons really listen to what parents of mentally retarded children say, we can take our clues from them. It was not unusual to find parents expressing relief as they learned their children could at least be toilet trained and could express such simple needs as to ask for water.

As one parent said, "I used to lie awake and pray that my child could say a little word like 'water' because I was so afraid he would be thirsty and could not help himself." It is interesting to note that two parents spontaneously commented that they were relieved in "spilling over to me," although they had had innumerable previous opportunities to talk about their problem.

Two observations worthy of mention are related to terminology. One is that parents showed severe reaction to such terms as idiot, imbecile, and moron and hoped for terminology that would avoid such negative connotation. Another is their request for simpler explanations in terms they can understand, particularly practical, tangible suggestions relative to everyday living. Perhaps we need a greater appreciation of the little achievements of the retarded child and its meaning to their parents. Still another request was for clearer explanations, the full meaning of which they can take in. Parents often interpret such terms as "the child is slow" to mean that the child "will catch up in due time." In my clinical experience, I have found that a better way of helping parents to understand what is really meant is to use the word "behind," connoting that the child will not catch up.

A discussion of the material would be incomplete without giving some illustrations of the continuous history of the parents' search for help. Comments taken out of context and categorized cannot possibly present the full meaning of the total impact of accumulated frustrations on the parents on the one hand, and their strength and capacity to handle their problems on the other. Only as we can appreciate and accept this can we be fully helpful in developing adequate services. Two records have been selected to illustrate this: the first one concerns a child diagnosed as mongoloid, and the second one a child diagnosed as brain damaged.

Mrs. Martin, the mother of five children, is a warm, motherly person of limited educational background but, nevertheless, of good intelligence. She is a thoughtful, sincere individual.

She begins as follows: "I knew Johnny was a slow child, but I thought he was a sick child. During infancy he slept for the most part and we couldn't awaken him." Early he was taken to the clinic;

however, no mention was made of retardation. "They said he was just sick. He was not a well baby, but would probably pick up, but they never gave me a reason." However, an attendant kept repeating, "If only I had your faith." Apparently this comment seemed so inappropriate at the time that, it made an impression on the mother.

When Johnny was about two years of age, a doctor was called about another sibling and casually commented that Johnny was mentally retarded. The Doctor referred him to the hospital, where the opinion was that the child was a mongoloid, very retarded, and that the best thing for us to do was to put him in an institution because he would forget us very quickly, and if we had other children, it would have an effect on the whole family, particularly our children who would be embarrassed because of Johnny. On this statement Mrs. Martin comments, "I thought that was abrupt and cruel."

Mrs. Martin continued, indicating her distress over this experience. She said, "After I got home, I wanted to know how retarded he was because I was too upset to ask any questions while I was at the hospital." She returned to her pediatrician because apparently she had a warm relationship with him. He disagreed with the opinion of institutionalization, suggesting that it was the parents prerogative to decide such a drastic move. His opinion was that the child needed the love which could not be received in an institution. He explained Johnny's mentality, cautioning her not to spend any money on Johnny, but to center her financial resources on the other children. The doctor's most meaningful comment, and Mrs. Martin says this with much warm feeling, was, "Remember, when your other children have left, you will always have Johnny." (In response to the question, "Who gave you the most help?" Mrs. Martin unequivocally said it was this pediatrician.)

The parents explored every school possibility without any success until he was ten years of age, when he was accepted in a special class in the public school. He stayed there four years and was withdrawn when the center closed, and was then placed in another school. According to the mother, considering his limitations, he has made a good adjustment at school. He mixes well with the other children, who have encouraged him in this respect. He even writes, spells, and does a little arithmetic. Mrs. Martin feels that the school has been instrumental in giving Johnny confidence and enabling him to do some of the things normal children are doing. She glowingly describes her relationship with the teacher as "wonderful," particularly the help she gives to the parents in allowing them to sit in class, observe, and learn.

In response to the question, "Do you feel that your contact with professional people have been satisfactory?" Mrs. Martin's first point was, "Parents need all the kindness you can give them."

She also felt that parents should know exactly what is wrong as early as possible. If known at birth, it should be told at that time so that one can be more helpful to the child. She regretted the information being withheld from her. She described it as "not fair." "It's yours, your baby, you want to know right at the beginning." Mrs. Martin had the feeling that everyone knew that her child was mongoloid except herself. It bears emphasis that she was not informed that the child was mongoloid until he was two years of age.

She further emphasized that "if there is a ray of hope, it should be told." When the pediatrician told her Johnny could reach the mental age of eight, it was helpful to her. "Every word we took hold of."

Still another area of importance is the handling of questions pertaining to heredity. The Martins were very much concerned whether to have additional children, and it was with great relief that after repeated contacts with professional people she finally got her questions answered.

"What type of service would you advise for people who are faced with this problem and are just beginning?" brought forth the seriously traumatic experience of first being told bluntly and insensitively. "I felt it could have been handled a little more kindly. If you can speak to anyone in the medical profession for a while, it's wonderful. If they can't help the child, maybe they can help the parent."

About institutionalization, she commented, "I think too many children like this are put in institutions. It frightens the parents to think of institutions. I don't think an institution should be mentioned at first. Couldn't it wait to see how a child progresses before it is mentioned? I am truly as proud of Johnny as I am of my boy who graduated from college."

The second record is as follows:

This is one of the few situations in which both parents participated in the interview. The Allans are intelligent, fairly young people in their middle thirties, and have a family of three children. In spite of all of their struggles, their charm and zest for living comes through.

Bobby was about seven months of age when they had some vague suspicion that all did not seem quite right. They consulted their pediatrician, who said that he was a little slow — not responding, not sitting up. "But the pediatrician said nothing to allay my fears, he said Bobby would be all right." Then with much feeling, Mrs. Allan adds, "He didn't say this because he didn't know — he did know."

After much "badgering," on the mother's part, and insistence that there must be something wrong, they were referred to a neurologist. Bobby was about one year of age by this time. The examination showed that he was nearsighted.

Further consultation with two doctors indicated that there was nothing wrong. Mrs. Allan said, "I thought I would work harder and teach him more. Then began the most frustrating period of my life. Trying to teach a child when it was not possible to teach him was like knocking my head against a stone wall. My heart just aches when I think what we have been through. I pushed him. I spent a lot of time with him. I would try to feed and toilet train him and we got just no place."

The Allans returned to the pediatrician, whereupon they were referred to an orthopedic man. At that time Bobby was about one and one-half years old, and Mrs. Allan estimates his intelligence at about one year. The orthopedic man found his feet were quite flat and suggested corrective shoes. He also offered the following advice, "He will catch up, he will be all right." Mrs. Allan, however, felt all was not so rosy because she mentions that at nineteen months he was beginning to walk, but "still there was not a flicker any place else."

When Bobby was two years of age the family was referred to a psychiatric clinic. Here she describes her experience as "wonderful." The doctor spoke to her at some length and "it was almost a relief for me to hear it. At least I knew where I stood." By this, Mrs. Allan means she had her suspicions confirmed, namely, that Bobby was retarded. However, he was described as being only mildly retarded, with a good prognosis, but the years have proved otherwise. At least she knew she didn't have a normal child.

Mrs. Allan described meeting her pediatrician on the street and berating him for not telling her the truth. His comment was, "You couldn't have done anything about it anyway. I knew that you would find out soon enough." Mrs. Allan emphasized how deeply disturbed she was during that time.

Although Mrs. Allan felt she was reasonably well handled by the psychiatrist, her questions were not answered. When questions arose regarding having other children, Mrs. Allan consulted her pediatrician and he advised her against having another child. Their obstetrician, however, encouraged her to have another one. She subsequently became pregnant, and describes this period as one of great fear of having another retarded child. In the sixth month of pregnancy she contracted mumps and "nearly went crazy." "The baby was wonderful. Anyway it had a happy ending."

At about three and one-half years of age, Bobby had his first convulsion. His condition was followed at the seizure clinic, where he was put on medicine for convulsions. The parents were told nothing about his condition and were critical of the fact that he did not have a complete work-up. They " . . . were not even told what the EEG showed."

There was further pursuit of medical exploration until finally they consulted another psychiatrist. The psychiatric consultation was described as being reasonably satisfactory, although the psychiatrist was "cold, he told us the brutal facts. At least I could start living after that rather than just hoping. Even so, he was optimistic." He recommended institutionalization, but the parents indicated their disapproval of this with much vehemence. The psychiatrist also pointed out that they were concentrating too much on the retarded child to the exclusion of the normal sibling. The indications were that they could accept this.

In answer to the question, "Was your contact with professional persons satisfactory?" the response was "absolutely not." Then they added, "In fact, we have lost a great deal of respect for the medical profession; we have had nothing but frustration every place we have turned."

"What type of services would you advise for people who are faced with this problem and are just beginning?" brought the immediate response, "Gently, but the truth." Mr. Allan felt that the counselor should evaluate the parents as to type and intellectual capacity, have a few visits with them if necessary, and handle them accordingly. They both agreed that the parents should be informed just as soon as the doctor knows. He said, "The attitude is of paramount importance. If the parents sense sympathy in the professional person and willingness to understand, this has a great deal of meaning. After all, most parents want to respect their doctor."

One further comment revealed the magnitude of the burden for parents when Mr. Allan said, "After all, you have a whole lifetime to worry about this, and you can only take it by degrees."

The discussion of the question of institutionalization produced much negative response on the part of the parents, especially when the counselor had no direct knowledge of the resources and, even more important, little understanding of the family, and indiscriminately advised it as a solution. Illustrative are such comments as, "They all spoke of institutional care as though that was the only thing we could do. They acted as though we had no choice." "If the child can be cared for at home and is not a burden on other members of the family, then they should keep him. I look at the happiness Billy has given us — he is so sweet and kind. The other children in the family adore him." "I honestly think that Tommy would not have gotten anywhere in an institution. There is no difficulty in having him at home." Without exception, these parents wanted what was best for their children. They wanted to know whether the resources would help their children to achieve their capacities, however, meager, and help them grow up as well as possible considering their handicaps. When necessary, they can come to terms with institutional care if that is the soundest way of helping their children. They asked whether their children need more than their share to enable them to assimilate whatever training and education are available. Also, they are able to provide the tender, loving care to make this possible. So many parents cannot be interviewed without the interviewer being greatly impressed with their love for their retarded children and their ability to accept and handle frustration. It is important to note that in twenty-one of the cases institutional care was recommended early, but in only one was it followed through. The obvious conclusion is that they were not ready for or interested in this solution to their problem.

It is significant to note that there is important research going on in the field on the families who can best use institutional care for their retarded children. One study, still in progress, considers the effects of a severely retarded child on family integration, the results of which can be of help to counselors in evaluating the kind of family that can keep their child with them and the kind that might best be directed toward institutionalization.

Apparently there has been more change in the attitudes of society toward retarded persons than we realize. The prevalent assumption has been that families cannot accept too much difference and that the higher the cultural and intellectual achievement, the less possibility there is for the retarded child to be cared for at home. This is not supported by this study. On the contrary, a place has been found for these children in their families, neighborhoods, and schools. I do not believe that it is being omniscient to say that many of these children have gotten as good a start in life as is possible under the circumstances. I should doubt that anyone would challenge the fact that the institutionalized child does not have his emotional needs met.

Needless to say, parents spoke glowingly of the local state society for retarded children. They have found a way to share their experiences, to be supportive to each other, to resolve their feelings of difference, and, most important, to speak for retarded children and crusade in their interest. This has been an invaluable group therapeutic experience for many parents, an important factor in enabling families to live more comfortably with these children and to be helpful to them. They have proved parents need to be no longer isolated as individuals and families, with the serious emotional problems which set them apart from the rest of the world. These parents have paved the way for community understanding and acceptance of the problem and have achieved an important role in community welfare by spearheading the need for specialized services in education, recreation, parent education facilities, and in programs of financial aid. They have discovered so much for themselves that they want to share their experiences and to be helpful to others.

Chapter 3

Parental Attitudes to Retardation

MARGUERITE M. STONE

W HEN, for the first time, the writer attempted to help parents accept mental retardation in their children, a search of published literature on the subject proved fruitless. The writer wanted information about what the parent might be feeling, why he might feel that way, and possible techniques for helping him to manage these feelings about his child more realistically. Since the writer found nothing published, original research in case records of a child guidance clinic was the only source available. This paper is a report of the results of such a study.

The purposes of the study were first, to classify parental types according to degree of awareness of retardation when the parent applied and when the interpretation was given; and second, to study the feelings of the parents as recorded in the interviews.

Forty-four cases were selected from the inactive file of the Child Center of the Catholic University of America by use of the following criteria: first, the diagnosis of mental retardation was made by the staff; second, there was a more or less detailed record of at least two interviews with one or both parents, namely the application interview and the interpretative interview.

TYPES OF REACTIONS AT INTAKE

Parents bring their children to a child guidance clinic for any number of reasons. In the case of retarded children, parents apply

*Note:*Reprinted by permission from the *American Journal of Mental Deficiency,* *53:*363-372, 1948. Copyrighted by the American Association on Mental Deficiency.

with varying degrees of awareness of the real problem. In the forty-four cases studied, criteria for classifying the degree of awareness were set up by careful reading of the records themselves and by conferences with other members of the staff.

The records of the intake or application interviews revealed three groups of parents: those with *considerable awareness,* others with *partial awareness,* and still others with *minimal awareness.* The criteria which were used to select each group and some examples from each type of record follow.

Considerable Awareness

1. The parent states that the child is retarded.
2. The parent recognizes the limitations of any treatment.
3. The parent requests information about suitable care and training, usually placement in an institution.
4. The worker who interviewed the parent states that he is aware of the real problem.

There were twelve cases in this group. Quotations from the records of several of these well illustrates this type of reaction. Throughout this study, at the beginning of each quotation from a record, identifying data will be given, that is, the case number assigned by the writer, the sex of the child, the age in years and months, as twelve years, three months (12-3), and the IQ of the child.

Case C3, Boy, 12-10, IQ 61

Mother said that they have recognized for the past few years that the child "is not like other children." She said they would just have to face it if he wasn't mentally right, so that they could find a way to help him. She also said, "If he ain't — isn't able to learn any better, I'll understand."

Case C12, Boy, 9-7, IQ 58

I asked her what she was most concerned about now and she promptly answered that it was because her child could not read and because he didn't develop properly. She thought the child was "retarded." I wondered if she would like to have us make a diagnostic study and to this she readily agreed, saying that she wanted to know all about the child and that she had hated to face this before. She wondered if we might suggest a boarding school for the child.

Partial Awareness

1. The parent describes the symptoms of retardation with questions about the causes.
2. The parent hopes for improvement, but fears that treatment will not be successful.
3. The parent questions his own ability to cope with the problem.
4. The worker evaluates him as having partial awareness of the child's real problem.

The following quotations from case records show instances of these reactions:

Case P12, Boy, 4-2, IQ 42

Mother says the child has always been different from the older brother. She is concerned because he doesn't talk, although he does make guttural sounds and says certain dipthongs distinctly. He needs constant assistance in dressing, bathing, eating, and the toilet. Mother wonders if measles and other illnesses have caused the patient to be retarded in development, but recognizes, herself, that during the infancy period the patient was quite different.

Case P19, 11-3, IQ 53

"It seems as though he just can't learn anything. I go over his work with him and try to help him and show him how things should be done, and the next morning he doesn't remember a bit of it. When you try to work with him he'll start giggling and laughing, and then if you keep on he'll begin to cry and then it's all off. He was always a sickly child. When he was young he used to have convulsions . . . "

This father seems to have a certain amount of insight but seems to be antagonistic toward his wife and possibly somewhat rejecting of the boy. The parents were separated for three years, and the father felt that one cause of the retardation was lack of discipline while the boy was with his mother.

Minimal Awareness

There were eleven cases in the third group, which had minimal awareness of the child's real problem. There were four criteria used to select this group, as follows:

1. The parent refuses to recognize that certain characteristic behavior is abnormal.

2. The parent blames causes other than retardation for the symptoms.
3. The parent believes that treatment will produce a "normal" child.
4. The worker evaluates the parent has having minimal awareness.

Sample quotations from case records are given below:

Case M4, Girl, 4-0, IQ 58

Mother says her daughter cannot talk and that she has had frequent abscesses in her ears since birth. She vomits when crossed or excited. Mother thinks there may be a hearing defect which causes these disturbances.

Case M3, Girl, 8-3, IQ 50

The child failed first grade and was transferred to a special class for children "that are supposed to be backward in study. After visiting this school and classroom I am satisfied it is not the proper place for my child." The mother believes that there is no other problem than backwardness in school.

TYPES OF REACTIONS AT INTERPRETATION

After the initial interview with the parent, the child is usually seen once or twice by the psychologist for a battery of tests, once by the psychiatrist for a diagnostic interview and, if the child is of school age, by the remedial education teacher for diagnostic and achievement tests. This entails several visits to the clinic, and usually the parent is seen by a social worker each time.

The dynamics of these interviews will be discussed later, but consideration will now be given to the reactions of the parents when the interpretation of the findings of the staff was made. Criteria were set up by the writer for this grouping in the same way as for classifying reactions at intake, that is, by reading the records carefully and confering with various staff members regarding proposed criteria. Some of the parents were able to make changes during the diagnostic process, but there were still three groups.

Considerable Acceptance

1. The parent says he accepts it.

2. The parent makes plans for suitable care and training.
3. The parent does not blame causes other than retardation.
4. The worker evaluates the reaction as acceptance.

The following are quotations from two of the nineteen case records of parents having this type of reaction:

Case C1, Boy, 12-5, IQ 47

She said she always realized that he was very handicapped, but did not think he was quite so low. She said, "I wonder about the future." I explained that he would always need supervision and care. She said she guessed that meant placement in an institution.

Case P5, Girl, 8-8, IQ 38

Mother listened tensely and then whispered, "I thought it would be like that." She wept quietly for some time, then dried her tears and said, "I really thought we could send her to school. Since that is impossible, what do you suggest?" She asked several questions about the school suggested, then sighed and said, "I suppose that's all that remains for us."

Partial Acceptance

The second group was also large. Twenty cases were found to fulfill the criteria for partial acceptance.

1. The parent agrees with the interpretation.
2. The parent continues to blame symptoms on causes other than retardation.
3. The parent rejects plans for suitable care and training.
4. The worker evaluates him as partially accepting the interpretation.

This type of reaction is illustrated as follows:

Case M5, Boy, 5-10, IQ 43

When placement was discussed, she stated very positively her belief that such a school would be an emotional upset, that he needed the security of his own home. She thought the housekeeper was too severe, but she herself spent as much time with him as she possibly could and tried to adapt her treatment to his needs. She said she had to acknowledge the validity of the findings, although she could not yet accept them as being entirely true.

Case P4, Boy, 2-4, IQ 54

She was visibly disturbed by what I was saying and broke in to say that she dreaded coming here for she had a feeling that she would receive bad news; however, she wanted to know how bad it was. She commenced to sob, and when she was able to say anything, she said they had prayed hard that God would help them and that the child would get better; in fact, she would not give up hope but believed something would happen to help him become normal. She also believed that while it was hard to come here today, she knew she had to face it and learn the truth from people who were capable of telling her, yet that she was going on hoping that something would happen to help her.

Minimal Acceptance

The following criteria were used for selecting the group of five cases having minimal acceptance of the interpretation:

1. The parent rejects the interpretation or the tests or both.
2. The parent refuses plans for suitable care and training.
3. The parent blames the symptoms on causes other than retardation.
4. The worker evaluates the parent as having minimal acceptance.

Some examples of this type of reaction will now be given.

Case M6, Girl, 7-4, IQ 34

I said that in the first interview she was worried about the child's speech; I wondered whether anything else about the child worried her or struck her as unusual. She said it was mainly her child's speech or her nerves, because she got so excited and irritable. I inquired if she thought the child could do the same things other children her age could do, and she answered No, but that she thought the inability was sufficiently explained by her speech problem and nervousness.

Case M2, Girl, 10-10, IQ 60

The parents appeared troubled and disturbed. They asked immediately for the results of the study. She was less hostile toward the interpretation than her husband; however, neither of the parents could accept the situation emotionally or even intellectually. They rejected any type of special school for retarded children but employed a tutor to assist her in a regular school. They continued to place much pressure on her at home to be scholastically successful.

These findings, then, answer the question, "What were the reactions of parents at intake and at interpretation;" Some were able to accept retardation in a child even before diagnosis, others moved into acceptance during the process, while others remained blocked.

RELATIONSHIPS WITHIN THE FAMILY AND THE CULTURE

Why do parents show the reactions that are recorded? What happens in the family where the child does not compete successfully? What meanings does he assume to father, mother, brothers, and sisters. What do the relatives and neighbors think of this child, and how do their opinions affect the family?

At the present state of our knowledge about the structure and function of the personality it is not possible to answer these questions adequately. Some clues may be found by examining individual records. It is also possible to give thoughtful consideration to certain characteristics in the culture and to discuss the possibilities of relatedness.

PSYCHIC PAIN OF THE PARENTS

In numerous records there is evidence that thinking and talking about a retarded child is painful to the parents. Excerpts from two records illustrate this behavior.

Case P7, Girl, 5-10, IQ 48

As soon as we sat down, the father explained that it was hard on the mother. Both had tears in their eyes. Father began by stating that mother had been very disturbed for the past few weeks since the doctor had referred them here. Father described how much anxiety he had experienced during the past when he had been deciding to apply to the clinic. It was difficult for him to come because both he and his wife would have preferred not to face the problem. He wondered if he were the only parent expressing fear about revealing his difficulty and felt more comfortable after I commented that in this situation he reacted like many other parents who would make every effort to handle their own problems until they found that outside assistance was definitely needed. He felt that it was a relief actually to be here. At the end of the interview he said that this had been "one of the hardest experiences of his whole life."

This father seems to indicate that he feels isolated from his fellow-parents and therefore lonely because of his trouble in relation to the child. When the worker reassured him that others felt the same way it helped to make it easier — that is, he felt less lonely.

Case P8, Boy, 9-6, IQ 66

She rose to her feet in a startled way when I spoke to her in the waiting room, and her manner was marked by quick, restless movements as she entered the office. It was very obvious that she was distressed and uncomfortable. She sat on the edge of the chair throughout the interview, nervously fingering her handbag and gloves. She seemed on the verge of tears at all times and cried several times during the interview. There was a noticeable tic.

(See also Cases P4 and M2 above.)

SYMBOLIC MEANING TO PARENTS

Some parents appear to identify so closely with their children that they feel as if a part of themselves is defective; they picture themselves mutilated or punished for some real or imagined failure on their part. Expressions such as those quoted below make this evident.

Case P4, Boy, 2-4, IQ 54

She said it was most difficult to understand how some people can have healthy babies and care nothing for them, while others do things to prevent having them, yet she wants to do everything that is right and she has a child who is deficient and not normal.

Case P7, Girl, 5-10, IQ 48

Mother said, "You can put this down in big letters, I am to blame for this girl's retardation, as I have done too much for her." Father paced the floor and looked out of the window, on the verge of tears which he didn't release, then asked, "Why does God do such things to us? Then the only alternative left is to get rid of the child. Perhaps it would be better for us not to have bothered at all when she was a baby. All those five years of treatment – futile. The best years of my wife's life were sacrificed for her sake, and it's all in vain!"

In the following example the mother appears to feel very guilty because of her operation during pregnancy, and this guilt is aggravated by her own mother. They both have questions about heredity.

Case C11, Girl, 6-1, IQ 56

She was very anxious about the cause of mongolism and asked many questions. She wondered about heredity and said she had an uncle who was deaf. She said she had an operation for hemorrhoids during pregnancy, and she had been advised by her doctor that it would not affect the child. However, her mother has expressed the opinion many times that the child's retardation is a result of the operation.

THE RETARDED CHILD IN A MARITAL PROBLEM

The retarded child may take on a special meaning in a problem of marital adjustment. Each parent may blame the other and use the child as a symbol of punishment. The following excerpt shows that the mother is lined up with the child against the father, yet she feels guilty and afraid of her husband because he is not pleased with her child. Some of the cultural differences are also evident when she discusses his national origin.

Case C3, Boy, 12-10, IQ 61

Mother seemed to feel that she must protect this boy from his father. She seemed to blame herself that her husband was not pleased with him. She helped him two hours a day with his school work and begged her husband not to force him to be athletic or to play with other boys when it makes him unhappy. She said, "No one can tell my husband anything. That is the trouble. He tries to drive the boy. He is afraid of his father who is Austrian, and he is used to strict discipline." The father felt that his wife and her family were too easy on the boy, letting him be a coward and lazy. It was very hard for him to accept the statement that there was some real deficiency. He never believed that the boy was not physically and mentally average, but blamed the mother and grandparents for pampering him. He wanted to know what to do now.

Another example of the use to which a retarded child may be put in a marital quarrel is evident in the next record quoted.

Case M4, Girl, 4-0, IQ 58

Parents quarrel not only over the presence of the maternal grandmother in the home but also over the disciplining of the children. Mother tells the father that if he does not like it he can take the children himself and leave — she will stay with her mother. (In a later interview) mother thinks the child's retardation is explained on the basis of emotional conflicts in the home and asks whether she may not become normal if she is removed from the environment. The father tried several times to interrupt his wife in her recital of grievances, but she brushed him aside saying that she had everything arranged the way she wanted to say it. (Later) mother telephoned several days later to say that the father had taken both children away to relatives in another city, and she was frantic with fear and anger.

NONACCEPTANCE IN THE CIRCLE OF ACQUAINTANCE

The meaning a retarded child has for relatives, friends, and neighbors may make it difficult for the parents. Do the parents feel some social stigma because they have a child who is retarded? In Case C11 the grandmother blamed the mother for permitting an operation during pregnancy, although medical advice had been that the operation would not harm the child. There are other examples in the records of the stigma attached to the child by people who mean something to the parents.

Case C1, Boy, 12-5, IQ 47

She revealed that her own family were critical of her because she had not placed the boy in an institution and had divorced her husband. She said they had offered to take her into their home but they would not have the boy because he was so difficult. She said that his teachers found him a problem to handle and that this had perhaps contributed to his being excused from school.

A strained relationship between the mother and her neighbors is described in the following record.

Case C11, Girl, 6-1, IQ 56

Mother said that the child is very difficult in that she does not play with other children, is quite cruel to younger ones, and is a source of considerable tension with the home and the neighborhood.

If the child does not make a good social adjustment in the school and among other children, the emotional load of the parents is increased a great deal.

Case P18, Girl, 14-9, IQ 46

The children at school call her "dummy," and she cries and begs to stay away. The mother thought she was stubborn because she would just look at her when told to do things.

Case P15, Boy, 15-6, IQ 63

He says he knows "he isn't as good as" his brother. He feels inferior and resents being awkward. It is not unusual for one of the family, while trying to show him how to do something to say, "Oh, you're too dumb — you can't do that." He gives up when someone tries to help him. Mother said, "this is hard to face, but one just has to make the best of it."

THE COMPETITIVE CULTURE

Not only are there elements in each individual case which may make rearing a retarded child painful to his parents, but also the pattern of the culture itself appears to contribute as well. The cultural anthropologist, Margaret Mead, has ably described the competitive nature of the American community in which parents live with their children. She says, "American parents send their children to school, to nursery school or kindergarten or first grade, to measure up and to be measured against their contemporaries."

The only standard which American parents use in judging their children is how they measure in comparison to their age mates. It starts when the baby sits up, teethes, of even sleeps through the night. They punish and reward by this relative standard.

Dr. Mead makes a further point that the mother does not feel free to love her child unconditionally unless he measures up to the age norm of his contemporaries; then the experts scold her because she does not love her child enough — a thing which she dare not do. Thus she is thrown into conflict with herself by her desire to be accepted in the culture and her desire to love her child. Is it strange, then, in view of all the personal and cultural animosities which may possibly be related to a retarded child, that parents seek and often find psychological mechanisms to escape from this dilemma?

LIMITED PERMISSION TO LOVE

Some parents are able to circumvent the many obstacles to a satisfying relationship with a retarded child and do find certain satisfactions which they could not get in the same measure from a normal child. The most obvious of these is the pleasure of mothering. The mother may achieve a sense of her own value because she is able to do so much for her child. The retarded child stays a baby much longer and needs more mothering than the average child. If the mother enjoys doing a lot for her child, she is able to love him more because of her work. However, eventually she comes to want him to grow up too, as illustrated in the following cases.

Case P13, Boy, 7-8, IQ 42

Mother said that she knew she had been overprotective because the child had been ill so much. She felt that he was extremely childish for his years. She said, "I liked it for a long time, but I know now that I would like him a whole lot better if he were more grown up."

Case P7, Girl, 5-10, IQ 42

Mother said that she has been engrossed in the child, that she has been doing everything for her and with her for the past five years.

If the child has been able to make a social adjustment in spite of the handicap, the parents may feel more free to love him.

Case M2, Girl, 10-10, IQ 60

In stating the problem, the parents said that the child had a history of convulsive seizures. They were aware that she was retarded in some areas, but also thought she was a genius in other areas, especially general socialization.

Case 10, Boy, 12-2, IQ 60

He plays football and baseball with the boys in the neighborhood and is popular with them. He gets along well with his sister who is eleven years old. The teachers have all liked him and "petted" him and given him extra help. He talks baby talk, but people understand him.

MOVEMENT DURING INTERVIEWS

No attempt has been made in this study to evaluate the skill of the worker who did the interviewing. That is one of the factors which may not be overlooked but which appears to the writer to require a separate study. However, there are certain statistical indications that parents changed in these interviews, and the skill of the worker undoubtedly contributes to that change.

These statistics indicate a movement toward awareness. There were eleven parents who had minimal awareness at intake as against five at interpretation. There were also seven more parents with considerable acceptance at the time of interpretation than at the time of intake.

IMPLICATIONS FOR CASEWORK

An important purpose for making a study of this kind is to learn something which may be helpful in doing casework with parents in other, similar interviews. There seem to be as many concepts of therapy in the casework interview as there are people who attempt to do it. In the writer's view, something happens during the interview which makes it possible for the client to think and feel differently about his child. What the caseworker *knows,* his body of professional knowledge, and what he *is* as a person contribute to the relationship in which this "something" happens. In interviews with parents regarding the diagnosis of mental retardation in their children, the caseworker has to educate the parent to the reality of his child's handicap and at the same time help him handle the emotions aroused by the facts.

Some of the reasons why parents find this learning process so painful have been discussed in this study. When the caseworker knows the facts of the diagnosis and also the resources in his community which are available to help the child, the caseworker's own feeling about these facts may become unusually important to the parent as they participate in this painful discussion together. With a broad understanding of the emotional meaning of this experience to both of them, the caseworker is equipped to share the parent's suffering in such a way as to reinforce whatever strength or inclination the parent may have to learn the facts.

However, the caseworker also needs to realize that growth and change in personality is often very slow and may take years, whereas the caseworker has only a few hours at most in which to help the parent to change. Perhaps all he can do is start the process, especially if there are many rigid hindrances in the way.

SUMMARY AND CONCLUSIONS

The reactions of parents during interviews concerning diagnosis of mental retardation in their children were carefully studied in forty-four case records. The cases were classified according to their awareness of the problem when they applied and when the interpretation was made. There was evidence of growth during the diagnostic process in the ability of some of the parents to face the real problem. This movement was shown by the changes in the numbers in the various groups (Table 3-I).

TABLE 3-I

	Considerable	Partial	Minimal	Total
Awareness at intake	12	21	11	44
Acceptance at interpretation	19	20	5	44

Factors in the individual family situations and in the culture were analyzed to discover possible relationships between these elements and the ability of the parent to learn the facts of his child's retardation. Evidence of much psychic pain was discovered in many of the interviews, and an effort was made to detect components in the situations which might be related to this suffering.

In the individual families studied, the symbolic meaning of the defective child to each of his parents tended to isolate the parent from his fellows and to make him feel guilty. The retarded child was also found to be used negatively in problems of marital adjustment. Each parent tried to protect himself and blame the partner. Some parents felt personally defective and others used their children as symbols to punish each other. In the larger circle of acquaintances, the meaning of a retarded child made it difficult for the parents. There may be social stigma and blame from relatives, teachers, and neighbors. The playmates of the child may ridicule him and the child in turn may fail to make any social adjustment.

The contributions of cultural anthropology concerning the competitive culture of the United States throw considerable light on these reactions. The norms for evaluating the worth of a baby or a child in school are based on what the group do at a similar age level, and parents feel that they dare not love their children completely unless they compete successfully. Then the experts scold the parents for not loving their children and often produce a painful conflict.

A diagnosis of the reality of this retardation would seem to be extremely painful to a parent where any of these factors were present. It was not possible to say definitely just how many were present in each case; nor would it be possible to rule out other unknown elements which also might contribute to the reactions which were recorded.

No attempt was made to evaluate the skill of the caseworker in the function of educating parents to this reality, but it was pointed out that learning does not take place unless the learner is at least partially ready for it. The caseworker's skill should include a thorough knowledge of the facts about mental deficiency and the specific handicap of the child under consideration. In addition to this, a knowledge of the hindrances to the readiness of parents to learn which have been pointed out in this study may further implement the caseworker to help the parents handle their emotions in working through these obstacles.

Chapter 4

Chronic Sorrow:
A Response to Having a
Mentally Defective Child

SIMON OLSHANSKY*

THE purpose of this article is twofold: (1) to propose that most parents who have a mentally retarded child suffer from a pervasive psychological reaction, chronic sorrow, that has not always been recognized by the professional personnel — physicians, psychologists, and social workers — who attempt to help them; and (2) to suggest some of the implications of the phenomenon of chronic sorrow for the parent counseling process. This discussion is based on the author's personal and professional experiences and on the experience of the Children's Developmental Clinic staff on counseling parents of severely retarded children.

THE PHENOMENON OF CHRONIC SORROW

Most parents who have a mentally defective child suffer chronic sorrow throughout their lives regardless of whether the child is kept at home or is "put away." The intensity of this sorrow varies from time to time for the same person, from situation to situation, and from one family to another. The sorrow may be more intense for one parent than for the other in the same family. Many factors, such as a parent's personality, ethnic group, religion, and

Note: Reprinted by permission of the author and *Social Casework, 43:*190-193, 1962, published by the Family Service Association of America.

*Study Director of the Children's Developmental Clinic, Cambridge, Massachusetts, which is suported by the U.S. Children's Bureau, the Massachusetts Department of Public Health, and the City of Cambridge.

The author is grateful to the following persons for their considerable help: Dr. Charles Hersch and Lillian Saltman, Cambridge Guidance Center; Dr. Samuel Grob, Massachusetts Association for Mental Health; Dr. Robert Flynn, Thelma Bloom, Gertrude Johnson, and Marjorie Kettell, Children's Developmental Clinic; Catherine Casey and Hilma Unterberger, Massachusetts Department of Public Health.

social class, influence the intensity of this sorrow. Some parents show their sorrow clearly; others attempt to conceal it, and sometimes they succeed. The need to keep a "stiff upper lip," especially outside the privacy of the home, is a common defense of parents. Anglo-Saxon parents in particular usually feel this need. Although chronic sorrow may be experienced by some parents of minimally retarded children, this reaction is probably more nearly universal among parents whose children are severely or moderately retarded — whose children would be considered retarded in any society and in any cultural group.

The helping professions have somewhat belabored the tendency of the parent to deny the reality of his child's mental deficiency. Few workers have reported what is probably a more frequent occurrence, the parent's tendency to deny his chronic sorrow. This tendency is often reinforced by the professional helper's habit of viewing chronic sorrow as a neurotic manifestation rather than as a natural and understandable response to a tragic fact. All the parental reactions reported in the literature, such as guilt, shame, and anger, may well be intertwined with chronic sorrow. Moreover, a parent's experiencing chronic sorrow does not preclude his deriving satisfaction and joy from his child's modest achievements in growth and development. It can also be assumed that the child's mental defectiveness has symbolic meaning, on an unconscious level, to some parents. The data that support this assumption, however, are rarely communicated by the parent except in deep psychotherapy.

The reality faced by the parent of a severely retarded child is such as to justify his chronic sorrow. When the parent is asked to "accept" mental deficiency, it is not clear just what he is being asked to do. The great stress professional workers tend to place on "acceptance" may suggest to the parent that he is expected to perceive his child from the point of view of the professional helper. This expectation may make him both resentful and resistant. In our clinical experience, we have seen relatively few parents so neurotic that they denied the fact that the child was mentally defective. We have seen relatively few parents who did not recover enough, after the initial shock of discovery, to mobilize their efforts in behalf of the child. It is understandable that some parents move slowly and erratically toward recognition of the mental defect and toward meeting the child's special needs. Some of them even "regress" to the point of denying, at certain times, the reality of the child's defectiveness. On other occasions they become unduly optimistic about the child's potentialities. In our view, such regression may help the parent to tolerate better the terrible reality that confronts him each day.

Why does the professional worker become so impatient with the parent's slowness or occasional regression, and why does he feel such a great sense of urgency to do something about it? After all, the parent has a lifetime in which to learn to deal with the needs and problems of a mentally defective child. In most cases one can ask what will be lost if the parent is unable for several years to view his child as mentally defective. The parents of one of our clinic patients have told us that their child was six or seven years old before they knew definitely that she was mentally defective. Although they had sensed that her development was slow, they had failed to act on their suspicions until her subnormality became self-evident. In what way had the parents been worse off in their "blissful ignorance?" In what way had the child been worse off, since she had had the capacity to meet the parents' expectations?

The parents of a normal child have to endure many woes, many trials, and many moments of despair. Almost all these parents know, however, that ultimately the child will become a self-sufficient adult. By contrast, the parents of a mentally defective child have little to look forward to; they will always be burdened by the child's unrelenting demands and unabated dependency. The woes, the trials, the moments of despair will continue until either their own deaths or the child's death. Concern about what will happen to his child after he is dead may be a realistic concern for a parent, or it may be associated with death wishes, either for himself or for his child. Release from his chronic sorrow may be obtainable only through death.

THE COUNSELING PROCESS

What are some of the implications of the parent's chronic sorrow for the professional person who attempts to help him?

First, the professional worker should abandon the simplistic and static concept of parental acceptance. Every parent — whether he has a normal or a mentally defective child — accepts his child and rejects his child at various times and in various situations. If both acceptance and rejection are universal parental responses, it is not clear just what the professional person is asking the parent of a mentally defective child to accept. Is the parent being asked to accept the fact that the child is defective? This the parent does, in general. Is he being asked to meet the child's needs realistically? This the parent tries to do, by and large. Is he being asked to abandon his chronic sorrow? This the parent wishes he could do, but cannot. The permanent, day-by-day dependence of the child, the interminable frustrations resulting from the child's relative changelessness, the unaesthetic quality of mental defectiveness, the deep symbolism buried in the process of giving birth to a defective child, all these join together to produce the parent's chronic sorrow. That so many parents bear this sorrow stoically is rich testimony to parental courage and endurance. (One might ask, for example, how much progress would have been achieved in the field of rehabilitation if the issue of "acceptance" had been made the primary focus of professional concern rather than the issue of managing the disability most efficiently through the use of prosthetic devices.)

Second, the professional person's perceptions of the parent will be different if he accepts the idea that chronic sorrow is a natural, rather than a neurotic, reaction. The worker's changed perceptions of the parent and his feelings may encourage the parent to discuss his chronic sorrow more openly and freely. There is a danger that some workers will become overinvolved and sentimental, so that they will serve as "wailing walls" rather than as helpers. This danger, however, is always present in any helping situation if a worker surrenders the discipline, restraint, and understanding he must have to fulfill his helping role. Although chronic sorrow is a natural rather than a neurotic response to a tragic fact, some parents do respond neurotically to their child's handicap and may require treatment for their neurosis. Judging from our experience, however, the number of neurotic parents is small. It is regrettable that this small number of people has received so much professional attention that the tragedy of having a mentally defective child has been viewed less as a tragedy than as a psychiatric problem.

The professional worker who learns to accept chronic sorrow as a normal psychological reaction will grant the parent a longer period of time than otherwise in which to adjust his feelings and organize his resources, both internal and external, to meet the child's needs. The worker will also plan to extend the length of the counseling process. He will alter the usual practice of telling the parent the facts about the child's mental defectiveness in as few as one to four interviews, since the worker will realize that the communication of facts is only one part of the counseling process and is not necessarily the most important part. Some parents may require months or even years of counseling before they can muster and maintain the strength and stamina needed to live with the tragedy of having a mentally defective child. What the parent requires, beyond a knowledge of the facts, is an opportunity to ventilate and clarify his feelings and to receive support for the legitimacy of the feelings he is expressing. In some instances the parent will need to be given this opportunity at various times throughout his life.

In addition to providing more time during which the parent can learn to face his problem, and to offering counseling at a slower pace, the worker should also make himself accessible to the parent over a long period of time. No matter how effective the counseling is, many parents need to discuss their feelings and the problems associated with a defective child on many occasions. This need for repeated counseling is natural and should not be considered a sign of either regression or neurosis. The experience of our clinic has demonstrated the importance of accessibility — an "open door" policy — for the parents of mentally defective children. A parent may telephone a staff member again and again about a recurring problem, a new problem, an emerging crisis, or his own distress.

Finally, if the worker accepts the validity of the concept of chronic sorrow, his goal in counseling the parent will be to increase the parent's comfortableness in living with and managing his defective child. In addition to providing psychological help, the worker will emphasize, more than formerly, the help the mother needs in order to learn to manage such problems as how to feed, discipline, and toilet train the child. Use of such facilities as preschool nurseries, special education classes, day-care centers, and sheltered workshops should be made available when they can be used appropriately. Moreover, the mother should be given an opportunity to be away from the child at recurring intervals. Although some workers tend to discount the value of "baby-sitting" services, these services can make it possible for the mother to get much needed relief and can enhance her sense of personal comfort. Greater comfortableness may help make her chronic sorrow more tolerable and may increase her effectiveness in meeting the child's continuing needs. Also, through increased comfortableness the parents may become more accessible to psychological help for themselves.

In summary, it has been suggested that the parent of a mentally defective child suffers from chronic sorrow. This sorrow is a natural response to a tragic fact. If the professional worker accepts chronic sorrow as a natural rather than a neurotic response, he can be more effective in helping the parent achieve the goal of increased comfort in living with and managing a mentally defective child.

Chapter 5

Parents' Feelings About Retarded Children

LEO KANNER, M.D.

T HERE was a time when, confronted with the task of dealing with retarded children, the educator's, psychologist's, or physician's main effort consisted of an examination of the child and advice to the family. No matter how expertly and con-scientiously this was done, it somehow did not take in the whole magnitude of the problem. Parents were told of the child's low IQ in mournful numbers and were urged to think in terms of ungraded classes or residential school placement. The IQ figures may have been correct and the suggestions may have been adequate, and yet very often a major, highly important and, in fact, indispensable part of the job was somehow neglected.

It is recognized more and more that professional and at the same time humane attention should be given to the attitudes and feelings of people who are understandably puzzled by the lag in their child's development and progress. Whenever parents are given an opportunity to express themselves, they invariably air their emotional involvements in the form of questions, utterances of guilt, open and sometimes impatient rebellion against destiny, stories of frantic search for causes, pathetic accounts of matri-monial dissensions about the child's condition, regret about the course that has been taken so far, anxious appraisals of the child's future, and tearful pleas for reassurance. It takes a considerable amount of cold, hard-boiled, pseudoprofessorial detachment to

Note: Reprinted by permission from the author and the *American Journal of Mental Deficiency, 57*:375-389, 1953. Copyrighted by the American Association on Mental Deficiency.

turn a deaf ear on the anxieties, self-incriminations, and concerns about past, present, and future contained in such remarks. We have learned to take them into serious consideration and to treat them as the genuine, deep-seated, intrinsic perplexities that they are. We have learned to distinguish between abrupt, brutal frankness and a sympathetic statement of fact, between a dictatorial, take-it-or-leave-it kind of recommendation and the sort of presentation which would appeal to parents as the most constructive and helpful procedure, best suited under the existing circumstances.

I know that it is difficult to speak in generalities about a subject which entails individual sentiments. I know from experience that every couple that comes with a retarded child carries along a set of specific curiosities which must be understood and satisfied. For this reason, it may perhaps serve the purpose of this address if I were to introduce a few definite instances and, in so doing, to discuss the principal implications as they come along in the life of the retarded child and in the minds of his family.

Johnny Jones was brought to our clinic at the age of eight years. He was referred to us by his pediatrician with the request for a psychometric evaluation. Johnny was in his third year in school, had been demoted once, and after that had been given courtesy promotions, even though he did not master the required curriculum of his grade. The psychologist's examination showed that Johnny had a test age of six years and an IQ of 75. It was obvious that, with his endowment, he could not possibly be expected to do better than low first-grade work. It would have seemed easy to say to the parents that Johnny should be in an ungraded class because of his low intelligence. It would have been very easy to give them the numerical result of the test and, if they balked, to offer them an authoritative explanation of the Binet-Simon or any other scale that had been employed. However, there was one big fly in the ointment. Mr. and Mrs. Jones were both college graduates and moved in highly intellectual and sophisticated circles. Mr. Jones was a competent representative of a pharmaceutical firm and his wife had been a librarian prior to her marriage. They could see logically that their son had not been able to accomplish the scholastic functions expected of a child his age. But for years they had struggled against the very thought that something might be amiss with their Johnny's academic possibilities. As a result, they had kept looking for interpretations of his failures other than the one interpretation which they dreaded because they could not accept it emotionally. They had found fault with the "school system." There could not be anything wrong with the child; the problem must lie somewhere in the *method of instruction:* Johnny's teachers were either too young and inexperienced or too old and unfamiliar with modern education. They were alternately critical of what they chose to call either old-fashioned drilling or newfangled frills. When, in the course of time, they had been convinced that the other children in Johnny's group got along all right under the same educational regime, they tried to seek the culprit in Johnny's *body.* After considerable search, they found one doctor who persuaded them that Johnny would do better if his tonsils and adenoids were taken out. They cherished this bit of wisdom because it fitted into their emotional pattern. They could say to themselves that, after all, their Johnny was all right and would learn better after the repair of a physical imperfection. This did not work. In order to satisfy their need for prestige, they began to pounce on *Johnny himself.* They decided that the child must be lazy. They scolded him, deprived him of privileges, and sat with him for hours trying to hammer his homework into him. They pointed out to him how well his numerous cousins did without all the help such as he received from them. The child, smarting from the constant rebuff and rebuke, sat there, unable to grasp the parental instructions and, not knowing why he could not conform, came to think of himself as a wretched, miserable, ungrateful creature who let his parents down. He gave up completely. He lost all confidence in himself and, in order to find some compensation for his anguish, he took to daydreaming. Eventually, the parents thought that Johnny's salvation stared them in the face when they came upon an article in *The Reader's Digest* which told them that a certain drug, named glutamic acid, could brighten up children and make them learn better. They obtained the drug and got him to swallow tablet after tablet. For a time, they called off the dogs of daily tutoring and pushing, with the idea that glutamic acid would do the trick. Johnny, relieved of the pressures, perked up for a while and seemed brighter. He felt that being offered the tablets, however ill-tasting they were, was better than being hovered over impatiently at the desk. The parents came to feel that the money they paid to the druggist was about the best investment they had ever made. But in the long run they realized that, as far as learning was concerned, there was no noticeable departure from the status quo. They felt disillusioned and finally decided to take the child to the clinic.

Betty Brown was a placid, likable little girl whose physical characteristics and marked developmental retardation had led the child's pediatrician to make the correct diagnosis of mongolism. He was able to help the parents to understand and accept Betty's limitations. The Browns were warm-hearted people and genuinely fond of their three children, of whom Betty was the youngest. Michael and Anne were healthy and bright and held out every promise of good academic achievement. They sensed their sister's handicaps, were helped by their parents to make the necessary allowances, and being secure in the warmth of a comfortable emotional climate, adjusted nicely to Γ   's need for her mother's special attention. Anne, in fact,   elcomed and invited opportunities to be mother's little helper in her ministrations to Betty.

This constellation of attitudes might have made for an ideal mode of family living. But a "bull in the china shop" charged into this peaceful home in the shape of Betty's paternal grandmother, who lived a few doors away from the Browns. The elder Mrs. Brown stubbornly refused to acknowledge the doctor's diagnosis. She had always been a bit critical of her daughter-in-law but had found it difficult to hold on to a specific hatrack on which to hang her expressions of disapproval. Betty's failure to develop properly came to her as a godsend. She made up her mind that there was nothing wrong with Betty herself and that the whole trouble stemmed from the child's mother's inadequate methods of training. She offered no concrete suggestions. She did not substantiate her recriminations. But every morning with clocklike regularity, she appeared at the home, looked at the child with a mien of profound commiseration, and uttered the same reproachful phrase: "When are you going to start making something of the child?"

Mrs. Brown took this as long as she could. She discarded as utterly futile her initial attempts to convey to her tormentor the reality of Betty's condition. She decided to remain silent. But eventually she could stand it no longer. It is not easy to be confronted daily with insult added to painful injury. She turned for help to her husband, imploring him to do something about his mother's stereotyped antics. All that he had to offer was the advice that she "pay no attention." After a few months, she brought Betty to our clinic. In reality, she brought herself and her misery rather than the child. She was obviously depressed and was seeking help for herself, which by that time she needed desperately.

Alan Smith was his parents' only child. He was severely retarded in his development. The Smiths, feeling that Alan would need all of their attention, had decided to deprive themselves of further offspring. There was also the dread of a possible repetition of the tragedy. But most pathetic of all was the boy's mother's constant self-searching for some shortcomings of her own which might be responsible for her son's intellectual defect. When she brought him to the clinic, she asked: "Doctor, did I have something to do with it? Did I do something wrong?" She eagerly gulped down the acquittal but went on: "Well, maybe before he was born — did I do something then?" When told that her child's retardation was not determined by anything that she had done, she was still puzzled. She wondered: "If it isn't what I have *done,* maybe it's what I *am* that brought it about." Again she seemed grateful for authoritative absolution. But still she went on. If she had not contributed to the fact of Alan's retardation, then she was surely guilty of not recognizing it in time, of pushing him beyond his capacity, of losing patience with him, of doing things for him which he might have learned to do for himself. Furthermore, she had been ashamed of his backwardness and tried to hide it from her friends and neighbors, and then she was ashamed of having felt shame. Of course, she could not gain peace through mere verbal reassurance, however thirstily she lapped it up. She needed many opportunities to talk herself out, more chances for this confessional type of expiation, and help in the suggested efforts to return to her previous social and communal life from which she had removed herself in sacrificial isolation because of her feelings of shame and guilt and remorse.

Larry White was brought to our clinic at the age of seven and one-half years. His parents were distressed by his poor progress in school and by the suggestion that he be placed in an ungraded class. Larry was their only child, who had come to them after eight years of married life. His birth, preceded by a miscarriage and much gynecological maneuvering, was greeted with jubilation. His mother, previously an efficient office manager, took Larry over as the biggest assignment of her career. Her feeding methods made and kept him nice and chubby. Speech development was somewhat delayed, but this, she reasoned, is true of many children who later become regular chatterboxes. His faulty articulation was handled by sending him to a "teacher of expression and dramatics." He did well in nursery school and kindergarten. He was a happy, sociable, and well-mannered child.

Then the parents experienced their great shock. Larry could not do his first-grade work, failed of promotion, and finally was recommended for a special class. At first, the mother blamed his eyesight, but three successive examinations convinced her that his vision was not at fault. The mother tried to do his homework with him, and each attempt made her more impatient. She then employed a tutor for him. When his scholastic performance showed no improvement, the parents began to transfer the blame to Larry himself. The father found comfort in the formula that Larry was "mentally lazy." The mother began to nag and punish him and deprive him of privileges. Larry became rebellious under the many-sided pressures, was increasingly restless, at times even destructive, and developed behavior ostensibly intended to get even with his critics and oppressors.

His IQ was 77.

The mother reported that her nephews and nieces all had superior intelligence and remarked significantly: "I can't understand. Why does this happen to me?" The father, more genuinely fond of the child, said: "I think he is perfect apart from school," and added that his wife was disturbed because Larry obviously was not a genius. Thereupon she said categorically: "I want him to go to college. We can afford it."

It is clear that one could not use a sledge hammer in dealing with Larry's parents. Merely telling them that their son was not ready for first-grade work did not solve the essential problem. They had known this for some time. But they needed help in learning to accept the child as he was without a sense of personal shame and failure. Larry's mother felt shamed and socially disgraced by having a child whom society considered inferior. She felt guilty because the unpleasant thought must have kept obtruding itself that, after all her gynecological difficulties, she should perhaps have remained childless. She felt frustrated because her one great asset, her efficiency, had suffered defeat.

Examples such as these can be produced almost indefinitely. But even the small number of cited instances suffices to bring out a few highly important considerations. It is, of course, necessary for the expert to make the best possible use of the available test methods in order to obtain a scientifically valid assessment of a child's developmental potentialities. The application of these tests requires skill, experience, patience, and a setting in which the tested child would be at his ease and cooperate to his best ability. Many pitfalls must be avoided, such as testing a child during his regular nap time, failure to take into account an existing impairment of hearing or vision, psychometric examination immediately preceding or following a convulsion, or difficulty in allaying a child's acute anxiety which may manifest itself in speechless timidity or noisy defiance.

When a test has been completed satisfactorily and the child's intellectual endowment has been ascertained with reasonable accuracy, it is the expert's duty to report and explain his findings to the child's parents. It should hardly seem necessary to point out that such a report, if it involves the disclosure of a child's retardation, should be made tactfully, lucidly, and truthfully. But I have known parents who, without any concern for their emotional readiness, were thrown into a panic by the words *feebleminded, imbecile,* or *moron,* hurled at them as if from an ambush. I have also known good-natured doctors who did not have the heart to confront the parents with the true state of affairs and mumbled something to the effect that Johnny or Janie may "outgrow" the developmental lag or "catch up" with other children of his or her age.

I once had a long-distance telephone call from a physician in a small town, who asked me to see a six-year-old boy who was markedly retarded. For several years he had "played along" with Billy's parents, who were his personal friends. He minimized, if not ridiculed, their apprehensions. When Billy did not begin to talk long past the expected time, he reminded the parents of a cousin of his who had not talked until the age of four years, but then made up for lost time and eventually graduated from high school and college. He advised: "If Billy won't talk, just don't give him the things he wants unless he asks for them verbally." When this method did not work and the parents wondered whether they should have Billy tested, he said some unkind words about "all that psychology stuff." But when Billy was to be enrolled in the first grade, the school authorities refused to accept him. The heartbroken parents were enraged at the physician who, they felt, had either been inexcusably ignorant or had knowingly betrayed their trust in him. When I saw them, they asked again and again: "*Why* didn't he tell us?"

Adequate examination and the issuance of correct information are indeed indispensable. But they by no means constitute the whole of the expert's responsibility. The cited examples show that the mere procedure of testing a child, the mere determination of an intelligence quotient, the mere pronouncement of the test results do not in themselves take care of the significant matter of family sentiments. It is true that each situation is unique and that different parents come with different problems. Yet it is possible to pick out from the large welter of cases several recurrent puzzlements which are voiced almost invariably. Allow me to enumerate some of the questions which are asked regularly with a great deal of feeling and to which the inquirers hope to get straightforward answers, without evasion and without hedging:

- What is the cause of our child's retardation?
- Have we personally contributed to his condition?
- Why did this have to happen to us?
- What about heredity?

• Is it safe to have another child?

• Is there any danger that our normal children's offspring might be similarly affected?

• How is his (or her) presence in the home likely to affect our normal children?

• How shall we explain him (or her) to our normal children?

• How shall we explain him (or her) to our friends and neighbors?

• Is there anything that we can do to brighten him (or her) up?

• Is there an operation which might help?

• Is there any drug which might help?

• What about glutamic acid?

• Will our child *ever* talk?

• What will our child be like when he (or she) grows up?

• Can we expect graduation from high school? From grammar school?

• Would you advise a private tutor?

• Should we keep our child at home or place him (or her) in a residential school?

• What specific school do you recommend?

• If a residential school, how long will our child have to remain there?

• Will our child become alienated from us if placed in a residential school?

• Will our child ever be mature enough to marry?

• Do you think that our child should be sterilized and, if so, at what age?

These are some of the questions asked commonly by the parents of retarded children. These questions vary, of course, depending on the degree of the child's retardation, on the presence or absence of other children in the family, on the parents' financial resources, on their ideas about social prestige, on their degree of acceptance or rejection of the child.

It is not possible to answer every one of these questions unequivocally. Science has not advanced sufficiently — and probably never will — to make omniscient persons of the consulted physician or psychologist. Aside from the fact that causes of retardation are not always the same in all instances and that there may be multiple contributing factors in the same instance, the search for an ultimate cause often runs against the barrier of our incomplete knowledge. I have never encountered a parent who respected me less because, in answer to the question about the cause of his or her child's retardation, I made no secret of my inability to supply a definite answer. Intelligent parents usually realize fully that would-be erudite terms, such as innate, congenital, or constitutional, though literally correct, often beg rather than answer their question. What most of them hope to hear is indeed not so much a piece of etiological wisdom in words of Greek or Latin origin as an authoritative and sympathetic endorsement of themselves, of their human and parental competence, of their right not to blame themselves for what has happened.

Parents whose first child happens to be seriously retarded are almost invariably plagued by the question of whether or not they should have another child. There is a conflict between the strong desire to enjoy the pleasure of having a healthy child and the simultaneous fear that things may go wrong again. The parents always wait for an opportunity to present this question to the person whom they consult about their handicapped offspring. They are disappointed if this opportunity is not forthcoming. It is not an easy thing to help in the solution of this conflict. For one thing, the question is not merely a desire for information. Behind it is sometimes a scheme, of which the parents themselves are not necessarily aware, to throw the whole burden of responsibility on the adviser. If the second child should also be afflicted, the parents are clear of any blame. They can point an accusing finger at the adviser who had told them what they wanted to hear. It has been my policy to remind parents that every childbirth entails a risk, that no one could possibly have predicted that their first child would be born handicapped. Though experience teaches that lightning does not usually strike twice in the same place, the risk, however small, must rest with the parents. But if they do decide in favor of having another child, they should do so only if they are capable of freeing themselves of any anticipation of disaster. Such constant dread before and after the arrival of the new baby would create an attitude not conducive to a wholesome relationship even with the healthiest and sturdiest child.

There is no time to go into a discussion of all the questions which have been enumerated above. But the introductory examples show how profoundly the feelings of parents are involved in their types of curiosity, in the handling of their retarded children, and in their need for understanding and guidance. Like all human beings, the parents of retarded children react to their feelings. Their own life experiences, which have helped to shape their personalities, have contributed to the manner in which they adjust to pleasant and unpleasant realities in general, and to the presence of a handicapped child in particular.

In essence, one may distinguish three principal types of reaction:

1. Mature acknowledgement of actuality makes it possible to assign to the child a place in the family in keeping with his specific peculiarities. The child is accepted as he is. The mother neither makes herself a slave to him, nor does she take her inevitable frustrations out on him. She goes on functioning in her accustomed way. She continues her associations with her friends and acquaintances. The father shares her fondness for the child. Both parents manage to appraise the needs of their normal children as well and to distribute their normal children as well and to distribute their parental contributions accordingly.

2. Disguises of reality create artificialities of living and planning which tend to disarrange the family relationships. The fact of the handicap is seen clearly but is ascribed to some circumstances, the correction of which would restore the child to normalcy. Some culprit is assumed in the child's character or body or in the educational inadequacy of the trainers. The child's poor scholastic progress in the regular grades is interpreted as a manifestation of laziness or stubbornness which must be exorcised with painfully punitive methods; the full burden is placed on the child himself. His low marks, his failure of promotion and the school's recommendation that he be placed in an ungraded class are taken as a result of the blameworthy effrontery of a

willfully unaccommodating child. Parental pressures to speed up his lagging speech development, to correct his indistinct articulation, and to improve his homework heap misery on the child, who finds it impossible to gain parental approval.

Instead of or in addition to the child himself, his body comes in for frantic attempts at correction. Tongues are clipped, prepuces are amputated, tonsils are evicted with the notion that somehow such measures will undo the reality of his handicap. Thyroid extract, caused to be swallowed by some physicians with hazy etiologic notions, and chiropractic adjustments of an allegedly misplaced vertebra are still much too frequently employed as a means of disguising reality.

3. Complete inability to face reality in any form leads to its uncompromising denial. The formula goes something like this: "There is absolutely nothing the matter with the child. Those who are anxious about his development are merely pessimistic spreaders of gloom. Some children walk or talk sooner than others, and some take their time." This is often the reaction especially of fathers who have no knowledge of children and do not wish to be bothered about them. They are away at work most of the day, have a glimpse of the child when he is asleep, hear the child's laughter on the rare occasion when they pick him up, and conclude with a shrug of the shoulder: "I can't see anything unusual."

A busy surgeon, the father of three children, could not see anything unusual about his youngest child, a severely withdrawn, autistic boy whom his mother brought to our clinic against her husband's wishes. The surgeon finally came, after several invitations. He had no idea of the child's developmental data; he left all this to his wife, he declared complacently. I tried to get an emotional rise at least by making him angry. I asked whether he would recognize any one of his three children if he met him unexpectedly in the street. He thought for a while, scratched his head, and then said calmly: "Well, I don't really know if I would." He felt that his wife's concern about the child was all nonsense, but if she wanted to bring him to the clinic, that was all right, too;

after all, this was her own business.

Any slightest acquaintance with the elementary principles of psychology is enough to indicate that all these different types of attitudes and resulting practices are deeply anchored in the emotional backgrounds of the individual parents and other relatives. Smothering overprotection, cold rejection, nagging coercion, or open neglect defended as proper tactics necessary to cope with the child's handicap are, in the main, fundamental, dynamically evolved reactions which seize on the handicap as a readily accessible, superficial explanation.

All of this leads to the inescapable conclusion that the study and treatment of exceptional children would be sorely incomplete if the emotional factors of family relationships were left out of the consideration. In every instance, the place of the exceptional child in the family structure calls for a thorough overhauling, often with the urgent need for interviews with the parents. Frequently enough, the parents themselves beg for such an overhauling; they do so by asking seemingly specific or insignificant questions, and are most appreciative if such hints are understood and they are given an opportunity to talk themselves out before an experienced and sympathetic listener.

PART II

THE INITIAL INFORMING INTERVIEW
WITH THE PARENTS

Chapter 6

Sensitivity of One Person
to Another

TAMARA DEMBO, Ph.D.*

W HY do parents of handicapped children feel that professional people are frequently insensitive to their needs? This question will be discussed first, and then suggestions will be made on how we might improve the relationship between professional people and these parents.

Only one frequently occurring case of unsatisfactory interaction of professional people and clients will be discussed here. Much of what will be pointed out, however, will be applicable to a number of other situations.

The case to be considered is the conduct of a professional person toward a client — a parent of a young, extremely handicapped child. The professional might be, for example, a physician, social worker, or psychologist. It frequently happens that on the first visit of the family to the hospital, the professional person suggests institutionalization of the child. He gives as reasons the inability of the child to improve under any circumstances and the fact that the institutionalization will be best for the whole family. Such behavior by a professional person, during a first visit by the client, is much criticized by parents.

Note: Reprinted by permission of the author and *Rehabilitation Literature, 25*:231-235, 1964; published by the National Society for Crippled Children and Adults, Inc.

*Dr. Dembo, professor of psychology at Clark University, Worcester, Mass., is also director of the Research Training Program in Psychology of Rehabilitation. This paper is a by-product of an investigation, "Psychological Development in Cerebral Palsy," supported in part by a grant from the Association for the Aid of Crippled Children and in part by U.S. Public Health Service Research Grant M1149 from the National Institute of Mental Health.

In the following, for brevity's sake, professional people will be referred to simply as professionals.

Social sensitivity or lack of it is frequently considered a characteristic of the personality. It seems to me, however, that the so-called insensitivity of the professional, as it is perceived by the client, is strongly influenced by a number of psychological determinants and by a discrepancy existing between the professional and the client in regard to these determinants. One such determinant is the *position* occupied by the professional in regard to the handicapped child. As we shall see, it is quite different from the position of the client. Another determinant is the *purpose of the visit*, differently thought of by the professional and the client. A third is the difference in evaluation of expectations concerning the *likelihood of improvement* of the handicap.

As a consequence of all these differences, the client and the professional arrive at different requirements concerning the proper behavior of a professional. If, then, the professional does not behave in accordance with the client's requirements, the parent will feel that the professional is insensitive to the client's needs, wishes, and values.

Starting with discussion of the difference in *position* occupied by the client and by the professional, we shall first describe the position of the professional. The professional himself does not experience the problems brought about by the handicap, that is, the professional is not the sufferer. It is one thing to know that *another person* has a handicapped child and quite another thing to be a *parent* of a handicapped child. Characteristically, the professional is in the position of an outsider, and as an outsider he looks at the relationship of the parent to the handicapped child from a distance. The parent is in quite a different position — he is inside the area or situation directly affected by the impact of the handicap.

The two positions of the outsider and of the insider carry with them two different roles. The role of the outsider is that of an observer, and the role of the insider is that of a participant. Carriers of a role usually carry a notion of an ideal role. The ideal of an observer is to be an objective observer, and he is supported in carrying this ideal by being taught to be objective.

To be an objective observer means to not get personally involved in what is observed. The observer feels that to be a *good* objective observer, he should not be swayed or influenced by the feelings of the insider. It is, then, understandable that the outsider may actually avoid finding out how it feels to be an insider. Applying the above to our case, not only is the professional by virtue of his position an objective observer, but his values concerning the ideal role make him resist paying attention to the parent's feelings toward the child.

Further, because the observer is an outsider, the impact of the situation in its immediacy affects him little. He is freer to concern himself with more general aspects of the situation and more remote problems than is the parent. In actuality, this is what he does, but he does it in a somewhat abstract way. Not experiencing, as he does the parent, the strong ties to the handicapped child in the immediate present, the professional is able to disregard them and emphasize the interests of the whole family. However, being an outsider to the family in question, he does not take the individuality of this particular family into account, and he thinks in abstract terms about what he regards as good for families in general.

For the insider the "here and now" is of great concern, and he has a particular, individual relationship to each member of the family. The parent feels, therefore, that the child who needs more thought, attention, and care than others should get it and that other members of the family can be asked to offer their help. We notice that the values of the insider and outsider are considerably different.

The difference in the positions of the insider and of the outsider, that is, of the sufferer and the observer, influences their judgment as to the *purpose* of the visit. Specifically, the professional sees the purpose of the visit as an objective, realistic evaluation of the situation, as a determination of *facts,* that is, as a determination of the severity of the handicap and of the most probable outcome in the future. If he knew how to alleviate the handicap, he would concern himself with the treatment of the child and discuss with the parents how to handle and help the child. In a case that the professional considers "hopeless," he feels he does not have any useful suggestions to make concerning the actual treatment of the child and does not need to pay attention to the problem of dealing with the child day by day. Characteristically, when the parent says that the child has shown some improvement in the past, the professional tends to disregard the remarks, judging the improvements to be either figments of the parent's imagination or so insignificant as not to be worthy of attention.

Turning again to the parent, we find that he agrees with the professional that it is important to have an objective, realistic evaluation of the situation, that is, to know how severe the handicap is and to know what to expect in the future. However, the factual determination is only one of two purposes leading him to go to the professional. The second — and it seems to be the major purpose — is to achieve satisfaction of his wishes. The parent's wishes are to find out that the handicap is not as severe as it looks, that the future entails promise, that there are ways of alleviating the handicap, and that the professional will show him such ways or direct him to somebody who will be able to show them to him. These wishes of the parent are much stronger than his need to know the realistic facts, especially so if the statement of the facts would bring nothing but disappointment. The major purpose of the visit for the parent is to acquire support in his belief in the possibility of improvement rather than to arrive at the knowledge of the certainty of a negative outcome.

These subjective demands of the parent are evaluated by the professional as hindrances to the management of the case. Faced with a "hopeless" case, the professional feels that it is his duty to tell the parent what the actual objective "truth" of the matter is. He feels he helps the parent when he tries to make him become realistic and accept the objective state of affairs. The professional, in what he believes to be attempts to help, might go so far as to pound into the parent that the wishes the parent has are useless and plainly harmful for planning. It is here that the professional and the client part, and it is here that clashes occur.

A client will feel that a professional is "insensitive" if he does not respect his wishes and does not even *try* to find a way to satisfy them. The professional will, at the same time, call the client "completely unrealistic" and offer the following argument: If a negative outcome is expected with as high a probability, say, as in 99.9 percent of cases, this is the outcome one has to expect will actually occur. Thus, it is most realistic, says the professional, to count on no improvement and to be guided in one's actions by the belief that no improvement will take place. The professional further asserts that such a realistic conclusion not only is valid for him, but has universal validity and thus has to be accepted by the parent as a guide in his actions.

The parent disagrees. His paramount desire is to be able to hope for the improvement of *his* child, and this leads him to interpret facts differently. He asserts that the professional should not consider the most highly probable outcome as the one that *will* occur. The existence of a fraction of a percent of probability of the positive outcome (disregarded by the professional) is of major importance to the client. To him this indicates that one out of a thousand cases, or even one out of a million, must improve and that this one child can be *his* child. When the professional says that there is "not even one chance in a million," the parent struggles for hope by asserting that errors in judgment, even by an expert, occur; that there are always exceptions to the rule, and that the professional might have been at fault in placing his child within the hopeless group. Further, there are chances that future discoveries will help the child. The parent demands, therefore, that the professional mention these possibilities to the parent and that he support the parent in his belief that no prediction of a negative outcome can be made with absolute certainty.

The struggle for hope just described is not limited to parents of severely handicapped children. Whenever a person suffers from a threatening loss of greatest importance to him, he struggles for hope. In a situation of despair a person, to succeed in gaining hope, tries and usually is able to make a step that he would normally reject; he exchanges the dictum of probability, which guides us in everyday life, for the dictum of possibility.

The probability dictum prescribes as follows: Be guided by the expectation of the most probable outcome, since it is most reasonable to believe that the most probable outcome *will* take place. It is paradoxical that a high probability of an outcome leads us to the belief that this outcome actually will occur. This belief might be supported by the requirement of unilateral guidance needed for orderly planning in life.

The dictum of possibility, which in hopeless situations the person actively attempts to accept as a guide, says, be guided in your actions and planning by the wished-for possible occurrence. One can arrive at this dictum by thinking in the following way: There is always a possibility that the negative evaluation of a situation is wrong; the future is never completely known; therefore, the positive outcome is actually possible — It *does* occur. Since it *must* sometimes occur, it might occur here and now, and it might occur to me; thus the hopeless situation is actually not a completely hopeless one.

In an everyday life situation, when we think about matters of relatively little importance to us, we are supposed to think "rationally." Actually, however, we ascribe to the most probable outcome an irrational certainty of outcome. When we face a loss of value highly important to us emotionally, we seem to become more accurate in our judgment, or if you wish, actually more "rational" in that we do not disregard an outcome of a minute probability of occurrence. The irrationality appears in the greater weight we have to give to the highly improbable, just possible, rather than to the most probable in order to acquire hope.

This ascription of great weight to the merely possible is brought about by emotional means, namely, by the impact of the paramount, all-inclusive desire. How this desire overcomes the weight of the impact of the most probable outcome upon our thinking is not yet well known. Doing away with the weight of the high frequency of the most probable occurrence and the acceptance of the dictum of possibility as a guide in thinking and planning is what is experienced by us as *having gained hope* in a desperately hopeless situation.

The parent, struggling for hope, demands that the professional accept the legitimacy of this struggle. The need for acceptance and understanding on the part of the professional is of paramount importance to the parent.

Here, if only in passing, let us mention that the client needs hope, not only to diminish his suffering, but also to be able to take care of his handicapped child and to engage, without undue strain, in other everyday activities. It is hope that saves him from paralyzing despair and despression. The content of this hope is that the child will improve; the parent does not demand support of the hope of complete recovery.

When professionals who strongly believe in an objective, realistic approach are faced with the statement that many clients object to being robbed of hope, they may give you one of two answers. Some professionals will deny that they rob the parents of hope and say that they only point out to the parents that no improvement can be expected. This, of course, means that, although they see the case as a "hopeless" one, they say they do not touch on the problem of hope as such. There are other professionals who are more extreme in their assertion of the value of a realistic approach; they insist that hope *should* be taken away from the parents because they believe that if hope is left, the parents will only unduly postpone the most important decision they have to make, namely, whether to institutionalize the child. These professionals insist that the parents should give up hope because this would save the parents from unnecessary trouble such as undue expenses and running from one expert to another.

The latter reasons presented to the parent are judged by the parent to be inappropriate and to show complete lack of understanding by the professional of the parent's needs. The parent made the appointment with the professional to get help with the child. The parent did not come to the professional to ask for advice on how to spend his money or for advice on how to manage his life in general.

From the parent's point of view, it is the professional who lacks in understanding the needs and feelings of the parent and who lacks in sensitivity in regard to social relationships. The parent feels this most strongly when, *unasked,* the professional raises the question of institutionalization. Such behavior on the part of the professional, the parent states, is both painful and shocking to him. Such behavior further implies to the parent lack of respect for his judgment as a parent and an undue attempt on the part of the professional to dominate him. Furthermore, the remarks of the professional that indicate a devaluative attitude toward the handicapped child cause further pain for the client. This is implied when the professional calls the child a hopeless case, not worthy of any effort, just a "vegetable," not a child. The parent feels not only that the lack of respect is expressed to the loved child, for whom the client suffers, but also that disrespect is shown toward him, the parent, who so strongly relates himself to a devalued being.

All of us might agree by now with the parent that the professional, at least the one who goes to the extreme in his realistic and objective evaluations, shows lack of sensitivity in regard to the most *complex* relationship of the parent to his handicapped child, full of meaning to the parent, full of negative but also positive feeling toward the child. This relationship requires slow working through and disentanglement before any suggestions, concerning the institutionalization of the child can profitably be made to the parent by a professional.

In the beginning of this presentation the question was asked, Why do parents frequently feel that professional people are insensitive to their needs? A brief, inclusive answer can now be given: The professionals frequently appear to be insensitive to the parents because the professionals' position and values as outsiders stand in opposition to the position and values of the parents as insiders.

And now the second question: How can the relationship between professional people and clients be improved? To answer this question, we have to take a stand toward the views of the professional and the parent. This is necessary because the parent's and the professional's dissatisfaction with each other stems primarily not from the way in which the two parties communicate with each other but rather from a basic disagreement in their evaluation of each other's values. The main difficulty lies not in the form of the communication between the professional and the parent but in the content of the communication.

In order to make suggestions that would promise to alleviate the severity of the disagreement between the two parties, a third party will have to take a stand as to the viewpoints of the two parties. There are several ways of taking a stand: One can take sides with one or the other party, or in part with both of them, or one can take no sides.

When we act as researchers investigating the relationship of the professional and client and try to suggest an improvement in this relationship, we are the third party. As investigators, we have to take the stand that science permits us to take, namely, the one that can be shown scientifically to be valid. However, actual knowledge concerning the effect of the "realistic" or the "hopeful" approach upon the child, parents, and siblings – knowledge that would permit comparisons – does not exist. Nor is knowledge available as to the effect institutionalization or home care has on a severely handicapped child and on the members of the family. Thus, let us admit and state bravely that we do not know whether, when, and under what circumstances the viewpoint of the professional or of the parent is to be recommended. It is a fact that as scientists or researchers, as experts in knowledge, we have at present no scientific basis for stating to the parent what approach to take.

Does this mean that we are doomed to passivity? No, we can make suggestions as to what we believe will lead to better relationships between professionals and parents.

Here are three sets of suggestions for consideration. One set concerns the parent; the second, professionals presently in practice; and the third, students training to become professionals.

Let us consider the suggestions concerning the parents first. The discord between the parents and the professionals would be diminished if the parents were prepared to expect professionals to make recommendations and to express opinions contrary to their own. Also, the parents could be informed in advance that the professionals frequently do not support hope as to a positive outcome in the future, nor do they pay attention to parents' remarks as to the recent improvements of the child. The parents could be shown how the position of the outsider leads the professional to a particular viewpoint as to the purpose of the visit and makes him evaluate most highly the most probable outcome. The parents could be informed that the question of whether their or the professionals' approach is better for all involved has not yet been adequately studied and that knowledge in this area is lacking. The attention of the parents could be drawn to the fact that the suggestions of the professionals in this respect sometimes may not be better than those of any other person.

If the parents are brought to the realization of all of this, one should expect that they would, as the saying goes, understand better "the position of the professional" and be less disturbed by the unwelcomed recommendations of the professionals. The parents' first visit to the professional is a particularly appropriate occasion for the communication of the above information.

To the professional in practice it is suggested that he himself take into account the following points when talking to parents: First, knowledge sufficient to decide whether a so-called realistic or hopeful approach is better is not available. Second, his own views on the matter are determined by his position, his expectations, and his personal values, just as those of the parents are due to their position, and their values, and their expectations. Third, parents come to him for comfort and support of hope, and he can alleviate, at least momentarily, the suffering of the parents by supporting hope. Fourth, even before starting to examine the child, he might inform the parents about the suggestions for the parents that were presented above. The professional might then, if he wishes, state his personal opinions by designating them as his· *personal* leanings toward a realistic or hopeful approach.

In offering a set of suggestions for students in professional training, we can go farther than those we give to an established professional person. At present, the development of viewpoints, opinions, and selection of values to be used by students in contacts with clients is left to the natural course of events, that is, it is left to the pressure of the position that the students will occupy as professionals and to their personal preferences. Therefore, when students become professionals, they frequently act without realizing the one-sidedness of their viewpoints.

A one-sided viewpoint is characterized by a lack of realization that there are possible advantages to be gained from taking the point of view of another person. When a student adheres to his own outsider's viewpoint, he of course realizes the existence of the parent's hopeful one. However, he sees this other viewpoint from his own position, that of an outsider, and therefore as having only disadvantages and as leading to difficulties. He actually does not understand what makes the other person believe in the advantages of his own viewpoint. He can, however, be taught to see with the eyes of the other and to see the advantages of the viewpoint to which the other adheres. This can be done by showing him how to take the position of the other, by teaching him about the conditions leading to the other's viewpoint, and by making him accept tentatively some values of the other as premises.

Through such teaching, the viewpoint of the other would appear to be quite meaningful and have some value. The understanding of both viewpoints, one would expect, would lead to a respect for both viewpoints. Briefly stated, the actual understanding of the other, which involves a tentative acceptance of premises and values of the other, should make the student "emotionally tolerant."

Let us add that if the professional and the parent had the occasion, at least temporarily, to take the viewpoint of each other, neither would feel prompted to accuse the other in an emotional way; the professional would not find the parent quite so "unreasonable" and the parent might not find the professional so "insensitive."

The temporary taking of the position of the other might not only lead to emotional tolerance but also might bring about an even more far-reaching change. It might lead to the reconsideration of one's own viewpoint and to a change in one's beliefs and actions. Whether the outsider or the insider could change more easily is a question for research on value problems. It is, however, only one of the many topics in the area of value research that are in need of investigation if one intends to achieve better understanding between professional people and their clients.

The above discussion has dealt with one serious difficulty between the professional and the parent. Of course, it is not the only one. To mention some others, let us point to the cases in which parents come with a request for a "valuable treatment" that the professional might consider inappropriate. For example, they might virtually insist on the necessity of early bracing of a child, having heard from someone that this is a promising treatment. If the professional feels bracing inadvisable, he legitimately will have to act against these "hopes" of the parent. In this article we have not asserted a necessity for the professional to support all the hopes of the parent but asserted only the necessity of supporting a general psychologically hopeful atmosphere, that is, a hopeful view of the future, a belief in the possibility of improvement that offers to the parents a way of coping with the immediate demands of living with the handicapped child and the gradual acceptance of the particular situation.

It may have seemed that in this article we have sided too much with the parents and that the problems facing the professionals have been slighted. The unwarranted demands of the parents, the professionals' feeling of helplessness in hopeless cases, the necessity of conveying disappointing news to the parents, robbing them of exaggerated hopes, and last but not least, the difficulties in guiding the parents who resist warranted advice are, of course, important concerns of professionals and they are problems requiring thorough consideration within professional-client relationships. Taking the point of view of the other, on the part of both professionals and parents, necessitates thorough knowledge of both viewpoints.

In conclusion, the problem of how to arrive at the most fruitful relationship between professionals and clients is not limited to the professional and the parent of the physically handicapped child; it exists in all professional-client relationships. In fact, the problem of insensitivity of one person to another is present whenever an outsider and insider meet.

Chapter 7

Initial Counseling of Parents with Mentally Retarded Children

ISRAEL ZWERLING, M.D., Ph.D.

THE problem of how much, when, and how to tell the patient or his family is an ever-present one in medicine. The situation varies with the diagnosis, the nature of the patient or family, and the personality of the physician. When the diagnosis is clear-cut, the prognosis favorable, the patient or family free from great anxiety, and the physician confident of his therapy, the problem of informing the patient or family either does not arise at all or else permits ready disposition. The concern of the present paper is with mental deficiency, a situation in which none of these favorable factors prevails. Here the prognosis is almost uniformly poor, the etiology only infrequently ascertainable, the parents regularly anxious, and the physician seldom confident of a therapeutic regimen.

The anxiety of the parents is of particular concern to the physician who must tell them his diagnosis* of mental deficiency. There are a number of reasons for this anxiety. To begin with, there is an awareness of the long-term implications of the dignosis and of the extremely limited therapeutic outlook. Another reason is the widespread awe of the "mental" as against the "physical" in human malfunction. However far we prefer to feel we have moved from the era of demonology, an irrational fear of intellectual deficiency is still manifest precisely because it is "mental." It must

Note: Reprinted with permission of the author and the *Journal of Pediatrics,* *44*:469-479, 1954. Copyrighted by The C.V. Mosby Co., St. Louis, Mo.
*Although mental deficiency is not, in the usual sense, a "diagnosis," it is in most instances so considered and is used in this manner in the present paper.

also be noted that there is seen with extraordinary frequency a marked guilt reaction on the part of the parents. The sources of the guilt feelings are complex and outside the scope of this paper, but their manifestations are familiar to the physician who has dealt with the parents of retarded children. Finally, as Doll (1953) has stressed, the core of any definition of mental deficiency is social incompetence, and much of the parental anxiety reflects the social stigma inherent in severe and prolonged social incompetence. Abel (1953) has recently written: "The mentally retarded is a deviant who is perhaps treated with greater rejection and less respect by parents, teachers, and the community than is any other deviant, perhaps with the exception of the person with Hansen's disease." Certainly, a number of additional diseases provoke rejection and loss of respect by family and community, but it remains true that the characteristic attitude of the community to the mentally retarded child operates to heighten the anxiety of the parents of the child.

At the same time, much can be done precisely at the time the diagnosis is presented to the parents to reduce this anxiety and to promote a more accepting and constructive attitude toward the child. It is the thesis of this paper that the initial counseling of the parents is of critical importance in this regard, and that appropriate handling by the physician can turn a potentially devastating experience into the foundation for a satisfactory adjustment to the problem and to the child.

PROCEDURE

The National Association for Retarded Children initially stimulated this study and cooperated in the procedure. Members of the N.A.R.C., who were themselves parents of retarded children, were asked to communicate with me with regard to the circumstances of their first learning of the diagnosis, their reaction at the time, and their feelings about whether the situation had been well or poorly handled. Eighty-five letters were received from parents scattered over twenty-three states and Canada. The contents of these communications were then tabulated and form the basis of the discussion presented below.

Several considerations render the data unsuitable for normal statistical handling. These experiences are presented as reported by the parents, with no independent data available as to what the physician actually said or did. In addition to the misconceptions and distortions seen with some frequency immediately after contact with a physician, there is here the added problem of an interval of a few months to several years having elapsed between the actual contact with the doctor and the report of this contact by the parent. Again, these are unusual parents in that they have been able to accept their retarded child at least to the extent of identifying themselves with the membership of the National Association for Retarded Children. The ability to write about the initial experience of being informed of the diagnosis of mental deficiency in their child is a further differential factor in this regard. One parent wrote, ". . . a person cannot sit down and write of this experience without opening old wounds. I think you would get more information through interviews than letters, for somehow it is easier to talk than to write." Finally, it is likely that experiences felt by the parents to have been poorly handled by the doctor would be more likely to prompt a letter than experiences felt to have been adequately handled. It must therefore be stressed that the letters cited are by no means offered as reflections of what physicians generally do in handling this problem, nor is it the intent to offer a tabulation of how representative parents react to being informed of the diagnosis of mental deficiency. Rather, the reported experiences have been analyzed for their individual content, and common concerns have been extracted for discussion as suggested areas of interest to the physician faced with parents with retarded children. These are presented below and are then compared with techniques for handling the initial counseling of parents with retarded children proposed by three recent contributors to the literature in this field.

RESULTS

The Attitude of the Physician

A striking number of letters (33 of the 85) refer to the

importance of the attitude of the physician. A representative letter noted: "Dr. J. was superb in his telling of Steve's limitations. . . . Mainly, the points I remember were of course his gentle treatment of us, his exquisite choice of words so as to avoid the obnoxious ones. . . ." Another wrote: "We shall be everlastingly grateful to our young pediatrician for his skillful, sympathetic handling of our case. He took as much interest in us as he did in our child and spared us what may have been a dreadful shock." The converse experience is reported by another parent as follows: "When his prophecies failed to materialize within the allotted time, he sent us to a very distinguished neurologist-psychiatrist. This man pronounced the accurate diagnosis with a hard, cold, almost surgical economy of words and feelings. To put it mildly, he was brutal. My wife and I walked through the streets of Brooklyn, weeping openly." The significance to the parents of the attitude of the physician is reflected not only in the frequency with which it is mentioned but also in the degree of concern which is expressed. One parent reported that her doctor had commented about her mongoloid daughter that ". . . they make nice pets around the house." Another wrote: "This doctor was a woman, and I didn't have my child with me at the time. She asked me many questions about her training and eating habits, then she asked me about her speech. When I said she didn't talk, she told me I should put her away and forget I ever had her, unless I wanted to limit myself to a dog's life. At least a dog could bark, she told me. . . . Every time I think about this doctor, I think how much more I have than her, and that is love for human beings." One letter made it clear that the parent was not seeking maudlin sentimentality:

> I was taken back to my room, and about twenty minutes later my doctor came in and the tears were running down his cheeks. He said there was something terribly wrong with my baby. He couldn't tell me at first, but finally told me that my baby was the type known as mongoloid. . . . My doctor had a compassionate heart, but it just seems to me that he did not have the right psychological approach. I was terrorized over the situation and remained so for about three years.

The concern of these parents with the attitude of their doctors is, of course, not unique to the field of mental deficiency. It is my impression, however, that few diagnoses provoke more anxiety in the physician than feeble-mindedness. A meaningful study remains to be done in defining the sources of doctors' attitudes toward mental deficiency. In any case, it is apparent that some parents react with great sensitivity to the warmth or coldness, the gentleness or harshness, the acceptance or rejection in the attitude of the doctor.

Thoroughness of Diagnosis

Twelve of the letters received from the parents comment upon the thoroughness of the study which preceded the announcement of the diagnosis. Several shared the direct comment of the mother who wrote, "I, as a thinking parent, was not content with anything less than a complete study of the child." Another wrote, "Dr. B's statement, on hearing my story, was, 'I cannot say from this one examination just what is wrong, but if it were my child I would make certain tests.' . . . Blood tests were made and x-rays taken . . . the consensus of neurological, psychological, and medical examinations agreed with her tentative diagnosis." Another parent, reporting a less favorable experience, wrote, "A lot of the shopping around that doctors deplore would be avoided if doctors would take patients into their confidence and not act threatened when a consultation is requested." A less bitter report by another parent was:

> Dr. L. saw her for five minutes. . . . He told us gently enough that she would never be able to assume adult responsibilities and that there was a theory that the same kind of lesions as she had on her face, that Dr. B. had called adenoma sebaceum, probably were inside her skull and pressed on her brain. . . . We should have accepted what he said, but we felt that he had not seen her for long enough. . . . Dr. C., a psychiatrist friend of mine, told me that one of the things he had learned with experience was not to give patients a quick diagnosis. Even if he knew what was wrong, he said, he went through the motions of more examinations because that gave people more confidence that he was not judging hastily.

It is, of course, obvious that not all clinical types of mental deficiency require equal investigative effort. Further, and precisely in cases in which diagnosis is immediately apparent, parents will recognize the perceptiveness of the physician and will be pleased that prolonged study was not required. Certainly, too, the suggestion that the physician who knows the diagnosis and prognosis make a pretense of thoroughly examining the child must be rejected. It remains true, however, that in many instances the special skills required for an inclusive evaluation of a retarded child exceed those possessed by the individual practitioner. Pediatrics, neurology, radiology, psychology, psychiatry, and orthopedics, each may contribute. The physician should certainly be prepared, where indications exist, for consulting specialists in these and other fields, to explain the need for those consultations, and to utilize all available relevant professional resources toward the end of complete diagnosis.

Clarity of Communication

Related to both the attitude of the physician and the thoroughness of the study preceding the diagnosis is the problem of the kind of information requested by the parents. In this regard, there are several interrelated problems. As is so often the case in the communication of technical information to lay persons, the problem of intelligibility is relevant. One parent wrote, "I feel that it is the doctor's duty to have the parents in for a discussion of what the full meaning of their diagnosis is. Instead, in their well-meaning way, they left us with such a mumbo-jumbo of medical terms that I had to find a medical dictionary to look up the meaning." Another wrote of being sent by the family doctor to a specialist, who ". . . gave us what amounted to a great deal of double-talk in medical terms that were above my comprehension." Concern with the content of the doctor's statement was more prominent. Eleven letters made reference to the fact that the doctor had stressed the negative aspects of the picture to the total exclusion of any assets in the child. One parent wrote, "I believe that when the doctor tells parents the child is defective he should point out the fact that it is possible to maintain a normal family life with such a child . . . and not point out the negative side so readily, which is done most of the time." Another parent listed some of the current accomplishments of her five-year-old daughter, and added, "The thought has occurred to me many times, but there is no way of knowing, that it might have been a different story for me if the doctor had told me a few things like that . . . just knowing that they do act like human beings would have helped, I think." A third parent wrote, "Tim is five years old now, very lovable, and he can say several words and even group a few together. He can ride a bicycle. . . . All of the doctors who saw Tim were kind, but not one of them gave one word of hope or reassurance." A related problem was the concern of the parents for more information with regard to the prognosis and management of the child. Several expressed views similar to those of the parent who wrote, "Doctors should be supplied with more material so they could advise you . . . on the proper ways to rear a retarded child so that you will not expect more of the child than he is capable." Another wrote, more emphatically, "If I were to summarize what we would want, it is . . . an explanation to the parents of what [diagnostic procedures] has been done . . . what positive conclusions can be drawn, what uncertainties remain, what general prognosis can be made. . . . The physician should give continuing, positive advice, well founded and of a practical nature, on the day-to-day handling of problems."

It is here again pertinent to add that parents present a wide range of capacities for accepting and understanding the doctor's discussion. One must agree with the parent who wrote, ". . . when a husband is a Ph.D. and the wife a college graduate, I think the doctor should lay the books on the table. He makes himself look foolish when he doesn't." At the same time, initial counseling must also be provided to the parent who wrote, "My reaction to the knowledge of my child's retardation was to lead an army, all alone if necessary, to help her live a normal life." This parent never did get beyond the expression of her powerful feelings of protectiveness for her child to describe the actual experience of being informed of the diagnosis. No single formulation of content can hope to serve so varied a population. A second point to be stressed in this regard is that the physician is being asked to provide information in fields in which he only rarely attains competence – child rearing and education of retarded children. A technique reported upon favorably by the parents is that of providing appropriate literature at the time of initial counseling. Several excellent pamphlets and books are available, and a bibliography for such purposes may be readily obtained by writing to the National Association for Retarded Children.* An additional suggestion of even wider applicability is for the physician to direct the parents to the local council for retarded children. Most units maintain programs directed precisely toward answering these questions and at the same time serve to integrate the parents into the wider community aspects of the problem of mental deficiency.

Role of Religion

A theme which appeared in twenty-two of the eighty-five letters written by the parents was the positive role played by religion in their adjustment. In most instances there was only a brief reference to the role, but several parents devoted considerable emphasis to this source of help. One noted, "It was really through the church that I gained two important insights: one, that we looked at things as punishment which might be our own guilt feelings . . . two, in connection with the Bible story of the man born blind, that these things were not a reflection on the parents, but could be used as a means of helpful endeavor."

In this connection it would appear that the physician might extend the collaboration with the minister, priest, or rabbi, certainly not infrequent in many areas of work, to the initial counseling of parents with retarded children when this appears to be indicated.

Institutional Care

The most bitter expression of feeling by the parents concerned their being advised to institutionalize their retarded children. This subject was approached in widely varied ways. Some, concerned with the frequency with which the advice to institutionalize the child was given, wrote on the factors within the doctor which they felt to be responsible. One parent felt that, "medical doctors work

---

*420 Lexington Ave., New York, N.Y. 10017.

with so much sick tissue that they think everything defective should be scrapped." Some parents remarked on the lack of factual information concerning institutions possessed by the doctors urging this disposition. One wrote,

> ... this has come up with other doctors; they do not know the institutional setup and do not take the trouble to find out what facilities are actually available and suitable for the child, nor do they refer parents to positive sources of information on these topics. One psychiatrist recommended the W. . . . School [a very expensive private school] to the wife of a machinist. In our case, the recommendation of Letchworth Village [a New York State institution] to New Jersey residents was quite frustrating.

Fifteen parents commented on the attitude of the physician toward institutionalization as one of finding some place to "put away" the child rather than as a positive procedure in the management of the child. A rather typical statement by one parent read, "He folded his arms across his chest and without batting an eyelash said, 'You're wasting your time. The only thing to do with this child is to place him in an institution.' " Another parent wrote, "The doctor there . . . advised that we should put him away and forget about him. I have never in my life heard such a cruel sentence." Five parents characterized the doctor's attitude toward institutionalization as demanding. One wrote, "I can supply you, practically verbatim, with the interview we had with the doctor . . . and with our reactions over that weekend when we thought our boy would be snatched away to an institution in a very short time." Twelve letters referred scornfully to advice for immediate institutionalization and then described a currently adequate home adjustment. One parent wrote, "Each time we went to the doctor, he would ask us if we had taken out the papers yet, and when we said No, he would harass us further. . . . Our boy walked at three, stood up alone and walked on his birthday! Were we ever surprised! You can imagine our joy! It took us quite a time to really accept him for the child he was, and to see he would never be the child we would have like to have him be. He is a happy, well-adjusted and self-sufficient child." The parent quoted above as interpreting the advice to institutionalize her child as a "sentence" went on to write, "My boy is now six years old. He goes to D. . . . School. He is talking very well and can carry out all the orders I give him in the home. He is sweet, very affectionate, and I guess the dearest little soul on this earth as far as his mother, daddy, and sister are concerned." A less frequently voiced complaint about advice to institutionalize concerned the timing. Characteristic was the statement, "I would say that a doctor should take it in easy stages in telling a parent. Tell them the child is retarded, yes, but don't go into a long talk about institutions. A parent is absolutely in no condition at the time of the initial shock to hear a verdict like that."

These statements serve to emphasize a most important area of concern to the physician who must tell parents of the existence of mental deficiency in a child. The decision to institutionalize a retarded child is complexly determined by the nature of the child, the available institutions, the parents, the siblings, and the timing of the procedure in the light of all these factors. The role of the institution in the management of the retarded child is variable; the proportion of actual training and of sheer custodial care will vary with the adequacy of the institution as well as the abilities of the children. Institutionalization is not a disposition to be cavalierly arrived at, nor one to be callously recommended.

When to Inform Parents

Among the parents who commented on the point, there was substantial agreement concerning the question of *when* they should be told of the diagnosis. Eighteen of the letters reported at least one, and generally several, experiences of being told that their child would "grow out of it." Thirteen of the letters make the specific complaint that the parents should have been told earlier: "He [the consultant pediatrician] also told us to go back to our family doctor and not to go chasing after miracles. At the time I was very depressed and bitter toward our family doctor. Since then we have gone back to him, but there is still a little resentment because he didn't tell us himself when he first suspected the baby was retarded." Another wrote bitterly, "I continually asked my pediatrician why Brian was so slow in sitting up, in standing, in walking; if there was any chance that his physical slowness would be accompanied by mental retardation.

Always I got a placating, 'No, he is just slow and will catch up.' There was no effort to refer me to a psychologist or psychiatrist for testing and advice. Do not the doctors know the signs of mental retardation and deficiency, or are they just afraid to tell us?" Several parents described the converse experience; one wrote, "I'm glad I knew from the start. Worry would have been worse." Another wrote, in a similar vein, ". . . learning the results of his tests was at the same time a tremendous blow and a tremendous relief from worrying and wondering just what, if anything, was wrong." In a few instances (5 letters) a stronger feeling is expressed on this matter in terms of the feelings of inadequacy developed by the parents. One mother reported, in dialogue form, a series of conversations with various doctors in which she asked about specific developmental lags and was continually reassured that the child merely needed more time, ". . . until I got to the point of feeling that I was a neurotic mother — a completely inadequate one — with no one paying any attention to me, not even my own husband." Only one letter expressed support for a delay in being told the diagnosis. This mother learned that she had given birth to a mongoloid child through a tragedy of errors in which the husband, obstetrician, and pediatrician each thought one of the others had told her and, therefore, greeted her successively on the morning after the delivery with expressions of sympathy. She wrote, "I do not think a mother should be told until she has had at least two weeks to recuperate from the actual birth of the child."

In the matter of the timing of discussions and advising institutionalization, the parents contributing letters to the present study are particularly unrepresentative samples of the population with which the physician must deal. First, these *are* parents of retarded children, and one would have to raise the question of how vigorous a protest against doctors who gave incautious diagnoses of mental deficiency could be culled from parents with children who did "grow out of it." Certainly, the anguish caused by needlessly alarming such parents can equal or exceed the despair of the parents contributing to this report. Again, these are parents who have accepted their children at least to the point of joining member units of the N.A.R.C. Denial is then not prominent in their collective defenses against the impact of the diagnosis, and denials on the part of their physicians are condemned. No conclusion concerning actual practice is, therefore, warranted from the letters in this regard. However, it may be emphasized that the letters express concerns which are central to good clinical practice. The task of the physician is to become fully skilled in developmental diagnosis so that clear indications of mental deficiency are not relegated to the lower end of the normal range. It is likely that the anxiety of the physician rather than a lack of knowledge concerning developmental norms or a lack of faith in the capacity of the parents to accept the diagnosis prompts some of the counsel for waiting for the child to "grow out of it." It is the further task of the physician to recognize and avoid such motive for his counsel.

A number of additional issues were raised by the parents who submitted letters, but these represented unique interests of these separate parents and have therefore been omitted from this discussion.

DISCUSSION

The initial counseling of parents with retarded children has received scant attention in the literature, particularly in the nonpsychiatric literature. Jensen (1950) has recently dealt with this problem. He emphasizes that the gravity of the situation is better appreciated when it is realized that between one and four million *families,* rather than individual children, are involved. He feels that errors made by physicians in handling the problem may increase the suffering of the parents, and lists as the three most frequent errors: "(1) Delay in defining the problem early in the patient's life, (2) encouragement of parents by holding out false hopes, which naturally results in disillusionment later, and (3) too much direct advice and/or urging adoption of a specific plan — too often institutionalization." He feels, with regard to the latter point, that the doctor may fail to take into account "the strong emotional ties that most parents center in the mentally handicapped person," and may thus invite resistance to his diagnosis. He lists as basic steps in the contact with parents: providing ample time, thoroughly studying the child, exercising care in the language used to the parent, respecting the right and the responsibility of the parents to determine disposition, maintaining an objective and analytic attitude, and using trained but not overaggressive psychologists and social workers for such contacts. In his final interview with parents, he offers the most likely explanation for the retardation, and offers four solutions: home care, boarding home, private school, and state school. He is careful to state the latter choice as taking advantage of the opportunity and facilities offered by the state. He stresses the actual saving of time which results from this procedure, both through a reduced need by the parents to "shop around," and an increased capacity for understanding the child and lessening destructive pressures on him.

Doll (1953) notes that the parent's question, "Is my child feeble-minded?" is really meant to be, "How feeble-minded is my child?" He sees the parents as asking four basic questions: "How is my child from the standpoint of suspicion of mental deficiency? What is the cause of it, if present? What have I to look forward to? How long will it take, and what shall I do in the meantime?" He introduces a concept which he terms "the cluster aspect of parental counseling," which he defines as taking into account all the factors in the family which bear upon the counseling process — the harmony in the marriage, absence of one parent, age and sex of other children, and so on. He states, "The basic point of 'cluster counseling' is that there is no simple, single solution," and stresses that counseling requires "realistic, sympathetic human attitudes toward the client and his family." Storrs has stated similar principles in dealing with parents making application for the state institution which he directs:

> Medicine is an art, and handling the relatives is one of the important functions of this art. In my opinion, every case is individual and should be investigated as such. I want to know all I can about the child, the family, and all situations connected with both the child and the family. . . . Doctors as a class do not seem to realize the enormity of the tragedy experienced by the parents when they find that their child is definitely defective. This should be appreciated by all doctors and they should size up the parents. . . . I have always felt that it was a mistake not to tell the parents the whole truth. . . . Parents have in

many instances been from doctor to doctor, spending their money;
have been given evasive answers; have built up hopes over and over,
only to have them dashed to the ground, finally. It always seemed to
me that they should be told the truth as early as possible — with, as I
have said, consideration of the family situation.

Kanner (1953) stresses the increasing recognition of the need
for "professional and at the same time humane attention" to the
parents of retarded children. His list of the questions most
commonly asked of him by parents is an excellent summary of the
wide range of issues likely to require attention in this situation,
and includes questions on causes, impact upon siblings, indications
for or against future children, the handling of friends and relatives,
available medical treatment, training possibilities, and prognosis.
He notes that unequivocal answers frequently cannot be given, and
states, "I have never encountered a parent who respected me less
because, in answer to the question about the cause of his or her
child's retardation, I made no secret of my inability to supply a
definite answer. . . . What most of them hope to hear is indeed not
so much a piece of etiological wisdom in words of Greek and Latin
origin as an authoritative and sympathetic endorsement of
themselves, of their human and parental competence, of their right
not to blame themselves for what has happened." His approach to
the frequent question about additional children is to place the
responsibility clearly upon the parents themselves, pointing out
the inevitable risk in any birth, and urging that the decision to
have additional children must be contingent upon a concomitant
freedom from anticipation of disaster. He describes parents'
reactions to mental deficiency in a child as variants of three basic
types — mature acknowledgement of the actuality and acceptance
of the child, disguises of reality with search for either scapegoats
upon which to blame the retardation or magic cures, and complete
denial of the existence of any retardation. Since these basic
attitudes will color all aspects of the care and management of the
retarded child, it becomes the obligation of the physician to
identify the attitudes present in the parents, and work for a
"thorough overhauling" in the direction of mature acceptance.

The large areas of agreement between the counsel of these
writers and the feelings expressed by the parents will be

immediately apparent. It was of special interest to me that two of the parents referred to two of the authors cited as having provided consultations in the cases of their children, and in both instances the parents described the experiences with enthusiastic praise.

There is a growing tendency to refer retarded children to special clinics for diagnostic evaluation and for treatment recommendations. In communities where such clinics are available, the problem of counseling the parents will be shifted from the individual practitioner to the clinic staff. However, such facilities remain few in number and inadequate in staff for more than token capacities. The individual physician — the pediatrician, neurologist, psychiatrist, or most frequently the general practitioner — will continue to serve as initial counselor for the great majority of parents with retarded children and must develop appropriate knowledge and skills for this difficult task. The reports of the parents who contributed letters are not felt to reflect the characteristic practices of physicians. They are, however, felt to be of value in providing principles for the correct handling of the initial counseling situation, and these are seen to be in accord with the principles announced by Jensen, Doll, and Kanner in recent contributions to the field.

SUMMARY

Eighty-five letters from parents with retarded children describing the initial experience of the parents on being informed of the diagnosis of mental deficiency have been analyzed from the viewpoint of the parents' feelings concerning the handling of the situation by the physician.

The letters stressed the importance of the physician's attitude, the thoroughness of the study which preceded the announcement of the diagnosis, and the clarity and directness of his communication.

Complaints were lodged against the tendency to stress only the limitations and not the assets of the child, and against the failure to discuss fully the developmental prognosis in both general and specific, day-to-day terms.

The positive role played by religion in their adjustment to the situation was stressed.

Strong condemnation was expressed toward the counsel to institutionalize the child without the physician himself knowing about institutions, and without consideration of the parents' urge to love and care for their retarded children.

Wide agreement was expressed in favor of early announcement of the diagnosis, in preference to temporizing statements to the effect that the child would "grow out of it."

Three recent contributions to the literature have been summarized, and the authors are found to be in close agreement with the parents concerning the principles for the correct handling of the initial counseling of parents with retarded children.

REFERENCES

Abel, T. M.: Resistances And difficulties in psychotherapy of mental retardates. *J. Clin. Psychol., 9*:107, 1953.

Doll, E. A.: Counseling parents of severely retarded children. *J. Clin. Psychol., 9*:114, 1953.

Jensen, R. A.: The clinical management of the mentally retarded child and the parents. *Am. J. Psychiat., 106*:830, 1950.

Storrs, H. S.: Personal communication.

Kanner, L.: Parents' feelings about retarded children. *Am. J. Ment. Defic., 57*:375, 1953.

Chapter 8

The Informing Interview*

CARL DRAYER, M.D. and ELFRIEDE G. SCHLESINGER, M.A.

IT is the object of this paper to acquaint others with the purpose and techniques of the informing interview which is held with parents following our clinic's initial diagnostic study of a child. This interview is designed to provide parents and other members of the family with an opportunity for thorough leisurely review of the findings, and to outline a suggested program of management. It is held, therefore, following the initial diagnostic case conference and precedes any active treatment, rehabilitation, or guidance work which may be planned with the child and his family.

The following brief description of our clinic and its total method of functioning may serve to highlight the important role this interview has come to play in our work and why we view it as a logical stop-off point of steppong-stone in the clinic's and family's mutual efforts on behalf of the child.

The clinic to which we refer is more formally known as the Division of Pediatric Psychiatry of the Jewish Hospital of Brooklyn. It is an outpatient facility which serves children ranging in age from infancy to fourteen years who represent a variety of the well-known psychiatric disorders. However, a large proportion of our patients are classified as mentally retarded and are served by that section of the Division known as the Morris J. Solomon Clinic for the Rehabilitation of Retarded Children. Thus, although our methods are similarly applied to all of our patients, the techniques to be described here have evolved primarily out of our

Note: Reprinted by permission from the author and the *American Journal of Mental Deficiency,* 65:363-370, 1960. Copyrighted by the American Association on Mental Deficiency.
*From the Morris J. Solomon Clinic for the Rehabilitation of Retarded Children, Division of Pediatric Psychiatry.

experience with retarded children.

The clinic serves only children who live in the Borough of Brooklyn. Patients are referred by a variety of sources, including other divisions of the hospital, schools, the local chapter of the Association for the Help of Retarded Children, social agencies, and private physicians. There has usually been a waiting period of anywhere from three months to two years before service can be initiated.

Every child who is seen at the clinic receives a diagnostic evaluation when first registered. This evaluation is always carried out by a team of specialists. While the needs of individual children vary, this "work-up" almost always includes a thorough review of development, social functioning, a specific history of the presenting problems, and psychiatric, pediatric, neurological, and psychological examinations. The clinic also maintains its own facilities for laboratory examinations, and speech and hearing evaluations. Where necessary, the facilities of the rest of the hospital can be utilized.

These initial studies, which usually take one to three months to complete, are followed by a case conference. The entire staff attends this conference, and thus, the staff members who have participated in the evaluation, as well as those who have not, are present. Representatives of the referring agency, the private physician, and others who might be interested are invited to attend. Before the parents and child are brought in, a summary of the pertinent findings is read by a staff member previously assigned to this task. When the family comes in, staff members have additional opportunity to observe the child and to ask questions which may remain unanswered by the material presented. When parents and child leave, the diagnosis and a treatment plan are formulated. While all staff members participate in the discussion, formulation of diagnosis and case supervision are, of course, the responsibility of the physician.

Before proceeding with a discussion of the informing interview, a word about the presence of the family at the case conference may also be in order. Although many questions have been raised about the possible adverse effects on the child and parents when faced with the array of personnel at the conference, we have found that most children enjoy the informal atmosphere which prevails around the large conference table. If the child is very timid or fearful, he is presented to the staff through a one-way viewing mirror while quietly interviewed in an adjoining room. Parents also have an opportunity to raise additional problems for the staff's consideration and can see directly that any formulation is the result of careful group deliberation. Parents are prepared for the conference and assured that there will be opportunity for discussion at a later point.

It is evident, then, that the informing interview represents the first point at which a responsible member of the team is prepared to answer the parents' many questions. Whenever possible, the informing interview is held directly after the conference, though occasionally, as a matter of preference, it may be arranged for the near future. Whichever time is chosen, it is of prime importance that a sufficient amount of time be available in order that the interview can be carried on in a leisurely, relaxed manner. Since the presence of the patient may serve to distract the parents, it is sometimes preferable to postpone the interview for a time when the child can be left at home. If the interview is scheduled for another day, it is important to meet briefly with the parents directly after the conference to allay the immediate anxiety which the conference may have engendered.

Usually the physician in charge of the case conducts the interview. Often he is assisted by another staff member. Although the clinic is primarily a medical facility, the problems presented by the children affect almost every aspect of their functioning, and in some instances the nonmedical problems loom large. Thus, in determining which discipline carries responsibility for a specific interview, the needs of the particular case, as well as the skill of an individual staff member, are taken into consideration. Where both the presenting complaints and the diagnosis involve a specific medical problem (i.e. when a child has convulsions, visual difficulties, or where the evaluation has uncovered the need for specific medical therapies), the physician always assumes primary responsibility for informing the parents. Where the child presents difficulties involving behavior, emotional development, adjustment in the community, self-care, or speech, other staff members, including the social worker, the public health nurse, the psychologist, or speech therapist, may join with the physician or carry major responsibility. We have found that an informing interview carried on jointly by the physician and one or more of the other team members who will have contact with the child and family during the rehabilitation process is most productive.

Each set of parents comes to the clinic and to such an interview at a different stage of development or awareness of their child's difficulty. Some are most realistic concerning the implications of his handicaps and have brought the child merely for confirmation of their own observations or those of a physician. On the other hand, they may have come because they learned of the availability of a specific service. Others come in desperate quest for a cure, or for the relief of their own apprehensions. Many, perhaps most, are aware of a difficulty, but have varying degrees of confusion concerning the implications of the problem and the best ways of helping the child. Despite these diverse attitudes, most are interested in obtaining some fundamental answers concerning etiology, therapy or management, and prognosis, all of which have been considered in the evaluation.

Thus, the informing interview in its most ideal form combines the science of medicine with the art of informing parents about their retarded child. Whoever the informant, he must have at his command an adequate amount of factual information pertaining to retardation. It is well to know, for example, what the statistical probabilities are that these parents will bear another retarded child, how late speech may develop, what educational and work opportunities are available, and what can be expected after a course of medical treatment or rehabilitation. Merely to convey such information, however, is rarely sufficient. The informant, utilizing both the data gained in the diagnostic process, and his own evaluation of the family's approach to the meeting, must gauge the course of the interview accordingly. He should evaluate just how much the family is prepared to know about the child at this time. What preconceived notions do they have about retardation? What are their feelings toward the child? Are they suffering from feelings of guilt about any part they believe they may have played? Are these pressures and tensions, intrafamilial conflicts, or economic and social inadequacies, each of which may interfere with their capacity to grapple with the problem?

Clearly, the techniques and the specific focus of such an interview will vary with the individual informant, depending upon his specific professional preparation, experience, and personality as well as upon the attitude of the individual family. Despite the emphasis on the importance of individualizing the conduct of such an interview, it is nevertheless possible to summarize some of the major techniques which have proved to be valuable in most situations.

We have found that during the first phase of the interview it is best if the informant conveys to the parents the findings and recommendations that were formulated at the case conference. It is not suggested that this consist of a mechanical recitation of the facts. Rather, some opportunity is given to the parents to restate their major questions and an attempt is made to focus discussion with these in mind. As the informant presents the findings, the parents must be given further opportunity to ask questions and to state their own opinion concerning the material being presented. The discussion is, therefore, continually adjusted to the parents' readiness to deal with certain aspects of the findings.

Whatever is told the parents should be put simply, directly, and honestly. The diagnosis must be phrased in a manner which parents will understand and must include a statement of what is known as well as what is not known. The extent of the retardation should be conveyed to them. Here one "skates on thin ice." Sometimes parents have brought the child to the clinic at a point when they are first beginning to recognize the developmental lag. However, on their own they have not yet begun to recognize that this lag may handicap the child in all areas of functioning throughout life and may simply not be prepared to deal with the possibility at this point. The interview may serve to help them make a beginning step in this direction. Often an attempt to have the parents themselves assess the child's level of development is useful. It is interesting how often their estimate corresponds very closely to our own. In this way the parents are themselves participating in the evaluation process. Generally speaking, we avoid giving a specific IQ score. The broad categories of mild, moderate, and severe retardation, and the concept of mental age, we find, have clarified the points raised in a more meaningful way. For example, the fact that the child has an IQ of 50 may shock and distress them, but gives them little concrete help in anticipating the general rate of development and functioning for the child either in long or short range terms. If, on the other hand, it is pointed out that at the age of five their child functions roughly like a two and one-half or three-year-old, they can deal with this much more effectively. Examples drawn from their own accounts of the child's past rate of development as well as from the clinic's findings help them further to grasp the meaning of the findings. However, here too, we have applied no rigid, unswerving standard. Where a parent has learned to think in terms of IQ scores, and has perhaps misinterpreted previous information given, we occasionally give the results of our tests, being most careful to caution the parents against uncritical acceptance of the meaning of a mere number. The constancy and prognostic implications of test results are not unduly emphasized, especially when we deal with younger children.

In discussing the child, we always attempt to evaluate him as a total individual rather than focus merely on his intellectual development or upon his medical problems. Thus, discussion of his behavior, personality, and sociability forms an integral part of these interviews. Where the child's behavior is severely disturbing and interferes with his learning capacities is pointed out to the parents. Where possible, we stress the patient's strong points, his physical appearance, commendable behavior, or his capacity for affection. When, as often happens, a child's social development exceeds his intellectual capacity, this too is stressed, particularly in relation to the more immediate prognosis. We stress the importance of demonstrating to the parents our recognition of a child's strengths for a number of reasons. The parent who is blinded to a degree to the inadequacies of the child may more readily accept our evaluation if we transmit the knowledge that we see his strengths despite the weaknesses and difficulties we have pointed out. For those parents who are too overwhelmed by the problems to see the child as a child, the demonstrated capacity of the informant to express positive feelings about the child as a person may help the parents to view the youngster in a new perspective.

Questions concerning etiology are in every parent's mind. In any discussion of this matter it must be anticipated that one or both parents may have feelings of guilt, and the greatest discretion must be practiced. They may have strong suspicions about the obstetrical delivery, early nursing care, pediatric management, their own role, or hereditary factors, and the part they believe these may have played in producing the defective child. Where the cause of the retardation is definitely known, it should be told to the parents; if unclassified, then this should be explained to them. The likelihood of a similar occurrence in future pregnancies should be statistically predicted to the best of our abilities. Frank confessions of scientific ignorance, where applicable, are better than dogmatic but ill-founded statements.

We implied earlier that although we have a responsibility to convey to the parents the prognostic implications of our evaluation, at no time should anyone attempt to prognosticate a child's development too far in advance or to give the parents more than they are emotionally prepared to hear at the moment. A prognosis may be made for the near future while it is explained to the parents that this will have to be reevaluated from time to time as the child is further observed. Thus, while we may be fairly certain that a young child lacks the capacity for becoming an independent, functioning member of the community, errors can be made. It seems more advisable to concentrate on the more immediately attainable goals. In the case of very young children, these are often in the area of helping the child to achieve some independence in self-care skills or to provide opportunities for socialization. When the parents of such a child raise questions concerning the long-range potential, it is perhaps more advisable to state rather frankly that the child is too young or that it is too soon to make definitive statements.

We emphasize this point, since in our zeal to help parents avoid pitfalls of overestimating their child, we have on occasion incurred their hostility because of their inability to accept too devastating a prognosis all at once. Perhaps even more important in consideration of this point is the fact that we have been in error at times in our long-range prognosis. Also, we have seen parents who are loath to accept any of our findings because of the mistaken, overly gloomy prognostications of others. The parents may have been informed earlier, by another center, that their child would never walk. Yet, they brought him to us because his incessant running and hyperactivity have become a major management problem. The younger the child, in general, the less certain is the prognosis.

We do not imply, however, that the informant goes along with the parent's most unreasonable hopes and expectations. Rather, he utilizes the parents' own observations of the child's current level of functioning and rate of progress to help them to come to a greater realization and understanding on their own. Ideally, the experience of being helped to assess the level of the child's development and rate of progress, both in terms of the clinic's estimate and their own observations, should help parents go through similar processes more independently at later stages of the child's development.

There are, however, specific situations which demand not only an evaluation of the child's current level of functioning and its implications for the more immediate future but discussion of long-range management. This is perhaps most true in the cases of preadolescents and adolescents. If the parents of a child in this age group are enrolling the youngster in a program of training for which he is obviously not suited, such as attempting to teach him a skilled trade, it is important to point this out to them. In situations of this kind, the technique of helping parents to comprehend the problem on the basis of their own observations or those made at the clinic is important. Thus, if the child has never shown any demonstrable skill in the areas required, this can be reviewed with the parents. When the child has reached the age when questions of independent functioning are pertinent, it is appropriate to discuss the child's capacities in relation to the skills required for independent living and to help the parents to review the problems from this perspective. For example, if the child has failed to achieve the most minimal reading skills and does not seem to be able to learn how to travel, this needs to be reviewed if they talk about his being a messenger boy. If his manual dexterity is shown to be most poor, their hopes that he might learn to work on an assembly line or do other semiskilled work should be pointed out more realistically.

In outlining a program of management and treatment, the family's capacity to follow through on suggestions, in terms of the total family situation, must be kept in mind at all times. The mother of a three-year-old retardate whose self-care functioning is at an infant level will view with skepticism any suggestion that she permit the child ample time at each meal to attain self-feeding skills if she has several other young children, all requiring considerable attention. It may, therefore, be more practical to recommend that she select only one meal during the day in which to concentrate on this particular skill. It would be beneficial, where possible, to give the parents an approximate estimate of the time required to accomplish a specific learning process.

It is important to commend any successes parents may have met in the handling of their child because their confidence is often battered by the up-hill course they have had to travel. The feeling that the child might have been "all right" had more time been devoted to his care must be corrected. Where the child's lags are accentuated by lack of parental understanding or attention, this should of course be mentioned diplomatically. These situations often require further counseling or concrete help to some nature. If the mother has, for example, failed to help the child to attain independence in self-care skills because of lack of patience and know-how, the difficulties involved can be acknowledged. Further, the accumulated experience of staff members and the availability of other resources can be pointed out. If other personnel, such as the clinic's visiting nurse, are called upon to aid the mother at home with a particular problem, it must remain clear that this role is purely supplementary to that of the family.

Parents often come seeking many therapies in the hope that a specific type of treatment will improve the basic problem. Frequently, the child is not ready to benefit from these services. For instance, the parent who insists that speech therapy will help the child, may have overlooked his own observation that the youngster's general level of development is comparable to that of his one-year-old sibling. Recalling his earlier statement may help him view his request more realistically. More important, it aids him in coming to a firmer grip with the reality of the child's disability and may refocus his thinking on those aspects of training which are more attainable at this point. Such an approach is also useful in consideration of the educational needs of the older retardate. If a special educational program is indicated, it may help the parent accept such class placement, if the child's inability to cope with the skills required in the regular grade is pointed out.

While parents often request specific services which are believed unsuitable, they often make realistic requests. All too frequently, these services would be most beneficial to the child but are not available. At the clinic there may be a waiting list for a specific therapeutic group. In the community there may be no opening in the local nursery school or in the special classes. The temptation to deny the importance of these services in order to prevent feelings of frustration is great. However, parents can easily sense such deception and show a justifiable resentment. We have found that forthright admission of these inadequacies is appreciated by a parent. Further, a discussion of the role played by parents' organizations in regard to unmet community needs for the retarded may be of additional help. While it must be pointed out honestly that a parent's participation will not guarantee the establishment of a facility from which his child could benefit, the organizations' overall achievements can be stressed. Furthermore, parents find it easier to deal with their own problems, both on a practical and emotional level, when they come in contact with others who are in the same situation.

During the course of the interview, the informant may get the impression that the parents have many problems which they hesitate to voice. Often there is a fear that the presence of a retarded child may have adverse effects on other siblings. The placement of a child in an institution may be attended by such pangs of conscience that the parents do not want to discuss it. In general, we know that parents of retarded children have questions on these matters at one time or another. How much of this is raised by the informant during the course of the informing interview is largely a matter of individual discretion. Of course, if the questions and problems in these areas have been brought up by the parent previously, they can be discussed very freely. Where this is not the case, and the parent has come to the interview primarily to gain an interpretation of our findings, a few well-placed questions or suggestive comments may make it possible for him to open such discussion. If there is a need for help in this area, it may be feasible to handle it briefly during the interview. Where the problems are more complicated, the informant merely acknowledges this and makes arrangements for further guidance.

An informing interview such as we have described deals essentially with the problems of an individual who is chronically handicapped and whose functioning will be impaired in one or more major areas throughout life. In dealing with a problem of such magnitude, a single discussion seldom suffices to answer all of the family's questions or to deal with the complexities of the situation. Nor should it be anticipated that the parents will come away from such a discussion fully accepting or understanding the child's condition. Rather, a well-conducted, informing interview sets a firm and sound foundation for further contacts.

In summary then, we view the informing interview held with parents following the diagnostic evaluation of their child as a medium for acquainting them with our findings and establishing a sound basis for future contacts. The informant who conducts such an interview must be equipped with much factual data concerning the major aspects of retardation. Sensitivity to the needs of the particular child and family, together with a sound understanding of the specific problems of the child, are crucial. The interview must be conducted in a leisurely manner and should provide the parents with ample opportunity to voice their fears and concerns. Positive aspects in the child's functioning and parental handling should be stressed. Long-range prognosis should at all times be presented in a guarded manner, particularly in the case of young children. How much is told the parents about the future must be geared to the family's capacity to accept the implications of such a prognosis. However, every effort must be made to prevent the raising of false hopes and to help the parents to deal realistically with their child's limitations. It is not expected that a single discussion will serve to answer all of the parents' questions, but rather that such an interview will help establish the basis for future work.

Chapter 9

Counseling Families During the Crisis Reaction to Mongolism

MARGARET J. GIANNINI, M.D. and LAWRENCE GOODMAN, M.S.W.

U NDER the auspices of the New York State Department of Mental Hygiene, the Clinic for Retarded Children at Flower-Fifth Avenue Hospital undertook in March, 1961, a two- to three-year demonstration treatment project evaluating the effect of comprehensive services to families who apply for state institutionalization of infant mongoloids. At this time we are presenting a description of the project, the rationale for undertaking it, and our initial clinical observations. We wish to emphasize that this is a preliminary report with tentative impressions that are subject to later statistical validation.

The policy of accepting children under five in New York State institutions, primarily Willowbrook State School, began in 1946. Within a brief period, however, the number of requested admissions to the nursery wards has necessitated the establishment of a waiting list of many months. About two thirds of the families involved (averaging about 300 at any given time) are New York City residents.

Concern with the extremely high mortality rate of infants led to the policy of deferring applications until the child was a year old. A retrospective study (Pense, 1961) showed that 66 percent of the children under one year of age admitted to State schools in 1956 had died — the great majority within a few months of admission. Most of these children, of course, had serious somatic ailments.

*Note:*Reprinted by permission from the author and the *American Journal of Mental Deficiency, 67:*740-777, 1963. Copyrighted by the American Association on Mental Deficiency.

(Of the total under-five population admitted that year, 32 percent had expired.)

There also has been increasing recognition of the advantages to the eventual developmental level of the retarded child who receives early home care. The classic works of Spitz (1945) and Bowlby (1951) emphasize dramatically the devastating effect in all areas of development of the maternally deprived child. A study by Centerwall (1960) comparing the development of mongoloid youngsters reared at home with those reared in institutions states that "it is obvious that the Mongoloid child will be adversely affected by early institutionalization." Of the matched groups, the children placed at birth were functioning in the severely retarded range — those who had been at home in early years were mainly in the "moderately retarded" range. Early home care thus was seen to be the difference between trainability and nontrainability.

The traumatic effect of early separation on the families of retarded youngsters is a less understood aspect of the total problem. Placement at the earliest possible time, with a satisfactory psychological resurgence from the experience, is not possible for most families unless they receive the kind of professional help that is rarely available at the time of decision. Many parents who appear to have been able to emotionally dissociate themselves from their child by placing him at birth carry with them conscious or unconsicious feelings of guilt and self-recrimination. Slobody and Scanlan (1959) point out that "it is a fallacy that the retarded child who is out of sight is out of the mind of the parent — it seems to us evident that early placement of the retarded child in an institution, although it often may seem the expedient method of dealing with the problem, can have foreseen and disastrous consequences for the child and family."

There finally is wakened concern with the mortality rate of institutionalized infants, the implications for the child's future development, and the long-range effect on families. We can see the moral, philosophical, humanistic, and psychological considerations involved in our belated recognition that the retarded child is entitled to the same opportunity for development as any other handicapped child — and that his family deserves the same sympathetic community understanding and comprehensive services as the families of other handicapped children. Yet concurrent with these strides is a counter-trend toward earlier and more extensive institutionalization of young children, particularly mongoloids. We can speculate on some of the reasons for this: (1) increased survival rate of infants with somatic complications, (2) earlier detection as a result of stimulated awareness of retardation, (3) lack of knowledge or acceptance of shifting attitudes in care of the retarded on the part of physicians, social workers, and clergymen, and (4) a lag in community facilities which would make readily available to families the kind of specialized services they require when facing the full psychic impact of the diagnosis. Some physicians may recognize that there are alternatives to placement — if immediate help can be obtained — but they feel frustrated when attempting to locate it.

The total population of the institutions for the retarded of New York State is 10 percent mongoloid, yet they represent a disproportionate 25 percent of all under-five admissions, and a majority of the youngest. A similar distribution is reported by Kramer (1959) in California. We know, pediatrically, that the mongoloid child's needs in infancy do not differ greatly from those of normal infants. He generally does not require elaborate physical care — but he does desperately need the same atmosphere of love and security possible only through maternal closeness. The mother, too, must experience an irreplaceable loss when deprived of the opportunity to nurture her child. These factors, which are so obvious to us who practice in the field of mental retardation, obviously become closed out and distorted in the context of medical misinformation (sometimes deliberate), preoccupation with social stigma, and the premature forcing of a vital decision in an atmosphere of catastrophe complicated by the already heightened emotionality of the birth experience. We recognize that there are certainly situations of social and psychological impairment where immediate institutionalization is vital, and that the community has the responsibility to provide such care. Yet we can state categorically that most mongoloid infants should be cared for at home — in the interest of both the child and the family — and that many such children have in the past been inappropriately placed.

In recognition of the deficiencies in meeting this many-faceted, serious social problem, our demonstration project was established with the following goals: (1) To evaluate the impact on families of the birth of a mongoloid child and the effect of introducing intensive services at the point of crisis. (2) To determine whether these services influence the flow of these mongoloid infants from the waiting list to the institution. (3) To determine if there are implications for future admission policies.

In setting up procedures for referral of cases to us, it was agreed that all families of infant mongoloids would be handled by the supervising social worker of the State Department of Mental Hygiene application unit, so that there would be uniformity in handling the question of referral. The New York City office processes cases from the five boroughs and surrounding counties. The services of the Clinic were to be suggested to all families except those who lived at too great a distance from the Clinic, or who, in the judgment of the supervisor, were so brittle that any discussion of the possibility of further exploration would be psychologically detrimental. The decision to use the Clinic was to be on an entirely voluntary basis — and it was clearly pointed out that it would in no way affect the child's place on the waiting list.

Initially we decided to offer service to families already on the waiting list, recognizing that many uncontrollable variables were present which would limit statistical inferences that could be made. We anticipated that psychological defenses of this group would already be rigidly drawn and self-protectingly defended against therapeutic intervention. The previous experience of the Department of Mental Hygiene showed that unless the child had died, when an opening became available, it was almost invariably accepted.

Of this waiting list group, 40 percent of the children were at home — 60 percent in private temporary placement, usually at great financial sacrifice. In nearly every such case the child had been placed at birth. It should be pointed out that applications are accepted when the child is under a year old in particularly emergent situations only. Usually parents of infants under a year are placed on a "deferred" list and must reapply later. They are then added to the waiting list. It was decided early in the project that the initial application was the point when families most needed help and that referral should be made of these "deferred" families. Previous experience also had shown that only rarely did these families not reapply and that very few sought specialized interim help. The proportion of youngsters in private placement was about the same as the waiting-list groups.

The present paper deals with the first one hundred families referred to the Clinic. More than half were on the waiting list when the project began. These families were, on the whole, less accessible to help than those later families with whom the Clinic was discussed at the point of application. Forty-five of these one hundred children were fully evaluated, including several youngsters who were removed from private institutions for the work-up. In thirty-three cases only the parents of children in private placement were seen, with a number of them continuing to use casework services. Twenty-two families, mainly from the original waiting-list group, did not respond or consistently failed to keep appointments.

The first appointments were with the social worker who was to maintain continuing contact with the family. Often several appointments were necessary before the family was able to restructure its thinking sufficiently to permit an evaluation of the child. For some the concept that this supposedly hopeless, grotesque child warranted the attention of a group of specialists carried with it the threat that their rigidified thinking about the child might be open to question and might reactivate the desperate uncertainty that they had originally experienced. This was sufficient to keep a number of families from going beyond the first contact. Others were so openly protective of their defenses that they kept a single appointment in order "to help research," but had no intention of continuing beyond the first session.

For those families able to use help, comprehensive services included pediatric examination and follow-up medical care, psychiatric evaluation and consultation, psychological testing through the adaptation of infant scales which would have some prognostic validity for the age group studied, and ongoing casework services. Our casework goals were viewed as follows:

1. To share with parents our understanding of what they can

expect from their child if he is placed immediately or at a later age, in terms of his potential intellectual functioning, physical condition, available services, special problems that may arise, and individual family considerations. We are thus giving them the opportunity to decide on placement in terms of a realistic appraisal of the total situation and to deal with it on a reality basis.

2. To provide counseling to help families understand the conflict and ambivalence that is almost always present — overtly or covertly — regardless of the final decision.

3. Where a family does not appear to have the strength to consider alternatives — or where placement is clearly indicated for a variety of reasons — to support them and to help them face and plan for separation as constructively as possible, with a minimum of guilt.

At this time let us examine the composition of the families. One highly significant observation is that the socioeconomic-educational level was considerably higher than the community as a whole (which also was true of the families we did not see). Ethnically, too, there were differences, with very few Negro and Puerto Rican families. Family integration and cohesiveness were generally high; practically all families were intact.

These observations are in sharp contrast to the findings of Saenger (1960). Parents of institutionalized children were found to be socioeconomically and ethnically representative of the general population and with a high incidence of family deterioration, broken homes, and parental inadequacy. The families of infant mongoloids planning to institutionalize are obviously of different composition and must, therefore, be seeking placement for different reasons. They are not unable or incapable of caring for their children at home, but yet they are blocked from doing so from inner pressures and external influences.

It is unlikely that middle-class families produce more mongoloid babies — what appears then to be happening? All families react to a retarded child in terms of their own life experiences and the values and attitudes of their own immediate environment. The mongoloid child, the most stigmatized of the retarded, physically and socially, represents and assault to middle-class strivings and aspirations and culturally determined goals. He is seen as a serious impediment to social mobility. The child is retarded for all the world to see — the family cannot find solace in euphemisms like brain damage or postencephalitis — and as a result the family's self-concept becomes seriously threatened. At the same time this is antithetical to the family's sense of justice and responsibility, which adds to the dilemma. Families with less status concern seem to be far less traumatized.

Another noteworthy factor is that these middle-class families are the ones who use private general practitioners, pediatricians, and obstetricians who are identified with the family and its values. The physician may feel a sense of having failed the family with whom he has a relationship — and his own emotions and feelings come into play — seemingly to a greater extent than with lower-class families. His recommendations may be influenced unconsciously by his discomfort with the situation and his strong desire to "save" the family. At this time of strain the physician can be viewed as an omnipotent figure, and the family feels compelled to follow his recommendation — which is usually an unqualified dictum for institutionalization.

There are, of course, examples of thoughtful and informed handling. On the whole, however, most physicians know little about mongolism, they do not see the guilt, denial, and struggle present even in parents who appear to have completely rejected the child, and they are not aware of community resources.

Previous papers dealing with the handling of mongolism by physicians (Schipper, 1959; Koch, 1959; Farrel, 1956) contain numerous dramatic illustrations of uninformed handling. Unfortunately, there appears to be no observable change in attitude. Families from our regular Clinic population, who have never considered placement, report parallel experiences. Some parents are still being told that their healthy child probably will die before he is two years old, that he will never be capable of any self-care skills, that there are no educational facilities for him, that the institution will be able to teach the child while they cannot, that it is harmful to keep him at home, etc. We shall give only two brief examples:

    1. Mr. and Mrs. A. were told that the child should be placed

immediately — that for their own sake they should tell everyone that the child had died. At a time when their judgment was seriously impaired, they followed his recommendations. They have continued to visit the child regularly. He is an alert, high-functioning, appealing child, whom they feel they have abandoned. They cannot find the strength to take him home and face their family and their own children and are experiencing intense guilt.

2. Mr. and Mrs. B. live in a semi-rural area. They were told that if they took their child home, he would have a devastating affect on their two adolescent children. He presents no management problems, but the cost of his private care has exhausted the money saved for the college education of their other children, this being the parents' misguided effort to save them from "the horror" of this infant who is so like every other young child.

It would be possible to go on at length with similar incidents to illustrate what parents can be subjected to that can only confuse further and add to an already overwhelming problem.

Our treatment of parents has utilized accepted, conventional casework methodology, with therapists who have acquired the necessary body of knowledge of mental retardation content and have worked through their own feelings and prejudices around institutional placement.

Social work methods being used are (1) individual counseling — both intensive and supportive, (2) group counseling for fathers and mothers (jointly), and (3) counseling at home.

Individual counseling has varied from weekly interviews with both parents to occasional "as needed" contacts. Some families were able to make optimal use of a limited number of sessions — while our more disturbed families required intensive treatment with less observable gain. Three mothers showed such pathological involvement that we tried to work with them toward accepting psychiatric therapy. None of them, however, were accepting of referral. In all cases, we attempted to include the father — and in nearly every situation he participated in treatment. The extent of the father's involvement from the very first contact has a number of implications that will be developed in later reports. It should also be mentioned that in order to accommodate fathers, evening and Saturday sessions were held.

Our counseling groups have included both parents — with six couples participating. For those families who are ready to involve themselves sufficiently in the group process, there have proved to be a number of advantages in group treatment. One obvious antidote to feelings of social isolation and uniqueness is to meet with other essentially adequate, intelligent, likeable individuals who are reacting to the same trauma and struggling, each in his own way, with a similar crisis. That the group was meeting a deeply felt need is evidenced by the almost perfect attendance record in spite of the considerable distance that most families had to travel.

We have structured the groups purposely so that there will be some balance between families who already are moving toward a decision to keep their child at home and those who will go ahead with placement. This introduces dynamic conflict, which the leader uses to point out that there is no single solution — each family must decide in terms of its own reality. Yet, in spite of the impartiality of the leader in relation to each individual family, the collective inclination seems inevitably to move toward a decision for home care. In the one completed group, three of the couples previously had indicated that they were considering withdrawing their application, and eventually did so. We think it will be of interest to discuss the three other families briefly.

> Mr. and Mrs. T. are an attractive, young, status-concerned Negro couple who in their individual contacts with us had presented a "united front." They felt deeply for their only child, but they could not face the social consequences of keeping him with them. He was at home, but largely under the care of his maternal grandmother. Mrs. T. had gone back to work, consciously recognizing that she had done so mainly to avoid her child and the guilt he aroused in her whenever she looked at him. Through their interaction in the group it became apparent that behind the surface agreement there was much conflict over placement between Mr. and Mrs. T., which threatened to permanently disturb their marriage. Mr. T. had been bitterly opposed to institutionalization but felt that he had to go along with his wife's unalterable decision. He began to seriously question her values — she felt he was insensitive to her feelings. Through their identification with other members of the group and expanded frame of reference in which to evaluate their thinking — as well as the active support of the leader and other group members — each was helped to better understand and accept the other's point of view. They came to the joint decision that they would place their child temporarily — see what it would be like without him — and then consider taking him

home. The youngster was placed in Willowbrook while the group was meeting, but Mr. and Mrs. T. continued until the sessions were completed. Shortly afterwards their child died of pneumonia, and they were able to discuss their feelings about it with their individual worker. It is quite possible that if this family had not been in treatment, the death of the child would have destroyed the marriage.

Mr. and Mrs. P. were extremely defensive about their decision to place their child, who already was receiving temporary private care. At one point Mrs. P. projected her guilt and self-anger on to the group by confronting those parents who were keeping their children at home with a callous vision of what the child would be like when he was past the "cute" age. In a later meeting when she understood her feelings, she was deeply apologetic to the group. They, in turn, could empathize with Mrs. P.'s conflict and could support her decision to place, and, in a sense, give their approval for what was right for Mr. and Mrs. P.

Mr. T. is a college professor — an overly intellectual, unemotional, somewhat pontifical man, who dominates his wife. There seemed to be no question about their decision to place Donald, who had been in a private institution since birth. He was coming to the group purely to give the other parents the benefit of his superior thinking. In the fourth or fifth session, however, Mrs. T. emerged from her passivity and — incorporating strength from the group — was able to say for the first time that she wanted her child and could never forgive her husband unless he recognized her need. While the group was still meeting, Donald was accepted into Willowbrook. Two weeks later the T.'s announced proudly that they were taking him home. After the meeting ended, the families in the group were invited to the T.'s home for a reception for Donald.

Recognizing the special values of the group method, in the coming year we plan to place greater emphasis on the group program. We also plan to expand our home-counseling facilities. This experimental part of the treatment program, which has provided service to seven families who were unable or too immobilized to come to the Clinic regularly, has had rich therapeutic overtones and obviously has had special meaning to the families involved.

Where families have shifted from their plan to institutionalize — some eagerly and with tremendous relief, some anxiously, hesitantly — they have sought reassurance from us that our help would remain available to them. In undertaking a demonstration treatment project, it is not sufficient to accept responsibility for care for the duration of the project only. The families involved become a part of the Clinic's population, and future help with planning must be made available to them.

Of the families we have worked with, twenty-four have indicated that they are no longer planning to place their child. In most instances they realize that this decision is subject to later reevaluation as they live further with the problem and test out their own reactions. In some cases the decision is neurotically based and these families will need a great deal of continuing help. In most situations, however, the decision appears to us to be sound and in the interest of the mental health of the child and the family. If help had not been provided at this time, it is likely that nearly all of these youngsters would have been prematurely institutionalized, obviously against the innate wishes of the parents. They could not have been influenced to keep their children — even if that had been our intention — unless there already was dissatisfaction with what they were doing. It could only have erupted into further doubt and guilt if the child had been placed without the opportunity for the parents to face and try to work out their conflict.

SUMMARY

We have reported on the first phase of a demonstration research project to evaluate the effect of intensive services made available to families of infant mongoloids at the time of initial crisis reaction.

Some inferences have been drawn which are subject to later statistical validation. There is little doubt, however, that parents able to participate have been helped to make a wiser choice between home and institutional care.

Of the first one hundred families studied, all of whom had applied for state institutionalization, the majority responded eagerly to the opportunity for looking beyond what had appeared to be an unalterable decision. Twenty-four of these families have indicated that they plan to keep their children at home, at least during the crucial early developmental period. In most instances the shift appears to be clinically sound. Continuing services to this group are strongly indicated.

In the next year there will be more systematic measurement of clinical procedure and intensification of those treatment methods that have proved most helpful. Group therapy and home-counseling facilities, for example, will be expanded. For the final report, coded data will be evaluated statistically to provide a socioeconomic-psychological profile of the families studied.

In conclusion, it appears strikingly apparent that parents at the critical time of considering institutionalization at any age need the most skilled kind of assistance in finding the solution that is most suitable for them and their child, and in obtaining support in carrying out whatever thoughtful and logical decision is made.

REFERENCES

Bowlby, J.: *Maternal Care and Mental Health*. Monograph, World Health Organization, Geneva, 1951.

Centerwall, S. A., and Centerwall, W. R.: A study of children with mongolism reared in the home compared to those reared away from the home. *Pediatrics, 25*:678-685, 1960.

Farrel, M.: Adverse effects of early institutionalization. *Am. J. Dis. Child, 91*:278-281, 1956.

Koch, R., *et al.*: Attitude studies of parents with mentally retarded children. *Pediatrics, 23*:582-584, 1959.

Kramer, M.: Measurement of the flow of the mentally retarded into institutions. *Am. J. Ment. Defic., 64*:278-290, 1959.

Pense, A., *et al.*: A cohort study of institutionalized young mentally retarded children. *Am. J. Ment. Defic., 66*:18-22, 1961.

Saenger, G.: *Factors Influencing the Institutionalization of Mentally Retarded Individuals in New York City*. Monograph Interdepartmental Health and Resources Board, Albany, 1960.

Schipper, M.: The child with mongolism in the home. *Pediatrics, 24*:132-144, 1959.

Slobody, L., and Scanlan, J.: Consequences of early institutionalization. *Am. J. Ment. Defic., 63*:971-974, 1959.

Spitz, R. A.: Hospitalism. In *The Psychoanalytic Study of the Child*, edited by O. Fenichel. New York U. Press, 1945, Vol. I, pp. 53-74.

Chapter 10

Medical Counseling of
Parents of the Retarded
The Importance of a Right Start

GERALD SOLOMONS, M.D.,* and FRANK J. MENOLASCINO, M.D.†

THE past few years have been seeing a great expansion in comprehensive programs for the indigent and the chronically handicapped, particularly the mentally retarded. New facilities are being built, multidisciplinary approaches are developing, and much interaction between communities and medical centers is taking place. Concomitant with this major progress is the burden of an increased case load upon a staff of trained professionals, already shorthanded before this process began.

One element which is being continually overlooked during the evolution of increased programs and facilities is the problem of communication — not only between the professional disciplines concerned, but between the professionals and the families seeking help. Evaluations are now more comprehensive and include such matters as speech and hearing and pedodontics, with the result that it has become necessary for the professionals in the field not only to enlarge their own knowledge in areas outside of their

Note: Reprinted with permission of the authors and *Clinical Pediatrics,* 7:11-16, 1968, published by J.B. Lippincott Company.

This investigation was supported by research grant No. HD-00370 from the National Institute of Child Health and Human Development and Project No. 405 from the Children's Bureau, H.E.W.

*Associate Professor of Pediatrics and Director, Child Development Clinic, The University of Iowa, Iowa City, Iowa 52240.

†Assistant Professor of Psychiatry, Developmental Evaluation Clinic, Nebraska Psychiatric Institute, Omaha, Nebraska.

individual disciplines but also to make sure that the findings of such detailed examinations are fully explained to the parents so that they in turn understand why and how to follow the consequent recommendations. If the work-up of a complicated case takes several days, but the interpretation of the patient or his family is given in only a few minutes in language replete with technical terms and professional jargon of several disciplines, the complaints of parents of handicapped children that, "Nobody told me anything," or "He's been seen many times, but I don't know what they found out," are understandable and legitimate.

Formerly, the chronically handicapped were not considered collectively as a clinical entity, and the present-day type of comprehensive collaboration between medical, paramedical, and educational disciplines was largely unknown. The blind were blind and were the concern of the ophthalmologist. Inasmuch as the mentally retarded were intellectually impaired, they were left to the psychiatrist, mainly for institutionalization purposes. The cerebral palsied were in the domain of the orthopedist, with the help of an agency known as Crippled Children's Services. In such circumstances the inability of parents to understand and cope with their child's problems via the explanations given by their physician was often ascribed thoughtlessly either to denial or to guilt feelings or to both.

It is the intent of this article to emphasize the importance of communication between the physician and the parents of a handicapped child

ISSUES

It is our contention that the time, expense, and effort involved in the evaluation of a mentally retarded individual can be largely wasted if the explanation to the parents is either inadequate or not understood. Indeed, an inadequate explanation can lead to such hostility in the parents toward recommendations and participating agencies that it entices them to "shop around" for further diagnostic services or to be attracted to special treatments of questionable value.

The initial interpretation interview is particularly crucial to all

further treatment and habilitation attempts. The "primary physician" (defined as the one who makes first contact with the
retarded individual and his family) is probably the most important
individual the family will meet. He sets the climate for the future
and, to a great extent, influences the overall prognosis of the child.
Indeed, a successful initial assessment and intelligent management
of family attitudes and problems may avoid institutionalization by
default.

The Physician

In the field of mental retardation the cornerstone for future
programming is the initial interpretation interview. If we fail to
help the parents understand their child's problems, the diagnostic
studies (and resultant recommendations) become an academic
exercise. The technics of diagnostic interpretation and parental
counseling in the area of mental retardation are the most
demanding ones, and the clinician needs certain skills in order to
be effective.

First of all, he must be aware of his own attitudes. The
physician with little empathy for or experience in the field of
mental retardation cannot avoid revealing both his disinterest and
his uncertainty in his discussion of diagnostic findings and the
resultant recommendations. Many physicians are aware of this and
refer their patients appropriately. Others continue to counsel,
apparently unaware of the negative effects of antagonism and
denial which their professional posturing and emotional reactions
to mental retardation evoke in the family.

Some physicians think that they are expected to "have all the
answers and do something about the problem immediately." This
often leads to peremptory advice and opinions based on the
physician's desire to get rid of the whole problem, instead of
initiating a thoughtful and long-term program for child and family.
Or the physician may overidentify himself with the parents and
conclude without justification that to retain a child at home
would be an intolerable burden for the family. A recent study by
Olshansky and Sternfeld (1963) has revealed that though most
pediatricians are not in favor of early institutionalization, only a

few looked upon the decision to institutionalize as belonging to the parents! Furthermore, in contrast to this attitude towards the severely retarded, the physician tends to overestimate the intelligence of children functioning in the higher ranges of mental retardation (Korsch et al., 1961). Although identification to some extent with the family is important, unrealistic attitudes on the part of the physician must not influence the therapeutic management.

Parents of the Retarded

An appreciation of the clinical problems common to families with retarded children on the part of the physician may help to avoid the frequently noted "shopping" pattern (for more diagnostic services) by the parents of a child who is mentally retarded. Specifically, this pattern consists of the parents approaching a number of different mental retardation evaluation clinics over a period of years in search of "the diagnosis," a pattern which leads both to duplication of services and to unnecessary expenditure of time on the part of professional personnel. To diminish or eliminate this, it is necessary to formulate an adequate system of counseling and interpretation to the parents.

A few general remarks on the entire subject of family counseling in mental retardation: There are over 150 publications dealing with or very relevant to this subject, mostly started since 1950, yet only a small number of experimental studies have been conducted (Wolfensberger, in press). Further, it is questionable whether the parents whose reactions have been reviewed in the literature are representative of the parents of the retarded in general, for two obvious areas may have been misrepresented. First, some authors have focused specifically on mothers of young retarded children in the severe to moderate range, from the middle and upper socioeconomic groups only. Also, the failure to assess the father's role in such studies, and over-reliance on maternal information with the associated assumption that such data are valid, has prompted Ross (1964) to state: "Reading the scientific literature in this field (counseling of parents of the retarded), a student unfamiliar with our culture might easily get the impression that fathers play no part in the rearing of our children."

It has been well established that parents of retarded children go through several distinct stages in their adjustments to their child's problem. An awareness of the state at which the parents are, is important for the physician's counseling of the family. These stages of parental adjustment to their retarded child have been succinctly outlined by the Group for the Advancement of Psychiatry (1963).

> The physician is dealing with parents who have a multifaceted problem: I. They may not have fully accepted the diagnosis of mental retardation. II. They have varying degrees of guilt feelings about the possible role and the causation of the child's condition. III. They resent the fact that this has happened to them and tend to try to find some outside influence on which they can blame the problem. IV. They hope for a magical solution. V. They have a wish, usually unconscious, to be rid of this burden. VI. They have come seeking advice.
>
> Each of these factors deserves separate consideration by the physician who must realize that he himself will have certain reactions to the child's condition and to the parents and their emotional problems.

A recent publication of the American Medical Association (1964) describes parental adaptation after receiving the diagnosis in three frequently noted stages. The *first stage* is one of "emotional disorganization." Great anxiety is produced; at times the stress is so great as to overwhelm the parents' usual adaptive mechanisms. The *second stage* is one of "reintegration," in which parental defense mechanisms become more apparent. The most common one is usually denial or hostility or both, and often towards the doctor who made the diagnosis. There may be complete opposition that the condition exists, or misunderstanding of the explanation given. There may even be a complete denial that the diagnosis was discussed at all — the "No one told me anything" response. This is the stage at which the parents are prone to initiate the "shopping" pattern, to go from doctor to doctor. Another type of defense may be to ascribe the blame to someone else. This may be the physician who delivered the baby, the neighbors, the school (for "not teaching properly"), or even society for neglecting the handicapped. These feelings of hostility and guilt, almost universal, were pointed out by Rembolt (1961) as being not different from those which all parents have on occasion towards their normal child. However, these last longer and are more intense in the parents of a handicapped child and can have a marked effect on the personality development and functioning of the child. Similarly, Denhoff and Holden (1954) insist that the attitude and cooperation of the parents are more important than the severity of the child's handicap in the prognosis. If parents are not allowed or helped to work through these feelings, they may respond by rejecting or overprotecting the child. This can be manifested either as outright neglect or as demands for an unrealistic level of performance. Overprotection may also stultify emotional growth and independence by restricting stimulating experiences and peer interaction.

It is therefore most important that the *third stage* of "mature adaptation" or acceptance is reached. Until this is accomplished no effective program can be proposed, and the family emotional climate for their child's developmental progress remains poor no matter what material comforts are available.

Therefore, the primary objectives of any program with respect to the parents must be to ensure (1) that their guilt and anxiety are allayed, (2) that they have a thorough understanding of their child's problems, and (3) that they appreciate that the treatment and management program recommended must alter as growth and development take place.

COUNSELING BY THE PRIMARY PHYSICIAN

There is no single formula for the physician in the management of a mentally retarded child and his family. But if the problem is approached as a complex and challenging one and early use is made of consultants and specialized diagnostic services, the rewards of successful management will more than out-weigh the additional efforts which may be required.

One common mistake is that of overdiagnosis. Most mental retardation facilities tend to be oriented towards diagnosis, prognosis, and recommendations (plans or actions), and the interpretation interview serves usually as the major vehicle for transmission of recommendations (Wolfensberger, 1965).

Excessive emphasis is placed on diagnostic activity at the expense of interpretation and family counseling considerations.

In many ways the therapeutic approaches to mental retardation convey an aura of passivity and helplessness on the part of the doctor. Such an aura is in direct contrast to the action orientation of the usual doctor-patient relationship wherein the physician has at his command several active treatment alternatives. Indeed, in many instances *few* medical actions can be initiated which will directly benefit the patient. In his relationship with the retarded patient the physician faces an extremely frustrating situation, for he must at times reconcile an action orientation with the lack of available actions. From a treatment perspective, many physicians concentrate on some treatable aspects (e.g. glasses, dental work), whether or not they are related to problems of mental retardation. Other physicians may concentrate their efforts on what might be interpreted as "objectively available" activities, such as diagnosis. Overemphasis on diagnosis usually occurs at the expense of formulating total and long-range plans of action.

Many physicians will get angry when their diagnosis is questioned. They feel that the parents are challenging them or are aware of their disinterest in the field of mental retardation.

Another dimension of the communication problem is evident here. The usual medical approach to these problems often does not give enough significance to the fact that, "just talking to parents" can be just as efficacious as a more tangible diagnostic test or treatment agent. Yet, *this* very necessary establishment of rapport, by communicating a genuine professional interest and concern in their child, often spells the difference between active parental implementation of recommended therapeutic programs and their rejection of same with subsequent future "shopping."

The attitude of the physician, the complexities of the diagnosis of mental retardation, and the aftermath of parental reactions to such a diagnosis all impinge directly on the child's ongoing personal-social adjustment and hamper his chances for achieving optimum developmental potential at any given time.

The reactions of parents of the retarded are kaleidoscopic. Many parents attempt to avoid the initial confrontation with the diagnosis. Many will talk about "special education" or "being slow," without calling their child mentally retarded. Hence the necessity to determine at which stage the parents are as they work through their reactions to the diagnosis of mental retardation and how this relates to their child. We must allow them to ventilate their feelings, help them to express unspoken concern about their child, and lead them (desensitize them) to the diagnosis by the matching of their own feelings with the clinical findings. Often one finds parents who can realistically describe their child's problems but cannot emotionally accept the disabilities they describe. If the child is more retarded than the parents describe him to be (denial) or, conversely, the child is less retarded than the parents state (rejection), then different counseling approaches are necessary.

Sometimes the shock of the diagnosis of mental retardation may result in denial of the child as a child, and here we must help the mother become aware of her negative feelings towards the child. The process of rejection is commonly voices as "why did this happen to me?" None of us has lived a perfect life, therefore there are unique personal reasons why things happen. Misinformation, guilt, and projection are quickly at hand for any parent, though not necessarily correct, relevant, or adaptive for them. At times the defense mechanism of rejection of the child's problems by the parents may be matched by the rejection of the physician. He may refer the patient to another physician or may recommend minor surgery or even institutionalization when it is not warranted. Thus the problem of rejection embodies both the parents and the physician.

The physician is the agent through which hope is communicated to the family (American Medical Association, 1964), and the dimension of hope must always be underscored.

The physician, while realistic and empathic when counseling with the parents, must also be always aware of the child's feelings and reactions and note any particular stresses to the child's personality as his parents go through the crises outlined above.

Family treatment considerations in parents of retarded children frequently underscore the need for general supportive measures and guidelines as to future management. The most common parental reactions noted are situational depressive features about their disappointment in the child's future potential built about their responsibility, disturbing mixed feelings which are commonly based on anger about the narcissistic injury done to them, and anxiety about the child's future. The problem of guilt presents a further unique dimension in counseling approaches to the parents of these children. With the primary emotional disorders of childhood the parents can usually project a good portion of their "blame" or guilt on the child, and scapegoat situations are frequently noted. With the retarded child there is usually no direct manner whereby this guilt can be externalized, and its continual lack of alleviation may present formidable resistance problems to any counseling attempts.

Thus we see that parents of children with mental retardation may have multiple levels and types of inner turmoil which may stem from the parental perplexity secondary to the child's unique developmental handicaps and which may lead to some of their child's future behavioral problems. Such considerations present a challenge to treatment and underscore the need for fuller appreciation of the family dynamics.

DISCUSSION

Although the handicapped child is his patient, the physician is a member of the "team," and in many ways its captain. He is the coordinator of community and medical services for the child and must take the responsibility of making decisions and monitoring long-term treatment-management programs. For example, an orthopedic operation for a handicapped child may be recommended, but it is up to the primary physician to determine the appropriate time for this procedure in view of the overall emotional and physical condition of the patient. How to deal with some of these recurring questions and problems has been reviewed in a previous article (Solomons, 1965).

The importance of communication is counseling parents of the retarded is worthwhile because it benefits the parents, the retarded member of the family, the family as a unit, and society as a whole. The parents benefit by achieving a higher level of understanding and acceptance of the problem, by recognizing and overcoming their conflicts, and by subsequently leading a better adjusted life. The retardate benefits by experiencing improved parental accept- ance and management. The family benefits because the adjustment of the retardate and the parents brings more harmonious inter- action between all family members. Society benefits because the chances of family dissolution, emotional problems, and institu- tionalization are diminished, and the likelihood of the retardate and other family members reaching their optimum potentials is increased.

Professionals should continue to focus on these problems so that different approaches can be properly evaluated and shared with colleagues. Such considerations are pertinent in regards to "old" and current approaches in counseling.

There has been an apparent shift in the availability and usage of mental retardation services (counseling and otherwise) from the upper and middle socioeconomic classes to the lower socio- economic classes. In this latter class the retardate, in contrast to the other two classes, is not usually viewed as a deviant. He has been termed the "invisible retardate" and encompasses a different spectrum of social and family forces of expectancy. Such considerations strongly suggest that continuing attention to delineating the changing differential patterns of family interaction would be most beneficial to the retardate, his family, and the professionals who seek to help.

Tizard (1966) has pointed out that the comparative ineffective- ness of some long-term treatment approaches as compared with short-term therapy is due to the fact that too much time, effort, and attention are paid to elucidation of the possible mechanisms which are thought to be responsible, rather than employing more direct (and creative!) approaches to advising parents, teachers, and the child himself on how to handle his problems.

There is a danger of all problems, however small, to be referred to the physician, and then common sense and parental action evaporate as the physician takes over. Mental retardation is a family matter and should remain a family matter, with guidance and counsel from professionals. The family should arrive at major decisions through talking things over; they themselves should decide the future of their child. Few families start out with the wisdom and fortitude to do this. Yet only when this ideal state is reached can the goal of optimal opportunity for optimal potential be attained.

Though primarily a problem of childhood, mental retardation is too complex to belong exclusively to one specialty. But the pediatrician or primary physician must be the coordinator of the community or professional team, which in turn must include representatives of all the disciplines which enter into the care of the handicapped.

REFERENCES

Denhoff, E., and Holden, R. H.: Family influence on successful school adjustment of cerebral palsied children. *J. Internat. Council Exceptional Child, 21*:5, 1954.

Korsch, B., Cobb, J., and Ashe, B.: Pediatricians' appraisals of patients' intelligence. *Pediatrics, 27*:990, 1961.

Mental retardation: a family crisis — the therapeutic role of the physician. Group for the Advancement of Psychiatry. Report No. 56, Dec. 1963.

Mental retardation. A handbook for the primary physician. Report of the American Medical Association Conference on Mental Retardation, Chicago, Apr. 9-11, 1964.

Olshansky, S. and Sternfeld, L.: Attitudes of some pediatricians toward the institutionalization of mentally retarded children. In *Institutionalizing Mentally Retarded Children. . . . Attitudes of Some Physicians.* U. S. Dept. of Health, Education and Welfare, Welfare Administration. Children's Bureau, 1963, p. 5.

Rembolt, R. R.: The "team" in cerebral palsy. Symposium on cerebral palsy. Thirty-seventh Annual Convention, American Speech and Hearing Association, 49, 1961.

Ross, A. V.: *The Exceptional Child in the Family.* New York, Grune and Stratton, 1964.

Solomons, G.: What do you tell the parents of a retarded child? Some personal experiences and reflections. *Clin. Pediat., 4*:227, 1965.

Tizard, J.: Mental subnormality and child psychiatry. *J. Child Psychol. Psychiat., 7*:1, 1966.

Wolfensberger, W.: Counseling the parents of the retarded. In Baumeister, A. (Ed.), *Mental Retardation: Selected Problems in Appraisal and Treatment.* Chicago, Aldine (in press).

Wolfensberger, W.: Diagnosis diagnosed. *J. Ment. Subnorm., 11*:62, 1965.

Chapter 11

Psychological Counseling with Parents of Retarded Children

PHILIP ROOS

In their painful search for answers to their dilemma, parents of retarded children frequently turn to the psychologist for counseling and guidance. Fruitful interaction between parents and psychologists requires special skill and sensitivity on the part of the psychologist. This presentation is an attempt to clarify important ingredients in the successful counseling situation.

The psychologist working with parents of retarded children should remember that he is probably dealing with highly distressed people. Reactions to the very real trauma of recognizing retardation in one's own child are, of course, infinitely varied, but certain general patterns recur with enough frequency to be considered more or less typical. Understanding of these patterns by the psychologist is helpful in dealing with the parents.

PARENTAL REACTIONS TO RETARDATION

Many parents suffer a severe loss of self-esteem when they recognize retardation in their child. In our culture children are often considered by parents as ego-extensions; that is, the parent closely identifies with his child, taking pride in his accomplishments and basking in his reflected glory. A serious defect in the child tends to be experienced by the parent as his own defect. Hence, the parent may feel responsible for disappointing his mate,

Note: Reprinted by permission from the author and *Mental Retardation, 1*:345-350, 1963. A publication of the American Association on Mental Deficiency.

133

his own parents, and other family members by "presenting" them with a defective child. The possibility of genetic etiology leads some parents to renounce plans for having other children. Self-esteem may be further lowered by threat to the fantasy of immortality through one's children — the individual is suddenly faced with the prospect that he will leave no descendants after him. Life goals and basic approaches to the world may be abruptly and radically altered.

Closely allied to loss of self-esteem is the feeling of shame experienced by many parents. They may anticipate social rejection, pity, or ridicule, and related loss of prestige. It is not uncommon to find parents withdrawing from social participation and altering plans which might expose them to social rebuff. They tend to view their child's school years with particular apprehension, since during this time his defect will become most apparent.

Parents' feelings toward their retarded child are typically extremely ambivalent. Not only are they constantly frustrated by the child's lack of achievement, but the child's inadequate control often leads to extremely irritating behavior. Resentment and hostility generated by repeated frustrations may be expressed in death wishes toward the child and feelings of rejection. Typically such feelings arouse considerable guilt in the parent, who then tries to atone for his hostility by developing overprotective and overindulgent attitudes toward the child. The inconsistent reactions by the parent of demandingness, hostility, and rejection, alternating with overprotection and overindulgence, are likely to disturb the child and thereby further reduce his efficiency, in turn increasing parental frustration. Such a self-perpetuating "vicious cycle" may further reduce the child's intellectual efficiency.

Hostility generated by frustration experienced in their interaction with the retarded child is often displaced by the parent onto other relationships. Parents may present a "chip-on-the-shoulder" attitude. Their irritable, resentful demeanor tends to alienate others and leads to rejection and avoidance by friends and relatives, further frustrating the parents and thereby increasing their resentment. The counselor should be alerted to the possibility that his clients may be in the grips of such a vicious cycle. Inappropriate attacks against the counselor are more easily accepted if recognized as manifestations of displaced hostility stemming from serious frustrations.

Feelings of depression are to be expected. The absence of such feelings, particularly when realization of the child's retardation is recent, is unusual enough to raise suspicions regarding the possibility of atypical techniques of handling emotions (e.g. repression and isolation of affect). Some parents react to the retarded child as if he had died, and manifest the typical grief reactions associated with the loss of a loved one. Such extreme reactions tend to be most prevalent in highly intelligent parents who tend to equate being human with the possession of intelligence. Disappointment in the child and concern for his future are appropriate reactions typically accompanied by some degree of unhappiness. Parents' ambivalence toward the child may contribute to depression, inasmuch as the hostility toward the child may be redirected toward the self.

Feelings of guilt and self-reproach may accompany depression and usually reflect internalization of hostility toward the child. It is not uncommon for parents to indicate that they feel responsible for the retardation, which may be described as a form of punishment for sins or as the outcome of transgressions. Cause of the retardation is sometimes erroneously attributed to guilt-ridden sexual activities.

Some parents adopt a masochistic position, almost welcoming the suffering they anticipate will accompany rearing the defective child. They may think of themselves as "martyrs" who will devote all their energies and sacrifice all pleasures for the child. The retardate may become the focus of a lifelong pattern of self-sacrifice and lamentation. It almost seems as if such parents "love to be miserable." They may dwell on the tragic and sordid aspects of their situation and often share their unhappiness with all who will listen. Such parents are typically reluctant to institutionalize their child — no matter how severely incapacitated he might be — and may neglect siblings, relatives, careers, and so forth, for the "welfare" of the child. In counseling with such parents, it usually becomes apparent that the retardate plays a very significant role in the parents' adjustment patterns.

Realization that a child is retarded often has disruptive effects

not only on the parents but on the entire family unit, and possibly
on friends, acquaintances, and neighbors as well. Siblings and
grandparents are very obviously involved, and increased tensions
typically develop within the family. Marital conflicts may be
aggravated, and the retarded child may become the focus of
mutual blame and criticism by the parents. It is as if the child were
a catalyst activating long-dormant conflicts into overt explosion.

Ambivalence toward the child may lead to defensiveness as
well as to overprotection. Parents may become acutely sensitive to
implied criticisms of the child and may react with resentment and
belligerence. It may be difficult in such cases to present factual
information which may be interpreted as depreciating the child.

A more extreme position is found in those parents who have
attempted to protect themselves against the pain of recognizing
retardation in their child by failing to become aware of its
existence. Human beings can become highly skilled at remaining
unaware of a certain aspect of reality, even when it is thrust upon
them with some force. Mechanisms of denial, repression, and
selective inattention have been described in detail as techniques
whereby people are able to exercise control over the extent of
their awareness. It is not unusual, therefore, to find parents who
claim that "there is really nothing wrong" with an obviously
severely retarded child. They may attribute the child's complete
failure in school to a vindictive teacher, for example, or to bouts
of tonsillitis. Parents may be helped in this self-deception by
relatives, friends, and at times even professionals, who have
reassured them of the child's "normality." Reluctance to face a
painful and irrevocable situation is not limited to parents, and it is
not surprising to find, therefore, that others have likewise failed to
recognize the situation.

The trauma of experiencing retardation in one's child may
precipitate serious existential conflicts. Concern with religion, the
meaning of life, the tragedy of death, the inescapability of
aloneness, and the relative insignificance and helplessness of man
may preoccupy the parents. Although these concerns are usually
less obvious than the other reactions described above, their
significance should not be underestimated.

THE THERAPEUTIC INTERVIEW

Since parents of retardates typically approach the psychologist with several of the reactions just described, it is important to furnish them with the opportunity for a therapeutic interview. In its simplest form, parents should be given the opportunity to express their feelings in a nonthreatening interpersonal interaction. The basic ingredients of such an interview include the following.

First, the counselee should be treated with acceptance and respect. By treating his client with dignity, the counselor helps decrease the feelings of worthlessness, self-blame, and shame which plague many parents of retardates. Feelings of loss of self-confidence and of helplessness are decreased when the parents feel accepted, understood, and respected.

Second, the psychologist should resist the temptation to assume an authoritarian role. Although the assumption of a godlike role may enhance the counselor's feeling of self-esteem, it tends to have the reverse effect on his clients. Furthermore, the authoritarian role tends to discourage parents from expressing their views and feelings; they tend instead to await expectantly the words of wisdom which the psychologist will bestow upon them.

Few competent psychologists regard themselves as authorities in the area of mental retardation, for, if one is at all in contact with the field, one cannot but be impressed with the vastness of our current ignorance. Therefore, assuming an omniscient role is a bit of a fraud, and most parents soon grow painfully aware of the counselor's real limitations.

Third, perhaps the essence of the therapeutic interview is that it is an interpersonal transaction wherein the interviewer allows the interviewee free emotional expression. In this respect, it differs rather markedly from the great majority of interpersonal inter-actions, since typically one is constantly reminded that many emotional reactions are rejected, condemned, censored, and so forth. As a result, of course, it becomes increasingly difficult to tolerate these "condemned" feelings within one's self, and one develops any number of ingenious mechanisms for disguising, disowning, and otherwise rejecting one's own feelings. The parent's statement that "sometimes this child makes me so mad!"

may have repeatedly been countered with statements that he "shouldn't feel that way," that the child "can't help" how he acts, and so on. After these reactions, the parent has never even allowed himself the much more "reprehensible" thought: "I wish this child was dead!"

By encouraging emotional expression without passing value judgments on the expressed feelings, the counselor helps the parent to tolerate his feelings with less guilt and anxiety and, consequently, to deal with the feelings more effectively.

Fourth, since the parents and not the psychologist will have to share life with the retarded child, decisions should be reached by the parents rather than the psychologist. By encouraging the parents to make their own decisions, the counselor enhances their feeling of self-confidence and helps them to assume responsibility for their actions. The counselor's goal should be to help the parents reach their decisions with as full an awareness as possible of their own feelings and of the reality of the situation.

Fifth, an important principle in conducting interviews with such parents is to let the parents determine the direction of the interview. That is, counseling seems most helpful when it is parent centered rather than counselor centered. The psychologists may have preconceived notions regarding the content and course which the interview should follow, and he may indeed experience feelings of accomplishment and satisfaction upon completing an interview successfully directed in this fashion. The parents, on the other hand, may have quite different expectations regarding the interview and may, consequently, leave disappointed, frustrated, or confused. After all, the goal of the interview is generally assumed to be to help the parents − not the counselor − and a parent centered interview seems most successful in reaching this goal.

The sixth and last important ingredient of a therapeutic interview is perhaps the simplest and most difficult, namely, honesty. Although most psycholgists do not plan to deceive their clients, their own needs and tensions may tempt them to distort, minimize, evade, ignore, and otherwise tamper with reality.

Not infrequently, the psycholgist's need for approval and for maintaining the myth of his own omniscience leads him to deceive his clients by disguising his own ignorance and by bombarding them with assorted bits of impressive information. To a parent's question regarding the etiology of his child's defect, for example, the counselor may vaguely indicate that the etiology of many forms of retardation is not yet fully understood, and he may then embark upon a truly engrossing review of chromosome studies in mongolism. Such a discourse may impress as well as confuse the parents, especially if their child is not mongoloid. In an attempt to "protect" parents against anxiety and depression, some counselors distort reality by minimizing the degree of retardation or by focusing upon unrealistic possibilities of eventual treatment or "cure."

IMPORTANCE OF LISTENING

Perhaps the most difficult skill for the psychologist to acquire is the ability to listen to his client. Listening not only implies attentiveness, interest, and sensitivity, but it also involves the capacity to remain silent. Many people find it difficult to refrain from speaking. Psychologists and other professionals often act as though their mission in life is to pass to the less informed the great wisdom which they possess.

Careful listening by the counselor has numerous beneficial results. The client's statements, for example, can be a valuable clue to the appropriateness of the counselor's comments. One does not respond in exactly the same way to an uneducated laborer as one does to a university professor. Detailed accounts of the latest studies of the reticular formation may be a bit inappropriate when directed to a truck driver, just as basic explanations of the meaning of electroencephalography are inappropriately condescending when directed to a physician.

By attentive listening, the counselor should succeed in reaching more or less valid conclusions as to the parents' current needs. If the counselor listens to the parents with the question, "Why are they seeing me here and now?" constantly in mind, he may frequently find that the initially stated reason for the interview is indeed far removed from the real reason which brings the parents to him. Having ascertained the parents' real needs, the counselor is better prepared to supply them with information which will be meaningful to them, and he can more intelligently make recommendations with regard to further evaluation and planning.

The psychologist who succeeds in controlling his need to speak is more likely to encourage his clients to express their own feelings, concerns, and opinions. The parents' observations of the retarded child are frequently of considerable value, and their estimates of functioning level are often quite accurate. It is not unusual to discover that parents come to the psychologist having already made important decisions and searching for support or a chance for catharsis rather than for information or evaluation. On occasion, encouraging parents to voice their opinions reveals surprising distortions and erroneous beliefs, indicating areas in which information is most needed.

USE OF EVALUATIVE FINDINGS

Since psychologists are frequently requested to determine the presence of mental retardation, psychological evaluation often becomes the subject of the interview with the parents. If the parents and the psychologist agree that formal evaluation of the child may be desirable, the parents should be informed of the nature and purpose of the evaluation. It is important to acquaint parents with the answers they may expect from the evaluation. If the results should prove to be relatively meaningless, the parents should be so advised. Parents' resentment at being told of uninterpretable results of complex and often expensive procedures is not entirely inappropriate, particularly if they were not forewarned of this possible outcome.

The psychologist should endeavor to expedite evaluative procedures. Allowing parents to linger in the agony of doubt is cruel and destructive. The period of evaluation is usually experienced as highly stressful and distressing by parents, and it should be kept as short as possible. As soon as the evaluation has been completed, the parents should be informed of the results.

Evaluative findings should be presented in terms that will be meaningful to the parents. Operational formulations and concrete examples are to be preferred to abstract and theoretical constructs. Presenting the child's level of functioning in mental age equivalents is usually considerably more meaningful than references to the intelligence quotients or social quotients. As a matter of fact, parents are often surprisingly accurate in estimating the child's level of functioning in terms of developmental level.

Description of probable accomplishments in terms of illustrative behavior is usually extremely helpful. Emphasis on those activities which the child may be able to perform is more helpful than dwelling on areas of limitations and expected failure. A statement such as "Your child will probably be able to master fifth- or sixth-grade work" is much less likely to cause pain than saying "Of course, your child will never complete junior high school," and it is equally factual.

Parents should be acquainted with the limitations of the evaluative findings. Parents usually have questions regarding etiology, diagnosis, and prognosis, and the counselor will, in many cases of course, have to indicate that in one or more of these areas he is making an "educated guess." Although the majority of parents are blissfully ignorant of such concepts as validity and reliability, it is meaningful to indicate the relative probability that the present findings are accurate, and particularly the likelihood that predictions will prove to be correct.

Although it is neither realistic nor appropriate to present exact probability figures, the counselor can indicate that his predictions regarding a severely retarded, ten-year-old microcephalic are made with considerable confidence, whereas his predictions regarding a two-year-old, mildly retarded child with no apparent neuropathology are made with less assurance. Comments regarding the possible value of future evaluations can be helpful, and they may include acquainting parents with suitable referral sources.

CONCLUDING THE INTERVIEW

Even if further referrals are not indicated, the psychologist should encourage parents to formulate tentative plans. Some parents are so overwhelmed with their tragedy that they seem to flounder in the present and to recoil from the future. With tactful encouragement and support, the counselor can help such parents to think constructively about the future. In attempting to plan for the child, the parents can be helped by presentation of factual information regarding community resources, referral agencies, institutions, psychotherapists, and so forth.

In concluding the interview — or series of interviews, as the case might be — the psychologist can be supportive by informing parents that he will remain available for further contacts should the need arise. The parents then leave the counselor with the feeling that they have been understood and that they are not completely alone in their misery.

PART III

GROUP COUNSELING WITH
PARENTS OF RETARDED CHILDREN

Chapter 12

Group Therapy with Parents of Mentally Deficient Children

JAMES C. COLEMAN

THE present study represents an attempt to evaluate the use of group therapy in working with parents of mentally deficient children. It grew out of (1) the need for a better coordination of activities between a private school for mentally deficient children and the home situation of these children, (2) the continual demand of parents for counseling time concerning their children, which placed excessive demands upon the time of school personnel, and (3) the many common problems which these parents revealed in counseling which seemed amenable to a group approach.

RECRUITMENT

No attempt was made to actually select from among the parents those who needed group therapy or would be likely to profit from it most. Rather, an opportunity was provided for all parents to participate in bimonthly evening meetings. Although the parents were sent postcards indicating the time and place of the meeting, the topic for discussion that evening, and an expressed wish that they would find the meeting of value, no direct appeal or pressure was put upon them to attend.

The parents in general were of lower middle-class socio-economic status, although they ranged from skilled tradesmen to businessmen, writers, lawyers, and other professionally trained

Note: Reprinted by permission from the author and the *American Journal of Mental Deficiency, 57*:700-704, 1953. Copyrighted by the American Association on Mental Deficiency.

persons. The average education of the parents was completion of the tenth grade. Approximately one-fourth had attended college.

At the first meeting some thirty, or about one third of the total parents of children in school, attended. Attendance at subsequent meetings varied between twenty and thirty-five, with some shift in personnel each time due to new additions and unavoidable absences of those parents who had attended preceding meetings. However, most of those attending the first two meetings continued through the six-month trial period with only occasional absences. Fourteen of the parents attended each of the twelve meetings.

PHYSICAL ARRANGEMENTS

The group meetings were held on the second and fourth Tuesday evenings of each month from 8:00 until approximately 9:30 p.m. No attempt was made to set up a definite closing time for the meetings, although 9:30 was usually considered the maximum length. The meetings actually varied from about one hour to one and three-quarter hours, with the average approximating one and one-quarter hours. The group meetings were held in a large room of the school made possible by combining two of the regular school classrooms via a movable partition. Regular classroom desks were removed and straight-backed folding chairs were substituted and placed in two semicircular rows around the periphery of the room. Ashtrays and necessary materials were made available for those who wished to smoke. A screen and projection equipment were provided for showing slides and movies. One of the regular school teachers acted as secretary-recorder for the sessions.

The group sessions were terminated at the end of a six-month period, and this fact was made known to the parents during the first meeting when the objectives of the meetings and other structuring was undertaken.

PROCEDURE IN THERAPY

In structuring the meetings to the parents, emphasis was placed on the coordination of home and school activities in the best interests of the children and upon freedom to discuss any and all problems which might have some bearing upon this basic objective. The term "group therapy" was not used, and no attempt was made to structure the situation as therapy in any form.

Each meeting was initiated with an educational motion picture or talk by local authorities, e.g. psychiatrists, pediatricians, dentists, school principals, on the problems of mental deficiency. The films and talks were limited to thirty minutes, followed by a question and answer period and general group discussion presided over by the group leader (author). The group leader made every attempt to promote a permissive, mutually supportive atmosphere in which the participants would feel free to bring up their problems and express their true feelings concerning them. The general approach to the group discussion was a flexible one, although an attempt was made to remain as nondirective as the situation seemed to permit. No attempt was made by the group leader to direct the discussion into certain channels or toward preconceived topics. The major emphasis was placed on bringing out the commonality of problems, in supporting individual discussants when this was necessary, and in pointing up group formulations of insights into and coping techniques for dealing with various problems worked on. This general orientation proved highly effective in eliciting group discussion and in making the parents feel that this was their meeting and their responsibility to get as much out of it as possible.

In a sense the interaction was maintained on a relatively surface level, since the group discussion was restricted to parent-child relations and did not take up various personal problems in other life areas. However, many of these parent-child problems went relatively deep in terms of personality conflicts centering around guilt, sex, and attitudes toward spouses.

GROUP INTERACTION

During the first three meetings the group discussion was highly intellectualized, focussing primarily on the formal topic which was

scheduled for that particular meeting of the general activities of
the school. However, now and again more personal problems came
to the fore in the form of personal experience or specific questions
of what to do in this or that particular situation. After the third
meeting the discussion became less and less restricted by the
particular topic scheduled for that evening and directed more and
more toward specific parent-child relations problems.

Among the major problems which were brought to the fore and
actively worked on by the group were the following:

1. Acceptance of themselves as parents of mentally deficient
   children without feeling guilty or devaluated. A large
   number of the parents expressed feelings of guilt concerning their possible role in the bearing of a mentally
   deficient child. Their guilt feelings were in the main
   engendered by false ideas of heredity, alcoholic consump-
   tion, and "immoral" sexual practices all of which they
   felt were largely their individual responsibility. The
   dispelling of these misconceptions, as well as the mutual
   support gained by group identification with other parents
   having this problem, were considered two of the most
   important values of the group sessions.

2. Acceptance of their mentally deficient child. Parental
   reactions to the realization that their child was mentally
   deficient seemed to vary from rejecting the child at one
   extreme to denying reality and refusing to believe that
   the child was really below normal in his intellectual
   potentialities. Several parents pointed to the tendency
   toward wishful thinking in the form of believing that
   some new method of treatment would soon be forthcoming or that some miracle would occur and bring their
   child up to normal. It was brought out also that the
   frustration of parental ambitions for their children
   undoubtedly was related to their tendency toward
   rejection of their child. Most of the parents agreed that it
   was a serious problem to view their children realistically
   and still accept them as worthwhile human beings.

3. Adjusting parental level of aspiration for child to his
   actual abilities. Closely related to viewing their children

realistically in the light of their actual abilities and potentialities was the problem of adjusting parental levels of aspiration to their realistic view. Many parents admitted that they had had such high hopes for their child and found it very difficult to face reality and accept his limitations, especially without rejecting the child or feeling differently toward him than toward their other children of normal intelligence. As noted previously, it was admitted that this in part resulted from the frustration of the parent's own ambition and aspirations.

4. Avoiding pampering the child and giving him all sorts of special privileges. It was pointed out that guilt feelings and feelings that their child was sick often contributed to a tendency to overindulge the child and to overprotect and baby him. This tended to inhibit the development of his potentialities toward actualization and independence.

5. Problems centering around normal siblings. A variety of problems were brought up by the parents centering around the mental deficient's relations to other siblings. Parents pointed out that punishment for misbehavior was particularly difficult, since their mentally deficient children did not fully understand the probable consequences of their misbehavior and hence were in a sense not morally responsible agents. This frequently led to the dilemma of punishing one or more of the siblings while excusing the same misbehavior on the part of the mental deficient. Since the other children often could not understand the justice of this procedure, problems in parent-child relations were automatically created. Other sibling problems centered around the intellectual effect on other siblings of having to play and work with a mentally deficient sibling, and emotional adjustments of siblings necessitated by children in the neighborhood making derogatory remarks about their mentally deficient brother or sister. This problem was sometimes accentuated by other parents in the neighborhood who would permit their children to play with the normal siblings but not with the mental deficient.

6. Sexual problems of the mentally deficient child. Here parents discussed the handling of masturbation and other specific problems faced by the mentally deficient child. Many of these children had been found out in sexual behavior of various natures with other children. In large part this was thought to result from their lack of normal inhibitions and understanding of sexual mores. Due to the prevalence of misconceptions concerning the harmfulness of masturbation and other sexual misinformation, a good deal of didactic therapy was undertaken at this point by the group leader. Topics related to the mentally deficient child's sexual adjustment which came up for discussion included sterilization, marriage and parenthood, and permissible sexual outlets.

7. Problems relating to keeping the child in the home or placing him in an institution. Parents pointed out the strain placed upon the home relationships by the various special problems introduced by the mentally deficient child and discussed the desirability of placing such children in an institution where they would receive some training and unburden the immediate family situation. Difficulties in resolving this problem were raised by the fact that the higher-level mentally deficient child is capable of loving and wanting to be with his family just like other children, by the overcrowded conditions of public institutions for the mentally deficient which made any adequate educational training difficult to obtain, and by the financial problems created by maintaining him in a private school.

8. Providing for child's future. Realizing that these children would never be able to function in the community without someone to supervise and care for them, the problem of their future was often a difficult one for the parents. Here matters relating to trust funds, community supervision for mentally deficients, and general methods of enabling them to live as adequate a life as possible were discussed.

9. Things the parents can do in the home to help the child.

Many of the parents had tried out on their children special educational techniques such as tracing in learning to read. A whole series of questions came up relating to the educational procedure and other activities the parents might undertake in order to better coordinate their activities with those of the school and to be of maximum assistance to the mentally deficient child. Here the importance of a practical, reality-oriented program to enrich the child's everyday experiences and related activities was discussed.

10. Things the parents might do to help the school. Toward the closing phases of the group sessions the discussion often centered around deficiencies in the school program, such as lack of desirable equipment, which the parents might assist in rectifying. Plans were undertaken on the initiative of the parents for school dinners and semisocial events to raise money for special equipment and other needed materials which the finances of the school did not permit.

It is interesting to note that the group interaction paralleled very closely that found in more typical group therapy groups, starting with a rather intellectual level of discussion, progressing to personal specific problems, and terminating in a more generalized and socially oriented approach to their problems. It was felt that most of the parents participated effectively in the group discussions. Some were of course more active than others, but even the most diffident seemed to be drawn into the discussion when problems closely affecting them were brought to light. Three of the parents were particularly active in the group in raising problems, supporting other participants, and enthusiastically backing the group sessions. They were considered most helpful by the group leader. In general, little conflict among members of the group was noted, although occasionally one participant would interrupt another to inject a comment of his own or to rather violently disagree with the opinions expressed. More characteristic were patterns of mutual support, group identification, assistance with problems raised, and immersion in the atmosphere of group understanding and acceptance.

EVALUATION OF THE GROUP SESSIONS

It is a difficult problem to evaluate group therapy results with the best available experimental controls, and in the present study such controls were lacking. However, there were a number of favorable indications: the range and importance of the discussion content, the parallel course of the group interaction to that in more typical groups, the continued high attendance, the accepting and understanding group atmosphere created, and the almost unanimous verbal testimonials to the value of the group sessions. Undoubtedly, much of the enthusiasm generated in the group members grew directly out of the supportive group identification with accepting and understanding fellows. For many this was a new and most welcome experience. This rather favorable view of the outcome of the group sessions was augmented by the requests of six of the participants for referrals to qualified psychologists or psychiatrists who might help them with personal problems not directly related to their mentally deficient children. This was interpreted as an expression of confidence in the value of bringing their problems out into the open and attempting with professional assistance to deal with them more realistically and effectively.

The findings of the present study indicate the possibility of utilizing group therapy with the parents of mentally deficient children for promoting better coordination between educational institutions and the home as well as in helping the parents themselves in developing understanding and healthier attitudes toward the various problems centering around the rearing of mentally deficient children.

Chapter 13

Attitude Change by Parents of Trainable Mentally Retarded Children as a Result of Group Discussion

JAMES A. BITTER

$\rm{T}$HAT the parents of a mentally retarded child need counseling is well recognized by educators, social workers, physicians, and other professional workers who come into contact with such parents. Counseling the parents of severely mentally retarded children is an especially acute problem because these children will be either dependent or nearly dependent throughout their lives. The attitudes of parents and the way they interact with their retarded offspring affect the mental health and happiness of the whole family. Farber (1959, 1960) studied the effects of a retarded child in the family and found that marital integration was negatively affected. He also found that institutionalization was less a crisis than was the orientation and education of the family concerning retardation. Other research reports by Rosen (1955) and by Worchel and Worchel (1961) also discuss the difficulties parents encounter in coping with a retarded child.

Research on programs conducted to help parents of mentally retarded children is reported by Popp, Ingram, and Jordan (1954) and Coleman (1953). The evidence presented by the investigators, however, is subjective in nature. In spite of the indicated

Note: Reprinted by permission of the author and *Exceptional Children, 30*:173-177, 1963. Published by The Council For Exceptional Children.

importance of parent education, very few studies of an objective nature have been undertaken to measure the worth of such programs.

PROBLEM

The purpose of this study was to determine the effectiveness of a series of parent group discussion sessions with regard to the attitudes of parents of a trainable mentally retarded child toward the child and toward the family problems occasioned by the retardation. It was hypothesized that parent group discussion sessions would lead to (1) positive changes in attitudes as a result of the parent education program, (2) greater changes in attitudes for parents attending three or more sessions than those attending one or two, and (3) no differences in change of attitudes between parents attending sessions in two different schools.

PROCEDURE

Two separate but similar parent discussion groups were conducted in each of two different schools. The parent education program consisted of seven monthly sessions in each of the schools during the normal school year. The subjects were sixteen parents (11 mothers and 5 fathers) of trainable mentally retarded children in two public schools located in economically middle-class communities in the same metropolitan area. All subjects involved in the study had a child with an IQ under 55 enrolled in a special class for trainable children. A summary description of the parent subjects is presented in Table 13-I.

In order to assess change, four measurement instruments were administered before and after the parent education program. The

TABLE 13-I

DESCRIPTION OF THE PARENT SUBJECTS

School	N	Mean Age	Mean Years of Education	Mean No. of Children	Mean Age of MR Child
A	10	41.9	11.8	3.1	10.7
B	6	39.8	12.8	2.8	11.2

Parent Attitude Research Instrument, Form IV, (PARI) constructed by Schaefer and Bell (1959) was used to measure parental attitudes toward child rearing. The PARI was supplemented with a Semantic Differential utilizing :.. technique developed by Osgood, Suci, and Tannenbaum (1957), and a Child Character Trait Questionnaire constructed by the investigator. The Semantic Differential was used to measure the parent attitudes toward ten concepts relating to mental retardation. The Child Character Trait Questionnaire was based on a list of forty character traits made by Worchel and Worchel (1961). The fourth measuring device was a fifty-item true or false test concerning facts about mental deficiency. It was derived in part from a pamphlet by Yepson (1956).

THE PARENT EDUCATION PROGRAM

The parent education program consisted of seven monthly evening sessions between November and May. The sessions were approximately two hours in length. The seven topics of discussion were selected by the parents at the first session from a list of eleven suggested topics.

The topics were:

First session: Special education: its purpose and goals.

Second session: Recreation for mentally retarded children.

Third session: Speech and language development of mentally retarded children.

Fourth session: Vocational potential of mentally retarded children and community resources for parents of the retarded.

Fifth session: Sociological aspects of mental retardation.

Sixth session: Family relationships and mental health in the home with a mentally retarded child.

Seventh session: Suggestions for training the mentally retarded by parents in the home.

The sessions were conducted by the teacher of the class in each school and followed the same general outline, i.e. (1) a brief orientation to the topic, usually lasting from five to twenty-five minutes, (2) questions for discussion, and (3) open discussion.

Resource people were used at sessions three, five, and six and included a speech therapist, a university professor of special education, and a supervisor of special education.

The order of the topics for the sessions was very carefully considered. The first topic was an appropriate topic early in the school year for three reasons. First, the parents are or should be interested in what the school does with their child; second, the topic provides for some cooperative planning for the school year; and third, as a result of this cooperative planning, rapport is developed between the teacher and the parents, the school and the home.

The second session fell just before the Christmas holidays. Thus, recreation was selected, since it offered the opportunity to exchange toy and gift suggestions in addition to learning of various community sponsored programs. Speech and language development was injected because of the interest by the parents in what the speech therapist was doing with the children in one school

The teachers of the classes felt that by the fourth session the parents should be ready to discuss their children a little more openly. In terms of realistic and frank discussion, vocational potential seemed to provide a stepping stone to the topics which were to follow. Sociological aspects preceded family relationship and mental health, with the rationale that parents would find it easier to discuss society's attitudes toward their children than their own attitudes.

The discussion of suggestions for training the mentally retarded by parents in the home was saved for the last session because it was felt the parents would like suggestions for the summer months when the child was not attending school.

The teachers as group leaders made every effort to maintain an informal atmosphere and to observe the principles of good group instruction and discussion as illustrated by Trecker and Trecker (1952). The teachers had no previous training or experience as adult group leaders. Preparation for leading group discussion was done through extensive reading by the teachers prior to the parent education program.

An observer was used to evaluate what happened in the group and who made what kinds of contributions. He sat outside the group, usually at the teacher's desk in the classroom, and did not participate in the discussion. Two observation instruments were used (1) an Interaction Process Analysis based upon observation categories suggested by Bales (1950) and (2) a form constructed by the investigator used to sum up the observations made by the observer. At the close of each session the teacher, serving as group leader, would write a brief report of the meeting noting reactions to the topic and participation in the discussion.

RESULTS

The statistical treatment of the data gathered on the attitudes of the parents before and after the parent education program revealed the following results:

Parents Before and After the Parent Education Program

As shown in Table 13-II, the parents demonstrated significant changes in Democratic Attitudes in a positive direction from before to after participating in the parent education program. No significant change occurred in the Authoritarian-Control or in the Hostility-Rejection attitudes. The three factors were determined for the 23 subscales as reported by Zuckerman, Ribback, Monashkin, and Norton (1958).

The results of the true-false test on mental deficiency revealed a significant (sign test, $p < .01$) difference between the pre- and post-tests. Since the parents made more rather than fewer errors, however, the obtained difference does not support the first

TABLE 13-II

COMPARISON OF THE TOTAL GROUP BEFORE
AND AFTER ON THE PARI

Factor	Before Mean	After Mean	Difference	t
Authoritarian-Control	13.27	12.48	−.79	.81
Hostility-Rejection	12.78	13.22	.44	.39
Democratic Attitudes	8.79	16.19	7.40	7.56**

$t_{.05} = 1.75; t_{.01} = 2.60$

hypothesis. This might suggest that a "little knowledge" is dangerous. However, no effort was made to increase a parent's knowledge of facts, but rather to develop and foster healthier attitudes through discussion. As a result of discussion with other parents, the parents perhaps realized that mental retardation does not consist of well-defined and clear-cut facts. If this feeling was engendered in the sessions then it would be reasonable to assume that more of the statements would appear ambiguous to the parents at the second testing.

Parents Attending Different Numbers of Sessions

Comparisons were made between the five parents attending seven sessions, the five attending four or five sessions, and the four attending one or two sessions. It should be noted that at the onset of the study it was difficult to foresee the number of parents attending different numbers of sessions. The results reported here are based on these three small groups.

Significant differences were found on four concepts of the Semantic Differential for parents attending different numbers of sessions.

The comparisons between those attending seven sessions and those attending one or two sessions are reported in Table 13-III. Parents attending seven sessions demonstrated more positive changes in attitudes on the concepts Trainable and Brain-Injured than parents attending one or two sessions.

The parents attending seven sessions demonstrated significantly ($t = 2.39$, $p < .05$) more positive changes in attitudes after the parent education program on the concept Teachers than the parents attending four or five sessions. The parents attending four or five sessions demonstrated significantly ($t = 1.87, p < .05$) more positive changes in attitudes on the concept Institutions.

Parents Attending Different Schools

There were significant differences between the two schools on one concept of the Semantic Differential and on the Child Character Trait Questionnaire. These findings do not support the third hypothesis.

TABLE 13-III

COMPARISON ON THE SEMANTIC DIFFERENTIAL
OF THE BEFORE AND AFTER DIFFERENCES OF PARENTS
ATTENDING SEVEN AND ONE OR TWO SESSIONS

Concept	Seven Sessions Mean Change	One-two Sessions Mean Change	Mean Differ- ence	t
Mental retardation	−1.40	−3.00	1.60	.33
Exceptional education	−2.20	−6.75	4.55	.65
Parent Groups	− .40	−2.75	2.35	.49
IQ	4.60	−1.25	5.85	.87
Teachers	1.40	3.75	2.35	.36
Institutions	−2.20	1.75	3.95	.48
Sterilization	−2.20	−4.25	2.05	.10
Sheltered workshops	− .20	.75	.95	.13
Trainable	.80	−1.75	2.55	1.83*
Brain-injured	8.80	−5.75	14.55	1.76*

$t_{.05}$ = 1.76; $t_{.01}$ = 2.62

On the Semantic Differential the parents of School B showed more positive changes after the parent education program on the concept Mental Retardation than the parents of School A. This difference was significant beyond the .05 level ($t = 2.67, p < .05$).

The parents of School A showed more positive change in acceptance-rejection patterns toward their mentally retarded child on the Child Character Trait Questionnaire than the parents of School B (chi square probability by factorials $< .05$).

It was observed by the investigator and the observers that the parents of School B showed a more anxious concern for the future of their retarded child than the parents of School A. Being less anxious, it may be that the parents of School A found it easier to make changes, thus suggesting a possible explanation for the measured differences between the two schools.

Of the forty-four parents represented by the two schools, twenty-nine took part in the discussion sessions and sixteen were tested. The average attendance per meeting was 7.5. School A had

48.08 percent participation, and School B had 28.06 percent. More effort was made by the teacher of School A to establish strong, friendly rapport between the school and the home before the onset of the parent education program. In the light of the differences between the schools in representation, this seems important to the success of parent programs.

DISCUSSION

Two factors which may have some bearing on the results should be noted: (1) on some scales, particularly the Semantic Differential, the expressed attitudes were positive on the initial test, thus leaving little room for measurable change; (2) on the Child Character Trait Questionnaire, 40 percent of the papers were unscorable, suggesting that it may have been difficult to complete and, therefore, the results might tend to be questionable.

One observation deserves mention. At the parent-teacher conferences at the end of the school year, three families mentioned a better outlook on life with their retarded child as a result of the discussion sessions.

As indicated in the literature, the results, objective and subjective, seem to confirm the importance of parent education in changing attitudes of parents of trainable mentally retarded children. However, the inconclusive results suggest a need for a longer experimental study using contrast groups.

The special-class teachers in the two schools felt that the relationship and cooperation between the school and the home as a result of the sessions resulted in a more effective and realistic special-class program. What effect this has on the trainable mentally retarded child can only be assumed and is an area for future research.

SUMMARY

The purpose of this study was to measure objectively the effectiveness of parent education for parents of trainable mentally retarded children.

The objective evidence, although not conclusive, would seem to indicate that a series of parent group-discussion sessions are effective in changing the attitudes of parents of trainable mentally retarded children toward their retarded child and toward family problems occasioned by the retardation. The subjective observations of the investigator and the observers seem to support the hypothesis that this change is to more positive attitudes.

REFERENCES

Bales, R. F.: *Interaction Process Analysis.* Cambridge, Addison-Wesley Press, 1950.

Bitter, J. A.: An experimental study of the effectiveness of a parent education program for parents of severely mentally retarded children as measured by attitude change. Unpublished masters paper, University of Wisconsin-Milwaukee, 1962.

Coleman, J. C.: Group therapy with parents of mentally deficient children. *Am. J. Ment. Defic., 57*:700-704, 1953.

Farber, B.: The effects of a severely retarded child on family integration. *Society for Research on Child Development Monograph,* 1959, No. 71.

Farber, B.: Family organization and crises: maintenance of integration in families with a severely mentally retarded child. *Society for Research on Child Development Monograph,* 1960, No. 75.

Osgood, C. E., Suci, G. J., and Tannenbaum, P. H.: *The Measurement of Meaning.* Urbana, University of Illinois Press, 1957.

Popp, Cleo B., Ingram, Vivian, and Jordan, P. H.: Helping parents understand their mentally handicapped child. *Am. J. Ment. Defic., 58*(4):530-534, 1954.

Rosen, L.: Selected aspects in the development of the mother's understanding of her mentally retarded child. *Am. J. Ment. Defic., 59*:522-528, 1955.

Schaefer, E. S., and Bell, R. Q.: Development of a parental attitude research instrument. *Child Develop., 29*(3):339-361, 1959.

Trecker, Audrey, and Trecker, H.: *How to Work With Groups.* New York, Woman's Press, 1952.

Worchel, Tillie L., and Worchel, P.: The parental concept of the mentally retarded child. *Am. J. Ment. Defic., 65*(6):782-788, 1961.

Yepson, L. N.: *Facts and Fancies About Mental Deficiency.* Trenton, New Jersey State Department of Institutions and Agencies, 1956.

Zuckerman, M., Ribback, Beatrice B., Monashkin, I., and Norton, J. A.: Normative data and factor analysis on the parental attitude research instrument. *J. Consult. Psychol., 22*(3):165-171, 1958.

Changes in Attitudes of Parents of Retarded Children Effected Through Group Counseling

MELVILLE J. APPELL, CLARENCE M. WILLIAMS and KENNETH N. FISHELL

T HE attitudes of parents toward their retarded children have been noted as leaving much to be desired (Katz, 1961; Thurston, 1960). These attitudes have been found to be of extreme importance in the rehabilitation of the retarded child. In a paper read before the New York State Welfare Conference, Weingold remarked, "Thus the first element in society that the retarded comes in contact with is the family group where the parents, of course, are the protagonists. If they do not act positively the child is doomed" (1960). It has been acknowledged by Thurston (1959) that the attitudes and emotional reactions of parents of the retardate are of crucial importance in planning for his effective treatment and rehabilitation.

Parent attitudes have been variously described. Reference has been made to parent "unrealism" by Weingold and Hormuth (1953). They report on the intense resistance of parents to any realistic recognition of the limitations or capacities of the retarded individual. According to Thurston (1960), "Initially all parents experienced emotional upset and anxiety when they learned they

Note: Reprinted by permission from the author and the *American Journal of Mental Deficiency,* *68*:807-812, 1964. Copyrighted by the American Association on Mental Deficiency.

had a handicapped child." He characterized these parents as "highly sensitive, suspicious, anxious and unhappy individuals, the opposite of what might be desired" (1960). In reviewing a variety of investigations Worchel and Worchel (1961) described findings of a similar nature.

As Cummings and Stock (1962) point out, "Many parents of retarded children are in need of a sustained counseling relationship. . . ." The need surpasses the ability of the various community agencies to supply the trained personnel. This inability has given impetus to the use of group guidance techniques, often referred to as group counseling, group discussion, or group therapy. These investigators in reviewing pertinent research concluded that the need for group therapy is substantial and is likely to increase (1962).

Even though a group guidance technique has been described and used, there are few investigations indicating attitudinal change on the part of parents brought about through its use. One study (Cummings and Stock, 1962) reported gains during group therapy in ventilation, sharing, and a more appropriate recognition of reality. Failure of this technique to effect change in long-standing problems which involved sex, guilt, and acceptance of self was also recognized. Similar findings were reported by Weingold and Hormuth (1953) and Coleman (1953).

The purpose of the present study was to investigate changes in parental attitudes brought about through the method of group counseling and discussion. Furthermore, it was hoped that an adaptation of an existing instrument might provide a valid method for inquiry into these changes.

SUBJECTS

The subjects were twenty-one mothers of retarded children. Their children were enrolled in the Day Care Center, Inc. The child's enrollment was conditional on the mother's willingness to participate in a counseling and discussion group for parents. This group ranged in age from 25 to 49 with the average being 38.5. All of these parents had had some high school and five had completed college. A description of the Day Care Center, Inc., Rochester, N. Y., has been reported by Nadal (1961).

PROCEDURE

For convenience, the parents were divided into two similar groups. Each met for a series of approximately sixty sessions extending over a period of two years. A modified version* of the Thurston Sentence Completion Form (TSCF) (1959) was given each group at the beginning and end of the series. Their responses were categorized and divided into the appropriate sections. These categories were (1) reactions and concerns of parents, (2) the handicapped individual's satisfactions and discomfitures, (3) the reactions of the brothers and sisters, (4) reactions of community, friends and neighbors, (5) the Day Care Center and its staff, (6) hopes and expectations for the handicapped. The seventh category, "Things of a General Nature" was not considered pertinent to this study.

The individual items in each section of the form were compared before and after by chi-square analyses for changes in quantities in response.

Reactions and Concerns of Parents

After two years of participating in these group sessions, parents showed a greater willingness to divulge their feelings about their retarded progeny. Their responses were less in terms of their own feelings and more in terms of their child's needs — not their love for him but more a concern for his happiness, self-sufficiency, and future. Even though the "wondering" increased in the post-administration, qualitatively, it was more structured and pointed. If a parent was "at a loss" or "confused" before counseling, the probability was that she would be wondering more about the future after counseling. In the preadministration more parents were concerned about his speech and physical disabilities. As these concerns subsided during the year, more basic questions involving cause and degree of retardation came to the fore.

It was somewhat surprising that prior to counseling only 52 percent of the parents were willing to admit they were originally

---

*Available from the senior author.

appraised of the retardation by medical doctors. This was increased to 71 percent on the postadministration. On learning of the handicap, these parents admitted to shock and disbelief. Other investigators (Masland, Sarason and Gladwin, 1958; Richmond, 1959), report similar findings. Richmond, however, goes on to say, "This is a normal reaction and can be adjusted to in time . . . through medical or other services . . ." (1959).

The findings from the present investigation were somewhat different. Even though they were more willing to admit to obtaining help from the medical profession and even though they had been involved in group counseling, many of these parents still seemed perplexed and confused about the cause of the retardation. The questions that were still being asked indicated their distress: "What causes it?" "What is the actual reason?" "Why?" "How severely retarded is he?" "Why is a child brought into the world like this?" To mitigate their concerns, they were still searching for more information to help them understand their handicapped children in spite of the exposure afforded them through individual and group counseling. Thurston's remark (1960) that "the methods and manners of physicians (and the present investigators would include all counselors) in this role are not known," might be worthy of investigation.

Although it might be suggested that information given these parents was vague or too general, their insatiability must also be considered. Undoubtedly, they did gain valuable information about their children during counseling. In the initial administration 43 percent of the parents said they thought no one knew the cause of the disability. This dropped to 33 percent in the postadministration, an indication that the cause of the disability was more realistically acknowledged. As compared to the original 33 percent, 52 percent thought "injury" was the primary causal factor. It was obvious that some facts were being communicated. However, it should be noted that in the postadministration, regardless of their greater knowledge, parents were insisting that the most difficult thing to accept was the disability itself.

A question concerning the worth of a professional relationship that appears to be predicated on information giving might be raised. It is possible that the "confusion," a part of the inability to

TABLE 14-I

ITEMS FROM A MODIFIED VERSION OF THE TSCF ON WHICH SIGNIFICANT DIFFERENCES WERE FOUND IN A PRE- AND POST-ADMINISTRATION

	X^2	df
1 (1) When I think of my child, I	42.6*	3
2 (1) The thing that I still don't understand about my child's handicap is		
. . . .	24.7†	3
3 (1) The future looks	31.5†	3
4 (1) The thing that most parents find hardest to accept about the handicap of their child is	21.6†	3
5 (1) When I first learned that my child was handicapped, I		
. . . .	15.0*	3
6 (1) The best thing that has happened to my child is		
. . . .	31.4†	4
7 (1) I (wanted) (did not want) (cross out one) my child placed in DCC because	10.5*	2
8 (1) The thing that would help me most in understanding my handicapped child would be	15.6*	3
9 (2) The thing that my child likes best about DCC is		
. . . .	15.8*	3
10 (2) The greatest difficulty for my child is		
. . . .	12.4*	2
11 (2) When my child comes home, he (or she) wants most to		
. . . .	37.4†	4
12 (2) My child becomes most easily disturbed when		
. . . .	29.9†	2
13 (2) My child is (happy) (unhappy) at DCC because		
. . . .	30.7†	6
14 (3) When the child's brothers and sisters ask about him I tell		
. . . .	16.0*	3
15 (4) The thing I'd like to see my community do for the handicapped is .		
. . . .	13.6*	4
18 (4) When people know you have a handicapped child, they		
. . . .	25.1†	6
19 (4) I (do) (do not) (cross out one) feel free to discuss my child's handicap with my friends and neighbors because		
. . . .	17.7*	2
20 (5) What they could do to make Day Care Center a better place is . .		
. . . .	21.6†	4
21 (5) The training program is		
. . . .	21.4†	3
22 (5) The thing I like most about DCC is		
. . . .	29.6†	3
23 (6) When I think of my child's future I . . . . ,		
. . . .	18.7†	3
24 (6) Although my child is handicapped, I would like him to		
. . . .	29.4†	5

Note. Numbers following the item numbers indicate the areas to which these items belong:

1. Reactions and Concerns of Parents.
2. Attitudes Regarding the Child's Satisfaction and Discomfiture.
3. Reactions of Brothers and Sisters.
4. Reactions of Community, Friends, and Neighbors.
5. Attitudes toward the Day Care Center and Staff.
6. Attitudes Related to Hopes and Expectations.

* Significant at the .01 level.
† Significant at the .001 level.

accept, was being used in an intellectual way. Knowledge of some aspects of mental retardation might then serve to keep the very concerned parents quite distant from the psychological realities that accompany this condition. A full acceptance of the retardation could conceivably be discouraged by information giving without adequate guidance.

Attitudes Regarding the Child's Satisfaction and Discomfiture

In the postadministration, parents expressed positive feelings that their children were more interested in interacting with their siblings. Although discussion centered on this point, it was more likely that interactions in the Day Care Center with parents watching behind a one-way vision screen had more bearing on this change.

As the parents gave more attention to their children's behavior, their concern about the ability to communicate decreased. Instead of communication they now saw self-control and peer acceptance as the areas of greater difficulty. In this regard they were supported by discussions which served to encourage realistic use of disciplinary measures which might serve to afford a degree of self-control in social situations.

Reactions of Brothers and Sisters

The counseling sessions gave the parents a more realistic interpretation of the child's disability, i.e. "He'll never be normal," "He's a little slow about learning." They then seemed more able to acknowledge these limitations in discussing the disability with their other children. "I'll tell them the truth as much as I know it," was a characteristic statement.

Reactions of Community, Friends, and Neighbors

Contrary to what might be expected of parents confronted with such a problem, both pre- and post-data indicated a feeling that the community understood and accepted their retarded children. Counseling served to enhance this feeling while at the same time it reduced the lesser impression that pity and sorrow were manifestations of the community's concern.

Postdata revealed some qualitative differences in response to the action parents wanted their community to take. Whereas in the predata, approximately 50 percent of the parents stressed the need for training facilities, in the postdata, a similar proportion seemed more aware of the need to attend to long range goals. Their more sophisticated desires were expressed as "long-range programs of schooling," "coordinated services," "more research to combat retardation in the future," and a "life care program."

Attitudes Toward the Day Care Center and Staff

In reference to the programs and the Center itself, counseling was evidently a cathartic. All sentences that referred to the Day Care Center produced a greater amount of response in the postdata. More parents gave expression to a critical approval of the facility and in their appraisal acknowledged the need for more space and more trained teachers. Their appraisal of the available staff as "understanding," "accepting," and "dedicated" did not change appreciably. Exposure to the programs provided these parents with a yardstick for evaluating the Center. In the postdata 62 percent of the parents compared to 43 percent in the predata thought the program was "good" to "excellent." In addition, 14 percent felt the program "good" with qualifications as to size of staff and number of sessions.

Attitudes Related to Hopes and Expectations

Group counseling seemed to promote more logical, realistic, and attainable aspiration levels on the part of parents. Some of the "wondering" about the future gave way to hope that the child would be more self-sufficient and thereby lead as "normal a life as possible." Even pessimism in relation to goals was more realistic. As one parent stated in apparent resignation, "I now think of Newark (State School)."

Where goals were originally somewhat unrealistic ("learn to read," "earn a livelihood", "learn to read and write"), counseling helped these parents to modify their aspirational levels so that becoming a "useful member of society" was more often referred to in terms of goals. Also the vague goal of "a happy life" became the more realistic "training in self-care." They clung to the hope that training toward self-sufficiency, the schooling, and the treatment, would all contribute toward life in the community. The more generally expressed optimism might possibly be the result of the recent legislation in the state that mandated public education for trainable retardates. Also their acceptance in the Day Care Center had undoubtedly confirmed their original high regard for this organization.

SUMMARY

A series of group counseling sessions with two similar groups of parents of retarded children was undertaken during the school years 1959-1960 and 1960-1961. Each group met for approximately sixty group sessions. The two groups were composed of twenty-one parents to whom a revised version of the Thurston Sentence Completion Form was administered before and after. The results indicated that the modified TACF was a valid instrument for determining changes in parent attitudes brought about through group counseling. Evaluations of these results point to both general and specific conclusions:

1. In general, the counseling served as a catharsis for the parents. There was a general decrease in the "no response" category in the postdata.

2. It is well known that initial shock and confusion prevent a frank recognition of the facts in a situation. The parents indicated initial confusion on diagnosis. After counseling, however, they were much more able to accept the medical diagnosis of mental retardation. The more the parents were willing to admit to the medical diagnosis, the less they were willing to insist on self-discovery of the retardation.

3. It was also revealed that counseling contributed to a freer and more realistic discussion of retardation between parents and the retardates' siblings and thereby increased their understanding of the condition.

4. According to the parents, counseling helped them to understand that others were sympathetic and not merely curious and pitying.
5. It was noted that parents' goal orientation changed after counseling, i.e. from immediate and short-range to more sophisticated and long range. The latter involved needs in research, trained personnel, coordinated service, and life-span programming.
6. Counseling enhanced the image of the Day Care Center as a helpful resource. Criticisms of the school were in terms of space and trained personnel rather than curriculum content.
7. Group counseling generally resulted in greater optimism related to a child's future. The few who saw the future as pessimistic were nevertheless realistic about its forebodings.

REFERENCES

Coleman, J. C.: Group therapy with parents of mentally retarded deficient children. *Am. J. Ment. Defic., 57*:700-704, 1953.

Cummings, S. T., and Stock, D.: Brief group therapy with mothers of retarded children outside of the specialty clinic setting. *Am. J. Ment. Defic., 66*:739-748, 1962.

French, A. C., Lavbarg, M., and Michal-Smith, H.: Parent Counseling as a Means of Improving the Performance of a Mentally Retarded Boy: A Case Study Presentation. In C. L. Stacey, and M. F.: DeMartino (Eds.): *Counseling & Psychotherapy With the Mentally Retarded.* Glencoe, The Free Press, 438-445, 1957.

Katz, H.: *Parents of the Handicapped.* Springfield, Charles C Thomas, 1961.

Masland, R. L., Sarason, S. B., and Gladwin, T.: *Mental Subnormality.* New York, Basic Books, 1958.

Nadal, R.: A counseling program for parents of severely retarded preschool children. *Social Casework, 42*:78-83, 1961.

Richman, S.: Parent-community interaction as a function for adjustment of the retarded child. *Am. J. Ment. Defic., 64*:556-560, 1959.

Thurston, J. R.: A procedure for evaluating parental attitudes toward the handicapped. *Am. J. Ment. Defic., 63*:148-155, 1959.

Thurston, J. R.: Attitudes and emotional reactions of parents of institutionalized, cerebral palsied, retarded patients. *Am. J. Ment. Defic., 65*:227-235, 1960.

Thurston, J. R.: Counseling the parents of the severely handicapped. *Exceptional Child., 351-354, 1960.

Weingold, J. T.: Parents Counseling Other Parents of Retarded. Paper read at

New York State Welfare Conference, New York City, Nov. 1960.

Weingold, J. T., and Hormuth, R. P.: Group guidance of parents of the mentally retarded. *J. Clinical. Psychol., 9*:118-124, 1953.

Worchel, T. L., and Worchel, P.: The parental concept of the mentally retarded child. *Am. J. Ment. Defic., 65*:782-788, 1961.

Chapter 15

Brief Group Therapy of Mothers of Retarded Children Outside of the Specialty Clinic Setting

S. THOMAS CUMMINGS and DOROTHY STOCK

THAT mentally retarded children and their parents face extremely taxing adjustment problems in our society is a patent certainty to every active participant in this field of study. In addition to the sizeable reality problems deriving from the life-long low social adaptability of the retarded individual, a combination of other factors further increases the psychological stresses bearing on the retarded person and his family. Limited knowledge of the origins and likely courses of many of the syndromes, conflicting and often ineptly given professional advice, the paucity of treatment and training facilities, the stigmatization of the disorders with resulting social rejection of the effected families by neighbors, friends, and relatives — all combine to increase psychological stress (Sarason, 1953; Stacey and DeMartino, 1957).

This total compound of stresses further attenuates the emotional health and adaptive competence of the retarded individual and his family. For the retardate himself, his reduced learning capacity is hampered further by the disruptive effects of anxiety, hostility, and low self-esteem. For his parents, the effectiveness of their training procedures with the retarded child is often lowered and their opportunities for deriving interpersonal satisfactions

Note: Reprinted by permission from the author and the *American Journal of Mental Deficiency,* 66:739-746, 1962. Copyrighted by the American Association on Mental Deficiency.

outside the family are reduced.

Much has been written of the needs for expanded treatment, training, and research facilities for mental retardates. In addition to these direct needs of present and future retarded individuals, many parents of retarded children are in need of a sustained counseling relationship to help alleviate their psychological stress load. An indication of the increasing recognition of this need is the increase of reports of the use of group therapy with parents of the retarded (Blatt, 1957; Coleman, 1953; Goodman and Rothman, 1961; Rankin; 1957; Weingold and Hormuth, 1953; White, 1959; Yates and Lederer, 1961). This early trend toward the application of group therapy techniques in meeting the counseling needs of parents is likely to grow, stimulated by the greater acceptance of the "total family" approach to problems of handicapped children generally, by the appropriateness of a group approach for patients whose problems derive from a common source, and by the greater availability of trained group therapists.

To date nearly all of the published reports of group therapy with parents of the retarded describe programs operated by one of the small number of specialty clinics. Occasionally, a program originating within a parents' organization has been described. The potential demand for group therapy services and the location of many trained group therapists in settings other than specialty clinics for the retarded, e.g. social agencies and general mental hygiene clinics, make it likely that an increasing amount of group treatment of parents of the retarded will be performed outside of the specialty clinic setting or at least have the opportunity to be performed in this way. What follows below – a description of our experience over an eighteen-month period in organizing and conducting brief group therapy series with two groups of mothers of retarded children and our preparations for a third such group – may be of special interest to those mental hygiene clinic or social agency personnel who plan to offer such group therapy services. In this paper we describe the problems of organization and adminis-tration of such brief group therapy groups, problems of therapy process, and research. We hope to illuminate some of the issues relevant to the feasibility and likely effectiveness of such brief group therapy for mothers of the retarded, specifically when it is conducted outside of the specialty clinic walls.

A few words are in order about our beginnings and our setting. We were interested in beginning this venture because of our common interests in the application of group techniques to the amelioration of problems of parents dealing with handicapped children. Concurrently, from our own individual clinical work we experienced some increasing awareness of the extensive needs of retarded children and their parents. Over a period of several months in discussions with established professionals in the field of retardation in our community, we received enthusiastic encouragement for the initiation of such a brief therapy program, to our knowledge a unique one in this metropolitan community at the time. The ultimate deciding factor leading us to begin the group therapy series was a compelling request from some individual members of a mother's organization for the retarded.

Our program is operated under the auspices of the Child Psychiatry Clinic of the University of Chicago, which is physically located in Bobs Roberts Memorial Hospital, the children's hospital of the University. We work within an institutional framework of medical and psychiatric clinics for patients of all ages, one in which there is no specialty clinic for retarded children at this time. The mothers with whom we have worked are typically self-referred, having come to us through hearing of the existence of our brief group therapy series from a parents' organization in the community, a community pediatrician, or from one of the two specialty clinics within the city. They usually have not had any prior diagnostic or treatment service from any one of our clinics, nor are their children seen. Seldom have the mothers had any experience with a sustained helping relationship through individual therapy or casework services. When they begin group therapy with us, they are relatively unfamiliar with a psychological helping relationship, and we have limited knowledge of them and their children. This is in comparison with the more typical conditions (diagnostic work-up and intake preparation) under which therapy begins.

PROCEDURES AND ADMINISTRATIVE PROBLEMS

We decided to begin with a time-limited series of sessions, about ten or twelve in number. Our reasons for settling on this number of sessions were two: first, one of the authors had had some experience in short-term group therapy with hospitalized veterans. For these patients, about twelve sessions proved to offer sufficient time for the formative issues to be worked through, for the group to "jell," and for some profitable work to take place. Intensive work, involving progression in depth and repetitive working through of problems was, of course, precluded. Previous experience had also suggested that when patients know in advance that the number of sessions is limited, they accommodate to the time available and tend to establish appropriate limits on the depth of their involvement and exploration. A second major reason for limiting the time was that we regarded this effort as exploratory in character. We did not know exactly what to expect of the mothers, nor whether group therapy in general was likely to prove profitable, nor what level of therapeutic work could occur. We therefore preferrred that our own commitment be limited.

To date, two short-term groups have been conducted — one of ten sessions and one of twelve. Eight mothers were recruited for the first group; five of these appeared for the first meeting and continued to attend throughout the series. Four mothers were recruited for the second group; one of these dropped out after two sessions. The relatively small size of our groups (we preferred groups of five to seven persons) was related to recruitment problems. We believe the slow recruitment was related to the newness of the program, the scattered character of the referral sources, and the unfamiliarity of the mothers with the ideal of group therapy as a source of help. For those mothers who conceive of help either as directed exclusively toward the child or as involving concrete advice about management problems and the advisability of institutionalization, the idea of getting help through talking together in a group seemed foreign indeed. A second and related psychological factor is the need for externalization of blame, which is a frequent reaction to the hurt, frustration, and hostility having a retarded child entails. Those mothers who handle their conflicting feelings by an externalization mechanism are likely to be unwilling to relinquish it by participating in procedures which turn one's attention to one's own thoughts and feelings. In any case, applicants came in slowly, and reluctance to keep the mothers waiting too long, coupled with our own impatience to begin, led us to start with relatively small groups.

Before the first group session each mother was seen individually by one of the therapists. In these individual sessions we hoped to get a bit acquainted with the mother and give her a chance to get acquainted with one of us. We explored the way she saw her problems, what she hoped to get from the group, and her image of what the group sessions would be like. At some point during the discussion we found an opportunity to explain that the group sessions would consist of open, unstructured discussion intended to provide opportunities for exploration and increased understanding of each member's feelings about herself and her child, her relatives and neighbors so that hopefully she might make more appropriate decisions and improve her training of her child. Here, our intention was to clarify as best we could the terms of the therapeutic contract, and to discourage those mothers interested solely in concrete information or advice. We also attempted to learn enough about the personality of the mother and her manner of handling problems with her retarded child to make an educated guess about her likelihood of making good use of an unstructured group therapy experience. During this interview we also requested the mother's participation in the research we are conducting.

This brief interview does not provide us with an extensive understanding of the mother or her background; nor does it provide the mother with a thoroughly adequate image of what the group will be like. However, it seems to offer a sufficient introduction to the group therapy experience so that the sessions themselves are not unduly unfamiliar, threatening, or disappointing. Some mothers screen themselves out during this interview. Either they realize and can tell us that the group experience is not for them, or they offer a series of excuses which we are inclined to respect.

The mothers who come to us are self-selected and are not necessarily typical of the general population of mothers of retardates. The mothers who do *not* come to us seem to fall into several groups:* those who have worked out satisfactory ways of

---

*This is a hunch derived from contact with mothers in parent groups who have not been interested in this kind of experience, and from exploratory interviews with mothers who have rejected the idea.

dealing with their child and who are at peace with themselves and their situation, those for whom the idea of talking over their feelings about their child is threatening, and those who feel they need concrete advice and recommendations rather than an opportunity to talk over problems. The mothers whom we have seen have shown great diversity in personality characteristics, life circumstances, and the severity of the child's retardation. What they have in common is some sense of stress, of unresolved issues, of impossible decisions which at the same time must be made, and of uneasy and ambivalent feelings. Almost all have felt let down by the experts, in that a number (sometimes a large number) of contradictory diagnoses have been made about the severity of the child's retardation. Often institutionalization has been recommended, but the parents have been unable to accept this, going through frequent seesaws on the issue. In some cases there was conflict within the family, with the father or grandparents finding it difficult to accept the diagnosis of mental retardation. Thus far, the children of these mothers have ranged in age from eighteen months to ten years.

THERAPY PROCESS

From our point of view, appropriate therapeutic goals for these mothers include an increase in awareness and acceptance of the child's condition and of the mothers' feelings about themselves, the retarded child, and others with whom they appear to be in conflict as a result of having produced a retarded child. Hopefully, this can lead to an increase in the adequacy and consistency of their own training measures with the child and of the decisions which they make regarding the use of schools and institutions. We begin group therapy by suggesting that the sessions are an opportunity to discuss problems and feelings about oneself and the child. No other formal structuring is provided. Choice of topics and the amount of time spent on them is largely determined by the mothers themselves, except where the therapists' interpretive comments indirectly influence these. Our most frequent comments refer to feelings which the mothers are expressing but which have not yet been made explicit. Usually these have to do with conflicts which they are experiencing as the parent of a retarded child, although not necessarily so.

One of the striking characteristics of our groups thus far is the tremendous push the mothers feel to ventilate their experiences and feelings about the child. During the early sessions, particularly, the complaints, fears, and hopes spill out at a great rate. The mothers interrupt one another and impatiently fight for a chance to have their say, the more timid ones are squeezed out, and the therapists have a hard time getting a word in edgewise. The material is largely focussed on the child and the problems involved in handling him, and the content shifts about in free association from problems about toilet training to institutionalization, play behavior with other children, attitudes of neighbors, how they felt when they found out, when they first suspected, etc. For many of the mothers this is their first real opportunity to talk themselves out without feeling guilty about burdening others with their troubles. Especially for some of the more isolated mothers, the first real benefit derives from the opportunity to find that others are faced with the same problems and are coping with them no better. During this early period, and often recurring throughout the sessions, there are appeals for expert, concrete advice from the therapists about how to handle specific management problems, whether or not to institutionalize, and how really to evaluate the future potential of the child. Such questions clearly cannot be answered by the therapists, at least not with the degree of specificity and sureness which the mothers would like. There is inevitable disappointment, but while the group is struggling with this issue, some (though not all) of the mothers can come to see that certain information is not available, or that certain decisions can be made only by the family taking into account its own situation and feelings.

As the group moves on, the content tends to shift away from an exclusive focus on the child and begins to include some material on the marriage, on problems with family and in-laws, on the mothers' own feelings and personality characteristics apart from her role as a mother, and on relationships which have developed among the group members. This shift seems highly appropriate to us, since many of the basic problems with the child do not exist in isolation but are also experienced in other interpersonal arenas.

Our experience so far has suggested that certain core problems may be associated with the presence of a retarded child in the family. One of these is the need to cope with inevitable yet personally unacceptable feelings of hostility toward the child. The child is a severe burden on the mother, and yet she often feels compelled to be enduringly loving and accepting. Decisions about institutionalization appear to be particularly difficult, since this becomes equated with "getting rid of the child" or playing a "dirty trick" on him. Even those for whom the child is highly rewarding through keeping them provided with a permanent "baby" in the home whom they can mother, are likely to experience an internal conflict over unacceptable hostile impulses. Another frequent problem is related to the disappointment, loss, and sense of bereavement associated with having a child who can never fulfill its own life in ways which a parent wishes. When a child dies, a mother can eventually deal with her loss, but in the case of these mothers, her sense of bereavement is unrelieved and exists continually as a background to her daily life. Some mothers experience severe narcissistic hurt in having produced a damaged child. To these the child is a reflection of their own inadequacies and imperfections. Some are preoccupied with a sense of guilt and experience a persistent uneasy feeling that perhaps they are somehow personally responsible for their child's condition. Many feel deserted and unhelped, left to deal alone with an excruciating and unrelenting problem.

The mothers whom we have come to know thus far share these problems to one degree or another. For some, they may be close to awareness; for others, they may be well buried or uneasily concealed. Each mother has uniquely found some set of defenses for coping with these conflicts. These include denial and reaction formation, projection of anger onto others, or acceptance of martyrdom.

In the course of the group sessions, some of the mothers can, to a somewhat greater degree, accept some of their own feelings and come to have less need to maintain painful, incapacitating, or self-defeating defenses. The extent to which this can happen depends on the health of the mothers' personality structure and the rigidity of her defenses, as well as on the character of the group sessions.

An important issue has to do with identifying those mothers who can utilize the group therapy experience profitably and those who cannot. Certainly, those mothers who are preoccupied with immediate practical reality problems such as transportation arrangements, the availability of baby-sitters, and the like, appear not to be good candidates. Such preoccupations typically mask a variety of resistances. Mothers who are still shopping for a refutation of their child's retardation or who want someone else to take over the responsibility for their retarded child form another less feasible group, as do the dependent mothers, many of whom have rescue fantasies of a magical nature.

Psychological defensiveness itself, at least in the early sessions, does not appear to be significantly associated with the less effective use of the group therapy experience, for nearly all of our mothers show a high degree of defensiveness. However, when the defenses appear to be extremely rigid, involving for example unchanging excesses of projection and denial, the likelihood of positive benefits being derived is slim. Some mothers bring with them inappropriate motivations, sometimes not apparent until late in the series of sessions. For example, one of our mothers apparently came to the group with the underlying hope that we would insist that she divorce a mentally ill husband. Another mother came with the latent hope that we would take punitive action toward a physician who had advised institutionalizing her mildly retarded child without taking account of her feelings in the matter. There is, of course, another group of mothers whose psychological problems are a part of long-standing neurotic personality organization for whom this form of brief group therapy is not enough and who should be referred for continuing psychotherapy.

The mothers who have been able to utilize the therapy experience display some common features: persistent interest in the diagnostic clarification of their child's condition and in procuring help for him, ability to acknowledge in some degree their hostility and hurt in having a retarded child, enough flexibility in their training modes to alter their approaches in overcoming problems with the child by accepting suggestions, and the ability to find and enjoy part-time work or recreational interests outside of the home.

RESEARCH

An integral feature of our conduct of these brief group therapy series is the carrying out of two research projects. In the first of these projects we are attempting to identify the common core conflicts inherently associated with having a retarded child, to determine the various patterns of coping with such core conflicts shown by individual mothers, and to evaluate changes in these coping patterns from the beginning to the end of therapy.* These analyses are being made from tape recordings and transcripts of the sessions.

In our second project we are concerned with the effects of the brief group therapy series on certain relevant attitudes in the mothers. We hope to be able to demonstrate some correlations between our subjective impressions of change/no change and responses to our attitude measures. The attitudes we are assessing are certain general child-rearing attitudes, self-attitudes, and attitudes toward the retarded child and significant others with whom the mother comes in contact in her daily life. These data are being derived from a battery of self-administered tests, three objective and two projective in nature, which include a child-rearing attitudes scale, a modification by Drews and Teahan (1957) of the Shoben inventory, the Self-Acceptance Scale of the Berger Acceptance Inventory (1952), a general personality inventory, the Edwards Personal Preference Schedule (1954), a "Family Drawing" task, and a sentence completion test constructed by the authors and designed to tap specific attitudes about the retarded child. The tests are administered in the week prior to the beginning of the group therapy series and three months following its completion. A control group composed of mothers of retarded children who do not participate in group therapy is being utilized. Other control groups of mothers of healthy and neurotic children will ultimately be added.

One of the problems we have encountered in conducting this research has been the mothers' reactions to the pretest batteries. For some the tests have fed their fantasy that the therapists know all and have only to reveal the results of the tests for all problems

---

*A focal conflict analysis of the sessions will be utilized to identify shared concerns and individual and group solutions (Whitman and Stock, 1958; Stock, 1962).

to be resolved. Thus, for some the tests become a diversionary, defensive tactic for temporarily avoiding self-exploration during group therapy sessions. A few mothers, firmly convinced that the tests must reveal their unacceptable hostility toward the retarded child and others, as well as other undesirable personality characteristics, press for what they assume will be a critical evaluation of them by the therapists through a candid review of these test results. As has been found by many others who have conducted research on their own therapy patients, highly ambivalent persons often see the research as adequate grounds for distrusting the sincerity of the therapists' investment in them as patients. Such issues have come up for discussion during the sessions and have not proved to interfere seriously with therapy. An incidental and unanticipated advantage of the use of the pretest battery has been its helpfulness in screening out mothers who are excessively defensive and therefore unlikely to profit from the group. Several mothers whom we had the greatest doubts about admitting to the group finally decided not to undertake therapy after finding some of the questions intruding or upsetting.

EVALUATION AND CONCLUSIONS

In discussing the feasibility of short-term group therapy in our clinic setting, perhaps the first point we should make is that we do not regard our setting as ideal. Ideally the treatment opportunities offered to the mothers ought to occur within a setting in which extended, perhaps lifelong contact is available for both the family and the child. In such a setting the contact with the family can be integrated more adequately with the needs and progress of the child. A thorough familiarity with both the child and the parents could provide optimum information on which to make judgments about the character, extent, and timing of treatment offered to the parents.

In our clinic perhaps the most striking features of our program are that it involves no contact whatsoever with the child and is short term in character. Our lack of direct knowledge of the child has not proved to be a serious handicap. In some ways the fact that we have no contact with the child helps to underline the fact that our primary interest is the mother and her feelings. One might assume that the lack of contact with the child makes it possible for the mother to introduce certain distortions about the child which remain uncorrected. However, it is our general feeling that in a short time we gain an accurate picture of the child's condition and problems. In large measure this is due to the presence of a number of mothers in the group. The explorations, challenges, comparisons, and questions soon yield a picture of both the child's actual condition and the distortions which the mother may introduce.

Within our limited number of sessions certain therapeutic goals can be accomplished and others cannot. During the sessions the mothers gain practical advice and new ideas from one another in the matter of management and training. They are also able to ventilate about their problems and often find reassurance in the fact that they are not alone either in the problems themselves or in their recurrent feelings of frustration, anger, and inadequacy. Ventilation, sharing, and some practical help constitute minimal gains which short-term group therapy can offer. On a second level, a potential gain consists in a more appropriate recognition of reality, both with regard to what is and is not real and what can and cannot be changed. Many mothers are out of touch with their own feelings about their child. Some arrive with the fantasy that their child will someday become normal or that others will or must change and become more accepting, less curious, more helpful, or more realistic. In some instances such wishful fantasies give way to a more realistic recognition that certain problems and situations are inevitable and recurrent. This paves the way for some mothers to gain a greater sense of mastery over their difficult situation, and in fact to find more adequate ways of dealing with their own feelings and problems. Once can identify a third and deeper therapeutic goal which cannot be achieved in short-term treatment. In the course of the sessions we become very aware of certain long-standing problems characteristic of each of the mothers. These have to do with such issues as means of coping with hostile and sexual impulses, management of guilt, sense of personal worth, sense of achievement and of deprivation, and acceptance of self as a woman. The mother inevitably reacts to the damaged child in terms which are consistent with her entire character development. Such persistent characteristics are revealed in the group both through the content of the discussion and the repetitive interpersonal behavior displayed by each mother. Some mothers can utilize the group to examine certain of their habitual ways of feeling and reacting and can begin to explore alternative and more adaptive coping modes. But even for those mothers who can begin this process, ten or twelve sessions do not provide enough time for the kind of recurrent experiences required for thorough exploration and consolidated change.

It has been our practice to offer each mother an individual session with the therapists following the series of group sessions. This provides an opportunity to review her problems and the meaning of the group therapy experience as well as to talk over plans for additional therapy if this seems indicated. Such a conference helps the mother round out and interpret the experience for herself. Some mothers feel they have gained some help from the group sessions and experience a sense of closure. For these, future contacts seem unnecessary, although we remain available should they wish to speak with us. For others, additional therapeutic contacts do not seem indicated for another reason, namely that we have become aware of a fairly rigid and brittle system of defenses with which it is inappropriate to tamper. For some mothers we feel that additional group therapy might be useful; for others, more intensive individual treatment seems required. In some instances it is clear that certain problems and feelings which had been denied previously or evaded have emerged during the course of the sessions. For these women it is inappropriate simply to arbitrarily terminate treatment. Where individual therapy seems indicated, referrals can be made within our clinic. For others, for whom further group treatment seems useful, we have considered inviting the mother to join the next series of sessions. Several mothers have suggested that we hold additional sessions on a less frequent basis. Another possibility, which would become feasible as our population increased, would be to provide a regular informal weekly session which mothers could attend or not as they felt the need. Certainly one of the problems we face with this kind of short-term group therapy is disposition and follow-up. It is a problem which is not settled to our satisfaction and will require further experience and experimentation.

Our experiences thus far have led us to a more realistic awareness of what can be achieved by short-term group therapy in alleviating the psychological stress load of mothers of retarded children. We plan to continue the series, experimenting further with modifications of our original procedure. Our continuing interest derives from observing the usefulness of the sessions to the mothers, as well as from increasing our own knowledge of the character of the problem and of the processes of group therapy.

REFERENCES

Berger, E. M.: The relation between expressed acceptance of self and expressed acceptance of others. *J. Abnorm. Soc. Psychol., 47*:778-782, 1952.

Blatt, A.: Group therapy with parents of severely retarded children: a preliminary report. *Group Psychother., 10*:133-140, 1957.

Coleman, J. C.: Group therapy with parents of mentally deficient children. *Am. J. Ment. Defic., 57*:700-704, 1953.

Drews, E., and Teahan, J. E.: Parental attitudes and academic achievement. *J. Clin. Psychol., 13*:328-332, 1957.

Edwards, A. L.: *Edwards Personal Preference Schedule.* New York, Psychological Corporation, 1954.

Goodman, L., and Rothman, R.: The development of a group counseling program in a clinic for retarded children. *Am. J. Ment. Defic., 65*:789-795, 1961.

Rankin, J. E.: A group therapy experiment with mothers of mentally deficient children. *Am. J. Ment. Defic., 62*:49-55, 1957.

Sarason, S. B.: *Psychological Problems in Mental Deficiency.* New York, Harper, 1953.

Stacey, C. L., and DeMartino, M. F. (Eds.): *Counseling and Psychotherapy With the Mentally Retarded.* Glencoe, Free Press, 1957.

Stock, D.: Interpersonal concerns during the early sessions of therapy groups. *Int. J. Grp. Psychother., 12*, 1962.

Weingold, J. T., and Hormuth, R. P.: Group guidance of parents of mentally retarded children. *J. Clin. Psychol., 9*:118-124, 1953.

White, B. L.: Clinical team treatment of mentally retarded child and his parents: group counseling and play observation. *Am. J. Ment. Defic., 63*:713-723, 1959.

Whitman, R. M., and Stock, D.: The group focal conflict. *Psychiatry, 21*:269-297, 1958.

Yates, M., and Lederer, R.: Small short-term group meetings. *Am. J. Ment. Defic.*, 65:467-472, 1961.

Chapter 16

Clinical Team Treatment of a Mentally Retarded Child and His Parents: Group Counseling and Play Observation

BERNARD L. WHITE*

T HE psychologist has had continued contact with all three members of the family: Teddy, his mother, and father. As mentioned by the caseworker, there was some question regarding the degree of Teddy's retardation on the basis of the original clinic examination.

Although two psychological examinations administered seven months apart yielded almost exactly the same IQ, in the high sixties, there were gross inconsistencies between the tests. Items which had been passed the first time were failed on the second examination. When directly presented with some items, he seemed unable to do them; however, when the same materials were intentionally left lying about the room, he picked them up and performed satisfactorily. A few items which were failed initially were correctly done when presented again. In addition, because of the child's lack of cooperation, the full test could not be completed. Social development also appeared to be below par when judged on the basis of the mother's replies to a standardized

Note: Reprinted by permission of the author and the *American Journal of Mental Deficiency*, *63*:713-719, 1959. Copyrighted by the American Association on Mental Deficiency.

*Clinical Psychologist, Guidance Clinic for the Retarded, East Orange, New Jersey.

questionnaire on social maturity.

The psychologist questioned the validity of the test results on the basis of the child's uncooperativeness and inconsistency. He was also concerned about the effects of the mother's attitude and behavior on Teddy. Play observation of the child was suggested for the purpose of clarification of his intellectual status. It was felt that further contact was necessary in order to gain Teddy's confidence and cooperation. Observation of the child at play might also give added information regarding the presence and the extent of emotional factors which might have been influencing his intellectual functioning.

Teddy was seen once a week for a few months while his mother was seeing the caseworker. He seemed to enjoy his contacts and cooperated fairly well in play activities. Selected items from a variety of tests were integrated into his play. Again he seemed interested in some materials and rejected others completely. Gradually these discriminations seemed to take on a pattern and make more sense. Teddy, like may youngsters, appeared to recognize his own limitations better than did his parents and psychologists. When faced with a situation where he expected to fail, he rejected it and tried to call attention away from the situation by acting up. This pattern of behavior was possibly developed because of the mother's reaction to his failures in the past.

In these sessions Teddy also displayed jealousy towards his younger brother, indications of difficulty in attitudes toward toilet training, a tendency toward self-punishment, and concern about his mother's attitude towards him. However, none of these problems seemed severe enough to account for his lessened intellectual functioning either singly or in combination. On the basis of observations such as these, it was decided that he was really slightly retarded. It was also felt that the mother's reaction and relationship to the child were preventing him from using his potential to the fullest. This situation was also evident in the mother's discussions with the caseworker and in her reactions to the child's behavior in the clinic. She became upset at his tendency to keep his mouth open and place objects in his mouth because "it makes him look stupid." When the child had toilet accidents while seeing the psychologist, the mother was mortified and extremely apologetic. "What will people think" appeared to be her slogan. Her reactions were discussed with the caseworker and integrated into the work that the caseworker was doing with the mother.

While the mother was being seen on an individual basis by the caseworker, a new series of parent group-counseling sessions was being organized. The father expressed an interest in these and after an individual interview was accepted into the group. The father seemed to be a stable person who was eager to do anything he could to help in integrating the child into the family and society. In the individual interview he was found to be accepting of the child, mature, and with a good common-sense attitude toward the problem of the retardation. In view of his maturity, it is natural to question why he should have been included in the group at all.

In order to understand this question, it is necessary to know something about the goals and the setup of our groups. The basic goal is to help essentially normal people gain added understanding of their own feelings about being parents of retarded children and through this understanding to become more effective parents. These groups are not substitutes for individual or group therapy. If candidates are felt to need more intensive help with their own personal problems, other facilities are recommended. Our groups are a compromise between the predominantly affective experience of group therapy and the intellectual experience of educational lectures. The terms "limited" and "structured" are probably most appropriate in describing the actual functioning of the group. The goals are limited. We would like to see the participants more comfortable in dealing with the problems associated with being the parent of a retarded child. Time is limited. The sessions last for an hour and a half for ten to fifteen consecutive weekly sessions. This number of sessions allows for adequate discussion of most problems, but does not allow the participants to become too engrossed in their own personal problems. The number of participants is limited. No more than ten members are included in any one group. This in itself is a compromise between the figure of seven, which seems to be most effective for intensive group therapy, and the larger numbers which can be accommodated in a lecture group. It allows individual participation but is large enough to be of value to those members whose participation in the group process is minimal.

The content is structured. Although in actual practice the group members maintain the flow of ideas and discussion, the leader exerts just enough influence to direct their attention to problems which through experience have been shown to be common to most parents of retarded children. Thus, in a series of ten to fifteen sessions, the major areas of concern can be covered. When talking about it, the process seems rather artificial; actually, in most groups it has been a smooth transition, so that the participants were usually not aware that certain "topics" were being introduced by the leader. The order of topics was also structured in the same manner so that we could gradually build up to those areas which were most affect laden and still have enough sessions left to deal with the emotions aroused by these topics. Another role was also filled by the leader; he acted as a resource person. When a topic had been discussed and accurate information was needed, or inaccurate information had been mentioned, the leader stepped in and supplied the needed information.

Teddy's father entered into the spirit of the group from the very beginning. He was one of the few members who maintained that discipline served more than the function of getting the child to conform. He felt that the child needed discipline in gaining a sense of stability and security in the home. Whereas the mother seemed more concerned about what others thought of the child and of her, he was child oriented. He recognized that if Teddy were to be accepted by others, he would have to follow the same rules and regulations expected of others.

While maintaining that he had accepted Teddy's retardation for quite a while, he nevertheless acknowledged that there was quite a problem in getting relatives and friends to accept the child's slowness. Well-meaning relatives, especially grandparents, were constantly berating the family for being too pessimistic and maintaining that Teddy "would grow out of it." The wife also vacillated between overoptimism and overpessimism. He recognized that he had to be the one to take a forceful stand. It was in this area that he sought and appeared to derive most help from the group. He needed reassurance and information to back up his stand. An interesting phenomenon of group functioning was evident in those sessions in which problems of this sort were discussed. While reassuring others, members often seemed to convince themselves of things which they had difficulty accepting. This seemed to be a vicarious form of "talking to themselves" and often a rewarding one. Actually, one member, after a particularly stirring speech, remarked, "I think I convinced myself more than I convinced you."

Mrs. T. also seemed to be engaging in this sort of self-convincing in his attempts to get others to recognize the child's limitations. He would accuse the mother of not accepting Teddy's retardation and would make an issue of this at home. His resulting anxiety was evident in the group, where he would often subtly accuse other group members, especially mothers, of not really recognizing the extent of their children's limitations.

In the particular group of which he was a member there were equal numbers of fathers and mothers, none of whom were each other's spouses. The group was set up in this manner for two reasons. More families could be served, and also we could provide spouse surrogates towards whom the members could express their feelings. Mr. T. took advantage of this to the point where one of the mothers pointed out that after all she was not his wife.

Although our impression from the beginning was that the father had made a rather good adjustment to his son's retardation, he nevertheless seemed to profit from the group experience. He was the most active participant and generally came out with realistic and accurate observations. Helping the others with their problems seemed to do as much for him as receiving help did for many of the others. Although he never quite verbalized it this way, it seemed that helping others compensated for the frustration of not being able to do more to help his son directly.

Approximately one month ago the mother also joined one of our groups and has attended three of the four sessions held. This group is rather different from previous ones. Two couples are included, that is, the husbands and wives besides the individual members. The group is also somewhat smaller than previous ones and somewhat more informal. There is less conscious structuring on the part of the leader and a greater emphasis on individual rather than group problems. In a sense the group has lost some of its "groupness." This appears to be a function partly of the reduction in size and the presence of the couples. Because of her previous contacts with the leader, the mother has exhibited quite a bit of freedom in the group. Basically a rather candid and somewhat naive person, she has expressed herself openly. When one of the other group members, a rather formal and rigid person, finished reciting a detailed account of the educational and social advantages provided for her own teen-age daughter, Mrs. T. Commented, "My, you have spoiled her terribly, haven't you." She still shows a tendency to vacillate between overoptimism and overpessimism but can now joke about it when it is called to her attention. There is now a concentration on Teddy's difficulties with his younger brother. When Teddy does something which she cannot accept, she is apt to blame it on his retardation rather than seeing it as part of the normal development of any child. Such problems as sibling rivalry, unwillingness to go to sleep on time, and other specific behavior traits bother her. Although she often mentions these with the implied request for specific ways of dealing with them, the group's orientation has been to focus on the normality rather than the abnormality of the behavior. At other times she mentions items of behavior phrased in such a way that other group members have questioned the child is retarded at all. Because of the leader's dual role, that of clinic psychologist and group leader, he has been specifically asked by Mrs. T. why he thought the child was retarded. After pointing out that this had actually been discussed many times and that she still had questions about it, the leader mentioned the slight degree of Teddy's retardation, the uncertainty of the family pediatrician, and the necessity of rather extended play observations before a diagnosis could be established. It was then that the leader recognized that she was falling into a semantic trap which seemed to be quite common among previous group members. When a diagnosis of retardation is made, many people allow the term "retarded" to obscure the term "child." They tend to think in terms of a composite retardate, a "typical" retarded child rather than the individual child. This led to a very worthwhile discussion of individual differences among retarded children, with emphasis upon the individual characteristics and personality of the child in question.

At the last session the mother related that her husband has accused her of not really accepting Teddy's retardation. This was of course denied, but she ended up by asking the leader if he and his colleagues were 100 percent certain that Teddy was retarded. The rhetorical nature of the question was called to her attention. Soon after this, the other group members became involved in a discussion of reasons for retardation. She seemed to wait until the others became involved in a side discussion, leaned over, and told the leader that she had been wondering whether some of her actions during her pregnancy might not have been responsible for Teddy's condition. When the leader commented upon her timing, that she had waited until the others were not listening to her, she immediately burst out laughing, called the others to attention and told them that she had often wondered whether her jumping rope during the sixth month of pregnancy might not have injured the child. A rather unusual and highly cathartic discussion developed. It became a "can you top this" situation with each of the members mentioning reasons they had thought of in connection with their own child's retardation. As each one finished, all went into gales of laughter with comments such as "if you think that's a silly idea, let me tell you what I thought." The laughter involved was not really appropriate but was indicative of the anxiety associated with feelings of guilt.

This is as far as the mother's group has gone. Although she still has many of the same problems with which she came to the clinic, she now seems to have clearer recognition of them. She seems relatively free in discussing her problems and in accepting the fact that she tends to misinterpret some of Teddy's behavior. She is a person who needs a great deal of support and reassurance and even after the group sessions are finished will probably remain in contact with the clinic.

The illustrations of group counseling given here are typical of the sort of interchange in our groups. Each group, however, seems to be different, and the techniques and format are adjusted to the composition and needs of each particular group. It is still too early to determine how effective they have been with this family and with others. We are continually experimenting with ways of enhancing the group process within the limitations of our setup. It is hoped that we may soon have a clearer understanding of the problems involved so that information concerning this technique can be disseminated and our own program expanded.

CONCLUSIONS

The family has gained from this coordinated treatment plan in the following ways: Teddy has been able to function more comfortably at his own pace, since his mother has gained some understanding of him through insight into her own reactions and has been able to stabilize her expressions toward and her handling of him. The father has definitely added to his own perspective and basically sound understanding of himself and his family through his group participation and thereby has assumed an even more helpfully supportive role within the family. Although the mother has not changed her basic personality patterns, she has been able, through conscious awareness and effort, to modify their overt expressions and foster a better family balance.

This case illustrates the use of time limits and realistic treatment goals. The level of treatment has been kept close to reality functioning but is based on an underlying understanding of the dynamics of human behavior. The effectiveness of integrating individual and group treatment has been demonstrated. Casework and psychological counseling methods have been usefully coordinated to provide a breadth of service, along with specialized diagnostic and training facilities, to help this particular family meet the problems associated with having a mentally retarded child.

Although the handicap of mental retardation is unique for this family, the problems which it evokes are not so different from those which might be associated with another handicap or adverse condition. The basic strengths and neurotic sensitivities which exist in any individual and family relationship need to be dealt with. When the burden seems too great to be borne alone, the helping hand and professional understanding of the caseworker and clinical counselor may tip the scales back toward a more comfortable balance of functioning.

It is interesting to note, in this case, the way in which the initial focus on the child's problems has been directed back toward consideration of underlying parental attitudes which frequently are an essential part of the child's difficulties and may actually prevent his functioning at his maximum capacity, despite certain inherent limitations. On the other hand, the need of parents for information about their child's condition, and the supportive effect of knowing that they are not alone in grappling with their particular problems, must be recognized and met therapeutically.

Chapter 17

Review of Group Methods
with Parents of the
Mentally Retarded

GLENN V. RAMSEY

GROUP methods used for meeting some of the
needs of patients and clients in the mental health field are
expanding rapidly (Rosenbaum and Berger, 1963). This development, combined with the current emphasis of extending counseling and therapeutic services to the "total family," logically leads
to more extensive use of group methods with family members of a
disturbed or handicapped individual. This paper presents a review
of selected articles which report on the use of group methods to
meet some of the needs and problems of parents who have a
mentally retarded child.

Probably the first major studies to report on the use of such
group approaches were made by Weingold and Hormuth (1953)
and Coleman (1953) Fifteen publications in all were located which
deal primarily with the use of various group methods to help
parents meet their various anxieties, frustrations, and problems
which arise because of a retardate in the family. In addition to the
two studies previously mentioned, the other studies found include
Anderson (1962); Appell, Williams, and Fishell (1964); Bitter
(1964); Blatt (1957); Cummings and Stock (1962); Goodman and
Rothman (1961); Nadal (1961); Popp, Ingram, and Jordan (1954);
Rankin (1957); Roche (1964); Rosen (1955); White (1959); and

Note: Reprinted by permission of the author and the *American Journal of Mental Deficiency,* 71:857-863, 1967. Copyrighted by the American Association on Mental Deficiency.

Yates and Lederer (1961).

Published studies in this area permit some consideration of such issues as the structure and composition of groups, selection criteria for membership, type of leaders employed, size and composition of groups, frequency and duration of sessions, parental issues and problems considered, and reports of outcomes. In the final section of this paper, the writer discusses several issues which seem relevant to any future planning for use of group methods in meeting some of the needs of parents of the retardate if any systematic advancement of knowledge in this field of endeavor is to be achieved.

Many parents of a retardate openly express a strong need for counseling assistance and guidance to assist them in dealing with their child as well as with the family's adjustment, both within and outside the home. Professionals in clinics, special schools, institutions, and private offices usually make some effort to meet the more pressing needs of such parents on an individual family basis, but most of these workers admit that, because of the time factor and needs of the handicapped child, their services to parents are often limited and usually far from adequate.

ANALYSIS OF STUDIES

The studies surveyed on the use of groups for meeting various emotional needs and problems of parents of retardates were analyzed for such factors as composition and organization of the groups, the number of members, length of a given session, total number of sessions, criteria for selecting group members, type of the group leader, nature of the group's structure, and reported outcomes. In the following section each of these factors will be considered.

Recruitment and Composition

Members for groups were recruited in several ways. Parents were often referred by a physician or the clinic staff that was treating the retardate. In one project parents were required to attend as one of the conditions set for admission of their handicapped child to the treatment program. Another group was easily organized by writing letters of invitation, asking parents to join. Still other parents requested they be permitted to join a group when it was opened to new members. None of the writers reported any difficulty in recruiting a sufficient number of members except Cummings and Stock (1962). A large majority of the groups were developed for mothers while the remainder were organized for both parents.

Number of Group Members

The number of members in the groups ranged from three to thirty-six, with the median number being ten. Groups having over ten members were to a large extent quite formal and organized. They were primarily designed as educational-informational meetings in which the parent role was primarily that of a listener. On the other hand, those groups composed of ten or less were largely informal and unstructured. These smaller groups were considered primarily as counseling and therapeutic sessions in which parent participation and discussion were encouraged.

Length of Session

Practically all studies stated that group sessions were scheduled for one and a half hours in duration. There was often some variation, as the time limit was not rigid. The sessions designed primarily for mothers were usually held in the daytime, while those for both parents met in the evenings.

Total Number of Sessions

The total number of sessions held for any one group ranged from three to sixty, with a median number of ten. Those groups involving the higher number of sessions were usually more therapeutic in nature. Those of ten or less were usually of the educational-informational type. One exception was the three session study of Yates and Lederer (1961) which was designed as a therapeutic project. The most frequently used schedule of meetings was weekly, but one series was held semimonthly and another monthly. Only about half of the studies reported on the time interval between sessions.

Criteria for Selection of Group Members

The studies surveyed were far from precise in describing the selection criteria for admission of parents into a group. The failure to delineate the selective process is clearly evident in the following excerpts from the studies. Generally, the groups were described as composed of mothers or parents of a "mentally retarded child," "a trainable retarded child," "a child on a clinic waiting list," "a child involved in clinic diagnosis," "a retarded child not acceptable to the public school," "a child diagnosed as mongoloid," "a child in a private school," or a "child under age eighteen (12 or 10)." Another factor sometimes figuring in the admission criteria was the clinical judgment of a professional or of clinic staff members as to the suitability of the parent for group memberships. Seldom were the criteria for clinical judgments stated. One stated he excluded parents who were psychotic, psychopathic, or severely neurotic. A few established some specific qualifications for admission such as acceptance by parents of the medical diagnosis of their child's mental retardation. In another, divorced parents were not accepted. In general, studies, while listing some of the factors which excluded parents from groups, seldom listed any positive selection criteria on which admission was based.

Type of Group Leadership

Most groups had one person as leader. A few were joint enterprises involving two professionals. The professional title of the various group leaders was reported as follows: Psychologists, listed five times; social workers, five; physicians, three; psychiatric nurses, twice; and a special education teacher, once. In groups designed to be more therapeutic in nature, the leaders were usually psychologists and psychiatrists. Other professionals were more frequently cited as leaders in the educationally oriented groups. In several of the educational-informational types of group programs, the leader often called upon various other specialists to lecture on topics related to mental retardation. Most of the studies gave little or no information regarding the special qualifications, if any, of the leader's training, experience and skill in directing such groups.

Structure of the Group

The organization of the various groups which parents attended ranged at one end from highly organized and formal meetings to very informal and unstructured groups at the other. About half the studies, however, attempted to combine both formal presentation and informal discussion in their structure. These three types were generally related to the goals set for each group.

The purpose of the more formal and organized type of program was to give parents facts about the retardate's care and training, sources of help, causes of mental deficiency, clinic procedures, and so on. The primary role of the parents in such groups was to listen and be informed. Programs of this type are reported by Bitter (1964) and Rosen (1955).

The informal and unstructured type of group, which was essentially designed to offer counseling and psychotherapy, was at the other end of group organization. The focus here was primarily upon the attitudes, feelings, and emotional problems of the parents. The goal of these groups was seen as release of tension, insight into difficulties, more constructive planning, and so on. A description of this type of group organization is given by Cummings and Stock (1962) who state, ". . . the group sessions would consist of open, unstructured discussions intended to provide opportunities for exploration and increased understanding of each member's feelings about herself and her child, her relatives and neighbors. . . ." Studies surveyed which involved the informal and open type of group structure are those reported by Appell, Williams, and Fishell (1964), Blatt (1957), Cummings and Stock (1962), Rankin (1957), and Yates and Lederer (1961).

The third type of group organization was a combination of the structured and formal with the unstructured and informal. In these groups, the goals were both the presentation of facts by experts and some controlled participation by parents. The latter aspect was attained by providing the parents with a question and answer period following a lecture or film, or allowing them some limited expression of attitudes and feelings through directed group discussions. White (1959), whose study follows these lines, states the structure of his group in these words: "Our groups are a compromise between the predominantly affective experience of group therapy and the intellectual experience of educational lectures." Such an approach is characteristic of the studies of Anderson (1962), Coleman (1953), Goodman and Rothman (1961), Nadal (1961), Popp, Ingram, and Jordan (1954), and White (1959). The topics covered in informational sessions have been fairly adequately reported by Popp, Ingram, and Jordan (1954) and Coleman (1953).

Reported Outcomes of Group Sessions

Evaluation of outcomes of the fifteen studies is based on subjective claims in twelve of them, while the other three offered some objective data to support their findings. All studies, however, report that the group sessions did meet some of the salient needs of the parents rather successfully. Most reports gave an enthusiastic endorsement of the use of group methods and were considered as effective approaches in meeting many of the needs of parents of retardates. All writers encouraged a more extensive use of group methods in designing programs in the future.

In reviewing the outcomes of group sessions, attention is directed first to those based primarily upon subjective evaluation. Among the unstructured groups involving counseling and psychotherapy, the subjective report given by Blatt (1957) is representative. He states: "Through catharsis, emotionally facing each other, identification of feelings of other group members, support from group members and from the therapist, they are able to derive maximum benefits." Another typical subjective report, based on the outcomes of a semi-structured project, is given by Weingold and Hormuth (1953), who state: "Our work with parents of the mentally retarded has definitely established the value of the group guidance for parents of the mentally retarded children as one of the most effective tools to bring about more adequate adjustment of the family to such a child, as well as reintegrating the family into the community."

Studies by Appell, Williams, and Fishell (1964), Bitter (1964), and Cummings and Stock (1962) introduced various test instruments into their groups in order to provide a more objective basis for assessment purposes. Among the more informal and unstructured types of programs is the one reported by Cummings and Stock (1962). They claim their objective data support such outcomes as providing ventilation, sharing practical advice, giving reassurance to one another, and achieving a more appropriate recognition of reality. Another program involving objective measurements and designed along the general lines of an unstructured group is the study made by Appell, Williams, and Fishell (1964). They report their data support such desired group outcomes as providing catharsis for parents, helping them accept the diagnosis of mental retardation, assisting them to shift from short-term goals to long-term goals, helping them realize others were sympathetic, and providing them with a greater optimism regarding the child's future. Among the more semistructured group projects, the report of Nadal (1964) is based upon some objective data as well as clinical opinion. She states: " ... on the basis of clinical and raters' judgment, it can be said that genuine improvement was made in such areas as attitudes toward the child, child-rearing practices, ability to handle the child, and the general level of the mother's communication of her concern and problems." Among the fairly structured groups in which objective data was used to assess outcomes was the one conducted by Bitter (1964). He states: "The objective evidence, although not conclusive, would seem to indicate that a series of parent discussion sessions is effective in changing attitudes of parents of trainable mentally retarded children toward their retarded child and toward family problems occasioned by the retardation."

DISCUSSION

The opinions and evidence presented by the fifteen studies covered in this review, in which group methods were used to meet emotional and other needs of parents of retardates, testify to the general value of such procedures and also support more extensive use of them in the future. No attempt is made here to question the successful outcomes reported in the published studies, as the nature of the reports and data do not lend themselves to such an evaluation. This statement is made because practically all studies were so poorly designed as research projects or so inadequately reported that any precise repetition of them, which would warrant comparison of results, appears improbable. However, the reports did provide a basis for other analyses and revealed certain issues and factors which demand more critical attention in planning future studies if any systematic understanding of the effectiveness of such groups is to be attained. Some of the deficiencies revealed in the design of these studies are discussed in the following paragraphs.

A most elementary requirement indicated for future studies is a more comprehensive taxonomic description of the population variables which might be related to outcomes. For example, the parent populations involved in such studies can be more clearly defined by citing data concerning age, sex, years married, number of children, ordinal position of the retardate, socioeconomic status, parental educational level, and so on. Also descriptive data regarding the retardate in each family needs to be more adequately reported such as age, sex, general degree of mental deficiency, resident at home or in an institution, additional handicaps, and other variables. Such simple taxonomic data permits at least some study of the relationship of such variables and outcomes as well as certain comparisons between different groups, and outcomes. None of the studies presented any findings bearing upon the relationship of such taxonomic variables and reported results.

Another major variable which demands more detailed attention and more precise description is the nature of each group's structure, functioning, and goals. First, such simple descriptive data is needed as to the length of sessions, frequency of sessions, and total number of sessions. Second, a more adequate statement need to be given concerning the nature of the group process to which the parents are exposed. In most of the studies reviewed, the group activity employed was simply described as group guidance, counseling, or psychotherapy. Does this mean directive, nondirective, psychoanalytic, or other theoretically based therapy or group process? Many questions concerning theory and practice can also be raised. Is one group method superior to another? Is there an opitmal number of sessions for any one method? Is there an optimal size for groups? Is the time interval between meetings important? What is the difference in outcomes between structured and unstructured group projects?

The studies also did little to describe the nature of the group leader other than to give his professional title. Many questions about group leaders can be raised. Should the leader be a professional mental health specialist? Does he need special training in group therapy or group process? Can simiprofessionals be trained to become group leaders? Does the group leader need to have direct information about the retardate in the family? Do different group goals require a different set of leader qualifications? The qualifications of the group leader and the types of group leadership skills he exerts are undoubtedly variables related to outcomes and, therefore, invite systematic study.

Another salient issue largely neglected except by Anderson (1962) concerns the immediate family situation and the time of group intervention. Are there times when a given group method is more effective with parents than at other times? Do groups function more effectively during crisis situations, such as when the parents go on the "waiting list," or when their child is given a medical diagnosis of mental retardation, or when the child is placed in an institution, or when the retardate becomes adolescent? Should certain types of groups for parents be scheduled at times of crisis? Should another type be offered parents who face long standing problems?

The greatest research need in this field is to introduce more objective measures so that more quantitative types of data can be secured. Such instruments could be used in selecting parent groups, measuring changes during group procedures and assessing final outcomes. A beginning has been made in the use of objective instruments for such evaluation as seen in studies made by Appell, Williams, and Fishell (1964), Bitter (1963), Cummings and Stock (1962), and Rankin (1957). Even these investigations, with the possible exception of the Bitter study, cannot be satisfactorily repeated by others because of inadequate research design or description in certain parts of each study. Therefore, most of the findings reported cannot be checked by independent investigators.

None of the studies used objective measures to aid in the selection and description of the populations admitted to group projects. Three studies administered certain tests, questionnaires, and rating scales to participants after they were engaged in group activities but only incidentally were the data obtained related directly to outcomes. The Bitter study (1963) was the only one which administered objective instruments before and after the group intervention and is possibly the only one that could be repeated again and results compared.

Cummings and Stock (1962) reported making tape recordings of group sessions. While these writers do not make any report of analysis of their tapes, the procedure certainly seems to offer a valuable source of data regarding the content and issues which evolve in group sessions, the nature of group and family dynamics, types of interventions by leader, and other variables which appear related to outcomes. More extensive use of tapes seems promising.

Another research design factor which needs to be incorporated in such studies is the use of control groups. None of the studies reviewed reported the use of such groups. It is essential to obtain subjective and objective types of data based on control groups if any substantial support is claimed for the efficacy of group projects. The best design for measuring outcomes would involve before and after measurements of selected variables for both the experimental and the control group. Research designs involving only measurements after a study is completed are difficult to evaluate. Another possible use of two or more groups is to compare them by measurement or self-reports for some major variation to which each is exposed, such as introducing different types of group leadership. Such studies can provide valuable comparative inferences and offer promising leads for further studies.

There are many basic issues which only control groups can begin to answer. Do different types of group structure produce different results? Is one type of leadership proven more effective than another? Is it really the group intervention that brings about claimed results, or is it simply the passage of time which solves many of the parents' problems, whether they are "in" or "out" of such groups? Do the professional qualifications of the leader elicit certain types of agenda and processes?

Finally, the need for long-term follow-up studies of results is beyond question. None of the studies reported any such attempts. Which changes noted at the end of group intervention tend to hold and which fade away? Are some changes not apparent until after six months or a year? Do parents who made gains through group interactions continue to increase in self-sufficiency and self-direction? Only long-term studies can answer a whole range of basic inquiries into the lasting effectiveness of such groups.

This review and discussion attempts to point out some possible improvements in designs of group projects which could aid in furthering our knowledge of the effective use of groups in meeting emotional needs and other problems of parents of retardates. It is hoped that this report will encourage a more extensive use of empirically planned group procedures as well as more tightly designed investigations.

REFERENCES

Anderson, A. V.: Orientating parents to a clinic for the retarded. *Children, 9:*178-182, 1962.

Appell, M. J., Williams, C. M., and Fishell, K. N.: Changes in attitudes of parents of retarded children effected through group counseling. *Am. J. Ment. Defic., 68:*807-812, 1964.

Bitter, J. A.: Attitude change by parents of trainable mentally retarded children as a result of group discussion. *Except. Child., 30:*173-176, 1964.

Blatt, A.: Group therapy with parents of severely retarded children: a preliminary report. *Group Psychotherapy, 10:*133-140, 1957.

Coleman, J. C.: Group therapy with parents of mentally deficient children. *Am. J. Ment. Defic., 57:*700-726, 1953.

Cummings, S. T., and Stock, D.: Brief group therapy of mothers of retarded children outside of the specialty clinic setting. *Am. J. Ment. Defic., 66:* 739-748, 1962.

Goodman, L., and Rothman, R.: The development of a group counseling program in a clinic for retarded children. *Am. J. Ment. Defic., 65:*789-795, 1961.

Nadal, R.: A counseling program for parents of severely retarded preschool children. *Social Casework, 42:*78-83, 1961.

Popp, Cleo B., Ingram, V., and Jordan, P. H.: Helping parents understand their mentally handicapped child. *Am. J. Ment. Defic., 58:*530-534, 1954.

Rankin, J. E.: A group therapy experiment with mothers of mentally deficient children. *Am. J. Ment. Defic., 62:* 49-55, 1957.

Roche, T.: A Study of the impact on child-family relationships of group counseling of mothers of mentally retarded. In: *Maintaining the Integrity of the Individual, the Family, and the Community: A Nursing Responsibility.* New York, Amer. Nurses Assoc., 1964.

Rosenbaum, M., and Berger, B.: *Group Psychotherapy and Group Function.* New York, Basic Books, 1963.

Rosen, L.: Selected aspects in the development of the mother's understanding of her mentally retarded child. *Am. J. Ment. Defic., 59:*522-528, 1955.

Weingold, J. T., and Hormuth, R. P.: Group guidance of parents of mentally retarded children. *J. Clin. Psychol., 9:*118-124, 1953.

White, B. L.: Clinical team treatment of mentally retarded child and his parents: group counseling and play observation. *Am. J. Ment. Defic., 63:*713-723, 1959.

Yates, M. L., and Lederer, R.: Small, short-term group meetings with parents of children with mongolism. *Am. J. Ment. Defic., 65:*467-472, 1961.

PART IV

FAMILY CASEWORK AND CHILD PLACEMENT

Clinical Team Treatment of a Mentally Retarded Child and His Parents: Casework with the Mother

NELLIE D. STONE, D.S.W.*

THIS presentation of the treatment of the parents of a four-year-old, mildly retarded boy, Teddy T., illustrates the use of casework and group counseling as part of a total plan for family help provided through the community guidance clinic operated by the Essex Unit of the New Jersey Association for Retarded Children in East Orange, New Jersey. This professional diagnostic and counseling service has been sponsored and developed over the past eight years by the associated parents and friends of mentally retarded children as the focal point around which community programs for dealing with this handicap have been built. It is significant that only within this short time have there become available specialized treatment resources for the mentally retarded child and his parents within their home community. Whereas much of the work in the past has been pioneered within the institutional setting, we are now able to report on current efforts to assist parents and child in their own home and community setting. It is to be hoped that impetus will

Note: Reprinted by permission of the author and the *American Journal of Mental Deficiency, 63*:707-712, 1959. Copyrighted by the American Association on Mental Deficiency.
*Director, Guidance Clinic for Retarded, East Orange, New Jersey.

be given to the broadening and strengthening of general community welfare services to include adequate attention to the needs
of parents and children affected by the handicap of mental
retardation along with those facing other social problems. A
further aim is to add to the professional understanding of social
workers and other counselors so that more effective helping
techniques may be developed.

The Guidance Clinic for the Retarded functions under the
supervision of a multidiscipline advisory committee, with a
neuropsychiatrist as medical director, and is administered by a
psychiatric social worker. Its staff includes pediatric, psychiatric,
neurological, speech and other specialists, as well as a clinical
psychologist and caseworker. The clinical team approach, integrating medical, psychological, and social casework disciplines, is used
both in the basic diagnostic evaluation and in subsequent
treatment services. The focus of this case presentation is the
coordination of efforts with parents and child through individual
and group treatment as carried out by the caseworker and
psychologist in the clinic setting. The team approach is used
throughout in the process of diagnosis, treatment and reevaluation
from stage to stage in the helping process.

INITIAL DIAGNOSTIC EVALUATION

Teddy, age four, was referred by his pediatrician for clinical
evaluation to determine the extent of his suspected mental
retardation. His parents, who are attractive and responsible young
people, were felt to need counseling in understanding Teddy and
their own reactions to his problem. The mother, in particular, was
experiencing difficulty in accepting Teddy's slowness in speech
and learning, which contrasted markedly with his baby brother's
rapid development. There were problems in Teddy's toilet training
and in handling of discipline. He suffered from a chronic skin rash
which did not respond to medical measures.

Medical history revealed prolonged and difficult labor due to
the mother's small pelvic measurements; and oxygen had been
required during Teddy's first day of life. He was an unusually
quiet baby, and his early development was slow. Physical
examination showed an eczematous rash on face and legs,

strabismus, poor lacrimation, marked salivation, slightly protruding tongue, malocclusion of teeth, undesended testicles with inguinal hernia, and slightly hyperactive reflexes as positive findings; other physical findings were negative. The diagnostic impression was of congenital mental retardation, possibly due to cerebral injury at birth.

In the psychological evaluation, Teddy did not cooperate well, and his test performance was inconsistent, so that it was questionable whether test results represented his true intellectual potential. He was found to be functioning at about two thirds of his age level capacity. Observations of Teddy's negativism, and of the mother's overconcern and ambivalence in attitudes and handling, suggested that emotional impediments might well be affecting Teddy's performance and relationships. Speech evaluation showed repetition of words and short phrases, along with slow development of speech. Prognosis for continued development seemed good.

In the social casework study, the parents were found to be concerned about the outlook for Teddy's training and development and anxious for clarification and guidance. The father was able to be fairly objective about Teddy, and appeared to be both stable and intelligently concerned about increasing his own understanding and helping Teddy. The mother displayed considerable anxiety through her constant talking and projecting of fears about Teddy's future, worrying about whether he would ever become self-sufficient. Both parents were eager to secure special training for Teddy through the Association's preschool class as soon as he was ready for this group experience. Teddy's retarded appearance, with his short, squat stature, his drooling and open mouth, was embarrassing to the mother, who constantly nagged at him to keep toys and fingers out of his mouth. Parental pressure for conformity to their standards of performance and behavior was felt to be a probable contributing factor in Teddy's present regression from early attempts at toilet training and in his confusion and negativism in response to directions and questions. It was felt that both parents could benefit from further examination of their feelings about Teddy and that the mother needed guidance in her handling of Teddy's training at home.

EXPLORATORY TREATMENT PLAN

After consideration by the entire clinic staff of the above factors, the following plan for further observation and exploration was suggested: Teddy was to be seen weekly by the psychologist during a three months' period for play observation in order to gain additional data which might define more clearly the child's ability and needs. At the same time, the mother would have weekly casework interviews to explore and clarify her feelings about Teddy and herself, and to discuss training problems. It was thought that the father could add to his understanding and perspective through participation in a parents' counseling group which would meet for ten weekly sessions, under the psychologist's leadership. At the end of three months, the situation would be evaluated and the treatment plan redirected as indicated.

The family physician, who would be continuing his medical treatment of Teddy, was informed of the findings and plan, which he felt would be helpful to the family. The tentative impressions and recommendations of the clinic study were reviewed with the parents, who were receptive to the suggested plan of exploration, which was then put into effect.

CASEWORK WITH THE MOTHER

The mother came regularly for the eleven interviews, in which she participated freely and constructively. The final interview in the exploratory series was held jointly with the father and psychologist to review conclusions and suggestions for a revised treatment approach.

Mrs. T. is an attractive, expressive woman with a strong need to verbalize her concerns. From the first, she showed a willingness to examine her feelings and reactions, although she also revealed, indirectly and subtly, her reluctance to face them squarely. During the initial interviews, she wore a tense expression and constantly fixed smile, which was not at all appropriate to the anxieties which she was detailing. Also, during this beginning period, the mother suffered from persistent laryngitis, which made it very hard for her to speak, yet she forced herself to do so. It is the caseworker's feeling that these defences were necessary for Mrs. T. during the time that she was getting to know her worker, and finding out to what extent she could relax and trust me. I saw my role with Mrs. T. to be that of an understanding, nonjudgmental mother person, who would facilitate Mrs. T.'s understanding of herself, and offer support, reassurance and suggestions as appropriate and helpful. My goal was to encourage her to examine and evaluate her patterns of reaction, trying to trace their roots, as she was able, to her earlier experiences. It was hoped that clarification and possibly some change in attitudes might be brought about by the understanding thus achieved.

We focused first on Mrs. T.'s concern about Teddy's regression in toilet control. After the mother was given an explanation of the complex nature of the physical controls required of a child in toilet training, and the differing rates of emotional and neurological readiness to achieve such controls, she herself concluded that she had been premature in pressing Teddy to conform in this area at nine months of age. His subsequent rebellion, through refusing to inform her of his toilet needs or of not responding at her suggestion, was seen as related to Teddy's lack of readiness and inability to conform, rather than purely as stubbornness or stupidity. The reassurance that toilet controls would develop as the child was able, both physically and emotionally, to assume responsibility for his own bodily functions relieved the mother of feeling that she was a total failure. She then could examine her own methods of handling Teddy's training, and become aware that she had been pressing him too much, and not allowing him to develop self-reliance in this area. As she was able to understand that accidents would occur as part of the learning process, the mother did not feel that each failure was solely a hostile expression directed toward her. When Mrs. T. was able to give up her punishment and berating of Teddy after each toilet accident, he was able to feel more relaxed and began to indicate his needs.

While Mrs. T. was gratified by Teddy's progress, she could not believe that the gains would be sustained. She was surprised that the improvement continued and was not able to feel any sense of personal achievement because of her better handling of Teddy's toilet training. It was at this point that the mother's pessimistic outlook and low self-regard began to be apparent. She could not believe that life could hold any happiness for her, yet she had tremendous needs and expectations. The worker's reassurance regarding the future for Teddy and concerning the mother's own capacities seemed so false to Mrs. T. that her anxiety was actually increased. As a defense, she tended to deny that there was any difficulty with Teddy, and expressed her own great needs through unrealistic expectations for his future development.

With the worker's encouragement, Mrs. T. began to examine the basis for her pessimism. She revealed that she felt quite responsible for Teddy's handicap, both because his skin condition is similar to the skin problem she experienced in her childhood, and also because of his difficult birth due to her own physical build. Mrs. T.'s skin condition had been a traumatic factor throughout her life, but had diminished considerably in severity following her marriage five years ago. She characterized herself in infancy, as a "naughty little baby" who caused her mother lots of trouble by not feeding properly. From the age of one year, she was subject to a breaking out on her hands and arms which practically incapacitated her. Since her hands needed to be bandaged, both parents and teachers had to do many things for her. While she enjoyed this dependence to some extent, she also felt ashamed and unlovable because of her condition. Because she was different, she felt that no one could really like her. Feeling thus unworthy and unloved, as well as helpless, she was unable to express her hostile feelings satisfactorily. When her parents were frequently harsh and restrictive toward her, she felt helpless and as if it were useless to express her protest, even though justified. She would cry in secret or else just not say anything, and suffered in silence. Mother was able to point out that frequently at such times of suppression of feeling, her rash would break out in renewed vigor, and then her mother or father would have to feel sorry for her and take care of her. It seemed thus to serve the dual purpose of self-punishment as well as retribution on her parents, ending up in dependent gratification based on suffering and helplessness.

This pattern of reaction was seen by the worker to be of rather deep and marked nature, and to be reflected in the mother's current reaction toward Teddy. Teddy's skin difficulty and slowness seemed to reactivate the mother's early feelings about herself. Even though she would become angry at Teddy because he could not measure up to her standards for him, she felt very guilty about expressing her negative feelings. As she put it, she realized that Teddy was helpless, even as she had been helpless as a child, and therefore she became uncomfortable in punishing him. On the other hand, she saw in Teddy's difference and slowness an uncomplimentary reflection of her own self-image, which was hard to accept. She was thus caught in the conflict between her high wishes for herself and her essentially low self-esteem. Through casework discussion, Mrs. T. gained some conscious awareness of how this inner conflict pressed toward opposite extremes of reaction, resulting in contradiction and inconsistency. To a limited extent, she was able to stabilize her expressions toward increased freedom and relief for herself, and at the same time let up her pressure on Teddy. This change was facilitated by Mr. T.'s encouragement and acceptance of Mrs. T. within the family relationship, while the caseworker was giving professional acceptance of Mrs. T. as a person through casework support and clarification.

Despite improvement in her overt manifestations, Mrs. T. continued to reflect severe doubts about her own capacities and what the future might hold for Teddy. In reality, she had made a good marriage, and her life had improved since her childhood sufferings. Yet Mrs. T. could not believe that she deserved any good out of life, despite her very great longings for excessive reassurance. She found it hard to accept the smaller, realistic gains which were at hand. Unless she could be guaranteed that Teddy would turn out to be completely adequate, she was unable to accept the capacities which he really had. The persistence of such fluctuations and doubts was seen to be an indication of the deep-seated nature of Mrs. T.'s difficulties, which lay beyond the scope of the casework treatment planned with her. And yet, Mrs. T. was able to absorb some greater understanding of Teddy and his condition, at least intellectually. Also, by the end of the casework series, she was herself questioning whether things were really as bad for her as she felt they were.

In relation to Teddy's sessions, the mother showed the

tendency to attempt to talk with the boy's worker at the conclusion of the hour. In this way she seemed to be expressing fear and apprehension about what Teddy might be revealing about her, as well as diverting the focus of her own efforts away from self-evaluation. This resistance to self-involvement seemed also related to her recurring unrealistic concepts of herself and Teddy. The consistent channeling of information about Teddy's progress to Mrs. T. through the caseworker was not sufficiently satisfying or reassuring to her, since it was not possible to give her the specific answers and extensive reassurance which she wished to have. In facing with Mrs. T. this implication, we were again made aware of how difficult it was for her to achieve a realistic acceptance and understanding of herself and Teddy.

EVALUATION OF CASEWORK TREATMENT

As the material and process growing out of the eleven interviews were reviewed, certain conclusions and indications emerged. Through exploration, interpretation and support afforded by the casework approach, Mrs. T. had gained some awareness of her own patterns of reaction, and had been able to modify them to a limited, yet significant extent. The result was more constructive handling of Teddy and a stabilization of the mother's overt expressions. While her basic underlying conflicts remained largely unchanged, Mrs. T. had become aware to a certain extent of their existence. The fact that she was able, toward the end of the exploration, to question the validity of her extreme reactions, indicated the possibility of still further modification, even if only in external expression.

The relationship between the caseworker and the mother proved to be helpful within the limitations of the exploratory period. Through acceptance and professional understanding, Mrs. T. was enabled to explore her earlier experiences and see how they related to her present discomforts. The level of treatment and relationship was purposely kept close to reality functioning, although based upon deeper understanding of human dynamics. While it was apparent that intensive psychotherapeutic effort would be required to bring about a major change in Mrs. T.'s firmly fixed personality patterns, this possibility was not considered to be available or appropriate for Mrs. T. Instead, it was thought best to help her sustain the gains she had made, and obtain a truer perspective regarding herself and Teddy.

In view of the mother's resistence to self-involvement which had been indicated by her tendency toward interjecting herself into the sessions with Teddy, it was doubtful that she would be willing to continue individual sessions without Teddy's being seen. Instead, it was felt that the mother was ready for and could benefit from group association with other parents in a counseling program. Such participation would afford her the opportunity for gaining perspective from other parents and the support and reassurance which such a group could provide. Having achieved some gains and awareness from the casework exploration, Mrs. T. was felt to be better prepared to use the kind of help which the counseling group offered.

REDIRECTION OF TREATMENT

By the end of the play sessions, the psychologist had confirmed his original impression of Teddy's capacity as lying close to borderline capacity. Since Teddy's functioning had improved with the mother's use of casework counseling, it was decided that he was ready for nursery class experience as a stimulation toward further development. Mr. T. had participated constructively in the counseling group, clarifying his own understanding through discussion with other parents, and was found to be operating helpfully within his own family.

A joint conference to implement this redirection of treatment for the mother and Teddy was planned between workers and parents. At this time the conclusions and suggestions growing out of the work with father, mother, and child were shared. Despite positive assurances regarding Teddy's outlook, the mother's basic doubts were again brought out. This time, however, it was the father who dealt helpfully with the mother's extreme points of view. She was quite eager to enter the counseling group, both because of Mr. T.'s enthusiastic reaction, and because of her preparation through casework exploration. The parents were pleased that Teddy would be able to attend class, and it was apparent that both of them had acquired a better understanding of Teddy and of themselves through the counseling help made available through this clinic.

Chapter 19

Some Problems in Casework
with Parents of
Mentally Retarded Children *

HOWARD R. KELMAN†

THE desire on the part of parents to keep their retarded child at home is certainly not a new phenomena, nor is it inconsistent, generally, with what is best for the child itself. Although it was once deemed socially desirable and necessary to isolate and exclude the retarded child from family and community life, we are now becoming more aware of the many serious shortcomings of this (or any other) unilateral approach to the varied needs and problems of the mentally retarded in our society. Indeed the antiquated and outdated assumptions that buttressed this philosophy stemmed as much out of society's ignorance and fear of the retarded as it did out of a deep humanitarian concern for their welfare.

Except for a few notable exceptions, the social work community has made little or no special provisions for services for retarded children who live at home and for their families. As a matter of fact, many of the psychiatric tenets underlying current

Note: Reprinted by permission from the author and the *American Journal of Mental Deficiency,* 57:595-598, 1957. Copyrighted by the American Association on Mental Deficiency.

*Based on a paper presented at the Annual Convention of the AAMD, Richmond, Va., May, 1956.

†Mr. Kelman was formerly Consultant in Community Services, National Association for Retarded Children. Now Instructor in Pediatrics, New York Medical College, Flower and Fifth Avenue Hospitals.

casework theory tend to reject and deprecate work with retarded individuals. Likewise, concepts and characterizations of parents of retarded children born of an earlier era, or those uncritically transferred from certain other disability groups serve to block further understanding and application of fresh approaches to the problem by concerned professional workers.

Despite the conveniences of these characterizations and their apparent resemblance to reality, it must also be stated that they can act as barriers to the development of clearer insights and greater understanding of parents of retarded children as people struggling with a serious and deeply personal social problem. The nature of this struggle and its eventual outcome will depend, in great part, upon how the professional person relates himself to it and the kind of influence he brings to bear upon it. Superficiality or brusqueness by some unthinking professionals in the past have, in too many instances, added to the woes of some parents and lent confirmation to others that they were "deserving" of condemnation and stigmatization for having given birth to a mentally deviant child.

It is vital, though, that caseworkers concern themselves with the parents and families of the retarded and not alone for humanitarian reasons. Of perhaps even greater importance is this necessary in order to satisfy the professional necessities involved in the rendering of sound and effective services of all types to the retarded child living at home. For in this area, as in other areas of chronic disability, the main burden of care for the handicapped individual falls upon the family unit (and ultimately the community), and if the caseworker is to assist the family in shouldering its rightful share of this social responsibility, he must himself have convictions about its possibilities and values.

The ability to individualize understanding and help which constitutes perhaps the unique contribution of the caseworker is particularly crucial in the field of mental retardation — an area in which stereotyped notions and damaging generalizations have for so long held such unchallenged sway.

It is difficult in speaking of any large disability group to describe schematically the deeply felt concerns of people, for we are dealing with human organisms whose very nature is such that they are alike in some respects and unique in others. Problems which seem generic to the group take on for the individual subtle shadings and colorations depending upon the interplay of all the varied factors which bring their influence to bear upon the matter. We are dealing, also, with situations and problems that are not themselves static and unchanging but which undergo modifications in kind and intensity with the passing of time.

Parents whose retarded child resides at home with them face many difficulties and are often handicapped in the carrying out of their desire to care for and manage their child properly for several reasons. They may lack precise knowledge of the unique nature of their child's disability and its personal and social implications. Then, too, there may not be available to them in their community the necessary services to assist the family in maintaining and training their child for social living. Or the family unit itself may not possess the necessary cohesion, stability, and resources to be able to withstand the chronic tensions and strains that so often befall the family of a mentally retarded child.

To be sure, the decision by some parents to keep and maintain the child at home is sometimes made without a careful weighing of all the factors involved and may be reflective in some cases of a subjective reaction to a hurt, profoundly felt, and constantly reexperienced in a society which is ill-prepared and unoriented to tolerate deviation and difference of this sort. But it is also true that most families have little or no prior experience in living with and having to restructure their lives to the varied demands and unique needs of a chronically disabled individual. The caseworker must come to grips with and be prepared to work through the differing degrees of realization, understanding, and conceptualization of parents regarding the nature and the meaning of their child's handicap. The way in which this realization is achieved and the type and degree of disability have an important bearing on how the parents later view their child and his place in the family and the larger society. The impact this handicapped child has had upon the lives of the parents, the parents real and imagined doubts about their own worth, coupled with their fears for the child's future, are all part of the immediate constellation in which the child functions and to which a judgment of his performance and potential must be related.

The retarded child himself must be regarded as an integral part of the family unit who mutually interacts and affects all the members of the group. Parents and siblings in turn affect the child and can contribute significantly, positively or negatively, to his larger social adjustment or to the progress of his immediate school or training program. Attempts must be made to properly orient family members and direct their behavior to what is beneficial, appropriate and constructive for the child.

In so doing, it soon becomes evident that supportive help or reassurance is insufficient and that it will be necessary to offer concrete, practical "tutorial" assistance, or guidance to parents and other family members who live with the child. This type of help should not only be aimed at making clear or uncovering for them the "inexplicable" behavior and actions of the child but should focus also upon the imparting of tested techniques for his home management and daily care. By thus focussing upon the everyday chores and problems of daily living and in helping the child to deal with and successfully master those tasks which he can be expected properly to handle, a more meaningful insight into the child's capabilities can be achieved by all concerned, and the greater is the child's chances for developing more constructively his social potential. It may also serve to prevent the later development of other difficulties as the child grows into adolescence and adulthood.

In a very real sense, the supportive and "tutorial" aspects of the caseworker's function blend properly into a meaningful and necessary whole. The supportive efforts enable parents and others to assume other and perhaps more important training obligations to the child. These training obligations to the child. These training obligations to the child will not be fulfilled unless the caseworker assists and aids the family members in a concrete way to use this knowledge.

Nor can the caseworker tie his goals to the illusive aim of achieving what has been termed *parent acceptance* of the child. He must instead help the parents to understand the child as he really is — his potentials for growth and development — as well as his limitations. He must not, because of a particular (and perhaps personal) investment in one solution to the problem, deny change where there is change nor deny growth where there is growth. It is for the caseworker to point out the nature, direction and rate of this growth, and its larger social meaning.

I believe that there is much unclarity about this question of acceptance and its implications. While it is true that there are some unusually harassed and perplexed parents who are apparently unable to grasp the significance of their child's disability or its implications, this behavior should not be equated with the desire on the part of other parents to fully explore the possibilities of assistance, training, or help which might be available. Nor should it be confused with the indignation felt by many parents who, having achieved a full realization of the nature of mental retardation and its comparative historical neglect, are concerned enough to try to rectify this undesirable abandonment. Indeed, were it not for this refusal to accept the status quo, much of the stimulation and broad signs of progress in this field that we are witnessing today probably would not have occurred. In so doing, the parent himself can gain a broader recognition of the full nature and the larger implications of mental retardation, see himself in a truer and healthier relationship to it, and derive, as a by-product, certain personal therapeutic benefits.

The caseworker, particularly, ought to ally himself or herself with these expressions of concern, since they lead to broader community recognition of the problem and to the establishment of services so essential to the well-being and training of retarded children. The caseworker should contribute his or her professional knowledge and skill to the furtherance and balancing of these programs and at the same time contribute positively to the strengthening of the community's health and welfare service systems.

The challenge that the retarded offer to the professional caseworker is most profound both in terms of the complex community planning involved as well as in the rich possibilities it offers in rendering needed individual services to the parents and siblings. If this challenge is to be met and its possibilities grasped, it will mean that caseworkers, if not the field of social work itself, will have to more carefully and systematically explore their skills and techniques in relation to the needs of this disability group.

It will call, I believe, for a distillation and some incorporation into casework practice of some of the content and knowledge of allied professions in the medical, psychological, and educational areas. It will mean too a critical reappraisal of some social agency structures and values (both apparent and hidden) which underly both the caseworker's approach to and his expectations of parents, the testing of skills and services that will be more in keeping with the needs of the retarded and their families, and the advances made by some allied professions.

The caseworker (in collaboration with social scientists and others) will also need to come to grips with those elements in our current social value system that place such heavy emphasis and high premium upon intellectual prowess and the quick mind and relegate those among us in our society who are incapable of this level of achievement to positions of lesser worth or status. Much needs to be learned about those factors which make for healthy social adaptions and the workings of larger environmental forces, which in their own inexorable fashion affect the stability of families and communities and influence the abilities of parents to successfully adapt themselves to the demands of a mentally retarded child.

In conclusion, I should like to say that the expansion and establishment of facilities of all types to better meet the needs of the retarded individual who resides at home and his family poses a profound challenge to the professional social caseworker and to the larger social work community. If this profession is to fulfill its responsibilities and obligations to this disability group, it will call for more systematic and intensive efforts in both understanding the nature of the problems faced by families in this regard and in the development of forms of help and community services that will enable families to more successfully assume their obligations to their child.

Mental retardation is both a deeply personal problem to a parent of a child with this type of disability and a large and complex health and social problem to the whole community. The caseworker's responsibilities include not only efforts designed to assist the individual child and his family but also participation in broad community efforts directed toward the study and articulation of positive programs looking toward their social integration into the larger society.

Chapter 20

Family Factors in Willingness
to Place the Mongoloid Child*

NELLIE D. STONE, D.S.W.

THE birth of a child with an obvious defect such as mongolism (or Down's syndrome) confronts the parents with a crisis which must be resolved constructively if the family's welfare is to be safeguarded. The question of institutional or home care for the mongoloid child is a particular issue with which the parents are faced at an early and vulnerable point following the birth because of the handicap's high visibility, the heightened ego-impact and emotional blow to parental self-regard, and the authoritative placement recommendations which are frequently received from physicians, relatives, and other influential persons. The chronic strain and crises, which recur throughout the retarded child's career, bring the question repeatedly to the fore. In view of the initial and subsequent impact of this kind of handicap upon the family, special study is merited to learn how parents can adapt to this problem, with particular reference to their decisions concerning institutional or home care.

Note: Reprinted by permission of the author and the *American Journal of Mental Deficiency,* 72:16-20, 1967. Copyrighted by the American Association on Mental Deficiency.
*This article is a summary of a study which was supported by the United States Public Health Service Grant MH-1185, and sponsored by the Essex Unit, New Jersey Association for Retarded Children, East Orange, New Jersey. Joseph J. Parnicky, Ph.D., Superintendent of the E. R. Johnstone Training and Research Center, Bordentown, N. J., acted as consultant while Dr. Stone was the principal investigator. This paper is a revision of a presentation to the annual AAMD meeting in Chicago, May, 1966. A full report of the study, including statistical tables, is available from the National Association for Retarded Children, 420 Lexington Avenue, New York, New York 10017, as a monograph: *Family Factors Related to Placement of Mongoloid Children,* 1965.

Since the professional literature surveyed does not yet furnish consistent and reliable guides in this kind of situation, advisers cannot be clear about their own recommendations in counseling parents. Several investigators have reported varying conclusions about the advisability of placement for mongoloid (Kelman, 1959; Kramm, 1963) and other types of retarded children (Farber, Jenne, and Toigo, 1960; Saenger, 1960; Tizard and Grad, 1961), but further investigation seems necessary to clarify and substantiate these indications in the search for more specific counseling guides. The study being reported examined the reactions of both fathers and mothers to the birth and continuing impact of the mongoloid child within the framework of crisis concepts as developed by public health investigators such as Parad and Caplan (1960) and Rapoport (1962). The family situations and relationships were assessed by professional casework judgment, as well as by the parents themselves, in a search for clues to adaptive response in deciding upon institutional or home care for the mongoloid child.

PROCEDURE

The study population was made up of 103 families who agreed to participate, each of which included a mongoloid child under the age of nine years who was living at home with both parents within the northern New Jersey metropolitan area as of the end of 1963. Fifty of these families had applied for institutional care and were on the state waiting lists. The remaining fifty-three nonapplicant families were located by intensive case finding, the majority being identified through two mental retardation clinics serving the area. Almost 70 percent of the families found to be eligible took part in the study. Among the forty-six eligible families who did not agree to participate, the proportions of applicants and nonapplicants were not significantly different.

Data were obtained directly from the fathers' and mothers' responses to a structured interview schedule as well as to paper and pencil attitude instruments. Interviews were conducted in the home by four trained social caseworkers with experience in mental retardation and averaged more than three hours in length. While each father and mother was interviewed alternately, the other completed questionnaires designed to tap parental attitudes and knowledge about their child's handicap and to reflect the nature of family interrelationships and current adaptation to the situation. The interview systematically covered the parent's reactions and experiences following the birth of the mongoloid child, elucidating the influences perceived to influence parental placement decision and willingness both initially and currently.

On the basis of his professional judgment, each interviewer rated the adequacy of family functioning on an eight-point scale, using the anchoring specifications for adequate, marginal, or inadequate social functioning outlined by Geismar and Ayres (1960). From the recorded observations of the interviewers and the parents' responses, the study director made a second, independent rating for each family. Only 2 percent of the two sets of judgments differed by more than one point on the ratings. Steps taken to reduce the bias deriving from the interviewer's knowledge of the family's application status included assignment of equal numbers of applicants and nonapplicants and the securing of direct parental responses to objective instruments.

The method of study was by cross-sectional analysis through statistical comparison of the data for the applicant and nonapplicant families. To increase the fruitfulness of the analysis, the applicant families were subdivided into two groups according to their current willingness to place the mongoloid child, as reported by the parents during the interview. The twenty applicant families who were highly willing for institutionalization were designated as *Placers,* while the remaining thirty families who wished to defer placement were called the *Postponers.* The quantified data for these two groups of applicants, along with that of the total group of fifty-three nonapplicants, were then compared with regard to parental responses, sociodemographic data, and professional ratings by analysis of variance on IBM equipment. Pearsonian coefficients of correlation were computed on the data for all families in order to determine strength of association between variables. Data obtained from fathers and mothers were examined in separate, parallel analyses to show similarities or differences. By factor analysis, the scores of both sets of parents' attitude responses were reduced to fifteen sets of highly intercorrelated factors.

The cross-sectional method of study meant that the families were studied at varying lengths of time after the birth crisis, from less than one year to over eight years. In an effort to offset this time differential to some extent, the data were analyzed separately for families whose mongoloid children were under or over five years old. This comparison provided some impressions of the early, as against continued, impact of the mongoloid's presence on the family. However, the limitations of retrospective data still apply to the findings of this study.

RESULTS

At or beyond the 5 percent level of probability, statistical analysis revealed significant differences between the three study groups of families (two of applicants and one of nonapplicants) in regard to their sociodemographic characteristics and situations. Cognitive, experiential, attitudinal, and interpersonal factors among these three groups were found to be significantly different and to be associated with level of family functioning, whether professionally rated or as reported by the parents, themselves. The findings suggest conclusions about the appropriateness of the placement intention of these three groups of families. The willing applicant *Placers* were found to have the least adequate socio-economic situations as well as the poorest relationships and overall family adaptation, according to their own reports as well as by the interviewers' evaluations. Placement of their mongoloid children might well be considered necessary to relieve and possibly improve the situations of these twenty applicant families.

The nonapplicants' generally adequate environment, personal, and family relations, along with their unity of purpose, implied that their consistent wish to provide home care for their mongoloid children represented appropriate and stable decisions by these families. While the *Postponer* applicants' social situations were found to be the most favorable, and they reported high levels of information and social adaptation, their premature application and subsequent placement indecision, as well as indications of weakness in family relations and maternal adjustment, suggested that these parents continued to be ambivalent about care of their mongoloid child.

The findings further revealed that parents indicated less tolerance toward the older group of mongoloids (between the ages of 5 and 9 years), particularly if they were boys, since the parents were more willing to institutionalize them, and their presence was associated with poorer reported family adjustment. The adequacy of parental knowledge about mongolism and mental retardation was inversely correlated with placement willingness. On the other hand, more adequate parental knowledge was positively associated with attitudes indicative of crisis resolution as well as with professional judgments of satisfactory family functioning. The general concurrence between the interviewers' judgments and the parents' reports indicative of family adjustment suggested confidence in the professional evaluations. Active participation in parents' organizations was associated with both accurate knowledge about mongolism and willingness to care for the retarded child at home.

The mother-father relationship was located by the findings as the most sensitive area of family life in regard to plans for home or institutional care of the mongoloid child as well as with respect to the continued adjustment of the whole family. The father's essential contribution was seen to lie in his supportiveness and encouragement of the mother through his capacity to withstand the impact of the crisis and subsequent stress. The mother's feelings toward the mongoloid child appeared to influence her attitudes toward placement or home care and were found to depend upon the nature of her relationship with the father as well as to affect the welfare of the children.

DISCUSSION

Overall, the findings revealed the interaction of social, cognitive, experiential, attitudinal, and relational factors in the application decisions and subsequent placement intentions of the study families. Despite statistically significant differences, all three groups of families studied showed fairly good overall functioning, averaging from near adequate levels for the *Postponers* and *Nonapplicants* to above marginal for the *Placers*. In view of such generally similar functioning, it is important to examine the factors which appear to have influenced initial parental decisions concerning institutional application as well as those which may explain subsequent parental outlook about placement.

With reference to initial decision about caring for their mongoloid child, the results strongly suggested that the character of the parents' experiences and relationships exerted more influence than did their social, situational, or personal resources. Applicant parents reported that they had received significantly more frequent urging toward placement, that they were much less hopeful about their child's future development, felt less close, secure, and united with their spouses, and in general were less encouraged to undertake the strain of having a handicapped child in the home than was true for the nonapplicant parents.

However, after the initial application decision was reached, then the effect of personal, social, and situational differences was reflected in the contrasting placement willingness or reluctance which marked the subsequent intentions of the two groups of applicants. The process of living with the mongoloid child revealed that the personal capacities and social resources of the *Placers* were less adequate for withstanding such stress than in the case of the *Postponers,* who found more supportive associations, were motivated to gain more accurate knowledge about their child's handicap, and seemed able to adapt more favorably to their situations.

One may speculate that the *Placers* might have been helped to make a more satisfactory adjustment if the community had provided more adequately for the personal, informational, and social supports which could enhance the family's own resources for coping with this crisis. It seems possible that such social intervention from the time of the child's birth might have enabled some of these families to absorb the defective child into their ranks instead of becoming discouraged to the point of seeking his placement to relieve home pressures.

In general, the results of this study supported the findings of Tizard and Grad (1961), Kramm (1963), and Giannini and Goodman (1963), all of whom focussed totally or partially upon mongoloid subjects. However, the comparability of present conclusions with those of Saenger (1960) and Farber *et al.* (1960) was considerably diminished by differences in the populations studied, since the present investigation included a wider age range and greater variety of mental retardation types. While social status and religion, considered separately, were not shown by this study to be differentially associated with placement willingness, as was indicated by these other investigators, the mongoloid's age and sex were found to have a more defined and specific relationship as reported above.

IMPLICATIONS

The results of this study contain significant implications for professional practice as well as for the provision of community services. The critical influence of the experiences which the parents reported as occurring immediately after the child's birth indicate the importance of their receiving adequate information and sensitive counseling during this initial crisis as well as subsequently. The apparent effectiveness of cognitive understanding as an aid to parents in withstanding crisis and in arriving at sound decisions is one of the most important findings, with definite indications for strengthening and extending the provision of information by counselors, physicians, and community services regarding the child's outlook and resources for helping him. To minimize the possibility of premature institutional application and admission of mongoloid babies, such requests should receive careful screening and evaluation with information and guidance to the parents about alternate means of coping with their problem. By such early and careful study, the families needing institutional care might be assured of prompt admission while the others could be enabled to care for their children at home, with the help of the community services made available to them.

The influence of the mongoloid's age and sex upon parental placement intentions and upon family adaptation to the stresses of living with the handicapped child, as indicated by the study results, calls for periodic professional evaluation and the extension of social supports to the family at crucial stages in the child's life, such as during the early school years. The interrelation of paternal and maternal attitudes and characteristics in regard to placement intention and to total family adjustment points up the need to counsel with both parents in helping them meet and deal with the crisis of mental retardation. The importance of strong family relations in surmounting crisis, confirmed by parents' self-reports as well as by professional judgments, emphasizes the need to make available adequate counseling for parents at points of crisis and recurring stress. The helping professions can join hands to provide this kind of preventive intervention in the interests of strengthening family life along with helping parents to make sound decisions and plans for the care of their handicapped children.

The present study points up the advisability of more extensive investigation of the problems faced by families with congenitally defective children through prospective, longitudinal design. Systematic examination of the patterns of family response to various types of birth crises, as well as evaluation of the effectiveness of interventive techniques, can most profitably begin at the time of birth and continue over a span of time with periodic follow-up and assessment. The indications emerging from this study might in this way be tested for broader applicability.

REFERENCES

Farber, B., Jenne, W. C., and Toigo, R.: *Family Crisis and the Decision to Institutionalize the Retarded Child*. Research Monograph Series A, No. 1. Washington, D. C.: Council for Exceptional Children, 1960.

Geismar, L. L., and Ayres, B. B.: Measuring family functioning. St. Paul: Family-centered Project, 1960 (Mimeographed).

Giannini, M. J., and Goodman, L.: Counseling families during the crisis reaction to mongolism. *Am. J. Ment. Defic., 67:*740-747, 1963.

Kelman, H. R.: The effects of a group of non-institutionalized mongoloid children upon their families as perceived by their mothers. Unpublished doctoral dissertation, New York Univer., 1959.

Kramm, E. R.: *Families of Mongoloid Children*, Children's Bureau Pub. No. 401. Washington, D. C.: U. S. Dept. of Health, Education, and Welfare, 1963.

Parad, H. J., and Caplan, G.: A framework for studying families in crisis. *Social Work, 5:*3-15, 1960.

Rapoport, L.: Working with families in crisis: An explanation in preventive intervention. *Social Work, 7:*48-56, 1962.

Saenger, G.: *Factors Influencing the Institutionalization of Mentally Retarded Individuals in New York City*. Albany, New York State Interdept.

Health Resources Bd., 1960.
Tizard, J., and Grad, J. C.: *The Mentally Handicapped and Their Families.*
London, Oxford Univer. Press, 1961.

PART V
PASTORAL COUNSELING

Chapter 21

The Religious Factor
and the Role of Guilt in
Parental Acceptance of the
Retarded Child

G. H. ZUK, Ph.D.

IT has been said that the handling of parents of retarded children is fraught with such danger that it is important that clinical impression be subjected to constant scientific scrutiny. Recently a study by this writer (1959) called attention to the selective perception of parents of retarded children. It was found that information supplied by parents about their children, when compared with similar information obtained from relatively objective observers, cast them in a more favorable light. The results were consistent with Sarason's impression that "the tendency to perceive and report in a selective manner is a human charcteristic which appears to become increasingly operative when strongly felt, personal problems are involved" (1953). The study reemphasized the need for caution when evaluating the information supplied by persons who may be involved emotionally with handicapped children.

In this study the writer pursues the investigation of the "parent problem." The question under consideration is, what factors affect the kind of adjustment parents will make to the retarded child?

Note: Reprinted by permission of the author and the *American Journal of Mental Deficiency,* *64*:139-147, 1959. Copyrighted by the American Association on Mental Deficiency.

Specifically, the study compares various factors with a measure of acceptance of the child by the mother. It is generally believed that acceptance of the child and adjustment of the parents to the child's handicap are positively related. One other assumption has frequently been mentioned in the literature of guidance work with parents, namely, that guilt is a central dynamic problem impeding adjustment. Guilt has been assigned a role of special significance in the clinical observations of such workers as Kanner (1953), Scheimo (1951), Waterman (1948), Rheingold (1945) and Hastings (1948). On this particular hypothesis, Kanner and Tietze, as noted by Sarason, have commented:

> It is, quite understandably, difficult for many parents, especially those who themselves have been blessed with a good IQ, to accept their child's retardation as an Act of God, as something unpredictable, inevitable and unalterable. There comes often the search for the possibility of paternal contribution to the child's inadequacy. The question "Why do we have such a child?" soon assumes the form of "What have we done to have such a child?" (1968).

Kanner and Tietze thus describe one of the dynamic bases for the development of guilt feelings. In addition, they implicate intelligence as a factor which tends to the development and exaggeration of guilt.

In the opinion of the writer, many factors influence the kind and degree of guilt feelings of parents. The present study will attempt to show that religious background is one among these. Because guilt is an important religious concept and because the major religions handle it somewhat differently, it was suspected that religious background would play a significant role in determining the level of acceptance (and indirectly the level of adjustment) of parents.

METHOD

St. Christopher's Hospital for Children, a nonsectarian institution, has had in operation for the last two years a pilot project*

*The project is supported by grants from the Children's Bureau, Department of Health, Welfare and Education and the Pennsylvania State Department of Health, Division of Maternal and Child Health. The writer thanks the following persons at St. Christopher's for their valuable critical comments and help in formulating the paper: Dr. John Bartram, Dr. June Dobbs, Dr. Samuel Granick, Mr. William Mark, Miss Doris Haar, and Miss Mary Martire.

concerned with the evaluation and guidance of the retarded child and his family. All types of children are seen in the Clinic, from those functioning at the lowest conceivable IQ level to those functioning at actually a normal IQ level but whose performance indicates certain deficiences or gaps in learning ability. Because of the location of the Hospital and the free services offered, most of the children seen are from lower-income families.

In the course of the regular case work-up on each child and family seen, the following information is gathered: (1) source of referral, (2) age of child, (3) sex of child, (4) IQ of child, (5) number of siblings, (6) present age of mother, (7) father's job, and (8) religious denomination. The study was designed to compare these more or less "objective" bits of information with a more or less "subjective" measure of acceptance of the child by the mother. It was felt that each of the variables described above (and very likely others not considered) was possibly related in some way or other with acceptance of the child.

The following information will define more thoroughly the variables listed above:

1. Source of referral. This refers to either the outpatient medical department at St. Christopher's or to another source in the community, such as private agency, physician, psychologist. Of 76 cases, 39 were referred from the outpatient medical department, 37 from other sources in the community.
2. Age of the child. This information existed for 81 children who ranged in age from 1 through 14 years. More than 50 percent of the children were in the 2 to 6 year age range.
3. Sex of the child. The children in the study were about equally divided as to sex.
4. IQ of the child. IQ's (derived in more than 90% of the cases from the Stanford-Binet, L) ranged from 15 through 86.† However, more than 50 percent of the children had IQ's in the 40 to 60 range.

Note. Special thanks are due Miss Helen Beck, psychiatric social worker, and Dr. Peter Lewinsohn, clinical psychologist, for their help in obtaining the necessary evaluations and groupings.

†A few children whose IQ's were determined to be in the 80's were referred to the project on the basis that they seemed to be functioning as retarded children.

5. Number of siblings. The number ranged from 0 to 5 with the median 2.
6. Present age of the mother. Ages ranged from twenty-four through fifty-one years, the median in the middle thirties.
7. Father's job. Roughly grouped, better than 75 percent of the fathers held semiskilled and skilled labor jobs. Three were classed as unskilled and three as professional.
8. Religious denomination. Of 76 cases for which information existed, 39 were Catholic and 37 non-Catholic. Of the non-Catholics, 19 were white Protestant, 9 were Negro Protestant and 9 were Jewish. Of the Catholics, 38 were white and 1 was Negro.

As for the evaluation of the level of acceptance, clearly such measurement must be based on a highly subjective impression. In 67 of 76 cases this subjective impression was obtained from the staff psychiatric social worker who consistently recorded her impressions of the parents (usually the mother, since it was she who most often brought the child in) on level of acceptance of the child. In 9 cases the evaluation was made by the staff pediatrician or public health nurse. At the time of her *initial* contact with the parent, the social worker would state whether she felt there was basic acceptance of the child. The criteria on which these judgments were based were those generally employed by other members of the Clinic staff when evaluating the parent-child relationship. Parents were felt to be acceptant if they (1) displayed minimal anxiety in the presence of the child or hostility toward him, (2) displayed minimal defensiveness about the child's limitations, and (3) neither obviously rejected the child nor fostered overdependence.

Obviously, these criteria are highly subjective. Impressions would be expected to vary as a function of professional training and experience. Also, acceptance in parents is probably not a rigid factor but could be expected to vary itself from time to time. The impressions of the social worker were utilized in this study because (1) they were available for a fairly good-sized group of mothers, (2) each impression was made independently in time from every other impression, i.e. at or near the time of the initial interview, (3) the focus of the social worker's interviews was more directly concerned with evaluating the parental adjustment than was the case with other staff members, (4) the social worker was unaware of the purpose to which her impressions would later be put, and (5) she was a member of neither of the predominant religious groups compared in this study.

As an attempt to control possible sources of variance in the social worker's impressions of parents, she was asked to rate them on level of intelligence and social status. Kanner and Tietze, it will be recalled, implied that parents with the higher IQ's were more likely to develop guilt feelings and therefore might be expected to be less acceptant. Social status might be expected to operate in the same manner. On the intelligence variable, the social worker rated the mothers on a four-point scale: bright, good, fair, limited. On the social status variable, the mothers were rated also on a four-point scale: upper middle class, lower middle class, upper working class, lower working class. As it turned out, only 22 percent (of an N of 76) were judged as belonging to either of the middle-class groups. This was as expected in view of the general geographic location of St. Christopher's and the free services provided. The "lower working class" and "upper working class" – roughly equivalent to the upper lower and lower middle socio-economic groups – were designated in 78 percent of the social worker's rating.

Table 21-I shows the results of the comparison of the social worker's ratings of intelligence and social status with her impressions of acceptance of the child. Row one shows, by means of the chi square test, no statistical relationship between intelligence and acceptance. (The 4-point scale for intelligence was reduced to a 2-point scale for purposes of the analysis.) Row two shows that acceptance and social status were not significantly related. (Here too the 4-point scale for social status was reduced to a 2-point scale on which the small percentage of middle class mothers was *not* represented). Row three shows that the ratings of intelligence and social status made by the social worker were themselves unrelated.

The first three rows of Table 21-II show, therefore, that the social worker's impression of intelligence and social status of the mothers did not influence in one direction or another her

TABLE 21-I

CHI-SQUARE ANALYSES TO DETERMINE RELIABILITY AND
INDEPENDENCE OF ACCEPTANCE VARIABLE

Variables	N.	Chi Square	P.	Interpretation
Acceptance with intelligence	67	.19*	.70	No relationship
Acceptance with social status	53	.009*	.90	No relationship
Intelligence with social status	52	.36*	.50	No relationship
Groupings of writer with soc. worker	25	12.0*	.001	Significant relationship
Groupings of writer with other psychol.	25	17.6*	.001	Significant relations

*Indicates chi square corrected for continuity.

evaluation of the mother's level of acceptance. This in no way refutes the hypothesis that intelligence of the parent and level of acceptance may be related: it merely shows that for the particular group of parents seen in the clinic, the impression of level of acceptance and impression of intelligence and social status were unrelated for one observer. It confirms also the writer's knowledge of the character of the group, that is, that it tended to be relatively homogeneous for the variables of intelligence and social status. All levels of intelligence and social status were not equally represented, in other words, in the Clinic population.

The writer grouped into two piles the 76 cases which had been evaluated. These evaluations had been made, it will be recalled, at the time of the initial contact with the mother. In one pile were grouped those mothers who were felt to accept the child; in the other pile were grouped those who had some problem in acceptance. Of the 76 cases, 30 were felt to be of mothers who accepted, 46 of mothers who were felt not to accept.

Rows four and five of Table 21-I show the results of the two procedures by which the writer attempted to check the reliability of his groupings. Two sets of 25 cases were randomly selected from the pile of 76. One set was handed to the social worker herself, and the other, to a fellow psychologist at St Christopher's.

They were instructed to sort the piles by level of acceptance, as had been done by the writer for the 76 cases. The level of agreement between the groupings of the writer and social worker (see row 4, Table 21-I) reached 88 percent. Concordance between those of the writer and fellow psychologist reached 95 percent (see row 5, Table 21-I). Somewhat better agreement between psychologists was to be expected in view of the fact that their basis of judgment for grouping the cases was the verbal statement of the social worker; whereas, it is likely that additional cues were available to the social worker, other aspects and nuances bearing on acceptance which were unknown to the psychologists.

By the procedure described, it was shown that the groupings mady by the writer reflected with fair accuracy the actual intentions of the evaluations of acceptance. It should be made explicit that neither the social worker nor the writer's fellow psychologist was aware of the basis for the writer's request. Nor was the social worker aware, during the collection of her material, that it would later be used as a basis for judgment on the acceptance dimension.

As a person trained in the field of psychiatric social work, it may be fairly stated that the psychiatric terminology and a knowledge of psychoanalytic principles were both available to and utilized by the social worker in her clinical evaluations. It should also be made explicit that the individuals involved in gathering or making the evaluations and groupings were themselves non-Catholic.

RESULTS

Table 21-II contains the statistical treatment of information on relevant variables. 2 by 2 tables were set up by which they could be compared and the relationships evaluated. Each of the analyses is briefly interpreted.

As shown in the first row of Table 21-II, there is a relationship beyond chance expectancy (P. less than .001) between mothers' acceptance of the retarded child and religious background. The direction indicates that the Catholic mothers were the more acceptant. Of the 39 Catholic mothers, 25 accepted the child and

14 did not. Of the 37 non-Catholic mothers, 5 accepted the child and 32 did not. Breaking down the non-Catholic group by denomination: of 19 Protestant whites, 3 accepted and 16 did not; of 9 Protestant Negroes, 2 accepted and 7 did not; of 9 Jewish

TABLE 21-II

COMPARISON OF ACCEPTANCE WITH RELATIVELY
MORE OBJECTIVE VARIABLES OF STUDY

Variables	N.	Chi Square	P.	Interpretation
Religion with acceptance	76	20.5	.001	Catholic mothers more acceptant than non-Catholic
Age of child with acceptance	81	5.4	.02	Mothers more acceptant of younger than older retarded children
Age of child with acceptance by Catholics	39	1.8*	.20	No relationship, but trend shows Catholic mothers less acceptant with older children than younger
Age of child with religion	80	.39	.50	No relationship
Sex of child with acceptance	81	1.0	.30	No relationship
IQ of child with acceptance	81	.03	.80	No relationship
Job status of father with acceptance	70	.08	.80	No relationship
Job status of father with religion	67	.65	.30	No relationship
Number of siblings with acceptance by Catholic	36	.63*	.50	No relationship
Number of siblings by acceptance in non-Catholic	33	.003*	.95	No relationship
Age of mother with acceptance	74	.004	.95	No relationship
Religion with source of referral	76	.002	.95	No relationship
Religion with acceptance in medical outpatient referrals	39	3.2*	.10	No relationship, but trend shows Catholic mothers more acceptant
Religion with acceptance in other sources of referral in community	37	10.6*	.01	Catholic mothers more acceptant

*Indicates chi square corrected for continuity.

mothers, 0 accepted and 9 did not. The consistency of reaction in the non-Catholic groups is noteworthy. None failed to follow the clear trend.

In the second row of Table 21-II, a significant relationship is shown between age of the child and acceptance. The direction indicates that the younger the child (i.e. those three years and younger as opposed to those four years and older), the more acceptant the mother. Row three suggests that, although lacking statistical significance, Catholic mothers were less acceptant of older children as compared with younger children. Of 9 Catholic mothers with children three years or younger, 8 accepted the child and 1 did not. Of 30 Catholic mothers with children four years or older, 17 accepted and 13 did not.

Row four of Table 21-II shows that religious background and age of the child were unrelated. Thus Catholic mothers, for example, did not tend to have the younger children as compared with the non-Catholics. Row five shows that sex of the child and level of acceptance were unrelated. Thus, for example, Catholic mothers did not tend to have more children of one sex, non-Catholic mothers more children of the opposite sex. Row six shows that IQ of the child and level of acceptance were unrelated. Thus, the brighter children were not found to be the more accepted in the group seen in the Clinic. Row seven shows that job status of the father was unrelated to the level of acceptance of the mother. Row eight shows that job status of the father and religious background were unrelated. Thus, for example, Catholic fathers were neither of higher nor lower job status than non-Catholic fathers. Row nine shows that Catholic mothers were not more acceptant if they had larger families. Row ten shows that size of family was unrelated to level of acceptance in both Catholic and non-Catholic groups. Row eleven shows age of the mother at the present time was unrelated to level of acceptance. Younger mothers, therefore, were found to be neither less nor more acceptant. Row twelve shows that source of referral and religion were unrelated. Thus, both Catholic and non-Catholic parents were referred to the Clinic by the out-patient medical department and by other sources in the community with approximately equal frequency. Rows thirteen and fourteen both show that acceptance was more frequent in Catholic mothers regardless of the source of referral. This finding establishes the important point that Catholic mothers were more acceptant even when they had relatively little control over the selection of the hospital they wished their child to be seen at.

CONCLUSIONS

This study has provided some evidence that religious background and acceptance of the retarded child by mothers are related. Catholic mothers were found to be more acceptant than non-Catholic mothers. It is undoubtedly true that many aspects and nuances of the acceptance dimension could not be fully evaluated in a single clinical impression. On the other hand, it is to be expected that the evaluation of a skilled clinician with years of experience in the field of social work would incorporate at least a few of the main features of such a variable.

It was determined that in her evaluations, the social worker's impression of the mother's level of intelligence and social status did not specifically affect her judgment of acceptance. This finding tended to confirm the view that the population seen in the Clinic was relatively homogeneous for the factors of intelligence and social status. Yet another point bearing on the reliability of the acceptance evaluations was the fact that none of those involved in making them or the groupings were themselves Catholic. Thus, if indeed a judgmental bias existed, it should probably not have been expected to gravitate in the direction of the major finding of the study.

Of the numerous variables compared with level of acceptance only age of the child appeared to be significantly related. Mothers of the younger aged children tended to be more acceptant regardless of religious background. This finding seems quite consistent with clinical observation. Sarason has aptly pointed out that "when the nature of the child's condition is explained to the parents, their tendencies to resist the explanation and react in an emotional way are strengthened rather than decreased" (1963). With younger-aged children, many of the parents are not rejecting of the child but of the diagnosis. Their rejection tends also to get projected onto those who, legitimately or illegitimately, evaluate the child: professional diagnosticians, in-laws, other relatives, neighbors, strangers on the street, and so on.

One other finding that deserves special mention was that the relationship between religious background and acceptance held regardless of the source of referral of the parent. This meant that it made no difference whether parents wanted their children seen specifically at St. Christopher's. It is suspected that, given a comparable sample of Catholic and non-Catholic parents, the same results would have been obtained from a similar study conducted in one of the other children's hospitals in Philadelphia. In other words, it is felt that the results are generalizable.

To what can the better acceptance of the Catholic mothers be attributed? In the writer's opinion, it is due to the explicit absolution from personal guilt offered by their religious belief. Catholic doctrine provides considerable emotional support for mothers by its insistence that every child, normal or defective, is a special gift of God bestowed on the parents. Indeed, the birth of a retarded child may be perceived by the devout Catholic mother as a unique test of her religious faith. It is the writer's impression that the Catholic mother is much less subject to the kind of searching self-examination that often results in the development of strong guilt feelings. She is not so likely to ask herself, "what have I done to have such a child?" She is more willing to accept the fact that the birth of the child was the result of a decision made by high spiritual authority. It is not hard to see how acceptance of this decision is a major step along the path to acceptance of the child. Almost a pure case of thinking of this kind has been described in Eaton and Weil's remarkable study of the Hutterite group: "The Hutterite way of life provides social security from the womb to the tomb. The religious creed of the group gives the members a further guarantee of security beyond the tomb. It promises absolute salvation to all who follow its precepts" (1955). As far as the management of Hutterite defectives is concerned it is of considerable significance that none of them are institutionalized.

There is considerable social acceptance of mentally defective persons among the Hutterites. . . . Feelings of rejection by the parents exist, but they are usually well repressed. Other children are punished if they ridicule or take advantage of the afflicted child. . . . Defectives are not thought to be morally responsible for what they do. . . . In two cases where mildly defective individuals violated a number of religious rules, the community 'cancelled their baptism' rather than excommunicate them. By cancellation of their baptism they were reduced to the status of children, who are thought to be incapable of sinning and therefore can attain salvation automatically (1955).

In the writer's opinion, there is a similarity between the Hutterite and Catholic attitude toward defectives.

It should be appreciated that parents of a retarded child are often subject to extreme conflict: they are caught between strong feelings of love and hate toward the affected offspring. These contradictory feelings tend to result in the arousal of a guilt reaction. In the writer's experience, few parents openly admit to guilt. It is more likely to be seen "projectively," that is, in such reactions as a rejection or fostering of overdependency, or putting too much pressure on the child to perform. Too often counselors or psychotherapists focus on these aspects of the problem rather than directly on the problem of guilt.

This study has raised many more questions than it can answer at this time. One would like to know what distinguishes the 25 acceptant from the 14 nonacceptant Catholic mothers. One would like to know what the long-term implications are of the greater acceptance of the child by Catholics. On the basis of the present results, one would expect some interesting religious differences in parents of children who are institutionalized. One would like to know more about what acceptance itself means to the Catholic and non-Catholic parent.

Further study of the problem is continuing at St. Christopher's. It is hoped that other investigators will be stimulated to solidify the results and interpretations of this study. At the theoretical level, this study offers some evidence to illustrate the profound impact that religious attitudes may have on individuals at times of special stress. At the practical level, the results suggest a need for the therapeutic probing of guilt feelings in parents of retarded children. Perhaps also the results are partially generalizable to parents of children with other types of handicaps, physical or emotional. This will have to be decided by work that is yet to be done.

SUMMARY

In a group of mothers studied in the Federal Mental Retardation Clinic at St. Christopher's, a relationship was shown between religious background of parents and level of acceptance of the retarded child. Catholic mothers were judged to be more acceptant than non-Catholic mothers. The finding is interpreted as reflecting the benefit of greater emotional support given the Catholic mother by her religious faith, which explicitly absolves her from a sense of personal guilt in the birth of a retarded child.

The literature states that one of the central problems impeding optimal adjustment of parents is their strong sense of personal guilt. Since guilt is an important religious concept and is handled somewhat differently by the major religions, it is not particularly surprising that religious background should be a factor of some weight in parental adjustment. This study suggests that psychotherapeutic handling of parents give due consideration to the religious factor, since it may partially determine the extent to which guilt is operating to impede progress in adjustment. It emphasizes also the need for skillful probing of guilt feelings as an initial step toward improving the level of acceptance of the child.

REFERENCES

Eaton, J. W., and Weil, R. J.: *Culture and Mental Disorders: A comparative Study of the Hutterites and Other Populations.* Glencoe, Free Press, 1955.

Hastings, D.: Some psychiatric problems of mental deficiency. *Am. J. Ment. Defic., 52:*260-262, 1948.

Kanner, L.: Parents' feelings about retarded children. *Am. J. Ment. Defic., 57:*375-383, 1953.

Rheingold, Harriet: Interpreting mental deficiency to parents. *J. Consult. Psychol., 9:*142-148, 1945.

Sarason, S. *Psychological Problems in Mental Deficiency,* 2nd ed. New York, Harpers, 1953, pp. 331, 333, 339.

Scheimo, S. L.: Problems of helping parents of mental defective and handicapped children. *Am. J. Ment. Defic., 56:*42-47, 1951.

Waterman, J. J.: Psychogenic factors in parental acceptance of feebleminded children. *Dis. Nerv. System 9:*184-187, 1948.

Zuk, G. H.: Autistic distortions of parents of retarded children. *J. Consult. Psychol., 23,* No. 2., 1959.

Chapter 22

A Parent Speaks to Pastors on Mental Retardation

DOROTHY GARST MURRAY

IT was a crisp spring day in 1952. A young couple, parents of a thirteen-year-old retarded daughter, had stopped by my home to talk over initial plans for the organization of an Association for Retarded Children in our state. In the course of our conversation I happened to mention the fact that the understanding and concern of our pastor had meant much to both my husband and myself during the bleak days when we were going through the agonizing experience of adjusting to the reality that our third child, a winsome little son, was mentally retarded. In essence, the reply of my guest was something like this: "Well, that's certainly different from what Jean and I experienced. Although our minister has seen Sue at church every Sunday for years, and though I am sure he certainly must have sensed some of the emotional and spiritual torment through which we were passing during those first few years, he has never so much as mentioned to us the fact that Sue is different from our other daughter who is now in college. On the rare occasions when he visits in our home, he just acts as though Sue doesn't exist even though there are times when she behaves in a somewhat bizarre way. On Sundays he shakes hands with her in a somewhat perfunctory manner and there are times that I think Sue fully realizes that he is uncomfortable and ill at ease in her presence." He concluded somewhat wistfully but not without a trace of bitterness in his voice: "It must have been wonderfully rewarding

Note: Reprinted by permission of the author and *Pastoral Psychology, 13*:23-30, 1962.

to have had a spiritual adviser when you most needed him. It certainly didn't happen to us."

Less than six weeks later I was serving as co-director of a youth camp which included several ministers on the staff. Two of them came to me during the week to discuss the very same problem — only in reverse! Said one of them: "I have this young couple in my church who are going through an almost devastating spiritual upheaval because of the birth of a retarded child in the family. Both sets of grandparents are rather prominent community leaders and of course this child was awaited with all the eager expectation imaginable. For two years I have watched the parents gradually grow more bitter, more withdrawn from human contacts and more indifferent to things of spiritual value. Is there *anything* I can do? When I visit in the home they simply act as though the child doesn't exist, or is in no way different from other children even though he has physical characteristics which quite definitely mark him as mentally retarded. Is there any way such parents can be reached or helped by the church?"

These two instances, both of them actual experiences, illustrate rather clearly the impasse which seems to exist between the parents of mentally retarded children and those who are in position to minister to them spiritually. On the one hand are the parents, heart-broken and often conscience-smitten, struggling with feelings of deepest grief and the black despair which result from the loneliness they feel because they erroneously believe that no one cares about their problem. On the other hand are their spiritual advisers, wanting to offer words of understanding and encouragement yet hesitating to do so for fear of either embarrassing or offending the parents. Were these two isolated instances, one could dismiss them lightly as just "one of those things." Unhappily, they are not isolated instances. Rather, they are almost a set pattern which has existed for years, and those of us who come in contact with hundreds of parents of retarded children hear the same stories with variations repeated over and over again. Neither the parents of retarded children nor the clergymen are responsible for the condition which has existed for so many years. It was so simply because since the beginning of mankind all conditions of mental abnormality have been viewed as

St. Paul might have expressed it, "through a glass, darkly." A glass darkened by misinformation, by sheer superstition, by fear of what could not be understood, and by a very natural human tendency to turn aside from any situation with which one felt unable to cope.

Today, however, the opportunity for obtaining a clearer and more objective view of mental retardation places upon every minister the obligation for more adequately meeting the spiritual needs of family units which include a retarded child. With the wealth of information concerning mental retardation which has been made available in the past ten years by the National Association for Retarded Children, professional persons in any walk of life can no longer excuse themselves for failing to meet the needs of the retarded. The plea of ignorance or of not knowing what to do is no longer a valid one. Those who fail in this respect today could more accurately be charged with indifference than with ignorance. To know not is bad, but to care not is worse.

This article has been written for the purpose of helping the pastor to develop a more compassionate concern for the families of the retarded within his fellowship. It is written, we believe, with some fair degree of understanding because the writer is not only the mother of a retarded child but is also the daughter of a Protestant minister, the sister-in-law of two ministers, the niece of six, and the aunt of two more! Furthermore, personal friends include ministers from at least seven different Protestant denominations, two Catholic priests, and a Jewish rabbi. A very large segment of my adult life has been spent working with clergymen on various boards and committees — so with this background we have some degree of understanding of the pastor's problems as well as with the problems of parents.

Perhaps it would be wise to emphasize here that our own family experience in relation to a spiritual ministry during this crisis in our lives was a most satisfactory one. We were fortunate in having not only our pastor but a number of other ministers as warm personal friends, and their concern for us at this time was conveyed in many ways. Our own case, however, was not typical of what happens to the majority of parents. After ten years of talking and working with hundreds of parents of retarded children,

I am convinced that there are certain things that clergymen should *not* do in their attempt to bring spiritual healing. Perhaps if we look first at some of the things we believe they should not do, this will provide a logical steppingstone to some of the things we believe they can and should do.

DO NOT ATTEMPT TO PLAY GOD

The first cry which goes up from the hearts of all parents of retarded children is the same that has haunted mankind through the ages when faced with the unanswerable question: "Why?" Perhaps it is selfishness which prompts us to cry out, "Why did this have to happen to us?" but it is sheer agony of soul which causes one to ask, "Why did this happen to this child? Why must this innocent one be denied the natural birthright of every individual of an intelligent and reasoning intellect? Why, God, why?" Sometimes in their anxiety to be of help, a few clergymen feel the necessity of trying to answer this most difficult of all questions. And in too many instances, parents are left more confused than ever by the theological answers which are given. One of my aged and much loved clergymen friends said to me one time: "We ministers finally have to learn that there is no pat little theological answer to *this* question and the sooner we learn it, the better for all concerned."

The following succinct observation was made by a young professional friend of mine in an article prepared for his local Civitan Newsletter in relation to this very pertinent and painful question. It is not necessary that we completely agree with the philosophy he has set forth, but I believe we can all agree that he has given us some worthwhile food for thought:

> A great deal of material has been written attempting to explain why retardation is visited upon humanity, and upon those certain parents. Some of these articles are written by laymen, many by religious leaders of all denominations. Some make the grave mistake of trying to prove that a retarded child is a blessing in disguise, or that he is somehow part of God's plan for the burdened parents. Other articles wrestle with the questions which philosophers have kicked around for centuries — the question of evil in the world, and of whom does it visit and why. It seems to me that the apparent need for

explanation for things like retardation reflects upon our maturity, if not, indeed, upon the maturity of some of our religions which may actually attempt to explain too many things which cannot really be explained. If we look the facts squarely in the face as mature adults, we must admit that we really know few of the answers we would like to know. Our intelligence and our observations tell us, with regard to retardation, that nature makes mistakes, that doctors make mistakes, and that accidents of infections can happen to anyone. Further explanation is simply unavailable to us. The person who can accept these facts and can accept the fact that this has happened to him because that is the way the ol' ball bounced, is rid of an inward struggle which would never lead to anything constructive. He is then free to turn his energies and his talents to *doing* something about retardation. Doing something for his child and for all children. If he spends his energies, instead, worrying about problems which cannot be solved or questions for which there are no answers, he will produce nothing and will perhaps destroy himself.

In my own personal struggle I was more fortunate than most. Many, many years before in my early youth a wise father had taught me the philosophy that "sorrow can either make you or break you; grief can make you better or it can make you bitter — its altogether up to the individual." I suppose I was somewhat stubbornly determined that this "individual" must be made instead of broken. Although my father had died more than ten years before the birth of our retarded child, having this ingrained philosophy to build upon, together with the complete and unfailing belief and trust that all things work together for good to those who love God, it was a much quicker step for me to leave the "Why?" stage and step into a more mature "How?" one. Parents will rise up and call blessed those clergymen who endeavor to gently but firmly lead them from the stage of asking, "Why did this thing happen to me?" to the stage of asking "How can I best use what has happened to the glory of God and my neighbor's good?" It is a more complicated and time-consuming road to follow than to just attempt a pat answer to the "Why?" but in the end it is a far more rewarding one for all concerned.

DO NOT TRY TO COUNSEL BEYOND YOUR DISCIPLINE

Do not attempt to counsel or give guidance in an area which

more properly belongs to a psychiatrist, a physician, a psychologist, or some other professional discipline working with the child and parents. We doubt that there is any area of human endeavor in which the trite saying, "A little learning is a dangerous thing" is more true than in the area of mental retardation. One may somewhat facetiously conclude that since the skeleton of mental retardation has been removed from the closet, many persons are "rattling dem bones" more for the sake of playing on this popular bandwagon rather than for the sake of any good they may be doing! We highly recommend that all clergymen take the time to read and digest some of the current material published in the field of mental retardation, but we also would gently suggest that they refrain from considering themselves final authorities on the matter after having done so. The clergyman who attempts to diagnose, to recommend treatment, to help make decisions in regard to the care of the retarded individual or otherwise give professional advice out of his field will more often than not fail in the very area in which he is most needed and is most qualified to serve: that of helping the parents to retain their faith in God as a loving and merciful Father. Many parents, when faced with this severe disappointment in their personal lives, lose faith in themselves and their ability to cope with a problem which they realize will never have a final and permanent solution so long as the child lives. Worse than this, they lose faith in God as a God of love, of mercy and justice. The clergyman who can lead them to a stage of spiritual maturity that enables them to see life as still worth living and God as still loving and worthy of being loved, has done his part of the job — and done it well.

DO NOT CATEGORIZE PARENTS BECAUSE THEY HAVE GIVEN BIRTH TO A RETARDED CHILD

For years too many professional persons have assumed that certain "symptoms" were characteristic of *all* parents of retarded children merely because they were characteristic of *some* of them. According to a popular and much overdone concept all such parents carried a "guilt complex" — but then who does not? To continue, many such parents had "rejected" their child so that little could be done to help either them or the child; such parents were supposed to be "on the defensive" against humanity; such parents believed that "this just couldn't happen to them" — and on and on and on. Some very well qualified persons have come to feel that the over use of these well-worn phrases usually arises from the fact that the professional person in question feels his own inadequacy in knowing how to counsel with the parents in a constructive manner. This matter of so-called typing of parents is something of an insult to the majority of them and will be studiously avoided by the wise and judicious clergyman. Few clergymen would like to be measured or judged as individuals by the most incompetent and inadequate members of their own vocation. Neither do they want their vocation as a whole to be judged by the quality of its third- and fourth-rate members. Just so, parents of retarded children resent being placed in neat little categories just because they have given birth to a retarded child. True, many of the same problems are common to all parents of retarded children. But our methods of dealing with them are as different and varied as the parents themselves. The wise clergyman will recognize this fact and make use of it in counseling with parents. He will not automatically accept some of the well-worn and overdone cliches which have frequently been used in describing the parents of retarded children.

Perhaps at this point some readers are no doubt impatiently asking themselves the question: "But what *can* we do to help such parents? Surely there must be something we *should* do as well as refrain from doing!" And there is.

LET PARENTS KNOW YOU CARE

First of all, in the initial stage of shock and grief, just letting parents know that you *care* helps more than you can ever know. A lot of words are not necessary at this point — counseling can come later, much later, but at least let the parents know that you know of their concern for the child, and that you are daily remembering them so that they may have the necessary spiritual courage to keep going from one day to the next. If you feel it wisest not to approach them verbally, write a letter. Details are unnecessary — merely let them know that you realize that they are carrying a deep burden of concern for their child and that you share this with them, waiting for the time when you may be of some concrete assistance. Do place in your church library several of the excellent books and booklets which are now available on the subject of mental retardation. But do not stop with merely placing them there. Read and study them yourself so that you can speak intelligently of the problem when the appropriate time presents itself. Call attention to this reading matter through book reviews, notices in the church bulletin, announcements at informal meetings, etc. Good reading material will not only help the parents to better understand their own emotions and those of their handicapped child, but it will also tend to make members of the congregation much more understanding of the problems and heartache with which the parents are coping. Do invite a member of the local Association for Retarded Children to meet informally with a group of your church schoolteachers and officers to interpret the work being done in your community for the mentally retarded. You will never believe what it does for the spiritual morale of parents to discover that their church really cares about the needs of children like their own.

A number of excellent films on mental retardation are now available, and a discussion based on one of these films could provide a most enlightening evening of study for your staff of church school teachers. Such a study may lead to the development of a Sunday morning church session for the retarded in your entire area in case such does not already exist. Many such classes are now being held throughout the country and the retarded have the privilege of attending a service of worship geared to their own needs and understanding while their parents are free to worship at the church of their choice. One father told me recently that neither he nor his wife had been to church regularly for years, but when their little four-year-old mongoloid son began begging to go to "his" church school every Sunday morning both parents rediscovered the value and need of religious nurture in their own lives. Truly, in this case, "a little child did lead them"!

ENCOURAGE SEEKING PROFESSIONAL HELP

Do encourage parents of these children to seek professional help and guidance for the child if you suspect they have not already done so. Many times parents are prone to postpone having their child seen by professional persons because they have not developed the necessary courage to come face to face with the unpleasant reality they may suspect. These parents should be helped to understand that the earlier a child is placed in the hands of competent professional persons, the greater will be the possibility for development of his limited faculties. Many states now have diagnostic clinics to which mentally retarded children and infants may be taken for a thorough diagnosis and prognosis. (You may obtain information on the location of such clinics by writing to the National Association for Retarded Children, 420 Lexington Avenue, New York, New York, 10017.) Often the visit to a diagnostic clinic is the first step in the direction of healing which comes to parents of the retarded. Once they have faced up to the situation as it is, and have had the opportunity to talk at length with the members of a diagnostic team, all of whom have a thorough understanding of the problems with which they are struggling, the parents are then better prepared to plan constructive action for meeting the needs of their child.

Do avoid advising parents either to institutionalize their child or to refrain from doing so. It may be well to give them the benefit of your thinking if they request it, but emphasis should always be clearly made that this is a decision which must be reached by the parents themselves without undue pressure from *anyone.* In past years some clergymen, as well as many physicians, routinely recommended to parents that they "put away the child and forget about him." Such advice was not only heartless but contrary to every God-given instinct with which human beings are endowed. We were not made to forget — we were made to remember. And remember we do — regardless of whether the child is with us or away from us. I have seen these children by the hundreds at the state institution where my own son makes his home. I have seen them in other similar institutions throughout the country — literally thousands of them utterly abandoned by their families on the well-meaning but tragically mistaken advice of professional people. The question of institutionalization as such is far too complicated and too lengthy to go into here, but the pastor should be aware of these facts: less than 7 percent of the mentally retarded individuals of the nation now reside in private or public institutions yet the vast majority of institutions are from 20 to 40 percent overcrowded, and many of them have lengthy waiting lists of from two to five hundred. Only a limited few can admit a child immediately upon application, and for the average state institution the waiting period is often from one to three years. There is not now, nor will there likely ever be, sufficient institutional space, either public or private, to provide care for all the mentally retarded regardless of how severe the home situation may be. In the face of this stern reality, every clergyman should cooperate with all efforts to establish local facilities to provide care and training for the mentally retarded.

These, then are some of the few things the pastor *can* do. Other ideas will suggest themselves as he becomes familiar with the overall aspects of mental retardation as the significant social problem that it is.

In conclusion, a few general observations relating to the problem may be valid. It has been most interesting to me to note that some of the most severe critics of the failure of the clergy in bringing help to the parents of retarded children have been ministers who, themselves, were fathers of retarded children. In ten years of work on a local, state, and national level, I have come to know many ministers who are parents, and almost without fail they agree unanimously that gaining the interest of the ministers in their area has been a difficult task. One consecrated minister who not only served faithfully in his local group but also served on our state board said to me several times: "We can get everyone in our area interested in our organization but our local ministerial association. The women's clubs, the P.T.A.'s, the Civitans, Kiwanis — all of these have shown a very definite interest in the programs we are trying to promote, but somehow the clergymen just don't seem to care."

This sentiment has been echoed not once or twice but many times by people from many different faiths and in many parts of the nation. All too often the explanation which follows goes something like this: "Our ministers are too busy trying to settle the problems of the masses to know or to care what happens to their communicants as individuals." Perhaps this indictment is too severe. No doubt in many cases it is an unjust criticism brought about by the spiritual immaturity or anxiety of the one uttering it, and I am certain that in some situations it is an indictment which is made because the speaker has a misconception of the role which should be most properly fulfilled by clergymen in general. But the expression or its equivalent occurs so very frequently that it should cause a conscientious clergyman to probe thoughtfully and deeply into his own relationship with those who look to him for spiritual succor.

Perhaps the real problem with which we are struggling is not to develop methods or techniques or advice on "how" to counsel the parents of the retarded. Perhaps the basic assessment we need to make is to ask ourselves if we really care about them enough to be truly concerned about their struggle toward achieving an element of faith and peace in learning to live with their problem. Most clergymen will probably agree that their success in helping a person to resolve any problem is in almost direct ratio to the warmth of the relationship that existed before the problem presented itself. If one has proven himself a dedicated shepherd to his flock with warm and sincere compassion for their needs, words are not too important in times of spiritual stress and techniques can frequently be pitched in file thirteen.

One's spiritual ministry is largely a matter of the heart, and what comes from the heart speaks to the heart. Compassionate concern will communicate itself not only to the parents but to the retarded individual as well, regardless of how limited he or she may be. But the concern must be a sincere and honest one and not rise from shallow pretense in an attempt to make parents feel good. Sorrow is an alchemist that strips aside all sham and pretense — not only from those who grieve but also from those to whom they bare their souls. Parents filled with grief know instinctively when an expression of concern is genuine or whether it is a perfunctory performance of one's obligation. As for being too busy about more important matters to share one's spiritual strength with those who need it most, may we modestly suggest that one should reflect deeply upon the fact that our Lord and Master never got that busy! Instead of asking, "Do I know enough?" or "Am I using the right technique?" or "Can I spare the time?" perhaps the *real* question with which we need to struggle is: "Do I *care* enough?"

Chapter 23

The Pastoral Care and
Counseling of Families of the
Mentally Retarded

ROBERT PERSKE*

THE mother of a thirteen-year-old mentally retarded son was heard to say, "My pastor is a good counselor. He counsels many of his parishioners. But, every time I go to talk to him about Jimmy, he refers me to the chaplain at the institution for the mentally retarded. Why won't he counsel me about my son? Are we that different?"

This statement was given to a social worker friend of mine who in turn shared it with me. As my friend and I discussed the situation of this family, we felt this particular pastor was more than capable of ministering to the needs of these people — if he only knew it. He did not need any new and strange counseling techniques. The counseling methods he now uses would be sufficient. It is true, he could have used some knowledge of mental retardation. But, it was our hunch that he could have learned all he needed to know about this human situation by letting himself get involved in a pastoral way with this family.

The following are a few considerations about the human predicament of mental retardation which pastors seem to need. It is hoped these considerations cast light on some of the major issues and problems in such a way that the pastor will recognize he already has the skill to deal with the situation. It is further hoped

Note: Reprinted by permission of the author and *Pastoral Psychology*, *19*:21-28, 1968.
*Chaplain Supervisor, Kansas Neurological Institute; Staff Affiliate, The Menninger Foundation, Topeka, Kansas.

that these clarifications will help the pastor feel more free to involve himself with these struggling families and to utilize the pastoral skills he already possesses that are so greatly needed. I have the very strong hunch that many pastors are on the verge of discovering how very helpful they can be to the families of the mentally retarded. It is my hope that what is written here will help them in this discovery.

THE ENORMOUS WIDTH OF THE
MENTAL RETARDATION RANGE

When one thinks of the many different types of people who can be labeled "mentally retarded" he cannot help being overwhelmed. A "mentally retarded" person can be a person in a bed, barely living off the cortex of the brain with a frightfully feeble heart, almost imperceptively pumping blood through the body. He may have little or no consciousness of himself or life around him. He literally must be kept alive by others. On the other hand, a "mentally retarded" person can be one who is near normal in his intellectual functioning. And yet, he's able to adapt to society and have specific talents that are superior to those who are labeled "normal." The label "mental retardation" is supposed to cover all persons who function between these extremes. In fact, the range of mental retardation is much wider than the range of those who are called normal!

Every now and then the clinical staff at the children's institution where I work must struggle with the problem of "patient placement." At these times we try to figure out where each child belongs in our hospital. The debate sometimes becomes hot and frustrating. It's an impossibly difficult problem. But we try to solve it as best we can for each child, or some children would have to live alone in the hall.

This may help the pastor to see that the wide range of mental retardation allows no general answers; there are no two mentally retarded persons who are alike. Every family confronted with the problem of a mentally retarded child will have their own tensions, their own weaknesses and strengths, their own limits and possibilities, all of which must be taken into consideration. Every one of these families will have to ask a staggering number of pat questions. But, they must be answered afresh as if they had never been asked before. "Is it best to keep Susie at home or send her to the institution?" "Will Jim be able eventually to live in the community or will he need sheltered care all of his life?" "Should Sally be placed in regular school classes requiring minimal study, or should she be assigned to a special education class?" "Why did God let this happen?" "What horrible thing have I done that Billy was born this way?" These are only the beginnings of a long series of questions that must be raised for which no general answer will be found.

To me, this is what makes pastoral work with families of the mentally retarded such an exciting thing. One must let himself get involved with a family in a pastoral way and struggle along with them in situation after situation as each comes up. Yet, no one can predict how the family will solve a certain situation until they've struggled with it for a time. The complete absence of pat answers forces the pastor to move into these situations in such a way that he must use his best senses and his greatest creative talents to help the family solve each situation as it arises. This makes it an intriguing pastoral work!

THE PARENT'S PROCESS OF
UNDERSTANDING AND ACCEPTING

Stop and think how you would feel if you were told your child is mentally retarded! At first, this would be very hard to understand and accept. You would begin a process in your life that would never completely end. At first, you would *deny* that anything is wrong. You simply wouldn't let yourself believe it. Later, you would start believing it and you would feel *guilty*. You would be sure that you must have done something wrong to cause your child's mental retardation. You would search for that one cause as if you could go back and make it right. Still later, you would try to place *blame* on others. You might blame your doctor, or your spouse, or anyone else who might have been negligent. You would become interested in people who claimed to cure mentally retarded children. You wouldn't care if other people did call them "quacks." You would want to believe in them for the sake of your child. During these struggles, you might play with the idea that your child is evil and the product of evil, or that your child is a special messenger from God sent to you for a "special" reason. At other times you might secretly wish the child would die.

Why does the parent of a mentally retarded child have all these different feelings and thoughts? Such different feelings and thoughts would come because the person is involved in a long-term psychological problem. He is struggling to move away from all urges to *rid himself of the problem* and to grow day by day to the point where he can *learn to live with the situation.* Such a parent would be growing toward understanding and *accepting his child as the specific and unique human being he really is* with both his realistic weaknesses and his realistic strengths.

I have known families over the years who have moved strongly away from the urge to get rid of the problem. Each year they seem to come to a newer and warmer understanding of the mentally retarded person in their midst or at the institution. The process in their life has been beautiful to behold: the gains, the strength, the personal warmth, and the skill in making creative decisions because of it. And even if I told them of the noble process I saw, they would be sure to reply, "Don't brag about me too soon. I'm still working on it, you know."

On the other hand, there are other families who are not able to accept and understand. They still work day by day avoiding, rejecting, trying to get rid of the problem. Knowing of the healthy process that can take place in some, a pastor cannot help trying to help the others be aware of it too.

Any pastor has an excellent opportunity to be aware of this process toward understanding and accepting that can take place, and to observe it with respect and awe. He also has the opportunity from time to time to assist them with this process in a strong but kind way.

Sometimes, a pastor can get caught up in theologizing about the process. I personally feel that the better job we can do in understanding and accepting the mentally retarded the better we can believe what God must feel toward us. For then we can come closer to believing that God loves, understands, and accepts us as we are and does not wait until we change into what He wants us to be before He starts loving us.

THE MENTALLY RETARDED CAN AROUSE REPULSIONS

Many hate to admit they can be repelled by the mentally retarded to some degree. Sometimes the "pulling away" is observed as an overt act. At other times it is done in more subtle ways. This can lead to a most interesting problem. Why is it that we sometimes feel repelled?

> Is it because we have never learned to live graciously with *failure* in our own lives? Failure can make us feel guilty.
>
> Is it because we have strong needs for *stimulating relationships* only? Is it hard to give to people who cannot give as much in return?
>
> Is it because our *feelings of omnipotence* are tested? We like to think we are powerful "life-changers." Because we cannot change them into what we want them to be, does this make us feel helpless?
>
> It is because emotionally we still see these things as the *results of evil?* We used to. We say we do not anymore. But, sometimes do we not look at them and wonder if "somebody sinned"?
>
> Is it because one of our greatest fears is that we will be found to be *stupid and insignificant?* Is this one of our most closely guarded fears: that we will be found to be a "nothing"? (Tillich did write about our fear of nonbeing, you know.) Do we sometimes refuse to associate with those who remind us of one of our own greatest fears?
>
> Is it because in America we hold high the *myth of human progress?* We try so hard to believe that man is always making positive development, always moving onward and upward toward achieving the brilliant mind, the beautiful body, and the pure heart which none of us will ever have fully in this life. Maybe we hate to admit that human process does move backward and downhill at times.
>
> Is it more comfortable and secure to keep our *relationships narrowed* to those who live, function, and think like ourselves? Can we dare do this when society has now begun to learn that greater creativity comes from struggling with the individual differences of people even if it is risky?

Notice that the questions raised do not force us to ask, "What is wrong with the mentally retarded person?" Instead, the tables are turned. They force us to ask, "What is wrong with *us* that makes us want to avoid the mentally retarded?"

In the motion picture "A Child Is Waiting," a sensitive story about mental retardation, a warm and healthy father of a retarded girl talks to the angry, frustrated and repulsed father of a mentally retarded boy. In the course of a somewhat heated conversation, the warm father exclaims, "Can't you see? *They* don't know they are a tragedy." The mentally retarded never know they are a tragedy until they see it in our faces and our actions. Someday, someone may do an intensive study of this repulsion and find that this is our problem and not the problem of the mentally retarded.

THE NEED TO FIND REALISTIC FUNCTIONAL LIMITS

How hard it is to find and accept our limits. But, if we are to be healthy emotionally, we must learn to know and live with the things we can and cannot do. How much harder it is if a boy is not an athlete but his father has high hopes that he will someday play fullback for Nebraska University. How hard it is if we have high hopes of being an "Einstein" but cannot even add the figures in our checkbook accurately. All of us have wishes to be the best person, the healthiest person, the smartest person we can be. But we must keep our struggles within limits, within the range of our own capabilities.

The family of the retarded person has a harder time with realistic limits. Every member of the family must work at knowing the limits of their retarded child, brother, or sister. All of them must work kindly and affectionately in helping the mentally retarded person to know what he really can and what he really cannot do in the life he is living. The pastor is another person who can be exceedingly helpful to all in helping them find and accept the limits of the retarded person. Then, when the limits are set and accepted, everyone seems to relax and the child can work on realistic goals.

Abnormal tension will always come when there is an inequity between what a mentally retarded person can realistically accomplish and what he or someone else believes he can do. I have vivid recollections of the horribly painful time a sixteen-year-old boy was having in a family where mother and father were both high school teachers and his three sisters were straight 'A' students. This family had to see that Jim had realistic limits, making it impossible for him to be what the other members of the family were, intellectually. In another case, a pastor continued to encourage an eighteen-year-old, mildly retarded boy in his urge to become a minister. Somehow the pastor was oblivious to the parents' subtle statements that "he'll never make it." Later, this boy's hopes were crashed. They had to crash. He had to find his realistic limits. The pastor could have done much to help him with this particular struggle.

THE THRILL IN SMALL GAINS

Once a pastor is aware of the realistic limits of a mentally retarded person, he can join the family in knowing the thrills that come from observing the small gains he or she accomplishes. This is true in early childhood as well as in adulthood. The retarded child has such a struggle to move from his crib and to live, move and adapt in the world, that each gain is a tremendous thing to him and the family. And when a pastor is aware of the fight and struggle that must be found in a retarded child in order to develop, he cannot help joining the family in cheering the child on.

These small gains are important:

When a child learns to sit up in his crib, he can raise his intellectual functioning and adaption at a tremendous rate. The ceiling is not half as stimulating as watching everything that goes on around him.

If the child can crawl, he can move about in his world and explore more things. Again, he can increase his functioning and adaption at a tremendous rate.

If a child can learn to walk — bingo! — he can really move about in the world. If he learns to run, it is even better.

If he can be toilet trained, he has gained a real milestone in our society. Now he's really ready to travel and learn!

If he learns to feed himself and clothe himself and take care of his own teeth, hands and face, how proud everyone in the family can become.

If he learns to come in out of the rain, he can be trusted even farther. He can feel proud.

If he can talk and ask for things or offer things or express himself — both likes and dislikes — he reaches the high status of being a verbal communicator!

In normal children all this is taken for granted. But members of the family of the mentally retarded can never take the gains in childhood development for granted. Every gain is important. It amounts to what can be called *survival learning.* In one family, everyone made it their task to help little Joe develop. And each gain Joe made was cause for a party, a real celebration!

But these small gains do not stop in early childhood. They continue throughout the life of the mentally retarded person. It is still a cause for celebration when a retarded person learns to ride the bus alone, or proves he can hold down a job shining shoes, washing dishes, serving as a farmhand, or a janitor, or building up his own bank account, buying his own television set or bicycle, maintaining himself in a rented room, paying his own income tax, attending church and serving as an usher, to mention only a few accomplishments.

One can envision that the pastors, the neighborhood friends, the other helping professionals will be the ones to mark the growth and conduct the celebrations for the middle aged and the elderly mentally retarded persons.

THEIR HUMAN EXPERIENCE CAN BE RICH!

We are learning from the mentally retarded that human experience is a relative thing. It depends on how hard one works to solve a problem or accomplish a goal:

> A mentally retarded teen age girl sang a solo from memory at a church youth fellowship meeting. She had never done it before. She worked and worked at learning it and singing it. When she finally sang it, she experienced the same thrill that you or I would have singing the solo lead in a Broadway muscial.
>
> A retarded boy with atrophied legs was learning to wheel his chair up a ramp. He worked for months at getting to the top. No one would help him even though he sometimes cried and begged for help. Then one day he did it. At that point this boy experienced the same thrill that you or I might if we reached the summit of Mount Everest.
>
> A teen age boy on industrial assignment was able to save and deposit two hundred dollars of his earnings. When he showed me his bankbook, he experienced the same sense of accomplishment that you or I would know if we were made the president of the bank.

How hard these persons have to work to be able to hold a job and to get along in society. For those who make it, they have every right to be thrilled.

Philosophers have struggled for years trying to find and describe "the good life." They have discussed "the highest good for the highest number," "the rewards and dangers of Hedonism," and such things as "truth, beauty and goodness." But, one wonders if the mentally retarded could teach us an axiom as well. For them, "the good life" is being able to solve one's own problems at one's own level with his own abilities. This is certainly true of the mentally retarded. It seems to be true of us as well. The only difference is that we struggle at a different level with different abilities.

PARENTS NEED TO FEEL THEY HAVE
FULFILLED THEIR RESPONSIBILITY

Because the predicament of mental retardation is such a painful yet enigmatic thing, the parents are always haunted by the question, "Did I do everything I possibly could for my child?" In some cases the parents go far beyond the call of their responsibility. In other cases, helping professionals and institutions take over and do many of the things the parents should have been doing. This can have tragic consequences to the relationship of the mentally retarded child and his family. In other cases, the parents feel so helpless that they do nothing. They may need help in seeing some of the realistic things they can do.

It is my hunch that the pastor, more than any other helping professional, will be the one to help parents evaluate whether they have fulfilled their responsibility to the child or not. One of the chaplains at our institution conducted the funeral service of a ten-year-old severely retarded child who lived on one of the wards. After the funeral, the parents had their final conversation with the chaplain. They felt the need to review the whole situation of their child from the time of his birth, early development, institutionalization, and the illness that caused his death. In the course of the conversation the father said, "Chaplain, there's a lot of things we don't understand about Mike. And, we never will. But, now that it's all over, I don't feel too bad. God knows we did everything we humanly could for Mike." Pastors have an excellent opportunity to help the family see if they have been doing too much, too little, or if they have been doing everything humanly possible in exhausting their responsibility for the mentally retarded person in their family.

AN OPPORTUNITY TO PERFECT THE
SKILL OF "SUSTAINING"

What a wonderful opportunity a pastor has to test this oft neglected Hiltnerian dimension of pastoral work.* All of us have been active in using our ministry as both healing and guiding forces. So often we get impatient when we cannot "move" things or "change" things. Here is a situation where the pastor must be able to be the stable, kind, and strong person who is not manipulated or "faded out," nor does he "move in" directly with "heavy feet." Instead he becomes the strong person who comes to the home and sometimes does nothing but be "with" the family and to listen without giving any easy solutions. In essence his warmth and stability can be the thing that keeps the family going.

A Christmas card was sent to a pastor who had an ongoing, healthy relationship with the family of a mentally retarded girl. The card contained the following note:

> You never pushed us.
> You never tried to explain anything away.
> You never tried to give easy answers.
> You just came and let yourself be yourself.
> Thank you for being what you are to us.

Hiltner emphasized the fact that there will be many times when we as pastors can do nothing more than be with people and "standing by." This is also a pastoral skill that takes much practice in order to "stand by" in a helpful and a stable way.

SOME CRITICAL SITUATIONS TO EXPECT

There are critical situations which bring about healthy or unhealthy changes in the lives of parents of the mentally retarded. The following are a few which the pastor may expect:

1. *A parent may attempt to "dump" the whole problem in the*

---

*Hiltner, Seward: *Preface To Pastoral Theology*. Nashville, Abingdon Press, 1957.

pastor's lap as if to say, "You're the strong one; take over my problem; you tell me what to do; you do the work for me." (God knows we all wish we could get rid of our problems that way.) This can force the pastor to be defensive and to withdraw from the problem. Then the parent can withdraw saying, "See, my pastor won't help me." Good pastors have the knowledge and the skill to deal with such behavior in a therapeutic way.

2. *Exacerbated conflict between man and wife* is always a danger. In the painful struggle to place blame, the spouse becomes a ready target in the irrational attempt to handle his or her own feelings of anxiety and guilt. It is sad to say that the divorce rate among the parents of mentally retarded persons is tremendously high. Many of these divorces are unnecessary! A pastor who is aware of this danger may be a very helpful person when anxiety and guilt feelings are running high.

3. *The child can become a scapegoat* for every failure and problem the family faces. "I lost my job because I'm always worrying about Jim." "I wasn't elected cheerleader because I have a brother in the special ed. room." "I could really love you like a wife should if it wasn't for Jimmy." Anyone can see how devastating this can be to the personality of the mentally retarded person as well as the members of the family who are unaware of what they are doing.

4. *The sibling problems* may or may not be serious. In some cases the brothers and sisters are stronger and more healthy persons because a retarded person is in the home. In other cases, the brothers and sisters suffer in their own growth and development because of the mentally retarded person in their midst. A pastor could be helpful in evaluating what the presence of the mentally retarded child is doing to the siblings.

5. There will nearly always be *death wishes* in the families of the mentally retarded. (This shouldn't be alarming since aggressive fantasies are present in even the most warm and wholesome relationships at certain times.) Often these death wishes are denied and pushed back. They can cause real problems in the relationship with the mentally retarded person. A skilled pastor may be very helpful in the struggle to recognize them,

understand, and deal with them.

6. *Religious attitudes and beliefs* often undergo radical change. In many cases, those who were not active in church will become active. Others who were extremely active become less active. They may even drop out or change church affiliation. Mental retardation comes as such a blow to most persons that their theological beliefs cannot help being shaken and reconstituted on another level.

LOCAL ASSOCIATIONS FOR RETARDED CHILDREN

I have yet to find a local association for retarded children which would not be glad to cooperate wholeheartedly with any pastor who asks for help and guidance regarding a specific problem of mental retardation. They know the community resources. They have read the recent popular books in the field and usually have a library containing them. They have a wealth of information at their fingertips, ranging from recent legislation for the handicapped to the most recent breakthroughs in the care and treatment of the mentally retarded.

This group of hard-working people serves as a major communication vehicle teaching the country the latest developments in the field. The National Association for Retarded Children, 420 Lexington Avenue, New York, N.Y. 10017, produces an excellent newspaper entitled *Children Limited.* This paper seems to let nothing of significance escape notice. One can find write-ups of the latest medical and psychological breakthroughs, reviews of the newest popular books in the field, as well as reviews of plays and motion pictures which deal with mental retardation.

Pastors are always welcome at the monthly meetings of the local associations. In fact, some pastors have become so interested in their work that they have joined and take an active part. But, whether he becomes involved with the association or not, the pastor can count on them as a ready resource at any time.

CONCLUSION

It is hoped that the foregoing has cast some new light on the issues and problems the families of the mentally retarded will face. And with these clarifications, it is hoped that the pastor will feel more free to involve himself with these struggling families who need him so very much.

This is a new and great day for the mentally retarded and their families. In less than fifteen years we have moved from smuggling the mentally retarded into the back doors of churches for special classes. Now, they walk into the front doors. The congregations and the communities are showing an added interest in their life situation, their development, and their welfare. Every up-to-date public school system is developing special education classes. Day care centers and residential care centers have progressed at a tremendous rate. Now we are beginning to see the retarded as human beings with weaknesses and strengths just as we are human beings with weaknesses and strengths. We now find these families have much to teach us about life and faith. The pastor has a remarkable opportunity to be an active participant in this hopeful process.

Chapter 24

The Pastoral Care of Parents
of Mentally Retarded Persons

SIGURD D. PETERSEN*

THE nature of pastoral care is well understood by the readers of *Pastoral Psychology* I do feel, however, that a brief reference to Seward Hiltner's discussion in his book, *Preface to Pastoral Theology*, of pastoral theology as "shepherding" provides a fitting background for any thinking about the pastor's concern for parents who have a retarded child. Hiltner's concept of shepherding as "healing," "sustaining," and "guiding" seems especially appropriate in our ministering to these people. They have been deeply hurt and desperately need healing of mind and spirit. They have a special, lifelong burden and for that reason need the sustaining influence of their pastor. The many perplexing questions and problems associated with mental retardation leave these parents bewildered as sheep without a shepherd, and therefore they need guidance through the hazy and dangerous valleys of doubt, guilt, and anxiety until they reach the highlands of faith and hope.

In our discussion it would also seem necessary to keep in mind the varying personal resources of the parents. People's ability to deal with stress situations differs radically. Even personality types become a factor in parental reaction to mental retardation. Some parents have sufficient understanding, emotional stability, and whatever else it takes to cope fairly adequately with their problem. Others seem to lack all these qualities, and therefore they meet their situation inadequately. Nor must we forget the variance in attitude of parents. Some care profoundly, others seem

Note: Reprinted by permission of the author and *Pastoral Psychology*, *13*:37-44, 1962.
*Chaplain, Parsons State Hospital and Training Center, Parsons, Kansas.

quite indifferent, all of which is readily reflected in their degree of willingness to assume responsibility for the care of the retarded child. As we find in all areas of life, there are those who live self-centered lives, who fail to respond to duty, and who simply do not care enough. In all probability such people need help in an overall readjustment of their religious and personal life, not simply in the matter of their attitude toward an unfortunate child. The majority of the parents, however, do care, even when they are lacking in personal resources and emotional stability, and as pastors, we must meet them where they are and try to understand, in each case, the manner in which their experience affects them.

My earliest recollection of mentally retarded persons goes back to my childhood. I recall a multihandicapped boy who was carried to church in the arms of his father, and who sat in his wheelchair watching other children play whenever my family chanced to visit at his home. Another retarded individual was my own sister who, as I recall very vividly, was one day expelled from the rural school with the teacher's comment, "She cannot learn." How much the hurt feelings I experienced reflected those of our complete family constellation, I am not sure, but they were traumatic enough to have remained constant in my consciousness since that day. My sister lived to the age of twenty-one.

Sister, however, was always with us in church, and I can recall the warmth of her relationship with adults, who all seemed to love her. How much our sister's condition burdened our parents was not known to my brothers and me. Apart from some minor sibling irritations, she seemed an integral part of our family, which, I am certain, was because our parents had the grace to accept her genuinely for what she was. The spiritual strength with which my parents met this vicissitude and many others seemed to stem from their Christian faith, which did not, however, exist in isolation but was greatly fortified in the fellowship of a church which consisted of a very homogeneous group of people closely knitted together in national, cultural, and religious similarities. These early recollections of mine have certain implications which will be mentioned later.

In my parish ministry, I recall these specific cases of mental retardation:

Three small children with physical malformations, two of whom died early. The other one was institutionalized.

A family of five children, all of whom were retarded, possibly because of familial, cultural, and environmental reasons.

Two brothers who were gainfully employed, but who were socially withdrawn and greatly dependent upon their parents.

Two mongoloid children, a boy and a girl.

Three adults, totally, or partially dependent upon their family. One of these was later institutionalized. All three had harmless, but peculiar, personality traits.

Five adolescent young people who over the years had been in my confirmation classes. Some of these were unable to read or write.

A brain-injured teenager whose condition had involved brain surgery.

Two young boys who failed to learn and to socialize in school.

A spastic, nonverbal, nonambulatory teenage boy who was a constant nursing care at home.

This group represents twenty-four mentally retarded persons and nineteen families, eight of which were in my last parish. Although these individuals represent a limited scope within the field of mental retardation, they do suggest what might be the average experience which any pastor might have, and their deficiencies are diversified enough to suggest the complexity of the problem. The particular needs of the parents varied greatly, and they varied with the parents, themselves, as the years passed. Likewise, a study of these parents' age, culture, social environment, and church life would seem to suggest further variation in the degree of suffering associated with the experience of having a retarded child.

My own parents, as well as some of the others, were a part of a church and social group where they found acceptance for themselves and their child. They escaped the feelings of isolation, reproach, and misunderstanding which many parents of retarded children experience. It would seem that any pastoral care for parents of retarded children should be broad enough to foster this group acceptance. Somewhere within this interaction of the group (the fellowship of believers), the parents will find understanding.

They will be able to talk of their burden, and they will find those who can love and accept their child for what he is, namely, a significant individual in the sight of both God and man.

There was an element in the faith of these parents which made it possible for them to face adverse facts of life with a wholesome resignation. Realistically they did not expect life to be perfect. They knew evil could befall them and their children, but they were so firmly rooted in the love of God that, although they must have asked questions, they could never link their tragedy to God's vindictiveness, although they might have felt God's will for them was therein revealed.

Could it be that we pastors try too hard to shield our people from the hurts of life? How can we have the heart to say to a young couple who come into our study to talk about their wedding, and who have high hopes of having some lovely children in the future, "Look, your hopes may become a life of sorrow, frustration, and despair"? Yet, somewhere this ought to be said, perhaps not the night before the wedding, but from the pulpit, or through group instruction, and in the context of an overall attempt to help people face the realities of life with a faith grounded in a sound theology. We are remiss in our care of people if we do not prepare them to die; also, if we fail to help them meet any other tragic experiences in life. When we confront people with life's possibilities in the framework of God's infinite care, we cushion them against the hard knocks of life. And when such occasions do arise, specific pastoral care can become far more meaningful and sustaining. Some parents do become the parents of a retarded child. For every such child, there are two parents, or, roughly speaking, 10,000,000 in the United States.

In the diversity of human experiences, there are few identical situations surrounding mental retardation. Each case must be considered very personal and unique, because it definitely is to the parents. But in order to say anything at all some generalizations must be made. These questions certainly can be considered: What will be the nature of pastoral care (1) when retardation is obvious at birth, (2) when parents gradually become aware of their child's deficiencies at a later date, (3) when institutionalization must be considered, (4) in the continuous ongoing parental concern and involvement which arises out of the presence of a retarded child in the home?

When retardation is obvious at birth, the tragedy and shock can be second to none. Not even the death of the child can be as severe. Obviously, this will be the test of the pastor's faith, personality, and maturity. One summer a group of ministerial students spent one week at our institution, during which time the pediatrician showed them a number of badly deformed retarded children. The comment of one of the students was, "I surely was shook up," to which the doctor replied, "I would rather have you shook up here than in your future parish." A mother said to me, "Our young pastor was more shaken than we were. He was of no help to us." As in all areas of life, the price a pastor must pay in order to meet any situation is to have worked through his own feelings of revulsion, anxiety, and shock, at least in some areas of human experiences, so he can respond in a mature way which alone will strengthen the parents' faith. No glib answers will meet the parents' need. The questions which they ask may not have ready answers. What do we say when they ask, "Why did God let this happen to us?" We dare not detach their experience of giving birth to a retarded child from the reality of the providence of God. If we do, life, indeed, will be meaningless. Although the answers come with difficulty, if at all, we must give the questions enough attention, in the secret of our own counsel and in the contemplation of the mysteries of life so that the parents can sense our genuine familiarity with them.

The answer we do give must be one which does justice to the integrity of the parents and the faithfulness and love of God. It must be asserted that the birth of a retarded and/or a deformed child is not an insult against the parents' quality as persons. The first visit with the parents after the birth of the child may not be the time for any words, but rather a moment in which there must be a giving of oneself in terms of genuine affect and understanding without any appearance of panic. In such moments, it is the positive aspects of the pastoral relationship that count. The fact that the pastor is personally concerned in their particular crisis will in itself be helpful. Apart from these generalizations, each situation will be different. There may be a need to listen while the parents talk and to be quiet while they weep, but always there is a place for a confident faith expressed in a prayer to God.

There are situations in which parents gradually become aware of their child's deficiency. This can happen any time from shortly after birth to within the first years in school. Associated with this growing awareness is an increasing apprehension and a related anxiety. Denial of the presence of retardation will be used as long as possible, often to the inevitable hurt of the child. Because the child presents difficulties, the parents may disagree about the right methods of management. Either husband or wife may refuse to recognize any cause for concern. Every aspect of the problem can cause increasing tension and stress which, if not released, will eventually generate marital strife. It is conceivable that serious difficulties may arise even before the pastor is aware of it.

It is, of course, impossible to anticipate the endless variety of circumstances that may arise in the home of a retarded child. One of the pastor's major problems may be to gain the confidence of the people involved. It certainly would be difficult to tell parents that their child is retarded and needs special help before they are ready to accept the fact. The sensitivity of people is often such that they resent any intrusion into their home life. The pastor may nevertheless feel the responsibility of offering his services, for he would rightly feel that the parents need the counseling and support he is professionally prepared to give. He may have to wait for the right moment which eventually will come. In the meantime, he can be alert to the conscious or unconscious hints which the parents give and which are prompted by their anxiety over a child who is not doing well. With some discernment and fact, it is possible to help the parents realistically to confront their child's special needs and to be supportive to them in their growing awareness.

He should be ready in a variety of situations to suggest some course of action which can lead to a reasonable approach to the problem. Rather than express his own "educated guess," no matter how right he might be, it would be much more helpful and wise to suggest to the parents that they seek professional consultation and guidance. In such an approach, he can give pastoral assurance which people frequently need when they must seek professional help.

When a medical and psychological diagnosis of mental retardation has been made in a specific case, a crucial period of adjustment lies ahead for the parents. The judgment comes with a stunning finality. It is this ultimate finality that is so hard to accept. Emotionally, the parents are unable to accept the tragic truth. Maybe, they reason, the doctors and psychologists are wrong! Maybe a miracle can be performed! Maybe! Maybe!

Most of us have learned through our pastoral experiences that we cannot command peoples' emotions to obey even rational exhortations. To say, "You should not feel this way" is generally useless, if not harmful. The emotional adjustment may come slowly and torturously, but it will come through the interplay within the pastoral relationship, which is always therapeutic. As in the case of a death in the family, the emotional upheaval following the full realization of a child's mental retardation can be a severe shock and, therefore, merits genuine pastoral care. In the case of retardation, however, there are many very important ramifications which suddenly or gradually dawn upon the parents and which leave life forever different. The initial adjustment may well determine the fortitude with which the parents meet the coming years. The pastor's role will be that of a counselor who consciously seeks to be available for any service he may be able to render.

When institutionalization must be considered, other problems arise for the parents. The need of such action may arise out of any one of several factors, or a combination of such factors, some of which are the child's needs, the mother's health, and the total impact of the child upon the family constellation. The need for making the right decision is generally complicated by a sense of guilt, the difficulty of separation, and sometimes, a more or less unconscious desire to be relieved of the care of the child. Once again, the pastor may be confronted with a combination of emotional factors which he must seek to untangle and alleviate. Professional counselors can deal with these problems on their level, but parents who seek in all things to do God's will want to come to a conclusion within the perspective of their commitment to God. It is within this framework of religious concern that the pastor functions in his care for the parents.

Their feelings of guilt can ultimately be resolved only on a religious basis, for there is always an element of reality in these feelings. In this situation, the assurance of forgiveness is not only appropriate but needed. It should, however, be made clear to the parents that they are not "bad" because they are unable to meet the needs of their child, and that it might be God's will that the care and training of their child should be entrusted to others. On the other hand, there may be parents who need help to accept the responsibility of the child's care as the most reasonable expression of God's will.

Institutionalization is not the answer to the overall problems of mental retardation. This is obvious when we consider that only a small percentage of the mentally deficient come to institutions. But apart from such a consideration, it has become my basic belief that, except for severe emotional disturbance and for difficult management reasons, no child should be sent to an institution. The advantages which are offered by the best state facilities do not offset the loss of separation from the home. The parent-child relationship is too fundamental, even for retarded children, for any agency to supply adequately a substitute. It is within his relation to his parents that a child "lives, and moves, and has his being," and his self-concept and ego formation develop within this relationship. Separation from parents, I do not believe, is ever rationally accepted by these children. Adjustment may come through a repression of emotional responses to the separation, but I am not sure that these psychic problems are ever truly resolved.

There is a further consideration which involves the return of an institutionalized person. The difficulty of coming back to the family and community increases with the length of separation. Social adjustment should be learned on the community level and the community is likely to think of the individual as an intruder who should remain the concern of the institution. In other words, the patient becomes a stranger in his home town. The pastor's role remains that of a counselor, but he might well become involved in arousing various agencies to take a progressive approach to the training of retarded children on a community level.

We come now to the consideration of the ongoing pastoral care of parents in their long-term concern and involvement which arise out of the continued presence of a retarded child in the home. The pastor is certainly not to function as a "family guidance center." He may want to refer the family to such a community service where it is available. Apart from that, his helpfulness lies in other areas. He certainly has a legitimate interest in the daily continuous psychic and spiritual drain which parents experience. He has a right to be concerned about their ability to accept the child realistically as he is, as an integral part of the family, and to aid in the formation of goals that seem suited to his potentialities. He will seek to help the parents to enjoy their child as a person in his own right, which he himself must do lest he become a "clanging cymbal." His own genuine love for the child will help to replenish the parents' own psychic and spiritual strength which will enable them to continue to love and care.

All these things will be his concern. He, however, will go beyond these to pursue, with the parents, the potentialities for growth and maturation which suffering can occasion. Suffering, per se, has always been a difficult intellectual problem, but it seems that God in His good providence, uses it for teaching His children the great lessons of life. "Suffering produces endurance, and endurance produces character, and character produces hope." (*Romans* 5:3-4.) We have in our day been enhanced by the possibilities of having our tensions and anxieties alleviated through some psychiatric technique and, in the meantime, we have been forgetting that which occurs in the lives of men and women in a real confrontation of God and in His dealings with the individual. Jesus stated emphatically, "I am the vine and my Father is the Vinedresser. Every branch of mine that bears no fruit, he takes away, and every branch that does bear fruit, he prunes that it may bear more fruit." (*John* 15:1-3.) I take this to mean that there are hurts in life which shear off man's complacency and become significant positive factors in Christian personality growth. No pastor ever wishes that his people must suffer, but he should acquaint himself with the potentials of grief to the point where he will be able to help turn sorrow into joy. In short, he will seek to use tragedy to good advantages in the life of his people.

I am certain that this often involves leading people, among these the parents of retarded children, to a full commitment to God, helping them to "Let God be God." This can be done within the framework of natural laws which allows for obvious accidents in child birth and development. The conviction can remain that God is "a very present help in trouble," (*Psalms* 46:1), and that "in everything God works together for good with those who love him." (*Romans* 8:28.)

What concerns me is that we give a genuine religious significance and setting to this difficult experience of many parents. They can learn that "in all these things we are more than conquerors through Him who loved us." (*Romans* 8:37.) All this indicates that as pastors we must be deeply involved in this growth process, consciously and continuously seeking to foster it. This will be done in person to person relationships, but it will also be done in the confines of the Christian congregation through the ministry of the Word and Sacraments.

Although it is difficult to chart the process of growth in any person, and still more difficult to stimulate it, the potentials are unique in parents or retarded children. If they can work through the feeling of utter helplessness and hopelessness, which is often associated with retardation, to a positive acceptance of their lot, a most significant step has been taken. It is an experience comparable to Christ's in the Garden of Gethsemane, in which the embrace of the inevitable becomes the will of God. This is not the same as believing that God willed their child's condition, but it is the way in which faith can transcend the many paradoxes of life and place people within the conscious confines of the providence of God.

I believe the experience of having a retarded child can sharpen the sensitivity of people by making them keenly alert to other people's trouble, deeply appreciative of little things, of the uniqueness of human life, of the fact that we are "fearfully and wonderfully made," and that each life, however simple and circumscribed, is a "pearl of great price." Such sensitivity is greatly lacking in many people. I, also, believe that a retarded child can teach parents something of the wonders of life which God has placed in every person. There is hardly a child so low mentally but what he seeks love and exhibits a will to live and fulfill his destiny. So with an increased sensitivity there develops in the parents a deeper insight into the marvels of the life that God has given man.

Quite frequently, too, parents of retarded children become active in meaningful endeavors. By their own tragedy, they become stimulated to using their talents for the sake of others. It is a sign of maturing when people can give of themselves to a cause and accept responsibility for the welfare of others.

Growth, as we think of it in Christian terms, is profoundly significant because it has many implications. It does not only profit the individual who is maturing, but all those about him. In our present discussion, this means that the parents of a retarded child will have more to give him in terms of security, love, and special care which he needs very much. A lack of this growth of which we speak, not only means stagnation, but often regression, a breaking down of personal assets. This means less and less ability to cope with the growing problems of having a retarded child.

The problem of mental retardation is deeply emotional. Parents will seek understanding and some even pity. Some will react with anger against fate, or God, which has dealt them the cruel blow. Others have not resolved the feeling that their retarded child is a punishment for some known, or unknown, sin. They are constantly plagued with disturbing questions such as, "What will happen to our child when we no longer can care for him? What is our child's status with God?" It is imperative that the pastor walks circumspectly in this world of emotions so that he does not lose his bearing, but from the vantage point of objectivity that he be able to act as a source of stability and security to these troubled people.

As I look back upon my parish ministry, it is with ambivalent feelings. Some of the parents whose children are enumerated at the beginning of this article responded to my pastoral efforts, others did not, and still others, long before I became their pastor, had advanced in their Christian growth to the point where their lives were firmly secured in God's grace. So, also, in this respect, my experiences may well parallel those of the average pastor.

In reviewing what I have written on this subject of pastoral care for the parents of retarded children, it seems to me that a few pertinent principles are evident: (1) there will be much direct counseling to meet an immediate crisis and a long-term involvement. (2) There will be an effort to turn an apparent tragedy into positive means of personal Christian growth. (3) This specific concern with these parents should not be detached from the general ministry of the church, but should find its roots well planted within the soil of the household of faith.

Chapter 25

Ministry and Mental Retardation

ROBERT PERSKE*

*In dealing with the mentally retarded
and their families, the minister finds
his theological presuppositions
seriously challenged. In accepting the
challenge he may be led to significant
new insights.*

W HEN a person seeks to love and care for another
human being who has been limited by a grim and irreversible case
of mental retardation, some interesting things can happen to what
he believes about God and his creations. A clergyman involving
himself in a pastoral way with such a family has an excellent
opportunity to see what this situation does to the theology of the
parents. But, as he works to develop a helpful relationship with
this family and the retarded person himself, he finds that his own
theological views are challenged as well.

If any of us feel we know all we need to know about God and
life and man, this would be a good time to get involved in a
pastoral way with a mentally retarded person and his family and
get to know them well. It is my hunch that any pastor who dares
to struggle with the grim, enigmatic, and sometimes repulsive
predicament of mental retardation has an excellent opportunity to
challenge and find growth in his theological views. The following is
an attempt (1) to show how I was first inspired by the parents of
the mentally retarded to take a second look at my theological
views; (2) to show how one begins to think theologically about

Note: Reprinted by permission of the author and *Pastoral Psychology, 20*:21-27, 1969.
*Chaplain Supervisor, Kansas Neurological Institute; Staff Affiliate, The Menninger
Foundation, Topeka, Kansas.

this situation, and (3) to cite only a few of many areas where my theological views have been affected.

It is hoped that the reader will find a new interest in the mentally retarded and their families and, subsequently, see the opportunity to enter his own creative struggle which may modify, enlarge, and enhance what he believes about God and his creations.

THE THEOLOGICAL CRISIS IN PARENTS:
AN OPPORTUNITY

In 1964, Harold Stubblefield did an excellent study utilizing 220 Protestant and Catholic clergymen in order to survey attitudes toward the mentally retarded. One of his striking discoveries was that almost all parents of the mentally retarded go into a period of theological crisis (Stubblefield, 1965). As I refer to my notes of former pastoral conversations with parents of the mentally retarded, I am well aware that Stubblefield was right. For example:

> Tom O'Brien,* a rather sophisticated church treasurer in a liberal Methodist Church, took his six-year-old daughter to a famous radio and television faith healer.
>
> Mary Jones became active in the Presbyterian Church, although she had no church background.
>
> Sam Smith, a regular attender of Sunday services and a church schoolteacher, slowly drifted away until all ties were severed.
>
> John Brooks resigned his job as an executive in a manufacturing firm and entered the Methodist Seminary.
>
> Nancy Jones left the Methodist Church and joined the Nazarene Church.
>
> Fred Fritz left his four-year-old child at an institution. He then moved to Texas, where he underwent a religious conversion and automatically became a pastor in a Pentecostal Church.

These major shifts in church affiliation help us to see that a lot is going on inside these parents with regard to what they believe. Somehow, the bittersweet wine fermented by mental retardation does not always seem to be held in the wineskins of their former faith. They are thinking theologically even though they do not

---

*All names of the mentally retarded and their families have been changed.

know the proper terms. *But, they do know the proper questions.* They are struggling to reconcile what they believe about God with what has happened to their child. This struggle — like all struggles — will force some to regress into bitterness and others to develop a healthier outlook. The pastor has an excellent opportunity to help these parents progress toward a stronger, renewed faith, and to join with them in their vital theological struggle.

THINKING THEOLOGICALLY ABOUT MENTAL RETARDATION

Seward Hiltner has contributed much to both the field of pastoral care and the field of theology when he challenged us to theologize about the human predicaments of man. His discovery and application of the pastoral notes of Ichabod Crane have provided an excellent method for developing a theology that is relevant today (1959). Ichabod Crane was a pastor in Brooklyn during the middle of the nineteenth century who painstakingly kept accurate notes of pastoral conversations with his people when they were in crisis. He showed how he struggled to bring theological meaning to their suffering. It is this method, inspired by Crane and developed by Hiltner, which we seek to use here.

When one attempts to think theologically about the situation of a particular mentally retarded child and his family, he can take a rigorous and mentally exhausting course. It is much easier to speak theological language out of one side of the mouth and to use psychological, social, and medical language out of the other. It is more comfortable for a pastor to talk about a mentally retarded child's situation in psychological, medical, and social terminology. But when he dares to draw theological understanding from this gutsy human situation, some of his theological beliefs will be shaken. This is painful. But it is good. He then has the opportunity to develop a more realistic and helpful theological view.

In a sense, one is held in suspension, being pulled in two directions. First, he must draw new conclusions about the nature of God and man and life from the struggles of the mentally retarded. Secondly, he must test them with the traditional theological concepts of the past. At first, one may feel he is a victim both of the theological cries of this human situation pulling him on one hand, and the theological demands of the church fathers pulling him on the other. But as he gains his own intellectual and emotional strength, he pays attention to both forces, and makes his own strong decisions about what he believes. He literally seeks to synthesize and make sense out of both the human cries of the mentally retarded and the admonitions of the church fathers while also focusing on the same predicament.

THE PARENTS' STRUGGLE: A NEW PERSPECTIVE ON DEATH AND RESURRECTION

Now that the theological crisis in parents has been pointed out, we will take a deeper look at the nature of their struggle. I have developed a profound reverence for the struggle of these parents. How complex and frustrating it is! The reader may wonder why this predicament is different from other crisis situations. The answer is simple. Almost immediately, the "myths of cure" are shot down (although we cannot say that someday some sort of talking therapy, or electric shock, or surgery, or physical manipulation, or special drug will totally cure this affliction). On top of this, the child may live a long life. This is not a short-term crisis. This is a lifelong crisis. To be sure, there is growth. But it is limited growth. There is something final about mental retardation.

When the parents get to the point of seeing this finality – although some struggle for years before they face it – the realization comes to them like death! There are some things in a parent that have to die before he or she can become a healthy parent of a mentally retarded child. One mother stated it this way:

> Before Billie was born, I was a different person. I was active as an officer in Junior League. I was involved in bridge circles, and I regularly attended the country club activities with my husband. I still go to the country club once in a while. But, something happened to me, to my image, so that Junior League and bridge did not mean as much. It's like some things had to die in me . . . some myths I believed about myself . . . some ways I saw myself. They had to die and I had to let them die. Now I'm glad. But at that time I fought against it.

This woman is now active in a local Association for the Mentally Retarded in Nebraska and is deeply interested in legislation for the handicapped. She is a warm, gracious, and creative wife and the mother of four children. Somehow, some things had to die in her before she could "come alive" in others ways.

This case could be contrasted with another family where both mother and father are high school teachers. Two of their daughters grew up and also went into the teaching profession. But, John, their mildly retarded boy, barely made it through the eighth grade. Because of the myths this family built about themselves as intellectuals and teachers, they are deeply "embarrassed" by him. They have not gotten over it. He continues to embarrass them to this day as he travels with a carnival throughout the United States, doing something he does well — riding a motorcycle in a barrel.

As I observe these struggles, it has been possible for me to gain a clearer understanding of the theological workings of death and resurrection. In essence, these people struggle to hang on to the false myths that this predicament has pinpointed, or they must strive to let them die. As this death struggle takes place, one can almost hear their cries: "O God, get me out of this . . . Nevertheless, not my will but yours be done." "My God! My God! Why have you pulled out on me?" "I'm finished. I'm helpless. I give up."

It's never easy to let some things we once experienced get swallowed up by death. But for those who have been able to allow certain parts of themselves die, there seems to be a God-given chemistry at work so that they can rise again as stronger, more mature, emotionally warmer and more understanding people of God! They are literally "new beings." This "resurrection" comes to them as a surprise! It was something they neither expected nor could predict. Resurrections seem to come in our human personalities only when certain parts of us are allowed to find a total death. I believe that I can see an excellent paradigm of death and resurrection in the struggle of the parents of the mentally retarded.

THE PARENTS' STRUGGLE: A NEW
PERSPECTIVE OF THE PROBLEM OF EVIL

As we look even deeper into the struggle of these parents, we feel the need to take a new and fresh look at the problem of evil. All of us have memories of painful crisis times when we were prone to cry out: "Why, God?" "Why did this happen to me?" "What evil have I done that this should come to me?" "Why did it have to happen to Billy?" "Why, God?"

William Temple (1934) reminds us that most of us ask these questions when we are suffering. When the suffering ceases we no longer feel the need to ask. Then there is no emotional need for an answer. But the cry of the parents of the mentally retarded is a persistent cry. It is a lifelong cry. A pastor will hear it over and over again, year after year. It forces us to take another look at the problem of evil, to find some reason for it.

My thoughts about the problem of evil began to change when one of my pastor colleagues, Dr. Kenneth Mitchell, Director of Training, Religion and Psychiatry Department, The Menninger Foundation, met with the KNI Chaplaincy Department for a seminar. Our staff had been struggling with some gloomy aspects of the problem of evil, wondering why some of our little patients had to be born the way they were. Dr. Mitchell seemed to sense the general feeling and introduced some alternatives that helped us to develop a new and more hopeful perspective. He struggled with the data we presented and playfully suggested that possibly this world is an unfinished place, and both we and the mentally retarded are unfinished people. Our unfinished, our unwhole, our imperfect nature is what causes us to suffer. But, when we share in one another's sufferings, and struggle with one another, we *create* some good things. After observing the struggles of these parents I have come to believe that *we share in God's Creation of this world!*

When we have the view that we share in the creativity of an unfinished world, answers to the problem of evil demand less detective work (i.e. who did it and how can we bring them to justice?). When we believe that the world is an unfinished place and still in the process of being created, we find new meaning in our struggles. Good creations cannot come without noble struggles. And, noble struggles must come from the human situations of suffering.

The world is filled with people and groups who share in

Creation. They are all around us. But, they are so commonplace we are not aware of them. A good example is the struggling group of parents who have banded together as the Association for Retarded Children in our town. (If I told them they were sharing in Creation they would be a bit surprised and say, "Aw, you're putting us on.") They are involved in Creation. From memory — without research and investigation — it is possible for me to make a list of their struggles that have brought new Creations to our town:

1. Reeducation and pressure on the school boards of our town, resulting in an ever-growing number of special education classes and a growing consideration for both the mentally retarded and the gifted.
2. Reeducation and pressure on legislators and all governmental agencies for the handicapped, resulting in a growing number of good laws regarding the handicapped and a growing number of helping facilities for them.
3. Interest in and pressure on the local institution for the mentally retarded with regard to care and therapy. It is my feeling that this pressure is needed.
4. A continuous program of reeducation for their own members and the community at large, resulting in a much warmer and more accepting attitude toward the mentally retarded in our town.
5. The development and constant expansion of a day care center for the mentally retarded.
6. The development of a sheltered workshop for teenage and adult mentally retarded, resulting in solving social and vocational problems for many.
7. The offering of concern and help to all parents struggling with this problem whether they are members of the Association or not.

Research and investigation could show more of their activity. But this is enough to demonstrate that here is a group of unfinished people struggling in an unfinished town in an unfinished world. They *do* struggle. Often, their struggles spill over on others, causing them to struggle. They sometimes struggle and push to the point that the comfortable will see them as being a bit obnoxious. But the day they cease to struggle, their share in Creation will cease. These parents have helped me to better understand the nature of their "problem of evil" and find a more satisfying understanding of the meaning of Creation.

For the most part, we have focused on the parents of the mentally retarded. Now we will consider some of the situations of the mentally retarded persons themselves.

THE MENTALLY RETARDED PERSON'S STRUGGLE: A NEW PERSPECTIVE ON MAN'S FINITUDE

Sammy is a wide-eyed and happy ten-year-old boy who lives in my neighborhood. He seems to be seeing so many wonderful things in the world with those wide eyes of his. In fact, he sees so many things that he sometimes chases after them and loses himself in his world. Then, some of us have to search for him. I have developed a reverence for little Sammy's struggle to understand everything he sees. In spite of his wide eyes, one can quickly become aware of the "hobbling" effect of a slow mind that limits his comprehension of many things he sees in the world. Many mentally retarded persons are like this. We are aware of the limits that keep them from comprehending many things that we can understand. But, that does not keep those like Sammy from trying! Their struggle is a most interesting one.

Jean Paul Sartre once said that life is like watching a group of people in a room through a keyhole. The longer you watch, the more interested you get. Then, all of a sudden, you are aware of an eye on the other side of the keyhole looking back at you! As I watch Sammy struggling to move beyond his *limits* of comprehension, I am suddenly aware of the limits to my comprehension as well.

Today, as we stand at this circumscribed point in time and space, we see so much we cannot comprehend. We can look farther into the past, higher into the sky, deeper into the nature of things. Wherever we look we are aware of an infinity we cannot comprehend or understand. But many keep trying, and they make slow but positive growth. Yet with what we know today, finite man is utterly helpless in his attempt to understand the nature of an infinite God and an infinite world. Man certainly has limits to his comprehension. He is very much in need of a Grace which he can neither predict nor expect if he is to gain a deeper understanding of what lies beyond. Wide-eyed Sammy's predicament is my predicament!

But there is something else that Sammy's situation can challenge us to consider. Sammy *knows* he is limited. He is not afraid to discuss the reason why he attends a special education class. (So many times we hesitate to discuss a condition with the mentally retarded person that both we and he know he possesses. Sometimes this merely serves to develop a tension in the relationship that does not have to be there.) Sammy knows he has both weaknesses and strengths. He knows he is imperfect. Sometimes, I am forced to smile when I think of the doctrines of perfection and sanctification that caused many of us much struggle and guilt in earlier days. It is interesting to note how much theology has been written so that between the lines we can perceive man's struggle for a brilliant mind, a beautiful body, and a pure heart. It is a struggle for a fantastic perfection none of us can achieve in this world. Sammy's condition, and that of others like him, helps us to see that every man is a conglomerate of weaknesses and strengths with which he must struggle and out of which he will bring Creation or a sinful lack of Creation as long as he lives.

No theological view can ever be realistic and relevant until the man doing the viewing has some understanding of his own human limits. In fact, it is my hunch that the better a man is able to perceive his finite limits and live with them, the closer he will be able to come to a relevant theological view.

THE MENTALLY RETARDED PERSON'S STRUGGLE: A NEW PERSPECTIVE ON THEOLOGY OF WORSHIP

After serving as leader to a group of mentally retarded boys and girls in the worship of God, one fact strikes me time and time again. Many of these boys and girls work very hard to offer a good worship. They do this in spite of their limits. One even can be aware of their expectations as they come to the chapel like refugees on the move. Some are walking and running. Others hobble on braces and crutches. Some ride in wheelchairs pushed by their friends. A great many have expectations about the worship service soon to begin. One cannot help feeling they work at having their expectations fulfilled. Although many are tone deaf, they still sing with enthusiasm. Others cannot speak, so they do what they can by moving their arms and legs and nodding their heads in meaningful ways. The rest know they are "with us." Some are so responsive, it made sense to plan every other movement in the ritual as something they could do, whether it be a hymn, a prayer, a responsive statement, or a choral response. On some days, I have felt these boys and girls are *working* as best they can. When the worship leader is aware of this, he finds himself working harder to facilitate their act of worship.

A friend with whom I discussed this attitude called my attention to the writings of Gregory Dix on worship. Dix, in his definitive volume, *The Shape of the Liturgy,* shows clearly and concisely that the early church theology saw worship as a work (1945). In the first 150 years of the church, worship was an *active* thing. Following that period, worship became more of a *passive* thing. In the early service, the liturgy was filled with words like "making," "giving," "doing." There was a great deal of action in the form of moving, sharing, and touching. There was even a "kiss of peace." In the early church, worship was a work in which everyone was working to do something as his human part in this divine/human encounter. Later these words dropped away and services were typified by words like "attending," "hearing," and "observing." Somehow, I have the strong feeling that the mentally retarded, because of who they are and because of their struggle to overcome limits, possess an attitude similar to that which prevailed in the early church.

Many mentally retarded *work* at "reaching out" in their struggle to do their part in this divine/human encounter. It's an interesting thought that the mentally retarded, because the limits they have, may help the rest of us to recapture a more relevant view of a theology of worship.

CONCLUSION

This has been an attempt to show how the parents of the

mentally retarded inspired me to take a second look at my theological views, to show the method I used, and to give a few instances out of many in which my theological views have been affected. If space had allowed, it would have been good to show how this human predicament can cast new light on our theological thinking about grace, redemption, and many other categories. On the other hand, each of us has a chance to pursue in depth any single doctrine, using the added perspective of this particular crisis situation.

Each of us has the "original theological perspective" which we had before beginning our pastoral involvements with the mentally retarded and their families. Then as we focus on this human situation, we become aware of an "added theological perspective" that helps us to take a second look from a different viewpoint. We then find our original view has been reinforced, modified, or enlarged. It is my feeling that a pastor who becomes involved with these particular persons — who need his services very much — will find a golden opportunity to grow theologically.

If any of us feel we know all we need to know about God and life and man, this would be a good time to become involved in a pastoral way with a mentally retarded person and his family and get to know them well.

REFERENCES

Dix, Gregory: *The Shape of the Liturgy*. Glasgow, The University Press, 1945, Ch. 2.

Hiltner, Seward: *Preface To Pastoral Theology*. Nashville, Abingdon Press, 1959.

Stubblefield, Harold: The ministry and mental retardation. *J Religion Health, 3:*136-197, 1964.

Stubblefield, Harold: Religion, parents and mental retardation. *Ment. Retard.* August, pp. 8-11, 1965.

Temple, William: *Nature, Man and God*. Toronto, Macmillan, 1934, p. 43.

PART VI

GENETIC COUNSELING

Chapter 26

Psychiatric Aspects of
Genetic Counseling

FRANZ J. KALLMANN, M.D.*

PERHAPS it is partly because of the limited amount of counseling in human genetics in this country and partly because of consequent limitations in pertinent experience that workers in this specialized field are inclined to be on the conservative side. This guarded attitude seems to express itself in one of two ways. The first is a scientifically detached approach to all phases of counseling relevant to family planning. The other is an overcautious position based on the notion that eugenic considerations in this area are apt to create conflict and criticism and should therefore be kept apart from genetic considerations (Neel and Schull, 1954; Reed, 1955).

Hence the current emphasis in genetic counseling is placed on tendering a genetic prognosis, with no attempt made to appraise the advisability of parenthood. Decisions as to reproduction are regarded as falling strictly within the province of eugenics and consequently are left up to the person or family seeking advice. The tacit assumption — often evidently wishful — is that intelligent people, who are morally entitled to truthful information regarding the prospects of their own health and that of their children, are capable of dealing with their family problems realistically and without special guidance.

From a psychological standpoint, realism may be defined as the tendency to view things as they are rather than as what we want

Note: Reprinted by permission of the author and the *American Journal of Human Genetics, 8:*97-101, 1956. Published by the University of Chicago Press.
*Department of Medical Genetics, New York State Psychiatric Institute, Columbia University, New York, New York.

them to be. As a principle of adult behavior, this tendency is indicative of a mature mind and a wholesome pattern of adjustment to human imperfection and stress. However, a realistic attitude in the face of severe threats to health and survival can never be divorced from the existing circumstances. Nor can these circumstances be dealt with impersonally.

In no situation calling for genetic counseling can it ever be taken for granted that the person is realistic or will be able to attain a realistic attitude without the counselor's help. The attainment of this goal is highly desirable but often requires considerable effort. Even well-educated persons may fail to achieve it without encouragement and guidance. In many instances, unguided reality enforcement is apt to create fear, anxiety, and inner tension, and not realism.

Frightened people either withdraw from reality by regressing to immature patterns of behavior, or they attempt to neutralize reality by means of pathological defense reactions such as repression and displacement, rationalization and projection. The final outcome will not be on the positive side, and an emotionally disturbed mind is a high price to pay for meek reality testing.

Psychological damage of equal severity may result from disregarding the emotional needs of the individual when parenthood seems contraindicated. For instance, merely because voluntary sterilization does not seem more objectionable on moral grounds than the practice of birth control is not sufficient reason to recommend it to persons who cannot know its future implications. Once again, we are dealing with a situation pitting intellect against emotions, where formal acquaintance with standard textbook descriptions of possible complications does not guarantee the ability to meet the actual experiences successfully. What is more, a sterilizing operation, even when performed without undue persuasion and conferring an important personal gain, such as eliminating the fear of pregnancy, is certain to have psychosomatic sequelae, if only because of the finality of the procedure (Ekblad, 1955).

Lacking stable life conditions or a reasonably defined motive — prerequisites which defy both analysis by abstract methods and expert advice proffered by main — sterilized adults of either sex are in danger of responding to their lost reproductivity with feelings of inadequacy and insecurity. Too often such persons become fearful and apprehensive, and it takes no formal psychiatric training to understand that a chronic anxiety state, brought about by the fear of developing the very gene-specific illness which is to be forestalled for the good of the family, may be as distressing and disabling as the disease itself.

The need for combining counseling with a personalized guidance effort is apparent throughout the field of medical genetics. It applies especially to inheritable traits which have a relatively late manifestation period and pose a real or imagined threat to the individual's health and adaptiveness, thereby affecting the emotional climate of the whole family. It also applies to defects such as early blindness or deafness, which are conducive to the formation of certain personal and intrafamily patterns of adjustment highly specific to the impairment. The existential conditions of handicapped groups are rarely stabilized. It is unfortunate, therefore, that emotional deprivation in these groups is often aggravated needlessly. It is an erroneous belief, for instance, that these people live in a sheltered world and thus require less, rather than more, adequate provision for expert guidance (Kallmann, 1955).

Two recent observations, which can readily be multiplied from previous data, may serve to illustrate the significance of psychiatric problems encountered in genetic counseling. The first was a case that came to us through a surgeon in a rural district of New York State. He requested information about the advisability of an elective sterilization procedure in a thirty-three-year-old woman who was desperately worried about the recent confirmation of a history of Huntington's chorea on her maternal side.

The young woman, a popular college graduate and happily married to a successful lawyer, was the mother of two healthy children, seven and nine years of age. Although she had not been pregnant for the past seven years, she was anxious to be sterilized. Deeply impressed by a letter from a counseling center, she felt obliged to follow the example set by her older sister who had voluntarily had herself sterilized.

When the young lady came to see us in response to our request, she presented the symptoms of an acute anxiety state but revealed no evidence of a neurological disorder. Bravely resigned to the idea of being already afflicted with Huntington's chorea in its preclinical form, she produced the counseling letter which read as follows:

"It is generally accepted that Huntington's chorea is transmitted as a simple dominant characteristic. In this case, the probability of an individual being affected when one parent is affected is 1 chance in 2. This would be the situation which would apply in your case."

The letter went on to say, "We recognize certain additional factors associated with the disease, which may be of some value in your case. It is well established that the onset of the disease tends to be at approximately the same age among related individuals. This may be translated into the following risk of the disease appearing in your children: until such time as you develop Huntington's chorea or successfully pass the age of onset characteristic in your family, the probability that each of your children will be affected is 1 in 4."

The letter further stated, "It is important to note that in the event you should develop Huntington's chorea, then the probability that your children will be affected will be the same as your own present probability, namely 1 in 2 . . . Unfortunately, at the present time we know of no way of detecting an individual who will develop Huntington's chorea in time to prevent that anxiety associated with the disease and the anxiety with respect to one's children."

The unmitigated tenor of this communication speaks for itself and requires no psychological interpretation. At the time of our examination it was apparent that the young woman needed reassurance more than anything else. She herself confirmed this impression by the comment she had jotted down in the margin of the letter: "Hope is what we want — not statistics."

With all due respect to science, I do not hesitate to underscore the idea implicit in this young woman's remark. Adherence to scientific principles in genetic counseling is fine, but it is compatible with a certain amount of gentleness and psychological understanding in dealing with human problems.

As to appropriate medicogenetic indications for an elective sterilizing procedure, they should be compelling, fair, and humanized. Without adequate motivation, the necessity for the operation will be rationalized in one way or another. Fearful conviction of inescapable ill health may associate itself with feelings of guilt and inferiority, or breed promiscuous tendencies by creating the need for acting out the problem (Knight and Friedman, 1954).

The second case was that of a deaf couple in their late thirties, one of many we have seen in recent months. Both had lost their hearing in early childhood, and both had been married before. One marriage had ended in the suicide of the mate, the other in divorce. The woman in this case had been married to a hearing cousin, a shiftless man with whom she had a hearing daughter. Her present husband had two deaf children by his former marriage to a deaf childhood friend of borderline intelligence. In his second marriage he had hoped for a hearing son, but instead his wife had borne him a deaf daughter. Curiously enough, the most unhappy and poorly adjusted of the household's four children was the hearing girl. She blamed much of her frustration on being continuously rejected by the deaf members of her family.

The genetic information given this couple prior to their marriage had been to the effect that their future children would probably have no hearing impairment in view of the fact that the half-sister's hearing was normal despite the cousin marriage of her parents. Another clinic had offered the opinion that hereditary deafness tends to be recessive, generally occurs in sporadic form, and should preferably not be spread through marriage into a hearing family.

Here again, apart from the obvious need for scientific accuracy, it is evident that counseling involves people and not abstract problems. What is often overlooked in a genetic counseling situation of this kind is that even the best-educated people with an early hearing loss require instruction in the management of their family problems far more urgently than they need a genetic prognosis. Without special education, a deaf person is doomed to pass his life in a state of inarticulate ignorance and social isolation — without speech, without skills, and without the capacity for meeting the emotional and intellectual demands of adult life (Best, 1943).

If fully educated and trained, the deaf individual may be able to adjust to his particular conditions of minority group living, but he should not be expected to solve his specific family problems without expert guidance. In many instances, especially under conditions of gross parental immaturity or social inadequacy, it is certain to be as frustrating for hearing children as for nonhearing ones to be the offspring of deaf parents.

At the risk of accentuating the ambivalent attitude prevailing among some professional groups toward the aims and scientific principles of psychological medicine, it cannot be stressed too often that emotional disturbances may render people just as ineffectual as do any other serious illnesses. It is unfortunate that even in modern societies the psychic factors in many physical ailments continue to be neglected (Dunbar, 1954; Strecker, 1945).

Definitely avoidable, however, are situations where severe harm is done to relatively well-adjusted persons seeking advice in matters of health or family welfare. To this end, every professional worker — especially those whose work entails direct contact with human beings — should be made aware that thoughtless remarks or strenuously realistic comments may have a devastating effect on the adjustment and working capacity of sensitive persons, to such an extent that they may become chronic invalids.

It should be borne in mind that under the impact of such an experience even intelligent and ostensibly self-reliant persons may develop a feeling of living in an alien world. As a result, they become gloomy and insecure in their personal relationships, and gradually revert to immature forms of behavior.

In holding to one of the oldest ethical principles which dictates that mankind shall not suffer unduly and shall be given relief when it is within our power to do so (Lemkau, 1955), we must learn to accept the fact that proficiency of counseling in human genetics cannot be attained without some solid understanding of human psychology and human relations. To be sure, the primary responsibility of a genetic counselor is not specifically the mental health of the population with which he deals. Nevertheless, as has been indicated, he can do much good in this direction. He may be proud to consider himself a member of the "related service professions" working in the public health field, even as the family doctor, the schoolteacher, the probation officer, or the policeman on his beat (Ridenour, 1955).

While the scientific accomplishments of our discipline are truly remarkable, there is little doubt that our training programs have yet to prepare future genetic counselors for activity in the public health field (Herndon, 1955). It stands to reason that these workers will be unable to take a real interest in human problems until they have been effectively oriented toward them. Perhaps, in order to have a conception of the scope of physical and mental illness, every student of human genetics should be afforded the opportunity to have meaningful experiences in dealing with troubled people (Kallmann, 1952). In this way he will learn how to talk *with* people rather than at them or about them. Above all, he will gain a philosophy of public health. Then and only then will he know how to avoid creating ill will or ill health in any phase of his counseling work.

REFERENCES

Best, H.: *Deafness and the Deaf in the United States.* New York, Macmillan, 1943.

Dunbar, F.: *Emotion and Bodily Changes.* New York, Columbia University press, 1954, pp. 85-87.

Ekblad, M.: *Induced Abortion on Psychiatric Grounds.* Copenhagen, Munksgaard, 1955.

Herndon, C. N.: Heredity counseling. *Eugen. Quart., 2:*83-89, 1955.

Kallmann, F. J.: Human Genetics as a Science, as a profession and as a social-minded trend of orientation. *Am. J. Human Genet.,4:*237-245, 1952.

Kallmann, F. J.: Proceedings of 1955 Convention of American Instructors of the Deaf at Hartford, In press, 1955.

Knight, R. P., and Friedman, C. R. (Eds.): *Psychoanalytic Psychiatry and Psychology. Vol. I.* New York, International Universities Press, 1954, pp. 288-303.

Lemkau, P. V.: Why are we interested in mental health? *Ment. Hyg. 39:*353-364, 1955.

Neel, J. V. and Schull, W. J.: *Human Heredity.* Chicago, University of Chicago Press, 1954.

Reed, S.: *Counseling in Medical Genetics.* Philadelphia, Saunders, 1955, pp. 11-16.

Ridenour, N.: Mental health in the training of related service professions. *Mental Hygiene, 39:*476-482, 1955.

Strecker, E. A.: *Fundamentals of Psychiatry.* Philadelphia, Lippincott, 1945.

Chapter 27

Genetic Counseling

NANCY GEMMELL, M.D.

GENETIC counseling is one of the areas of applied mathematics in clinical medicine, and in some instances the mathematics, such as in Mendelian ratios, is reasonably straight-forward and easy to apply. In other instances only an empirical prognosis can be obtained. This prognosis is arrived at by determining the percentage chance of a given person bearing a certain familial relationship to the afflicted person of inheriting the disease concerned, and here the probabilities arrived at are more general and not as satisfactory either to the counselor or to the patient. The reasons for this are many, for such information is procured by an investigation of the initial case (propositus) and requires some pretty fancy footwork mathematically speaking. The results of various investigations must be pooled to arrive at a sufficiently large enough sample from which to draw conclusions, and there may be a lack of uniformity of investigation between the pooled samples, which will make the conclusions arrived at less plausible. Also the lack of ability to make a precise diagnosis — cryptogenic epilepsy comes to mind — means that the pooling of apparently similar samples may be wrong; that is, cryptogenic epilepsy in the future may be subdivided into several different diseases.

Where Mendelian ratios can be invoked, a further complication may occur — that is, what is apparently the same disease may have different modes of inheritance in different families. Gargoylism is such a case. In some families it is a Mendelian sex-linked recessive and in others it is a Mendelian autosomal recessive.

Despite these shortcomings, however, some relatively reasonable answers can be given to people seeking genetic counseling.

Note: Reprinted by permission of the author and the *Manitoba Medical Review*, 42:522-525, 1962.

Who are these people? The majority are parents who have had an afflicted child and they will ask one of several questions:
1. What are their chances of having a normal child?
2. Should they be sterilized?
3. Should they consider artificial insemination?
4. Should they have their present pregnancy terminated?

Except for the first question the answers given must be tailored to the individual. It is with the first question that the mathematics of the geneticist is used. I hope that you have noticed that one question is missing: "Should I marry this person when I know there is hereditary disease in their family or my family?"

This is the question that could prevent future heartache, and once lay people have a better understanding of heredity, I think this question will arise. It is here that the family doctor can play a vital part.

But to return to those people who seek counseling and their concern about having a normal child. As in any medical examination a thorough, well-checked family history is of the utmost importance. Ideally the counsellor should interview and, where necessary, examine physically (including all the necessary biochemical tests) as many members of the family, including uncles, aunts, cousins and grandparents, as are available. Medical records of deceased members should be obtained where possible. I have found that people just do not know the medical histories of any relative outside their immediate family – even when they claim that they do. So all reportedly positive cases must be confirmed by the counselor.

The results of such enquiries allows the counselor to draw up a family pedigree, and it is from this pedigree that conclusions concerning the chances of the next pregnancy being normal are drawn.

If a disease is caused by a single mutated gene, a form of Mendelian inheritance may show up in the pedigree.

If it is a Mendelian autosomal dominant, it will usually appear in more than one generation and will occur equally frequently in males and females. Occasionally a Mendelian autosomal dominant gene will apparently skip a generation. In this case the person who transmits the gene without any obvious effect on himself or herself is called a carrier and may, on close inspection, be found to have a forme fruste of the disease. The cause of this lack of penetrance of the action of the dominant gene is not known, but it is postulated that the total genic environment of this person has suppressed the malignant gene's action. The chances of parents, one of whom is afflicted and one of whom is normal, of having an afflicted child is 50:50 with each pregnancy, providing the gene always shows full or 100 percent penetrance. If the literature can report on the penetrance values of the gene under scrutiny, then the counselor must multiply the 50 percent chance of affliction with the percent degree of penetrance to arrive at the right answer. The chances of two afflicted parents of having an afflicted child are 75:25. Here penetrance need not be considered because both parents show the disease, therefore it is doubtful that the children can inherit a genic environment with a suppressor action.

If it is a Mendelian autosomal recessive gene, then all affected members of the family will occur in one generation and the parents may be consanguineous. In Mendelian autosomal recessive inheritance both parents are carriers of the disease.

The disease will not become manifest unless the child inherits both the bad genes from its parents. Forme frustes may or may not occur in the carriers. The chance of having an afflicted child by such a union is 25 percent or 25:75. But the chance of the parents producing another carrier is 50 percent. Therefore the total ratio concerning all types of offspring borne becomes: 25% normal: 50% carrier: 25% afflicted.

One mother who was a carrier of a Mendelian autosomal recessive gene asked about artificial insemination and was reminded that she still ran a 50 percent risk of having a carrier child.

A more complicated but not too uncommon form of Mendelian inheritance is the sex-linked recessive form. The classical example of this is hemophilia — although now there are other forms of hemophilia-like disease that may be inherited in a different way. In sex-linked recessive diseases the pedigree usually shows afflicted males who are the sons of carrier mothers. No male will pass the disease to a son. No female will be affected unless her parents show an afflicted male married to a carrier female. This is an extremely rare event. The usual mating is a carrier female to a normal male. This will cause 50 percent of all males to be afflicted and 50 percent of all females to be carriers. The marriage of an afflicted male to a normal female will produce 100 percent female carriers and 100 percent normal males.

There are some other very rare forms of Mendelian inheritance — sex-linked dominant and holandric types that may or may not exist in fact. The geneticists cannot make up their own minds at the present time about them, so that until the issue is settled, they may be ignored.

It is possible, but much rarer, that a pedigree showing more than one afflicted member may not represent the results of a single mutated gene, but may be produced by a chromosomal abnormality. This type of inheritance is not governed by Mendelian laws and will be enlarged on later.

What do you do with a pedigree that shows only one diseased child and no other afflicted member of the family? First, look up the literature and find out what is the usual mode of inheritance of the disease. Find out whether carriers may occur and if there is some technique available for bringing them to light. If one parent is a carrier and a male, the obvious inference is that this is an autosomal dominant. If the one carrier parent is a female and the diseased child is a male, the inheritance may be either autosomal dominant or sex-linked recessive. The literature should help out here. If both parents are shown to be carriers, the only assumption that can be made is autosomal recessive. When carrier states are not detectable, then reliance on the literature is the only resort.

If the literature reports the disease under investigation to be a Mendelian autosomal dominant, then you must assume that this child is a new mutation. A gene in an ovum or sperm has undergone spontaneous mutation, and the chances of another child being born with the same disease is rare. But the child with the mutation should be warned that 50 percent of his or her offspring will have the same disease.

If the disease is inherited as a Mendelian sex-linked recessive, then the only afflicted child will be a male and a new mutation. It is unlikely that other new mutations will occur in the same family, but he should be warned that 50 percent of his male offspring will be diseased and 50 percent of his female offspring will be carriers.

If the pattern of inheritance has not been well-established, the child may have a chromosomal abnormality. This can be confirmed by examination of the child's chromosomes.

Chromosomal abnormalities may appear spontaneously in the ova of women over thirty-five years of age and are directly linked with the aging process. The family pedigree may show the appearance of an abnormal child at or near the end of a succession of normal children. At any rate, the child will be the offspring of a mother over thirty-five, and there will usually be only one abnormal child per family.

Occasionally a chromosomal abnormality may be familial. In the July 14th, 1962, *Lancet,* there is a preliminary communication on chromosomal abnormalities in a mother and her two mentally retarded children. The pedigree was not drawn, but would look like the following:

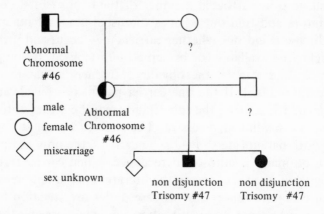

Figure 27-1.

In this pedigree the grandfather had a chromosomal translocation affecting all his cells. That is, a piece of one autosome broke off and became attached to another autosome, and under these conditions there is little or no loss of genic material — simply a rearrangement. In this case, one of the autosomes of group 17-18 donated a segment of chromosomal material to one of the chromosomes of group 13-15. This rearrangement will not affect cells undergoing mitosis because the homologous or matching chromosomes need not pair before undergoing cell division, but this picture changes abruptly during meiosis. Because of the translocated chromosome, one of the chromosomal pairs in group 13-15 will not match perfectly, and abnormal pairing will occur. This means that only one half of the grandfather's sperm will receive the normal amount of genic material with or without the translocated chromosome. Theoretically, one half of all his possible offspring will be miscarriages, stillbirths, congenitally abnormal, or he may be relatively infertile. Whether this occurred in this pedigree is not mentioned, but his one offspring that is mentioned is a daughter with the same translocation. Her offspring illustrate the other complication that may occur with abnormally shaped chromosomes. When her cells underwent abnormal pairing during meiosis, the stunted or foreshortened chromosome of the 12-15 group refused to separate from its normal homologous mate and went with its mate to the same cell. This is called nondisjunction of chromosomes and causes twice the normal amount of material from one pair of chromosomes to remain in one ovum or sperm. When that cell is fertilized, another chromosome containing similar genic material is introduced into the cell and this adds up to three doses of the same type of genic material present in a single fertilized cell.

This is known as trisomy and is, as far is known, incompatible with normal human development.

From the clinical standpoint the next question that arises is "How often will nondisjunction occur?" This question cannot be answered as yet, because too few cases of familial chromosomal abnormalities have been published. But even without nondisjunction, the chances of a normal offspring are only 50 percent.

In cases of reciprocal translocation, where two nonhomologous chromosomes exchange segments, the picture grows darker. Without nondisjunction only one third of all possible births will be normal and two thirds will be miscarriages, etc. So it can be said of familial chromosomal translocation that the chances of a normal birth with each pregnancy are less than 50:50. These chances will decrease still further when the maternal age reaches thirty-five.

A pseudofamilial pedigree may be observed when one or more children of normal parents are shown to possess chromosomal abnormalities while their parents' chromosomes are normal. This is produced by chromosomal mosaicism in one of the mother's ovaries. Here a primordial germ cell has undergone a chromosomal aberration during a cell division. Commonly only one child will be afflicted, but rarely there may be more than one. There is no positive way of predicting the chances of the birth of a normal child, because there is no way at the present time of knowing how many abnormal primordial cells are involved. In a general way, it can be said that usually only one child will be affected.

Another very rare form of familial chromosomal abnormality is described by Penrose as being "a primary nondisjunction facilitated by a maternal homozygous genetical constitution." In plain language, a female with a normal chromosomal constitution may inherit from both her parents a bad gene which increases the chances of nondisjunction of the chromosomes of her germ cells. This type of inheritance was postulated when a male mongoloid was born who was trisomic for autosome number 21 and also had Klinefelter's syndrome with an XXY chromosome pattern. The boy's total chromosome count was 48. This type of abnormality was the offspring of a young mother and, if she does inherit her tendency to nondisjunction as a Mendelian autosomal recessive, then 100 percent of all future offspring should be affected because of her homozygous state, but this situation has not been proven as yet.

There is one type of chromosomal aberration which may appear in one child of a young, normal mother that does not bode ill for future births. This is a somatic nondisjunction producing a chromosomal mosaic which is initiated by the child's own genetic constitution. That is, a normal fertilized ovum in one of its first cell divisions during metaphase loses control over the orderly subdivision of its chromosomes with the end result that an extra chromosome is present in one cell and lost from its cell twin. In this way approximately 50 percent of the somatic cells of the developing foetus will have a chromosome count of 47, and 50 percent will have a chromosome count of 45. This type of abnormality can be diagnosed by doing chromosome counts of cells from different parts of the body.

Finally, I must return to those inherited diseases for which only an empirical prognosis can be made. Many of these diseases require more than one factor to bring them to fruition. For example, diabetes mellitus may be inherited either as a Mendelian autosomal dominant or a Mendelian autosomal recessive. It is postulated that juvenile diabetes is the recessive form and adult diabetes is the dominant form. The juvenile form seems to need little environmental encouragement to put in its appearance, but the adult form sometimes requires the onset of obesity to bring it into the open. Sometimes the juvenile and adult forms occur in the same pedigree in such a way as to confound the recessive-dominant theory. Because diabetes mellitus can put in an appearance anywhere from birth to old age — this can confound an accurate prediction. In other words, such disease entities are multifactorial and ratios of abnormal: normal can have only a general accuracy. There is one safeguard to help shape a prognostication and that is the particular family pedigree that has been drawn up. Multifactorial diseases have a tendency to behave similarly within a single family group. If one parent has had mild epilepsy, the empirical risk for each child will be from 1:20 - 1:40, but even if the child becomes epileptic, the chances are close to 100 percent that it will be the same kind of epilepsy as his or her parent. Looking again at the pedigree — if there seems to be many affected family members, I would make the ratio 1:20 rather than 1:40, and when cryptogenic epilepsy can be subdivided diagnostically, these ratios will become more accurate. I am not going to discuss in detail multifactorial disease, although this group is the one most commonly encountered. There is a good book called *Counselling in Medical Genetics* by Sheldon C. Reed, which deals adequately with this problem. Its chapter on mongolism is out of date, but the rest of the book is useful to the doctor who has to counsel one of these multifactorial diseases. Another book which attempts to cover the whole field of medical genetics is *Clinical Genetics* by Arnold Sorsby, but it should be supplemented by a search of recent literature because it deals with some diseases in a very brief way, and there may be more recent information in the literature to confirm or deny the previous evidence. If the information obtained seems conflicting or does not fit the family pedigree drawn up, then full reliance must be placed on that pedigree. It would be wonderful if every doctor would report on every case of familial disease, accompanied by all the appropriate tests, that occurred in his own practice, for then medical genetics would take a giant step forward.

REFERENCES

Penrose, L. S.: Mongolism. *Brit. Med. Bull., 17:*(3), Sept., 1961.

Reed, Sheldon C.: *Counseling in Medical Genetics.* Philadelphia and London, W. B. Saunders, 1963.

Sorsby, Arnold: *Clinical Genetics.* London, Butterworth and Co., Ltd., 1953.

Visile, Hallvard, Wehn, Margarethe, Brogger, Anton, and Mohr, Jan: Chromosomal abnormalities in a mother and two mentally retarded children. *Lancet, 60*(2): 76-78, July 14, 1962.

Chapter 28

Mongolism and Genetic Counseling

ROBERT E. MERRILL, M.D.*

MANY physicians have not had the opportunity to acquire sufficient basic information to allow the interpretation and application of rapidly accumulating advances in genetics. Many medical students need more instruction in genetics, reflecting the inability of many institutions to adjust the curriculum in consonance with the increasing clinical importance of the discipline.

Mongolism (Down's syndrome; mongoloidism) is a condition which lends itself readily to a discussion of genetics, since new technics and new knowledge have provided a foundation upon which realistic genetic counseling may be based. To show how the physician may advise the parents of a child with mongolism, and the reasons therefor, are the objects of these comments.

The science of genetics has emerged during the twentieth century. The laws of segregation and independent assortment as described by Mendel, and the identification of chromosomes as the structures responsible for these phenomena are basic to all that has followed.

The very large salivary gland chromosomes found in *Drosophila melanogaster* and other qualities of this species have led to important discoveries permitting accurate mapping of chromosomes. Mapping represents the correlation of various observed attributes with specific segments of specific chromosomes. To date mapping has been virtually impossible in the human.

Note: Reprinted by permission of the author and *Clinical Pediatrics, 2*:531-533, 1963.
Assistant Professor of Pediatrics, Vanderbilt University School of Medicine, Nashville, Tennessee.

Information pertaining to human genetics has lagged far behind that derived from other species. The inability to control human procreation, the long life cycle of the human, and the relative unavailability of suitable material for study have contributed to this lag.

The use of molds, corn, animals, bacteria, and viruses has contributed to the general fund of knowledge, so that we now have available significant information on the chemical nature of genetic material. Also we know how it is transmitted and something of its mechanism of action. Some of this information has clinical significance, as in sickle cell disease. However, for most of the inherited diseases the physician must be content with the application of Mendelian laws as in hemophilia and fibrocystic disease. Specifically, these are useful for estimating the likelihood of another affected child.

The bone marrow and peripheral blood culture technics have led to accurate chromosome counting and identification in the human. Nevertheless, correctly prepared specimens for accurate interpretation require meticulous technical skill, and the time required has been an important reason why chromosome counting has remained primarily a research tool.

The general principles of classical genetics have been found to be the same for humans as for other species. In almost every case, the apparent exceptions have contributed to the understanding of the basic mechanisms of pathogenesis of clinical disturbances.

Alterations of genetic material either in amount or in ultrastructure will result in some change in the organism, either in function, structure, or both. One possible alteration is the loss of a complete chromosome. If the deleted chromosome is an autosome, a term applied to any chromosome other than a sex chromosome, the result is usually lethal. This result is evident either because the gamete (the egg or the sperm) with the missing chromosome does not survive or because the zygote (the union of the male with the female gamete) with the missing chromosome does not survive.

The loss of extremely small fractions of a human chromosome apparently may be tolerated with little or no discernible alteration. What portion of each chromosome may be lost with impunity must vary with the chromosome and the segment involved and is, in general, a matter of speculation.

On the other hand, too much genetic material is not necessarily lethal as illustrated by the description of several syndromes associated with extra genetic material.

With mongolism, this extra autosome (that one designated number 21) has been found unattached in virtually all of the cells of the affected individual. In a fewer number of cases, it is attached to another autosome, or rarely it may be unattached in a large proportion of the cells.

In the first instance, the extra chromosome has been ascribed to nondisjunction. During normal meiosis, when gametes are formed, the chromosomes line up in pairs, following which the genetic material is divided equally between two cells. These cells, in turn, give rise to the gametes. Normally, the number 21 chromosome lines up opposite the other number 21 and as the process evolves, one of these autosomes goes to each daughter cell. Figure 28-1 illustrates this normal phenomenon.

When this very critical process does not proceed normally, both of the number 21 chromosomes may migrate to one of the daughter cells leading to gametes which have two number 21 chromosomes rather than the normal single one. The cell line with the missing chromosome apparently dies. This abnormal process is illustrated by Figure 28-2.

The failure of normal separation (or disjunction) is termed nondisjunction and has been accepted as the basis, depending on the chromosome involved, of a variety of clinical syndromes. Various autosomes and the sex chromosomes have been implicated. It is probable that the extra genetic material (the extra chromosome) causes, in ways largely unexplained, the many manifestations of the particular disease under study. Nondisjunction involving chromosome number 21 is associated with mongolism. Nondisjunction is associated with advanced maternal age in humans and in other species (particularly Drosophila). We find that most mongols have three number 21 autosomes and that the mothers are well advanced in the childbearing age.

It is also true that the mothers of the common type of mongoloid have a normal number of chromosomes. This is

NORMAL MEIOSIS
21
21
21
21

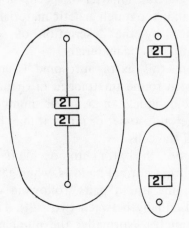

Figure 28-1. Diagrammatic representation of the normal separation of a specific pair of normal chromosomes.

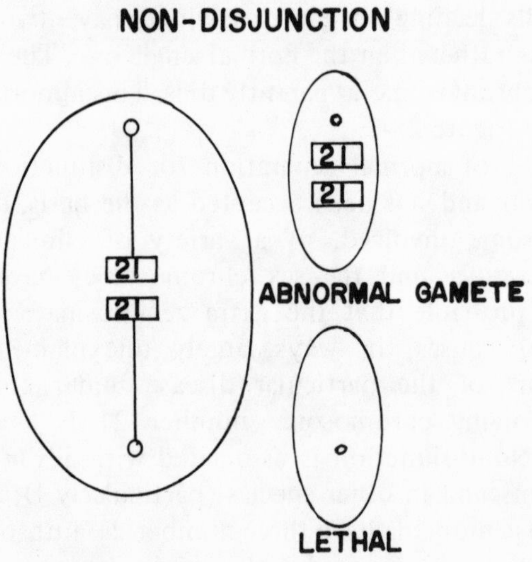

NON-DISJUNCTION
21
21
21
21
ABNORMAL GAMETE
LETHAL

Figure 28-2. Diagrammatic representation of the failure of normal separation of a specific pair of chromosomes.

expected because nondisjunction occurs during the formation of ova and is detectable only in those individuals derived from gametes with the extra chromosome. The abnormal ovum, normally fertilized, becomes the child with mongolism. That the demonstration of this abnormality in the blood cells of a child with mongolism can be of value in establishing the diagnosis is obvious.

Of more importance, although relatively rare, is the mongoloid who shows the normal number of chromosomes (46) but actually has extra genetic material (a number 21 chromosome or large portion thereof) attached to another autosome. This abnormality is called translocation. The effect in regard to the abnormal child is the same since the individual has three portions of genetic material designated chromosome 21 and is, therefore, clinically indistinguishable from the more common type. How the translocation is induced in the human is unknown.

In this form of the disease, it has been determined that frequently the mother is a carrier of the condition. She has the normal amount of genetic material but has the number 21 chromosome attached to another autosome (frequently number 15), Her genotype in regard to chromosomes number 21 and 15 are illustrated in Figure 28-3 under the term carrier parent.

When this woman produces ova, they may be expected by chance alone to be characterized in four ways with respect to the two specific chromosome pairs under discussion. The other chromosome pairs will also segregate and assort independently in the normal fashion but can be ignored here for illustrative purposes. Figure 28-3 shows that the following combinations are possible.

1. A normal 15 and no 21. This plus a normal sperm is likely to be lethal. A chromosome (21) is missing.
2. A normal 15 and normal 21. This plus a normal sperm would result in a normal child.
3. The 15/21 complex and no 21. This plus a normal sperm would result in a carrier. This is the same as the carrier parent.
4. The 15/21 complex and a normal 21. This plus a normal sperm would result in a child with mongolism. This child

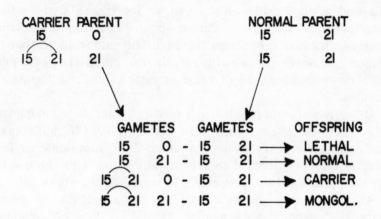

Figure 28-3. A scheme to illustrate possible combinations in regard to chromosomes 21 and 15 only. The other chromosomes are omitted for illustrative purposes. The 15/21 attachment is represented by *15 21*. *0* indicates that the number 21 chromosome is either absent or attached elsewhere and unable to migrate independently.

has an extra chromosome (number 21).

Since only three identifiable products of conception would be observed, because the lethals are seldom identified as such, the apparent chance of each to appear is one out of three.

More recently, a factor has been identified which may alter the projected risk. Male carriers have been found who produce other carriers but few actual mongoloids; this suggests that whether the gametes produced by the carrier are ova or spermatozoa has a direct bearing on the risk. Presumably, other factors will be identified to refine the risk figures further.

The importance of identification of this parent carrier among the usually young women (and their husbands) who have given birth to children with mongolism is evident if one proposes to answer any question in regard to further pregnancies with some assurance. It is particularly appropriate to request chromosome analysis with mongoloids born of young parents.

A third variety of mongolism, apparently associated with

nondisjunction (chromosome 21) during mitosis very early in the developing embryo, results in an abnormal cell line which can influence the organism enough to present a picture of clinical mongolism. The cell line with the missing chromosome probably dies. This form is apparently very rare but may also be more common in the offspring of the young mother. This condition is called mosaicism and can be defined as any condition in which a large proportion of the somatic cells vary in chromosome complement in comparison to the predominant type of cells. Mosaicism has been described associated with other chromosomes and other syndromes. The identification of these children has no practical application at this time, but efforts to determine what maternal factors may influence this abnormality may have far-reaching clinical application.

Similarly, the increased incidence of leukemia in children with mongolism has been well established. What relation this apparent susceptibility has to the presence of extra genetic material is unknown, but it may present an opportunity for mapping specific genetic loci on human chromosomes.

These new facts concerning the chromosomal abnormalities, which are seen in association with mongolism, make possible more realistic counseling for families in which children with mongolism appear. In the light of present knowledge, it is suggested that every mongol born of a mother less than thirty years of age be subjected to chromosome analysis. Similarly, the second mongol in any family should be so examined. With the information obtained, the physician may more accurately estimate the chance of a recurrence and may share these estimates with the family.

It is probable that more clinical syndromes will be described in which the same basic approach will be applicable. An understanding of what is known now may provide a basis of ever widening clinical application as this cloudy picture is clarified.

REFERENCES

Carter, C.O., and Evans, K. A.: Risk of parents who have had one child with Down's syndrome (mongolism) having another child similarly affected. *Lancet,, 2*:785-788, 1961.

Hirschhorn, K., and Cooper, H.L.: Chromosomal aberrations in human disease. A review of the status of cytogenetics in medicine. *Am. J. Med., 31*:442, 1961.

Polani, Paul E.: Cytogenetics of Down's syndrome (mongolism). *Ped. Clin. N. Amer. 10*(No. 2).:423, 1963.

Smith, D.W., Patau, K., and Therman, E.: Autosomal trisomy syndromes. *Lancet, 2*:211, 1961.

Chapter 29

Genetic Counseling for
Down's Syndrome (Mongolism)

SHELDON C. REED, Ph.D.

IT is perhaps typical of the dilatory interest in human genetics that the correct number of chromosomes in man was unknown until 1956 and the first trisomy (mongolism) was not found until 1959. This sort of cytological information had been available for thirty years in Drosophila and various weeds, such as Datura. When the chromosome breakthrough finally came for man, it was explosive because of its tardiness. The effect of the chromosome breakthrough on genetic counseling is well illustrated by the first really exciting bit of information obtained, namely, that Down's syndrome (mongolism) results from the presence in the fertilized egg of an extra 21st chromosome (Lejeune et al., 1959). This trisomy for the 21st pair of chromosomes results from the failure of the egg cell to reduce its number of chromosomes to only one member of each and every chromosome pair. When both members of the 21st pair of chromosomes are still present at the entrance of a sperm with its usual single 21st chromosome, a total of three members of this particular pair of chromosomes will be present, and Down's syndrome will result, even though all the other chromosomes are present in normal pairs.

It is interesting that the extra chromosome is more often marooned in the egg of an older woman than in a younger one. We do not know what causes this chromosomal lethargy in women as they grow older, but the phenomenon is thoroughly established. Indeed, if all women over forty years of age refrained from pregnancy, the number of children born with Down's syndrome

Note: Reprinted by permission of the author and *Eugenics Quarterly, 10*:139-142, 1963.

would be decreased by one-third. The eugenic advice that women complete their reproduction before age forty is sound and of importance to them and to the nation. The "age of mother" effect has been known for years, but it is doubtful that as many as one woman in ten thousand ceases reproduction after the age of forty for fear of having a mongoloid child. Let us hope that eugenic education will proceed more swiftly, beginning now.

Genetic counseling before the chromosome breakthrough was based entirely on empiric risks but was decidedly successful nonetheless. The clients were usually older mothers of a child with Down's syndrome who were relieved to learn that the chances were small that they would have a repetition of their misfortune even for the older ages. To be sure, they were warned that there was a real chance, even if a small one, that they might have another child with Down's syndrome and that the "lightning never strikes in the same place twice" cliché is the worst kind of false security. The younger mothers and the occasional mother with familial mongolism were disturbing because they had many years of fertility ahead. My counseling in these rare cases was always frustrating because the same empiric risk figure of about a 3 or 4 percent chance of a repetition of Down's syndrome at the next pregnancy had to be used for all.

The advent of chromosome study of the leucocytes and skin cells has thrown great light upon a previously dark and mysterious situation. The children with Down's syndrome fall into three chromosomally very distinct groups.

The first group of children have the "free" 21st chromosome in addition to the regular pair of 21st chromosomes, which is the classical human trisomy referred to above. There will still be some uncertainty in counseling older mothers because, unless there is a history of other mongoloids or miscarriages in the family, or among close relatives, we regretfully decline to make a chromosome study. It has been estimated that the actuarial cost of making a chromosome study is about four hundred dollars. Chromosome studies cannot be purchased like blood-typing work because few technicians are competent to do them. How many clients can be accommodated depends upon the supply of technicians available. Some physicians and scientists have asked me why one should take the trouble to make a chromosome study anyway. This question always makes me shudder because it is clear that the asker has no comprehension of the agony endured by the mother of a mongoloid child. The parents of a child with Down's syndrome want very much to know what the child's chromosome picture is, and it is difficult to explain why they should be deprived of such specific information.

The second group of children with Down's syndrome are most perplexing in that some of their cells have the extra free chromosome while other cells in the same child are normal. If they were completely normal, the parents of this "mosaic" child would usually not expect any further children with Down's syndrome.

The different chromosomal picture of the third group of children with Down's syndrome is fascinating to say the least, and the counseling is agonizing for the counselor and some members of these families, but most exhilarating for some of the others. Here we have the "familial" cases of the anomaly which result from a chromosomal translocation or fusion. In this group we find that, at some time in the ancestry of the patient with Down's syndrome, two chromosomes of unrelated pairs came in contact with each other and in some way fused together, or as we say, were translocated. If a person has two chromosomes fused together, they will be counted as one chromosome in the cytological preparation. Thus, if the two smallest chromosomes are fused, namely the 21st and 22nd, we will find one 21st chromosome, and one 22nd chromosome and a new unique chromosome composed of the fused 21/22 chromosomes. The total chromosome count will therefore be 45 instead of the normal 46. This will be crystal clear in any good preparation, particularly in women where there is no Y chromosome to clutter up the picture.

The person with a total count of 45 chromosomes, one of which is the 21/22, is called a normal carrier and has no obvious difficulty in conceiving. The results of reproduction are likely to be disasterous. It is not clear precisely what types of embryos will result from the possible products of meiosis in the carrier person. However, more than half of them will be undesirable, and therein lies the importance and gravity of the counseling situation for the third group of children with Down's syndrome. The reader is referred to the paper of Macintyre *et al.* (1962) for a diagram of the expected gametes produced by the normal carrier person. After fertilization has occurred, it is my assumption that about one quarter of the eggs will be chromosomally deficient and result in miscarriage, about one quarter will have Down's syndrome, one quarter will be normal carriers of the translocated chromosome, and only one quarter will be completely clear of the situation. Presumably, of the children coming to term, one third would be mongoloid, one third normal carriers, and only one third would be absolutely normal. Thus, there will be no good news for the normal carrier of a translocated chromosome. These percentages may not be precise but they are practical.

At last we come to the specific of the three quite different counseling situations, depending upon the type of extra 21st chromosome present.

In the first group of children, where there is a "free" third chromosome of the 21st pair, we would not expect a much greater chance of a repetition of the anomaly than in any other mother of the same age. For younger mothers the chance would be roughly one in one thousand of a repetition at each subsequent pregnancy, and for older ones the risk would be in the neighborhood of 3 or 4 percent.

The second group of mosaic children is such an irregular group that the counseling would be entirely dependent upon individual circumstances, such as the proportion of aberrant chromosome counts in each child, and the parent's chromosome picture.

The third group, where we are counseling a normal carrier, is the most threatening and is worth consideration on a casework basis. We have studied three families with fused chromosomes at the University of Minnesota. One is a 15/21 translocation and two are 21/22 translocations. An element of surprise to us was that two of the three families turned out to have the supposedly rare 21/22 translocation. We have studied less than thirty cases of young mothers with one or more mongoloid children, and have found the three translocations, which is better than 10 percent of the group of vulnerable young mothers who turn out to have this grave problem. It is most unlikely that there were more than one hundred children born with Down's syndrome in our area during this period of time, so that the frequency of translocation mongoloids among all mongoloids must be at least 3 percent. All three of our young normal carrier mothers were residents of Minneapolis.

The 15/21 translocation normal carrier mother is a Roman Catholic, and due to circumstances of no particular biological significance, I have not seen this couple for counseling yet.

One of the two 21/22 normal carrier mothers is a twenty-three-year-old Roman Catholic and has had two pregnancies, both resulting in children with Down's syndrome. She was referred after the birth of her first child at age twenty-two, and was already pregnant again at referral. However, I was on an extended trip at the time and nothing was done until my return when the second affected child was born. The young couple came for counseling as soon as the mother was out of the hospital. The various categories of chromosomal possibilities were explained to them, and they realized very well that there was a real chance that one or the other of them was a normal carrier of a fused chromosome. They were very much more apprehensive of this than I. Both members of the couple were from large families with no miscarriages or affected children as far as their parents were aware. After the chromosome study was completed by Dr. Jorge Yunis and Mrs. Ness, I asked the couple to return so that I might show them the pictures of their chromosomes. I thought that I did a smooth job of breaking the news that the wife was the carrier of the 21/22 translocation and could not guess why I seemed more concerned about it than they were. It soon turned out that they had decided before coming to see the chromosome pictures that they did not want to take any further chances, regardless of what they were going to find out from their visit.

The discussion then turned to methods of preventing further pregnancies, religion obviously entering the picture. The wife's menstrual periods have always been regular and they think that they can win with the rhythm method. I suspect that this case will be reopened.

The final case was easier to handle, as the young mother has a brother with Down's syndrome and had produced two miscarriages and a daughter with Down's syndrome. She already knew about the chromosome translocation types from reading the newspapers. The couple assumed that she had a translocation and expected me to demonstrate it. Fortunately, I did not try too desperately to dissuade them from this idea because it turned out that she is a normal carrier of a 21/22 fusion. This twenty-seven-year-old woman has a normal brother who was shown *not* to be a carrier of the fused chromosome by Dr. Herbert L. Cooper of the National Institute of Dental Research. The fact that the normal brother can be freed from apprehension is one of the positive and enjoyable aspects of genetic counseling.

This couple is Protestant and desires no further pregnancies. They have applied to the appropriate agency for the privilege of adopting a child. The agency requires proof of lack of fertility before placement. I was called upon to explain what the situation was to the agency, which had had no previous experience with translocated chromosomes.

There is no question but that the two young mothers and their husbands came to the conclusion, without any urging, that it would be unwise for them to have further pregnancies. In both cases the advantages of permanent contraception, sterilization, were pointed out and the Protestant couple has asked me for assistance in obtaining this final solution of their problems.

The cytological details of these three families are of great interest and, when other relatives have been studied, will be published elsewhere by Drs. Jorge Yunis, Herbert Cooper, and Kurt Hirschorn, and Mrs. Inez Ness. This present report merely introduces a few of the points involved in the "familial" cases where counseling is of great value both in helping the normal carrier of a translocation to understand his plight correctly, and particularly in freeing the relatives without the translocation from the apprehension which they otherwise could not escape.

REFERENCES

Lejuene, J., Gautier, M., et Turpin, R. Les chromosomes humains en culture de tissus. *C. R. Acad. Sci.,* (Paris) *248*:1721, 1959.

Macintyre, M. M., Staples, W. I., Steinberg, A. G., and Hempel, J. M.: Familial mongolism (Trisomy-21 Syndrome) resulting from a "15/21" chromosome translocation in more than three generations of a large kindred. *Am. J. Hum. Genet., 14:*335-344, 1962.

Chapter 30

Reproductive and Marital
Experience of Parents of
Children with Down's Syndrome
(Mongolism)

ARNOLD T. SIGLER, M.D.,* BERNICE H. COHEN, Ph.D.,
ABRAHAM M. LILIENFELD, M.D., JEANNETTE E. WESTLAKE, R.N.
and WILLIAM H. HETZNECKER, M.D.

RECENT cytogenetic observations stimulated an epidemiologic study of the possible relationships between certain factors postulated to cause chromosomal aberrations and the occurrence of clinically diagnosed Down's syndrome. Among the factors studied were parental radiation exposure, reproductive

Note: Reprinted with permission of the author and the *Journal of Pediatrics,* *70:*608-614, 1967. Copyrighted by The C.V. Mosby Co., St. Louis, Mo.

From the Department of Pediatrics, Harriet Lane Home, Children's Medical and Surgical Center, School of Medicine; and Department of Chronic Diseases, School of Public Health, The Johns Hopkins University.

Supported by United States Public Health Service, Research Branch, Division of Radiological Health, Contract No. SAph 76367, and in part by National Cancer Institute Grant No. CT 5085 and National Heart Institute Grant No. HE5297.

Some of the computations in this paper were done in the Computing Center of the Johns Hopkins Medical Institutions, which is supported by Research Grant FR-00004 from the National Institutes of Health.

*Part of this study was performed while Dr. Sigler was assigned to the Research Branch, Division of Radiological Health, United States Public Health Service.

333

patterns, and marital history. The observations in respect to radiation exposure and parental age have been published in detail (Sigler, *et al.,* 1965 a,b). Briefly, the mothers of children with Down's syndrome had a history of significantly increased exposure to fluoroscopic and therapeutic radiation prior to the birth of the child with Down's syndrome. No significant difference in the radiation exposure of the fathers was observed. A surprisingly high frequency of exposure to radar, however, was noted among the fathers of the children with Down's syndrome. Though there was no positive statistical association of paternal age and the birth of a child with Down's syndrome, there was a significant relationship with advanced maternal age.

Many of the earlier studies have examined the reproductive and fertility patterns of parents of children with Down's syndrome (Berda, 1960; Murphy, 1936; Beidleman, 1945; Engler, 1949; Down, 1909; Smith and Record, 1955; Coppen and Cowie, 1960; Ingalls, *et al.,* 1957; Oster, 1953; Lunn, 1959). This investigation reexamines these characteristics not only in mothers of affected children but also in a comparable series of mothers of control children.

METHOD

A detailed description of the methods used in this investigation is contained in previous reports (Sigler, 1965a,b) and this is only briefly reviewed here.

Several Baltimore sources made available the names of 421 children with a diagnosis of mongolism. For the parents to be eligible for interview, the child must have been Caucasian and born in greater Baltimore after Jan. 1, 1946, and before Oct. 1, 1962.

After eliminating those who did not meet these requirements, 288 children with Down's syndrome were available for study. Those eliminated either could not be located in the city directory, were not born in Baltimore, were not Caucasian, or were too old.

Birth certificates of the children with Down's syndrome were located. To ascertain control subjects, the birth certificate of each "case" was systematically matched with another birth certificate on the basis of (1) hospital of birth (or birth at home), (2) sex, (3) date of birth, and (4) maternal age at the time of birth of the child. All "cases" were matched with controls of identical sex, race, and place of birth. In 84.7 percent of the matched families, the birth dates of the children and ages of their respective mothers were the same. The mean age for the mothers of the children with Down's syndrome was 32.6 years and for the control mothers was 32.5 years.

Each eligible child reported to have Down's syndrome was examined by the senior author (A.T.S.). When the index child was deceased, confirmation of the diagnosis was based on data in medical and hospital records (Sigler, 1965b). Of the 288 children, 9 who were deceased or unavailable were eliminated because their medical records did not list the required number of signs to confirm the diagnosis. Another nine were rejected after personal examinations because of negative or equivocal diagnosis. In addition to those 18 rejected on the basis of diagnosis, 54 more were eliminated for the following reasons:

Parents of mongoloid child refused to cooperate.	17
Parents of control child refused to cooperate.	20
Unable to locate family of mongoloid child.	15
Parents of mongoloid child were unable to give adequate interview.	2

Thus of the original 288 cases available for study, 72 were eliminated, leaving 216 accepted for study. In every instance in which a family refused to cooperate, the corresponding matched control was also eliminated.

The interviewing of case and of control families was performed by five well-qualified women and in special instances by a physician. The approach to the families with an affected child and to the families of the controls was uniform. The interviewers were not informed as to which family had the abnormal index child; recognition of the family of the child with Down's syndrome was not usually made until the actual interview was conducted. Obstetrical hospital records as well as birth certificates on all pregnancies were checked for miscarriages, stillbirths, and the presence of other congenital abnormalities.

RESULTS

Reproductive History

The lifetime reproductive history of the mothers of the children with Down's syndrome and of the controls is summarized in Table 30-I. There is a striking similarity between the two groups with respect to fertility experience and pregnancy wastage. There were no significant differences in the number of pregnancies, abortions, or stillbirths either before or after the birth of the index child. Prior to the birth of the index child, 1.7 percent of the pregnancies of the mothers of the Down's group and 2.5 percent of the mothers of the control group ended in stillbirth, whereas 14.2 percent of the pregnancies of the mothers of the Down's children ended in abortion as compared to 12.2 percent of the mothers of the controls. Following the birth of the index child, the incidence of stillbirths was 1.1 percent in each group of

TABLE 30-I

PREGNANCY WASTAGE IN MOTHERS OF CHILDREN WITH
DOWN'S SYNDROME AND IN MOTHERS OF CONTROLS BY MATERNAL
AGE AND BY TIME RELATIONSHIP TO INDEX CHILD

| Maternal Age groups | Prior to Index Child | | | | Subsequent to Index Child | | | |
| | Total Pregnancies | | Abortions and Stillbirths* (%) | | Total Pregnancies | | Abortions and Stillbirths† (%) | |
	Down's	Controls	Down's	Controls	Down's	Controls	Down's	Controls
15-19	1	4	100.0	0	10	16	10.0	0
20-24	32	36	25.0	19.9	52	64	11.5	18.8
25-29	43	57	16.3	17.6	41	47	9.7	23.4
30-34	127	105	15.8	14.3	44	32	20.5	9.4
35-39	185	167	15.7	14.4	28	24	28.6	12.5
40-44	135	148	13.3	13.6	1	5	0	40.0
45-49	4	0	25.0	0	0	0	0	0
50 +	0	0	0	0	0	0	0	0
Total	527	517	15.9	14.7	176	188	15.9	16.5

*For percent of stillbirths, p > .30. For percent of abortions, p > .30.
†For percent of stillbirths, no difference. For percent of abortions, p > .80.

mothers, while 14.8 percent of the mothers of the affected children and 15.4 percent of the mothers of the controls had abortions. In addition, there were no significant differences for either birth or pregnancy order of the index child. Similarly, there were no important differences in the interval of time between the preceding pregnancy and the birth of the index child, or in the interval of time following the index child's birth and subsequent pregnancies. The number of neonatal deaths and of deaths during later childhood occurring in the siblings of the mongoloid children and controls was also very similar: 95.6 percent of the siblings of the children with mongolism and 95.2 percent of those of the controls were still alive at time of interview.

Menstrual History

Slightly fewer mothers of the children with Down's syndrome were still menstruating at the time of interview; the mean age at menopause for the mothers of the affected children was lower than that of the mothers of the controls. However, these differences are not statistically significant (Table 30-II). The two groups also showed no differences with respect to menstrual irregularities, such as a change in duration of menses or in the interval between menses. Furthermore, there was no increase in any type of menstrual irregularity just before the birth of the

TABLE 30-II

MENSTRUAL HISTORY OF MOTHERS OF CHILDREN WITH DOWN'S
SYNDROME AND OF CONTROL CHILDREN

Data	Down's N = 216	Controls N = 216	P value
Mean age at menarche (years)	13.56	13.44	.412
Mean age at menopause (years)	45.21	45.93	.276
Still menstruating (%)	70.60	77.60	.101
Operative menopause (%)	39.30	38.30	.907
Always regular period (%)	87.50	87.00	.878
Consulting physician for menstrual difficulty (%)	17.10	10.70	.060
Mean duration of menstural period (days)	5.72	5.54	.204
Mean interval between periods (days)	28.96	28.90	.741

index child. However, slightly more mothers of children with Down's syndrome reported having to consult a physician at some time during their lives for "menstrual difficulties" — usually menorrhagia.

Marital History

A significantly greater number of multiple marriages before the birth of the index child was recorded for the mothers of the children with Down's syndrome. There were 16.2 percent of the mothers of affected children who were married two or more times, as compared to only 6.9 percent of the mothers of the controls $(.01 > p > .001)$ (Table 30-III). Of the multiple marriages, six in the case group and five in the control group remarried because of the death of the previous mate; in addition twenty-eight marriages in the case group ended by annulment or divorce as compared to nine in the control group. However, as was observed in the total series of mothers, the examination of the reproductive histories of the mothers who were divorced or separated failed to reveal differences in fertility of occurrence of pregnancy wastage.

The difference in marital history of mothers of the children with mongolism and of controls was puzzling. Since mothers of children with mongolism have been shown also to have more radiation than mothers of control children (Sigler, 1965a) it seemed worthwhile to determine whether the greater number of multiple marriages for case mothers might be due to some factor

TABLE 30-III

MARITAL AND REPRODUCTIVE HISTORY OF MOTHERS
OF CHILDREN WITH DOWN'S SYNDROME AND OF CONTROL CHILDREN

Data	Down's N = 216	Controls N = 216	P value
Married twice or more before birth of index child (%)	16.2	6.9	<.01
Married once or more following birth of index child (%)	1.4	0.5	>.30
Median number of years married before birth of index child	8.13	8.48	>.30
Median number of years married before first pregnancy ended	1.93	1.99	>.50
Median interval between previous pregnancy and birth of index child	2.93	3.21	>.50

TABLE 30-IV

FREQUENCY OF MULTIPLE MARRIAGES AND/OR ALLIANCES ACCORDING TO RADIATION
HISTORY OF MOTHERS OF CHILDREN WITH DOWN'S SYNDROME AND OF CONTROLS

	All Mothers Irrespective of Radiation History*			Mothers not Irradiated			Irradiated Mothers†			Irradiated Mothers Fluroscopic and/or Therapeutic		
	Known Marital History	With Multiple Marriages		Known Marital History	With Multiple Marriages		Known Marital History	With Multiple Marriages		Known Marital History	With Multiple Marriages	
	(No.)	(No.)	(%)	(No.)	(No.)	(%)	(No.)	(No.)	(%)	(No.)	(No.)	(%)
Mongols	215	35	16.3	104	15	14.4	104	19	18.3	54	10	18.5
Controls	215	15	7.0	124	7	5.6	83	8	9.6	27	3	11.1

*Total mothers including those with unknown radiation history, but excluding 1 case mother and 1 control
mother with unknown marital history.
†Including all types of radiation: diagnostic, therapeutic, and/or fluoroscopic.

related to both radiation exposure and marital dissolution. From Table 30-IV, it is apparent that among those mothers with *no* reported history of radiation, the mothers of children with Down's syndrome had a significantly higher frequency of multiple marriages than mothers of the control children (p < .05). Although there was also a higher frequency of multiple marriages for irradiated mothers of children with mongolism, the difference is not statistically significant (.10 > p > .05). When only fluoroscopic and therapeutic irradiation were considered, the trends were similar but the differences were still not significant (p > .30). Thus the higher frequency of multiple marriages prior to birth of the index child among case mothers as compared to control mothers cannot be attributed to an association with radiation, but rather appears to represent an independent relationship.

Religion and Education

A larger proportion of both Catholic and Jewish parents were found in the group of children with mongolism, but the differences from the parents of the controls are not statistically significant (Table 30-V). Of the parents of the children with Down's syndrome, 24.5 percent were of differing religions, as compared to 19.2 percent of the parents of the controls. In the

TABLE 30-V

RELIGIOUS PREFERENCES OF PARENTS OF CHILDREN
WITH DOWN'S SYNDROME AND OF CONTROL CHILDREN

Religion	Mothers*		Fathers†	
	Down's, N= 214 (%)	Controls, N = 215 (%)	Down's, N = 206 (%)	Controls, N = 212 (%)
Catholic	50.9	43.3	44.7	41.0
Jewish	8.4	6.5	8.7	5.7
Protestant	38.8	48.8	44.7	50.9
Other	1.9	1.4	1.9	2.4

*X = 4.50; p > .20.
†X = 2.64; p > .30.

case group, 13.9 percent of the marriages involved a Catholic mother and a father of some other religion, as compared to 9.7 percent of the controls. Conversely, 5.6 percent of the marriages of parents in the case series involved a Catholic father and a mother of another religious preference, while this same combination applied to 6.9 percent of the parents of the controls.

In view of the higher frequency of multiple marriages among mothers of the cases, we thought it would be of interest to determine the religious distribution of those mothers who had multiple marriages. Of such mothers, 38 percent of the case mothers were Catholic and 12 percent Jewish, as compared to 33 percent and 0 percent for the control mothers; these differences were not statistically significant.

Similar educational backgrounds were reported by each group of parents: 77.8 percent of the mothers of the affected children and 76.9 percent of the mothers of the controls had no education following high school, while 67.1 percent and 72.2 percent of the case and control fathers, respectively, had no post–high-school education.

DISCUSSION

With the use of controls matched for maternal age at the time of birth of the index child, date of birth, sex, and hospital of birth of the index child, this study demonstrated that the reproductive, menstrual, and religious experience of mothers of children with Down's syndrome was not different from that of mothers of controls.

Of particular interest is the significantly greater number of multiple marriages due to separation and divorce prior to the birth of the index child found in the mothers of the Down's children as compared to mothers of controls. Although broken marriages might be expected *following* the birth of a defective child, they are not as easily explained *before* the birth. This increase in multiple marriages is noteworthy since the frequency of Jews and Catholics, known for their low divorce rates, is relatively higher in the Down's group, although this difference is not statistically significant. The etiologic basis of a relationship between multiple marriages and the occurrence of Down's syndrome in offspring is not clear. It is quite possible that in examining a great number of factors, one or more "chance" associations may appear. Whether this multiple marriage association is a "chance" finding or a real one, therefore, remains to be determined.

Pregnancy wastage, fertility, and menstrual irregularities have been the subject of frequent comment in studies of Down's syndrome. Unfortunately, most comparisons dealing with reproductive history have been made either with unsuitable controls or with no controls at all. Benda (1960) found his group of mothers of children with mongolism to have an abortion frequency of 31.2 percent and compared this figure to that of 10.6 percent for the general population. Other authors, including Murphy (1936), Beidleman (1945), and Engler (1949), also reported that mothers of Children with Down's syndrome have an abnormally high abortion rate. Down (1909), Beidleman (1945), Benda (1960), and Engler (1949) also indicated that the pregnancy-free interval prior to the birth of the affected child was longer than normal. Each of these studies, however, failed to take into account the importance of controlling maternal age when dealing with age-related reproductive factors. Smith and Record (1955) also reported higher abortion rates for mothers of children with mongolism than for controls and made an attempt to control for maternal age, but the scarcity of older control mothers led to the selection of a smaller and younger control group.

Similarly, Coppen and Cowie in 1960 observed that of 93 pregnancies in 55 Down's mothers, 31 percent ended in abortion or stillbirth. However, Ingalls, Babbott, and Philbrook (1957) found a 15.5 percent abortion rate in mothers of cases versus 9.4 percent in the controls. In contrast, Oster (1953) reported that 9.7 percent of 1,523 pregnancies of Down's mothers ended in stillbirth or abortion, and more recently Lunn (1959) found no difference in fertility and no higher rate of abortions in Down's mothers when compared to age matched controls in Glasgow.

Since the increased frequency of abortions is at least in part related to advancing maternal age (1964), and since the frequency varies in different populations and with different modes of data collection, the importance of an adequate comparison group controlled by maternal age cannot be overemphasized. The finding in this study that mothers of children with mongolism show no higher frequency of abortions, stillbirths, or other offspring with congenital abnormalities, suggests that meiotic nondisjunction occurs in relatively few viable ova in any one female during a lifetime.

SUMMARY

An epidemiologic study of the families of 216 children with Down's syndrome and 216 control children matched on the basis of maternal age at the time of the child's birth demonstrated no difference in abortions, stillbirths, congential abnormalities, or increased sibling deaths from acquired causes in the case group as compared with the control group. Fertility in the mothers of affected children, both before and after the birth of the child, was similar to that of the controls. No significant difference in maternal menstrual history was found. These data suggest that in families containing a child with Down's syndrome, except where the mother is young at the time of birth of the affected child, the risk of having a subsequent pregnancy end in abortion, stillbirth, another child with mongolism, or any other congenital abnormality is largely related to the risk associated with the maternal age at that time, rather than with the Down's syndrome itself.

The significantly higher incidence of multiple marriages prior to the birth of the index child observed in mothers of Down's children as compared to control mothers is noteworthy and requires further study.

*   *   *

We wish to acknowledge the contributions of Mrs. Susan Baker who was responsible for the computer programming, and of Drs. Robert Cooke, Barton Childs, and Simon Abrahams, and Mrs. Charlotte Benesch for their helpful suggestions. In addition, generous cooperation and support were given by Mr. Sidney Norton of the Department of Vital Statistics, by the Baltimore Society for Retarded Children, the principals of the many schools for the retarded, and the administrators and medical records personnel of the Baltimore hospitals.

REFERENCES

Beidleman, B.: Mongolism: a selective review, *Am. J. Ment. Defic., 50:*35, 1945.

Benda, C. E.: *The Child with Mongolism.* New York, Grune & Stratton, Inc., 1960.

Coppen, A., and Cowie, V.: Maternal health and mongolism. *Brit Med. J., 1:*1843, 1960.

Down, J. L.: Discussion of Shuttleworth, G. E.: Mongolian imbecility. *Brit. Med. J., 2:*661, 1909.

Engler, M.: *Mongolism (Peristatic Amentia).* Baltimore, Williams & Wilkins, 1949.

Ingalls, T. H., Babbott, J., and Philbrook, R.: The mothers of Mongoloid babies: A retrospective appraisal of their health during pregnancy. *Am. J. Obst. Gynec. 74:*572, 1957.

Lunn, J. E.: A survey of Mongol children in Glasgow. *Scottish Med. J. 4:*368, 1959.

Murphy, M.: The birth order of Mongol and other feebleminded children. *Human Biol., 8:*256, 1936.

Oster, J.: *Mongolism: A clinicogenealogical investigation comprising 526 Mongols living in Seeland and neighboring islands in Denmark.* Copenhagen, Danish Science Press, 1953.

Sigler, A. T., Lilienfeld, A. M., Cohen, B. H., and Westlake, J. E.: Radiation exposure in parents of children with mongolism (Down's syndrome). *Bull. Johns Hopkins Hosp., 117:*374, 1965.

Sigler, A. T., Lilienfeld, A. M., Cohen B. H., and Westlake, J. E.: Parental age in Down's syndrome (mongolism). *J. Pediat., 67:*631, 1965.

Smith, A., and Record, R. G.: Fertility and reproductive history of mothers of mongol defectives. *Brit. J. Prev. Social. Med., 9:*89, 1955.

Warburton, D., and Fraser, C. F.: Spontaneous abortion risks in man: Data from reproductive histories collected in a medical genetics unit. *Am. J. Human Genet, 16:*1, 1964.

Chapter 31

Attitudes of Parents of
Retarded Children Toward
Voluntary Sterilization

MEDORA S. BASS

THE purpose of this investigation was to explore the attitudes of "normal" parents of retarded children toward voluntary sterilization and to examine some of the factors related to these attitudes. An attempt was made to measure the degree of favorableness or unfavorableness, the intensity with which the attitude was held, and the level of information on which it was based.

The need to investigate the problems associated with family limitation for the mentally retarded was pointed out at the White House Conference on Mental Retardation in 1963. Dr. Lloyd M. Dunn (1963), Director of Special Education at George Peabody College, remarked that family planning for retarded individuals must be faced openly and frankly in order to reduce mental retardation:

> I am not asking you to consider family planning . . . primarily on eugenic grounds, though some genetic aspects probably exist. I would contend that other arguments are more compelling and cogent. First, this woman (retarded mother with seven children — all in institutions) and others like her may well be able to function adequately in society if they are not overburdened by parenthood. Secondly, such persons are not likely to be adequate parents, especially for children who are intellectually adequate. What responsibilities do we have to help people prevent or reduce the birth of children into such conditions?

Note: Reprinted by permission of the author and *Eugenics Quarterly, 14*:45-53, 1967.

In my view, if we could persuade low IQ parents, and those with average intellect who have already given birth to two or more low IQ children, from having additional youngsters, we would reduce by half the number of children destined to be classified as educable mentally retarded during their school years ... We who have a special concern for the prevention of mental retardation have even greater need to examine this delicate issue. For too long human reproduction has been a puritanical taboo. Unless answers are forthcoming in this area, other measures will avail us limited gains.

Almost forty years ago an investigation was made of mental deficiency on practically the entire population of the state of Vermont. Of eighty-two unions of a retarded individual and a normal spouse, 26.4 percent of the children were retarded; when both parents were retarded, 44.1 percent of the children were retarded (Reed and Reed, 1965, p.2).

The Brock Committee in England in 1934 recommended the legalization of voluntary sterilization after a study of 3,733 mental defectives showed that 22.5 percent of their children were retarded and another 22.5 percent had died (Brock, 1934).

The Danish program to prevent the reproduction of the retarded indicates after twenty-five years of genetic counseling and voluntary sterilization that the incidence of retardation is reduced approximately 50 percent a generation. Approximately one third of the mental defectives have been sterilized. Kemp studied retarded women who had had children and had been sterilized subsequently. Of the 352 living children, 31.8 percent had IQ less than 75, 36.1 percent were between 75 and 90. Of those 113 above 90, 16 were psychopathic and 50 had nervous disturbances; only 5 seemed to be without mental problems and with IQ above 100 (Reed and Reed, 1965, p. 77).

Benda et al (1963) studied retardates of the cultural-familial type in the Fernald School and found 48.8 percent had one or both parents retarded.

Reed and Reed (1965) made a longitudinal study of the frequencies of mental retardation in several categories of relatives of 289 mental defectives who were in the Faribault Minnesota State School in 1911. The 82,217 relatives of their grandparents were studied, beginning in 1911, discontinued and reopened again in 1949. The study covered as many as seven generations. Between

1 percent and 2 percent were retarded and these produced 36.1 percent of the retardates in the next generation. Normal individuals with normal siblings produced only .5 percent of retardates. There was no evidence of any undesirable results of the sterilization among the forty-two individuals who had been sterilized. Among the authors' conclusions were the following:

> One of the important humanitarian implications of our demonstration of the importance of the transmission of mental retardation is that a better legal basis must be provided for the voluntary sterilization of the higher grade retardate in the community . . .
>
> Few people have emphasized that where the transmission of a trait is frequently from parent to offspring, sterilization will be effective and it is irrelevant whether the basis for the trait is genetic or environmental . . .
>
> When voluntary sterilization for the retarded becomes a part of the culture of the United Ststes, we should expect a decrease of about 50 percent in the number of retarded persons, as a result of all methods combined to reduce retardation. (Reed and Reed, 1963, pp. 77-78.)

A poll of physicians in 1963 showed that 79 percent approved of sterilization in cases where mental deficiency was hereditary; 66 percent approved when there were too many children in relation to income. There was no specific question as to approval in cases where retarded adults were not likely to transmit the defect but were not capable of rearing children properly *(New Medical Material,* 1963, p. 19).

In spite of the recommendations of two committees appointed to study sterilizations over thirty years ago (Brock, 1934; Myerson, 1936), despite the continuing recommendation of experts over the intervening years (Halperin, 1946; Penrose, 1932; Whitney, 1958), and despite recent approval of physicians, there has been a steady decrease in the number of operations performed in institutions since 1946 (Russell, 1962). One factor in this decrease in operations may be the attitudes of parents of retarded children toward sterilization.

There are no statistics available for operations performed outside of institutions for the retarded. The incidence of sterilization may be greater than is generally believed now that 95 percent of the retarded are living in the community. More programs are presently directed toward creating opportunities for retarded young adults to live a more normal life and to meet others in workshops and in recreational activities where strong and lasting attachments are often formed.

The ability of the better adjusted retarded individuals to maintain a fairly stable and happy marriage, and the supportive and beneficial results of marriage have been discussed in a previous paper (Bass, 1964). This investigator also reviewed the literature on the adequacy of retarded persons as parents and the role of sterilization in the rehabilitation of the mentally deficient (Bass, 1963). There was a consensus among the few existing studies of sterilization that it was the most appropriate method of family limitation and should be made available on a voluntary basis for the protection of retarded individuals. The experience in Sweden has demonstrated that retarded individuals who are capable of living in the community are also capable of understanding the meaning of sterilization and can give a valid consent (Weintraub, 1951).

Social workers report that parents and the young retarded individuals themselves are asking for assistance in securing the operation. Many of the young couples who plan marriage seem to realize that the responsibilities of parenthood are beyond their abilities. Before counseling these families on the advisability of marriage, more information is needed on the attitudes of parents toward voluntary sterilization.

In summary, an investigation of the attitudes of parents toward sterilization is important for two reasons: to determine whether it is a factor in the decrease in the number of sterilizations performed despite the agreement among experts that it may be beneficial to the retarded; and because a greater understanding of these attitudes would enable counselors working with the retarded to give them more meaningful advice. There is no record of any similar investigation.

SUBJECTS

The original subjects were tested in 1959 as part of an investigation of the effect of attitudes on judgment. In order to enlarge the sample, other groups of parents were recruited with the help of organizations for retarded children, as had been done previously. Because sterilization was considered controversial, it was most difficult to obtain the cooperation of parents' associations. The sample is biased by the fact that those groups which were most opposed to sterilization were unwilling to participate. However, the number of Catholics approximates the proportion in the general population and the subjects represent a wide geographical area. The 132 subjects were "normal" parents of retarded children who volunteered through their local parent association. There were so few fathers in the groups that sex was not used as a variable.

METHOD

The method was adapted from the construction of the Thurstone type attitude scale (Thurstone *et al.,* 1929). Subjects were given eighty-eight cards, each one bearing a different statement concerning voluntary sterilization. They ranged from "most unfavorable" to "most favorable." (Further details are available upon request to the author.) Subjects were also given eleven envelopes marked from one to eleven. Examiner gave a brief definition of sterilization and defined "voluntary" as meaning with the consent of the individual or, in the case of a retarded child, as with the consent of the parent. Subjects were asked to judge the statements as to whether they were favorable or unfavorable to voluntary sterilization. Subjects were then asked to sort the statements into eleven piles, from one, most unfavorable, to eleven, most favorable. Examiner stressed that they were not to judge the statement as true or untrue, nor whether they agreed or disagreed with it, but whether they thought the statement supported sterilization or was opposed to it. After subjects had finished sorting, they were asked to pick out the pile of statements which most closely represented their own attitude toward sterilization. Subjects were next asked to place these cards in the corresponding envelope and mark it with an "X." As a further check, they were asked to put a rubber band around that envelope. Subjects were next asked to put all the other cards in the envelope corresponding to the pile. Examiner then distributed a card marked with a thermometer (the scale ranged from 0 to 100) and asked subjects to mark how strongly they felt about sterilization, irrespective of approval of disapproval. They were next given sheets with twenty true and false statements to check. Subjects were asked to give their religion and were again told that their names would not be needed as the test was anonymous. After subjects had checked the statements, they were asked to write briefly on the back of the sheet why they felt the way they did about sterilization. Some of the groups indicating the most interest in the investigation were asked whether they felt their children would be capable of a reasonably happy marriage; others were asked at what IQ level they believed a retarded individual could understand enough about the operation to give a valid consent.

RESULTS

Of the 132 subjects, 26 or 19.5 percent were Catholic, 10 or 7.6 percent were Jewish, 74 or 56 percent were Protestant, and 22 or 16.6 percent failed to give their religion or in⸱⸱ated that they had none. The proportion of Catholics appro⸱imated the national figure often estimated as 20 percent. The Jews were overrepresented and the nonaffiliated underrepresented. The percentages of the total sample and of the four religious groups giving their attitudes as being in the upper five categories of approval, the lower five, and those giving the neutral category are given in Table 31-I. The highest rate of approval was for the nonaffiliated group;

TABLE 31-I

PERCENTAGE OF RELIGIOUS GROUPS APPROVING,
NEUTRAL, AND DISAPPROVING

Groups	N	Ap-prove	Neu-tral	Dis-approve
Protestant	74	71.62	2.6	26.6
Catholic	26	16	19	65.4
Jewish	10	60	10	30
Religion not given	22	72.72	9.9	18.1
Total sample	132	59.85	7.57	33.3

the lowest for the Catholics. Almost twice as many in the total sample approved of sterilization as disapproved — 59.8 percent to 33.3 percent. The Jewish rate of approval most closely resembled that of the total sample.

The attitude scores based on the eleven-point scale, the intensity scores based on a ninety-nine-point scale, and the information scores based on twenty true and false statements are given in Table 31-II. As might be expected, the Protestants score higher on the attitude scale than do the Catholics, and the nonaffiliated score the highest. There is little difference in intensity scores. The information scores show the Protestants were the highest and the Catholics the lowest. This difference was not significant but was in the expected direction. Thirty-four percent (34%) of the sample did not know whether sterilization was the same as castration.

TABLE 31-II

MEAN SCORES OF FOUR RELIGIOUS GROUPS ON
APPROVAL, INTENSITY, INFORMATION

Groups	Atti-tude I–II	Inten-sity 0–100	Infor-mation 0-20
Protestant	8.43	67.88	11.20
Catholic	3.88	67.46	10.00
Jewish	7.30	58.20	11.00
Religion not given	8.59	66.95	10.64
Total	7.48	66.91	10.86

Comparison of scores by geographical area is given in Table 31-III. There does not appear to be any consistent trend. Of the highest scores one is in the east and the other in the midwest. Of the two lowest scores, one is in the east and the other in the west. The only Catholics who approved of sterilization were from the midwest or the west. It is interesting to note that the Delaware sample had the highest information score and one of the lowest intensity scores while Dallas had the highest intensity scores and one of the lowest information scores.

TABLE 31-III

MEAN SCORES ON ATTITUDE, INTENSITY AND
INFORMATION BY GEOGRAPHICAL AREA

Area	% Catholic	Attitude	Intensity	Information
Pennsylvania	13	7.47	73.67	9.27
New Jersey, Cumberland County	10	7.00	63.80	9.60
New Jersey Gloucester County	20	5.05	52.75	11.40
Delaware	17	8.75	62.25	12.67
St. Louis	11	18.72	64.72	11.17
Dallas	17	10	78.28	9.44
Alameda	35	7.65	69.65	11.65
San Leandro	26	5.74	69.47	11.26

Twenty-two *t* tests were performed. The significant comparisons are listed in Table 31-IV. For purposes of comparison, low intensity was defined as from 1 to 33, moderate intensity 34 to 66, and high intensity 67 to 99. "Unfavorable" included subjects who designated piles 1, 2, 3, 4; "neutral" was represented by piles 5, 6, 7; and "favorable," piles 8, 9, 10 and 11. The lower mean is listed first on each variable. Subjects with unfavorable attitudes have lower intensity scores and lower information scores.

TABLE 31-IV

SIGNIFICANT t TESTS ON VARIABLES OF ATTITUDE,
INTENSITY, INFORMATION AND RELIGION

Attitude	Sig	Intensity	Sig.	Information	Sig.
Cath.-Prot.	.01	Unfav.-Fav.	.01	Unfav.-Fav.	.01
Cath.-Jew	.02	Neut.-Fav.	.01	Mod.Int.- High Int.	.05
Cath.-No Religion	.01				
Low. Int.-Mod. Int.	.01				
Mod. Int.-High. Int.	.01				
Low. Int.-High Int.	.05				

TABLE 31-V

CORRELATIONS OF THREE VARIABLES:
ATTITUDE, INTENSITY AND INFORMATION

N	Variables	r	Sig.
132	Attitude & Intensity	+.3939	.01
	Attitude & Information	+.2670	.01
	Intensity & Information	+.0705	..

TABLE 31-VI

MEAN ATTITUDE AND INTENSITY SCORES FOR S's
ANSWERING TRUE AND FALSE TO STATEMENT:
"STERILIZATION IS THE SAME AS CASTRATION,"
AND S's GUESSING

Groups	N	Atti-tude	t	Sig.	Inten-sity
False (not castration	85	8.26			71
Guessing	26	5.80			64
True (castration)	19	5.89			53
Not castration vs. castration			2.58	.02	
Not castration vs. guessing			2.97	.01	

The correlations for the variables are given in Table 31-V.

On examining the data and noting the positive correlation between information and approval, it seemed that the information as to whether sterilization was the same as castration might be an important factor. The scores of 85 subjects who indicated that sterilization was not the same as castration and 19 subjects who indicated it was the same were compared. The results appear in Table 31-VI. The mean attitude score of subjects who had correct information and responded that sterilization was not the same as castration was 8.26 as compared to the attitude mean of the entire sample of 7.48.

The higher approval scores for those who knew sterilization was not castration compared to those scores of subjects who thought it was the same were significant at almost the .01 level of significance. The *t* score was 2.58, the significant *t* being 2.63.

It is interesting to note that those subjects who gave any certain answer, indicating they were sure it was castration or not castration, had a higher approval score of 7.82 as compared to 5.80 for the 26 subjects who indicated that they were guessing.

The written remarks often indicated a higher rate of approval than was evidenced in the scale. One Protestant mother, who rated her attitude as neutral, wrote:

> I approve of voluntary sterilization but I do not approve of involuntary sterilization. I feel that a person who has as many children as they want should be allowed to be sterilized if it is his wish. I myself would not care to be sterilized because I had all the children I wanted because if some unfortunate tragedy should occur and cause the death of all my children. I would surely want more. Of course, if it was a type of operation that could be reversed, that would be different.

A Protestant who judged his attitude as "two" on the eleven-point scale wrote, "I am patially [sic] for sterilization in cases where the individual is incompetent in raising and supporting a family or understanding what it is all about." Another rated herself as neutral and wrote, "Sterilization could be a good thing in controlling births among unfit (such as retarded) and over-population in general. The land can't continue to support the people." A Catholic father rated his attitude as "three" but wrote, "If the individual understands the operation, I would say yes."

In general, all those parents who were opposed to sterilization gave religious or moral reasons, such as, "I believe sterilization is against the laws of God and man," or "Sterilization is immoral."

ADDITIONAL REMARKS

One group of parents was asked whether they believed their child would be capable of marriage. Most of the parents replied "No." The answers would have been more meaningful had it been possible to secure the parents' rating of their child's IQ. This was attempted with one group of parents, most of whom replied that they had never been told their child's IQ. However, it would have been possible to have determined whether the older children were educable or trainable.

The question was asked of another group as to what IQ level would be required to understand enough about the operation to be able to give a valid consent. This was an attempt to determine whether parents believed the decision to be sterilized could be voluntary. The estimates of IQ level were much higher than those found by Sabagh and Edgerton (1962) in their study of mental defectives. Dr. Edgerton told the investigator that some retarded persons with IQ's in the 50's could understand the nature of the operation. This supports the experience with the Swedish sterilization program. Further research is needed on this point in order to determine which factors contribute most to the understanding of the operation. Emotional and personality factors may well be as important as intelligence. If it could be shown that a large majority of the educable retarded could understand the operation and were willing to have it when it was recommended, it might be possible to eliminate all compulsory sterilization statutes for this group. Since there is a general consensus that persons with IQ's of less than 50 are incompetent as parents, compulsory sterilization might be limited to the trainable retarded who are able to live in the community.

DISCUSSION

One of the interesting findings for research in general was the ability of a small minority in an organization who considered the subject controversial to prevent others from participating. Perhaps the finding that almost twice as many persons approved of sterilization as disapproved will help overcome this resistance to serve as subjects in scientific investigations.

The positive correlation of information and approval may well be reciprocal. Those who are interested in the subject and approve are more apt to inform themselves and to remember what they have learned. However, this correlation may mean that educating persons concerning sterilization may increase approval. Therefore, in states where there are laws requiring the sterilization of persons of childbearing age before they can be released from an institution for the mentally deficient, educational campaigns might facilitate the acceptance of sterilization by the parents and the patients. In India it has been found that persons who had been sterilized, or a doctor with prestige in the community, were best able to convince potential patients of the benefits of the operation.

The findings that subjects who stated they had no particular religion — or who failed to give their religion — had the highest rate of approval would suggest that religious teaching is one of the deterrents of sterilization. It would have been interesting to have had a question asking whether there were conditions under which their church would approve of sterilization. The National Council of Churches of Christ in America, the Methodists, the Episcopalians, and other Protestant churches have expressed approval of sterilization where there are valid indications. Some parents sincerely believed their child needed the operation and at the same time believed it was considered immoral by their church. If these facts were better known, the conflicts and anxieties of many parents faced with the decision of having their child sterilized might be relieved.

Another finding of general interest is the lack of information on sterilization. Over a third of the subjects were not aware that sterilization was not castrative. Some, who answered that sterilization was not the same, were of the opinion that the operation would produce masculinizing effects. Despite the fact that they thought it was castration, many were in favor of the operation. The rate of approval of those Protestants who thought it was the same as castration was a little less than 50 percent and exactly 59 percent for those of no religion. This last figure compares with 87 percent approval for the total "no religion" subjects who knew it was not castration. Thus, the belief that sterilization is the same as castration is an important factor in the rejection of sterilization. Some parents indicated their attitude as unfavorable; then after answering the questions wrote favorable attitudes. It would be interesting to test a group who knew little of sterilization, give them a few facts and then retest their attitudes.

This investigation was limited in that it was originally designed to measure the effect of favorable and unfavorable attitudes toward voluntary sterilization on the judgment of statements. More specific attitudes toward sterilization could have been obtained had less time been allotted to sorting. It would be helpful to know what the subjects attitudes would have been toward sterilization of their own child rather than to voluntary sterilization in general. The fact that some of the parents had very young children suggests that their attitude was not based on a thoughtful consideration of an existing situation. It would be interesting to determine whether parents of adolescent children would differ significantly from parents of young children and whether parents of children with higher IQ's differed from parents of children with lower IQ's. The few parents who believed their child to be capable of sustaining a reasonably stable marriage expressed approval of sterilization.

It might be meaningful to group parents according to the IQ's of their children and investigate which parents believed their children to be capable of marriage and of properly rearing children, which parents thought their children capable of marriage but not of properly rearing children, and which parents thought their children would be capable of understanding the meaning of the operation and of giving an affirmative consent. Some additional remarks indicated the child's ability to understand the operation did not concern the parents as much as the question of the operations being performed with the parents' consent rather than under a compulsory law.

This investigation points to the need of establishing criteria to predict and evaluate the ability of the retarded individual to provide proper care for children. This ability might be studied in a prekindergarten class where the young retarded people could help with the care of the children under careful supervision.

SUMMARY

The attitudes toward voluntary sterilization of 132 parents of retarded children were investigated. Approval, disapproval, intensity, and information were measured. The attitudes were related to each other, to religion, and to geographic area. The results showed that 60 percent of the total sample approved of sterilization, 72 percent of the Protestants, 60 percent of the Jews, 16 percent of the Catholics, and 73 percent of those who did not indicate their religion. Approval was positively related to intensity and information. Over a third erroneously believed that sterilization and castration were synonymous and had lower approval scores. The lack of information on this subject was offered as evidence of the need for counseling these parents. The need for further research was stressed.

CONCLUSIONS

Respect for a religious minority appears to be impeding research in the field of voluntary sterilization.

Almost twice as many parents approved as disapproved; therefore, it would not seem that parental attitudes are responsible for the decrease in sterilization operations.

Approval of sterilization is significantly related to expressed religious preference. It is lowest for Catholics and highest for those without religious affiliation.

Approval of voluntary sterilization is positively correlated with information level.

The intensity with which these attitudes were held is positively related to degree of approval but is not significantly related to level of information.

Many parents are unaware that sterilization is legal in almost all states and that it has had the approval of many Protestant denominations in cases of valid need.

Many parents believe sterilization to be the same as castration or to have similar effects. These parents have a significantly lower approval score than those who can accurately distinguish the two operations.

In spite of believing that it is illegal and immoral, many parents persist in believing that their child should have the protection of sterilization.

Counseling of parents of a retarded child on the scientific, legal, and moral aspects of sterilization would relieve the anxieties they experience when faced with some of the problems of an adolescent child.

There is need for further research to analyze attitudes and relate them to such variables as the age and IQ of the child, and to the ability of the child to sustain a stable marriage, to rear children and to comprehend the meaning of the operation.

REFERENCES

Bass, M. S.: Marriage, parenthood, and the prevention of pregnancy for the mentally deficient. *Am. J. Ment. Defic., 55:*318-333, 1963.

Bass, M. S.: Marriage for the mentally deficient. *Ment. Retar., Aug.:*198-202, 2, 4, 1964.

Benda, C. E., Squires, N. D., Ogonik, M. J., and Wise, R.: Personality factors in mild mental retardation. *Am. J. Ment. Defic., 68:*24-40, 1963.

Brock, L. F.: *Report of the Departmental Committee on Sterilization.* London, Joint Committee on Voluntary Sterilization, 1934.

Dunn, L. M.: *White House Conference on Mental Retardation Proceedings.* U. S. Govt. Printing Office, 1963, pp. 104-105.

Halperin, S. L.: Human heredity and mental deficiency *Am. J. Ment. Defic., 51:*153-163, 1946.

Kemp, T.: Genetic-hygienic experiences in Denmark in recent years. *Eugen. Rev.,* 11-18, 1957.

Myerson, A.: *Eugenical Sterilization.* New York, Macmillan Co., 1936.

New Medical Materia, New York, Hearst Corp., 1962, pp. 4, 11, 19.

Penrose, L. S.: Propagation of the unfit. *Lancet, 259:*425-427, 1950.

Reed, E. W., and Reed, S. C.: *Mental Retardation: A Family Study.* Philadelphia, W. B. Saunders Co., 1965.

Russell, K. P.: Indications in sterilization. *New Medical Materia,* New York, Hearst Corp., 1962, pp. 4, 11, 17.

Sabagh, G., and Edgerton, R. B.: Sterilized mental defectives look at eugenic sterilization. *Eugen. Quart., 9:*213-222, 1962.

Thurstone, L. I., and Chave, E. T.: *The Measurement of Attitude.* Chicago, Univ. of Chicago, 1929.

Weintraub, P.: Sterilization in Sweden: Its laws and practices. *Am. J. Ment. Defic., 56:*364-374, 1951.

Whitney, E. A.: Present-day problems in mental retardation. *Am. J. Ment. Defic. 63:*387-398, 1958.

APPENDICES

THE materials presented in this section of the book are provided as additional sources of information and aid for individuals who counsel parents of mentally retarded children.

Part One contains information on the two major associations dealing with the problem of mental deficiency. Both associations provide valuable professional and parental services of an informational and supportive nature. Current information on and addresses of state and national organizations are provided.

Part Two lists by states the special clinical facilities for mentally retarded children. This current listing is abridged from prepublication material graciously supplied the writer by Rudolph P. Hormuth, Specialist in Services for Mentally Retarded Children, Maternal and Child Health Services, U. S. Department of Health, Education and Welfare.

Part Three describes and explains some of the information found in the *Directory of Exceptional Children* as it applies to the mentally retarded child.

Part Four contains a descriptive listing of the many films, filmstrips, and tapes available on the subject of mental retardation. While few deal specifically with the counseling of parents of retarded children, they do provide an excellent source of information on the overall subject of mental retardation. Properly selected and presented, they can provide an invaluable service to those who need to know more about the origin, nature, and characteristics of the various types of mentally retarded individuals. Also shown in some of the films are examples of recent research and rehabilitation efforts and of programs provided by private and state residential facilities. Where available, a rental source of the films is included at the end of the description. The user is urged to preview any audiovisual aid being considered for group showing prior to presentation to parent groups, students, or others, to insure its appropriateness to the group and the group's goal. For additional information on selected films, the reader is referred to the booklet *Audio-Visual Media and Materials on Mental Retardation,* published by the National Association for Retarded Children, 420 Lexington Avenue, New York, New York 10017.

Major Associations for Parents
of Mentally Retarded Children

AMERICAN ASSOCIATION ON MENTAL DEFICIENCY (AAMD), 5201 Connecticut Ave. NW, Washington, D. C. 20015

In addition to a variety of informational services, the AAMD publishes two professional journals: the *American Journal of Mental Deficiency,* and *Mental Retardation.* A *Directory of Residential Facilities for the Mentally Retarded* is available from the Publications Office, 49 Sheridan Ave., Albany, New York 12210

NATIONAL ASSOCIATION FOR RETARDED CHILDREN, INC. (NARC), 420 Lexington Ave., New York, New York 10017

This organization publishes *Children Limited,* a newspaper devoted exclusively to the field of mental retardation, and provides a variety of informative services. Their publication list, available on request, includes directories, bibliographies, and articles on topics such as parental care, public health and medicine, education, residential care, recreation, social work, religion, vocational rehabilitation, and research. State associations accredited at the national office are listed below:

ALABAMA ASSOCIATION FOR RETARDED CHILDREN
Marvin P. Mantel, Exec. Dir., P. O. Box 6202, Montgomery, Alabama 36106

ARIZONA ASSOCIATION FOR RETARDED CHILDREN
Robert W. Shook, Exec. Dir., 2929 E. Thomas Rd., Rm. 206, Phoenix, Arizona 85016

ARKANSAS ASSOCIATION FOR RETARDED CHILDREN, INC.
Sam C. Sanders, Exec. Dir., University Shopping Center, Mall, Asher at University, Little Rock, Arkansas 72204

CALIFORNIA ASSOCIATION FOR RETARDED CHILDREN
Fred J. Krause, Exec. Dir., Forum Bldg., Rm. 1020, 1107 9th St., Sacramento, California 95814

COLORADO ASSOCIATION FOR RETARDED CHILDREN, INC.
Joseph Ruddley, Exec. Dir., 1540 Vine St., Denver, Colorado 80206

CONNECTICUT ASSOCIATION FOR RETARDED CHILDREN, INC.
Ann Switzer, Exec. Dir., 21 R-High St., Hartford, Connecticut 06103

DELAWARE ASSOCIATION FOR RETARDED CHILDREN, INC.
William T. Weist, Exec. Dir., P. O. Box 1896, Wilmington, Delaware 19899

HELP FOR RETARDED CHILDREN, INC.
David Silberman, Exec. Dir., 405 Riggs Rd. NE, Washington, D.C. 20011

FLORIDA ASSOCIATION FOR RETARDED CHILDREN, INC.
Jack W. McAllister, Exec. Dir., 220 E. College Ave., Suite 6, Tallahassee, Florida 32301

GEORGIA ASSOCIATION FOR RETARDED CHILDREN, INC.
Mrs. L. H. Stewart, Exec. Dir., 87 Walton St. NW, 425 Walton Bldg., Atlanta, Georgia 30303

HAWAII ASSOCIATION FOR RETARDED CHILDREN
James A. O'Brien, Exec. Dir., 245 N. Kukui St., Honolulu, Hawaii 96817

IDAHO ASSOCIATION FOR RETARDED CHILDREN
Mrs. Gailen B. Soule, Admin. Sec., Box 816, Boise, Idaho 83701

ILLINOIS ASSOCIATION FOR RETARDED CHILDREN
Gordon B. Snow, Exec. Dir., 343 S. Dearborn St., Rm. 709, Chicago, Illinois 60604

INDIANA ASSOCIATION FOR RETARDED CHILDREN, INC.
Frank E. Ball, Exec. Dir., 752 E. Market St., Indianapolis, Indiana 46202

IOWA ASSOCIATION FOR RETARDED CHILDREN, INC.
S. R. Christensen, Exec. Dir., 255 Jewett Bldg., 9th and Grand Ave., Des Moines, Iowa 50309

KANSAS ASSOCIATION FOR RETARDED CHILDREN, INC.
Mrs. Robert Wright, Exec. Dir., 5830 Nall Ave., Mission, Kansas 66202

KENTUCKY ASSOCIATION FOR RETARDED CHILDREN, INC.
Bob R. Rundell, Exec. Dir., 315 W. Main St., Frankfort, Kentucky 40601

LOUISIANA ASSOCIATION FOR RETARDED CHILDREN
Mrs. Carrie R. Saia, Exec. Dir., 4448 N. Boulevard, Baton Rouge, Louisiana 70806

MAINE ASSOCIATION FOR RETARDED CHILDREN, INC.
Donald Allison, Exec. Dir., 269½ Water St., Augusta, Maine 04330

MARYLAND ASSOCIATION FOR RETARDED CHILDREN, INC.
1514 Reisterstown Rd., Pikesville, Maryland 21208

MASSACHUSETTS ASSOCIATION FOR RETARDED CHILDREN, INC.
Manual J. Mello, Exec. Dir., Suite 402, 680 Main St., Waltham, Massachusetts 02154·

MICHIGAN ASSOCIATION FOR RETARDED CHILDREN
Roscoe W. Scott, Exec. Dir., 510 Michigan National Tower, Lansing, Michigan 48933

MINNESOTA ASSOCIATION FOR RETARDED CHILDREN, INC.
Harvey Glommen, Exec. Dir., 1191 Nicollet Ave., Minneapolis, Minnesota 55403

MISSISSIPPI ASSOCIATION FOR RETARDED CHILDREN
Harry R. Scott, Exec. Dir., 145 E. Amite St., P. O. Box 1363, Jackson, Mississippi 39205

MISSOURI ASSOCIATION FOR RETARDED CHILDREN
Mrs. Dorothy Woods, Acting Exec. Dir., 1001-C Dunklin Blvd., Jefferson City, Missouri 65101

MONTANA ASSOCIATION FOR RETARDED CHILDREN
Mrs. Jean A. Durham, Exec. Sec., P. O. Box 625, Helena, Montana 59601

NEBRASKA ASSOCIATION FOR RETARDED CHILDREN
Verlin Boldry, Exec. Dir., 1674 Van Dorn, Lincoln, Nebraska 68502

NEW HAMPSHIRE ASSOCIATION FOR RETARDED CHILDREN
Charles Dunn, Pres. 95 Market St., Manchester, New Hampshire 03101

NEW JERSEY ASSOCIATION FOR RETARDED CHILDREN, INC.
97 Bayard St., New Brunswick, New Jersey 08901

NEW MEXICO ASSOCIATION FOR RETARDED CHILDREN, INC.
William J. Green, Exec. Dir., 7017 Carriage Rd. NE, Albuquerque, New Nexico 87109

NEW YORK ASSOCIATION FOR RETARDED CHILDREN, INC.
Jospeh T. Weingold, Exec. Dir., 175 5th Ave., Rm. 1000, New York, New York 10010

NORTH CAROLINA ASSOCIATION FOR RETARDED CHILDREN, INC.
Carey Fendley, Exec. Dir., 1311 Morehead St., Suite #7, P. O. Box 11042, Charlotte, North Carolina 28209

NORTH DAKOTA ASSOCIATION FOR RETARDED CHILDREN, INC.
Vern Lindsey, Exec. Dir., Box 1494, 62½ Broadway, Fargo, North Dakota 58102

OHIO ASSOCIATION FOR RETARDED CHILDREN, INC.
James P. White, Exec. Dir., 131 E. State St., Rm. 308-9, Columbus, Ohio 43215

OKLAHOMA ASSOCIATION FOR RETARDED CHILDREN, INC.
901 Office Park Plaza, Oklahoma City, Oklahoma 73106

OREGON ASSOCIATION FOR RETARDED CHILDREN
Robert McNulty, Exec. Dir., 3085 River Rd. N, Salem, Oregon 97303

PENNSYLVANIA ASSOCIATION FOR RETARDED CHILDREN, INC.
J. E. VanDyke, Exec. Dir., 112 N 2nd St., Hall Bldg., Harrisburg, Pennsylvania 17101

RHODE ISLAND ASSOCIATION FOR RETARDED CHILDREN
820 Atwells Ave., Providence, Rhode Island 02909

SOUTH CAROLINA ASSOCIATION FOR RETARDED CHILDREN, INC.
Mrs. Hardin V. Stuart, Exec. Dir., 1517 Hampton St., Rm. 301, Box 1564, Columbia, South Carolina 29202

SOUTH DAKOTA ASSOCIATION FOR RETARDED CHILDREN, INC.
Keith Newcomb, Exec. Dir., 1612 W. 41 St., Sioux Falls, South Dakota 57105

TENNESSEE ASSOCIATION FOR RETARDED CHILDREN, INC.
Kenneth J. Young, Acting Exec. Dir., 21 Whitley Bldg., 1701 21st Ave. S, Nashville, Tennessee 37212

TEXAS ASSOCIATION FOR RETARDED CHILDREN, INC.
David B. Sloane, Exec. Dir., 706-08 Littlefield Bldg., 6th and Congress, Austin, Texas 78701

UTAH ASSOCIATION FOR RETARDED CHILDREN
Neal F. Christensen, Exec. Dir., 2311 Highland Drive, Salt Lake City, Utah 84106

VERMONT ASSOCIATION FOR RETARDED CHILDREN, INC.
Lyle Miller Sr., Pres., 10 Nash Place, Burlington, Vermont 05401

WASHINGTON ASSOCIATION FOR RETARDED CHILDREN
M. C. Kreider, Exec. Dir., Capitol Center Bldg., Suite 914, Olympia, Washington 98501

WEST VIRGINIA ASSOCIATION FOR RETARDED CHILDREN, INC.
Mrs. Ellen Brown, Pres. 4010 10th Ave., Vienna, West Virginia 26101

WISCONSIN ASSOCIATION FOR RETARDED CHILDREN, INC.
Merlen Kurth, Exec. Dir., 1 S. Webster St., Madison, Wisconsin 53703

WYOMING ASSOCIATION FOR RETARDED CHILDREN
Ed Evers, Pres. 711 C St., Rock Spring, Wyoming 82901

Clinical Programs for
Mentally Retarded Children

THE following extensive listing is an abridgement from an original compilation by Rudolph P. Hormuth, Specialist in Services for Mentally Retarded Children, United States Department of Health, Education and Welfare, Public Health Service, Maternal and Child Health Service.

In general, the clinics which have been listed are those which can be defined as outpatient medical facilities providing comprehensive evaluation, treatment, or follow-up services primarily to children suspected of or diagnosed as mentally retarded by an interdisciplinary team, of which a physician takes the medical responsibility for all patients seen while in attendance at regularly scheduled hours.

In developing this listing, the government Maternal and Child Health Service functioned only as a nonevaluative reporter. The information about each facility was provided by the clinic itself. Thus inclusion of a facility does not constitute an endorsement.

ALABAMA

*CLINIC FOR DEVELOPMENTAL AND LEARNING DISORDERS
University of Alabama in Birmingham
1919 Seventh Avenue South
Birmingham, Alabama 35233
Telephone: (205) 325-4974
Medical director: Andrew Lorincz, M.D.
Area served: Alabama State except eight counties served by Montgomery Project.
Ages accepted: Birth to 12 years (older children seen under special circumstances).

*DIAGNOSTIC AND GUIDANCE CLINIC
Children's Center of Montgomery, Inc.
310 North Madison Terrace
Montgomery, Alabama 36107
Telephone: (205) 262-5744
Medical director: David B. Monsky, M.D.
Area served: State of Alabama (priority given to Autauga, Barbour, Bullock, Elmore, Lowndes, Macon, Montgomery, and Russell Counties).
Ages accepted: Birth to 21 years (priority to children under 12).

*Facilities being supported fully or in part with funds from the Maternal and Child Health Services, United States Department of Health, Education and Welfare.

ALASKA

*CHILD STUDY CENTER
525 East Fourth Avenue
Anchorage, Alaska 99501
Telephone: 279-1551
Clinic director: Elizabeth Tower, M.D.
Area served: Alaska.
Ages accepted: Birth to 8 years given priority.

ARIZONA

*CHILD EVALUATION CENTER
2214 North Central Avenue
Phoenix, Arizona 85004
Telephone: (602) 254-4146
Clinic director: Clarence R. Laing, M.D.
Area served: Maricopa County and Central Arizona.
Ages accepted: Birth through 18 years.

*DIAGNOSTIC CENTER
Children's Evaluation Center of Southern Arizona
One South Quadrante
Tucson, Arizona 85711
Telephone: (602) 793-9414
Clinic director: Jospeh C. Heinlein, M.D.
Area served: Southern Arizona counties: Pima, Santa Cruz, Cochise, Graham, Pinal and Greenlee.
Ages accepted: Birth through 9 years.

ARKANSAS

*CHILD DEVELOPMENT CENTER
State Health Department Building
West Markham at Monroe
Little Rock, Arkansas 72205
Telephone: (501) FR 4-7489
Clinic director: John A. Harrel, Jr., M.D.
Area served: State.
Ages accepted: Birth to 21 years (priority given to those under 8).

CALIFORNIA

*CHILD DEVELOPMENT CLINIC OF KERN COUNTY
Kern County Health Department
Post Office Box 997
Bakersfield, California 93305
Telephone: (805) 325-5051
Clinic director: Millicent Johnson, M.D.
Area served: Kern County.
Ages accepted: Birth to 6 years.

*MONO COUNTY CHILD DEVELOPMENT CLINIC
Mono County Health Department
Post Office Box 476
Bridgeport, California 93517
Telephone: (714) 932-8841
Clinic director: Mrs. Ruth Phillips, PHN.
Area served: Mono County.
Ages accepted: Through childhood as needed.

*CHILD DEVELOPMENT CLINIC
Inyo County Health Department
Independence, California 93526
Telephone: (714) 878-2411
Clinic director: Victor H. Hough, M.D.
Area served: Inyo County.
Ages accepted: Infancy through childhood, as needed by the individual patient.

*RIVERSIDE COUNTY CHILD DEVELOPMENT CLINIC
Riverside County Health Department
Indio, California 92201
Telephone: (714) DI 7-8511
Clinic director: Antoinette Harris, PHN.
Area served: Desert area, Riverside County.
Ages accepted: Less than 6 years.

MANREFA CENTER
11 Spring Valley Road
La Selva Beach, California 95076
Telephone: (408) 722-4616
Clinic director: Jack Wendt, M.A.
Area served: Santa Cruz, San Benito, and
northern Monterey Counties.
Ages accepted: All ages.

LONG BEACH CHILDREN'S CLINIC
Diagnostic Services for Mentally
Retarded
430 West 14th Street
Long Beach, California 90813
Telephone: (213) HE 5-7529
Clinic director: Mary Jane Reynolds.
Area served: Long Beach, Lakewood,
Dominquez, Signal Hill, Catalina, and
Bellflower.
Ages accepted: 6 years and under
(priority to children under 3 years).

*CHILD DEVELOPMENT CLINIC
Children's Hospital of Los Angeles
4650 Sunset Boulevard
Los Angeles, California 90027
Telephone: (213) 663-3341
Clinic director: Richard Koch, M.D.
Area served: Los Angeles County and
surrounding counties.
Ages accepted: Less than 6 years.

GUIDANCE CENTER
Exceptional Children's Foundation
2225 West Adams Boulevard
Los Angeles, California 90018
Telephone: (213) RE 1-6366
Medical director: C. Brooks Fry, M.D.
Area served: Los Angeles greater area.
Ages accepted: All ages.

REGIONAL DIAGNOSTIC COUNSEL-
ING AND SERVICE CENTER
Children's Hospital of Los Angeles
4650 Sunset Boulevard

Los Angeles, California 90027
Telephone: (213) 663-3341
Clinic director: Richard Koch, M.D.
Area served: Los Angeles County.
Ages accepted: All ages.

*SOUTH DISTRICT MENTAL RE-
TARDATION CLINIC
1522 East 102nd Street
Los Angeles, California 90007
Telephone: (213) LO 4-5811
Clinic director: Alonzo B. Cass, M.D.,
Coordinator, Mental Retardation
Screening Clinics, Los Angeles County
Health Department.
Area served: Compton, Harbor, San
Antonio, South, Southeast and
Torrance.
Ages accepted: Birth through 5 years.

*NORTHERN CALIFORNIA
REGIONAL CHILD DEVELOPMENT
CENTER
Children's Hospital Medical Center
51st and Grove Streets
Oakland, California 94609
Telephone: (415) 654-5600, Ext. 351
Clinic director: Richard Umansky, M.D.
Area served: Northern California.
Ages accepted: Up to 7 years.

*PASADENA CHILD DEVELOPMENT
CLINIC
City Hall
100 North Garfield Avenue
Pasadena, California 91109
Telephone: (213) 449-1886, Ext. 284
Clinic director: Paul Osiek, M.D., Health
Officer.
Area served: Pasadena, Alhambra, Glen-
dale, Altaderk.
Ages accepted: 6 years and under.

MT. DIABLO THERAPY CENTER
100 Golf Club Road
Pleasant Hill, California 94523
Telephone: (415) 682-6330, Ext. 23
Clinic director: Carol M. D'Angelo, MSSW, MPH.
Area served: Contra Costa County.
Ages accepted: Infants through adolescence.

*POMONA CHILD DEVELOPMENT CLINIC
750 South Park
Pomona, California 91766
Telephone: (714) NA 9-4171
Clinic director: Alonzo B. Cass, M.D., Coordinator, Mental Retardation Clinics, Los Angeles County Health Department.
Area served: El Monte, Monrovia, Pomona, and Whittier.
Ages accepted: Birth through 5 years.

DIAGNOSTIC, COUNSELING AND SERVICE CENTER
568 North Market Street
Redding, California 96001
Telephone: (916) 243-4791
Executive director: Harold Barnett, M.S.W.
Area served: Lassen, Modoc, Shasta, Siskiyou, Tehama, Trinity, Butte, and Glenn Counties.
Ages accepted: All ages.

*CHILD DEVELOPMENT CLINIC
Health and Finance Building
Riverside, California 92501
Telephone: (714) 787-6646
Clinic director: Antoinette Harris, PHN.
Area served: Metropolitan Riverside area.
Ages accepted: Less than 6 years.

*BIRTH DEFECTS AND NEUROLOGICAL CENTER – CHILD DEVELOPMENT CLINIC
351 Mt. View Avenue
San Bernardino, California 92401
Telephone: (714) TU 9-0111
Clinic director: Irving Allen, M.D.
Area served: San Bernardino County.
Ages accepted: 6 years and under.

*CHILD DEVELOPMENT CLINIC
Children's Hospital
8001 Frost Street
San Diego, California 92123
Telephone: (714) 277-5808
Clinic director: G. Burch Mehlin, M.D.
Area served: San Diego County.
Ages accepted: Birth through 5 years.

CHILD DEVELOPMENT CENTER
Children's Hospital
3700 California Street
San Francisco, California 94119
Telephone: (415) BA 1-1200
Clinic director: J. P. Mednick, M.D.
Area served: Northern California.
Ages accepted: Up to 21 years.

DEVELOPMENTAL CLINIC
University of California Medical Center
Third and Parnassus Avenues
San Francisco, California 94122
Telephone: (415) 666-2971
Clinic director: Peter Cohen, M.D.
Area served: Primarily northern California.
Ages accepted: Up to 16 years.

GOLDEN GATE REGIONAL CENTER
456 Fulton Street
San Francisco, California 94102
Telephone: (415) 567-0928
Clinic director: Peter Cohen, M.D.
Area served: Alameda, Contra Costa, Marin, San Francisco, and San Mateo Counties.
Ages accepted: All ages.

**ALAMEDA COUNTY MENTAL RE-
TARDATION SERVICES**
131 Estudillo Avenue
San Leandro, California 94577
Telephone: (415) 483-7520
Clinic director: Virginia Blacklidge, M.D.
Area served: Alameda County.
Ages accepted: All ages.

**DEVELOPMENT EVALUATION
CLINIC**
255 37th Avenue
San Mateo, California 94403
Telephone: (415) 341-1361, Ext. 2379
Clinic director: George F. Hexter, M.D.
Area served: San Mateo.
Ages accepted: All ages.

***CHILD DEVELOPMENT CLINIC OF
ORANGE COUNTY**
Eighth and Ross Streets
Santa Ana, California 92805
Telephone: (213) 776-5551
Clinic director: Merle J. Carson, M.D.
Area served: Orange County.
Ages accepted: 2 to 5 years.

***MENTAL RETARDATION SERVICES
OF SANTA BARBARA COUNTY**
Santa Barbara County Health Depart-
ment
4440 Calle Real
Santa Barbara, California 93105
Telephone: (805) 967-2311, Ext. 379
Clinic director: Louis J. Needels, M.D.
Coordinator: Lois E. Lindt, M.S.W.
Area served: Santa Barbara County.
(Clinics are held in Santa Barbara,
Santa Maria, and Lompoc, as needed.)
Ages accepted: No age limitation.

KENNEDY CHILD STUDY CENTER
1339 20th Street
Santa Monica, California 90404
Telephone: (213) EX 3-9585
Clinic director: Evis J. Coda, M.D.
Area served: Greater Los Angeles.
Ages accepted: Birth to 17 years.

**WEST VALLEY CHILD DEVELOP-
MENT CLINIC**
14340 Sylvan Street
Van Nuys, California 91401
Telephone: (213) ST 1-8970
Clinic director: Alonzo B. Cass, M.D.
Coordinator, Mental Retardation
Screening Clinics, Los Angeles County
Health Department.
Area served: East Valley, West Valley,
and San Fernando.
Ages accepted: Birth through 5 years.

***VENTURA COUNTY CHILD DEVEL-
OPMENT CLINIC**
3147 Loma Vista Rd.
Ventura, California 93001
Telephone: (805) 648-3063
Clinic director: Stephen A. Coray, M.D.
Area served: Ventura County.
Ages accepted: Priority extended
through age 6 years.

COLORADO

***BOULDER COUNTY DEVELOP-
MENTAL EVALUATION CLINIC**
Boulder City-County Health Department
Boulder, Colorado 80302
Telephone: (303) 444-4095
Clinic director: William Y. Takahaski,
M.D.
Area served: City and County of
Boulder.
Ages accepted: Birth to 21 years.

MENTAL EVALUATION CLINIC
El Paso City-County Health Department
Colorado Springs, Colorado 80909
Telephone: (303) 634-3771
Clinic director: Paul G. duBois, M.D.
Area served: El Paso County and envi-
rons.
Ages accepted: Birth to 21 years.

CHILDREN'S HOSPITAL DEVELOP-
MENTAL AND EVALUATION
CLINIC
The Children's Hospital
1056 East 19th Avenue
Denver, Colorado 80218
Telephone: (303) 244-4377
Clinic director: Jean L. McMahon, M.D.
Area served: State and children from out
of State in special circumstances.
Ages accepted: Birth to 21 years.

*JOHN F. KENNEDY CHILD DEVEL-
OPMENT CENTER
Department of Pediatrics
University of Colorado Medical Center
Denver, Colorado 80220
Telephone: (303) 394-8407, 8408, 8409
Clinic director: Harold P. Martin, M.D.
Area served: Primarily the State of
Colorado and Rocky Mountain region.
Ages accepted: Up to age 8.

*THE MENTAL RETARDATION
CLINIC
San Juan Basin Health Unit
Durango, Colorado 81301
Telephone: (303) CH 7-5702
Clinic director: Richard Geer, M.D.
Area served: San Juan Basin.
Ages accepted: Birth to 21 years.

*MESA COUNTY CHILDREN'S DIAG-
NOSTIC AND CONSULTATION
SERVICE
515 Patterson Avenue
Grand Junction, Colorado 81501
Telephone: (303) 242-7145
Clinic director: Paul Kuhn, M.D.
Area served: Mesa, Garfield, and Moffat
Counties.
Ages accepted: Birth to 21 years (pre-
ference to children under 12 years).

*MENTAL RETARDATION CLINIC
Pueblo City-County Health Department
151 Central Main Street
Pueblo, Colorado 81003
Telephone: (303) LI 4-6031
Clinic director: Rodney Smith, M.D.

Area served: Pueblo and Pueblo County.
Ages accepted: Birth to 21 years (preference given to children of preschool
age).

CONNECTICUT

BRIDGEPORT REGIONAL CENTER
115 Virginia Avenue
Bridgeport, Connecticut 06610
Telephone: (203) 368-2593
Clinic director: Salvatore M. Clarizio,
M.A.
Area served: Milford, Straford, Bridge-
port, Fairfield, Monroe, Easton, and
Trumbull.
Ages accepted: 3 years and up.

COMMUNITY SERVICES CLINIC
Mansfield Training School
Mansfield Depot, Connecticut 06251
Telephone: (203) 429-9391, Ext. 311
Clinic director: Charles P. Fonda, Ph.D.
Area served: Tolland County and adja-
cent portions of Hartford and Wind-
ham Counties.
Ages accepted: All ages.

GROVER F. POWERS CLINIC
Yale-New Haven Medical Center
Department of Pediatrics
333 Cedar Street
New Haven, Connecticut 06510
Telephone: (203) 562-1161, Ext. 2220
Clinic director: Martha F. Leonard, M.D.
Area served: State of Connecticut.
Ages accepted: Infants to 5 years.

*NEW HAVEN EVALUATION AND
COUNSELING PROGRAM FOR
DEVELOPMENTAL PROBLEMS IN
EARLY CHILDHOOD
860 Howard Avenue
New Haven, Connecticut 06519
Telephone: (203) 777-5401
Supervising medical director: Sally A.
Provence, M.D.
Area served: State of Connecticut.
Ages accepted: Birth through 6 years.

OUT-PATIENT CLINIC
Southbury Training School
Southbury, Connecticut 06488
Telephone: (203) 264-8231, Ext. 204
Clinic director: Edward Benjamin, M.S.
Area served: Northwestern, Waterbury,
Danbury, Stamford, Bridgeport, and
New Haven Regional Center areas.
Ages: All ages.

DEVELOPMENTAL EVALUATION
CLINIC
Aid for Retarded Children, Inc.
1372 Summer Street
Stamford, Connecticut 06905
Telephone: (203) 323-6633
Medical director: Charles M. Murphy,
M.D.
Area served: Principally Lower Fairfield
County. No geographical limitations.
Ages accepted: Age two and up.

DELAWARE

*CHILD DIAGNOSTIC AND DEVEL-
OPMENT CENTER OF DELAWARE
1202 Jefferson Street
Wilmington, Delaware 19801
Telephone: (302) 652-4088
Executive director: Henry H. Stroud,
M.D.
Area served: State of Delaware.
Ages accepted: Birth to 16 years.

DISTRICT OF COLUMBIA

*CHILD DEVELOPMENT CLINIC
Department of Pediatrics
Howard University College of Medicine
Washington, D.C. 20001
Telephone: (202) 797-1888; 797-1889
Clinic director: Pearl L. Rosser, M.D.
Area served: Greater Metropolitan
Washington.
Ages accepted: Birth through adoles-
cence (new cases restricted to 13 years
with priority to preschool children).

*D.C. CLINIC FOR RETARDED
CHILDREN
65 Massachusetts Avenue N.W.

Washington, D.C. 20001
Telephone: (202) 629-4773
Clinic director: Mary McKenzie-Pollock,
M.D., D.P.H.
Area served: District of Columbia.
Ages accepted: Birth through 21 years
(priority to preschool children).

GEORGETOWN UNIVERSITY
HOSPITAL CHILDREN'S DIAG-
NOSTIC AND DEVELOPMENT
CENTER
3800 Reservoir Road NW.
Washington, D.C. 20007
Telephone: (202) 625-7138
Clinic director: Robert J. Clayton, M.D.
Area served: District of Columbia,
Southern Maryland and Northern
Virginia.
Ages accepted: Birth to 21 years.

FLORIDA

*CHILD DEVELOPMENT CENTER
University of Miami
1150 Northwest 14th Street, Suite 200
Miami, Florida 33125
Telephone: (305) 350-6631
Scientific director: Samuel T.
Giammona, M.D.
Associate director: Frances McGrath,
A.C.S.W.
Area served: Dade County primarily, and
selected cases from other counties in
the State.
Ages accepted: Birth to 14 years with
emphasis on preschool children.

ONE DAY DIAGNOSTIC AND EVALU-
ATION CLINIC
All Children's Hospital
801 Sixth Street South
St. Petersburg, Florida 33701
Telephone: (813) 894-4701, 898-7451
Project director: Ray C. Wunderlich,
M.D.
Area served: St. Petersburg, Fla. and
surrounding area.
Ages served: All ages.

*TAMPA DIAGNOSTIC AND EVALU-
ATION CLINIC
4420 Tampa Bay Boulevard
Post Office Box 15797
Tampa, Florida 33614
Telephone: (813) 872-9361
Clinic director: Arthur K. Husband,
M.D.
Area to be served: Greater Tampa Bay
area.
Ages to be accepted: Priority given to
preschool age and early school age
group. Applicants under 21 may be
accepted.

GEORGIA

*CHILD DEVELOPMENT AND EVAL-
UATION CENTER
District Health Department
Health District No. 35
Columbus, Georgia 31902
Telephone: (404) 327-1541
Clinic director: Jane Rivers, M.D.
Area served: Muscogee, Harris, Chatta-
hoochee, Troup Meriwether, Talbot,
Sumter, Marion, Schley, Stewart,
Webster, and Taylor Counties.
Ages accepted: Preschool and selected
children under teenage.

*DEVELOPMENT EVALUATION
CLINIC FOR CHILDREN
118 Barry Street
Decatur, Georgia 30030
Telephone: (404) 378-8002 and
377-8156
Clinic director: Elaine Donnellan, M.D.
Area served: DeKalb and Rockdale
Counties.
Ages accepted: Up to 14 years of age.

EVALUATION AND REHABIL-
ITATION CENTER
Gracewood State School and Hospital
Gracewood, Georgia 30812
Telephone: (404) 798-4374
Clinic director: H. S. Whitaker, M.D.
Area served: State of Georgia.
Ages accepted: All ages.

*DEVELOPMENTAL SERVICES FOR
MENTAL RETARDATION
Chatham County Health Department
721 Abercorn Street
Savannah, Georgia 31401
Telephone: (404) 236-9582
Acting medical director: Walter W. Otto,
M.D.
Area served: Bryan, Chatham, and
Liberty Counties.
Ages accepted: Birth to 21 years, with
emphasis on preschool children.

HAWAII

*EVALUATION CLINICS FOR MEN-
TALLY RETARDED CHILDREN
Mental Retardation Division
Hawaii State Department of Health
Post Office Box 3378
Honolulu, Hawaii 96801
Telephone: HOnolulu 5-07711, Ext. 550
Clinic director: Margaret R. Soliman,
M.D.
Area served: All Islands.
Ages accepted: All ages. (Priority for
children under 10.)

IDAHO

*SOUTHWESTERN CLINIC
City-County Health Department
Boise, Idaho 83706
Telephone: (208) 375-5211
Clinic director: Bert Reed, M.D.
Area served: South Western Idaho.
Ages accepted: Birth to 21 years.

*SPECIAL MENTAL RETARDATION
PROJECT
Idaho State Department of Health
Boise, Idaho 83707
Telephone: (208) 344-5811
Acting director: J. E. Wyatt, M.D.
Area served: State.
Ages accepted: Birth to 21 years
(priority to preschool children).

*COEUR d'ALENE CLINIC
Panhandle District Health Department
Coeur d'Alene, Idaho 83814
Telephone: (208) 664-9296
Acting clinic director: Robert S.
McKean, M.D.
Area served: Idaho Panhandle.
Ages accepted: Birth to 21 years.

*CITY-COUNTY CLINIC
City-County Health Department
Idaho Falls, Idaho 83401
Telephone: (208) 523-2244
Clinic director: Ronald LeChelt, M.D.
Area served: North Eastern Idaho.
Ages accepted: Birth to 21 years.

*NORTH CENTRAL CLINIC
North Central District Health Department
Lewiston, Idaho 83501
Telephone: (208) 743-5501
Clinic directors: William C. Mannschreck, M.D., and Robert L. Olson, M.D.
Area served: North Central Idaho.
Ages accepted: No age limit.

IDAHO STATE SCHOOL AND HOSPITAL
Box 47
Nampa, Idaho 83651
Telephone: (208) 466-3588
Clinic director: Clarence A. McIntyre, M.D.
Area served: State of Idaho.
Ages accepted: No limitations.

*SOUTH EASTERN CLINIC
Southeastern District Health Department
Pocatello, Idaho 83201
Telephone: (208) 232-8231
Clinic director: Roger W. Boe, M.D.
Area served: Southeastern Idaho.

*SOUTH CENTRAL CLINIC
South Central District Health Department
Box 281
Twin Falls, Idaho 83301

Telephone: (208) 733-6711
Clinic director: Ben E. Katz, M.D.
Area served: South Central Idaho.
Ages accepted: Birth to 21 years.

ILLINOIS

*CHILD DEVELOPMENT CLINIC
Children's Memorial Hospital
707 West Fullerton Street
Chicago, Illinois 60614
Telephone: (312) DI 8-4040
Clinic director: Jerome L. Schulman, M.D.
Area served: Chicago.
Ages accepted: Birth to 16 years (priority to preschool children).

DR. JULIAN D. LEVINSON RESEARCH FOUNDATION FOR MENTALLY RETARDED CHILDREN
1850 West Harrison Street
Chicago, Illinois 60612
Telephone: (312) MO 6-8388
Administrative director: Delilah L. White, Ph.D.
Area served: Cook County.
Ages accepted: Birth to 16 years.

*DYSFUNCTIONING CHILD PROGRAM
Michael Reese Hospital and Medical Center
29th Street and Ellis Avenue
Chicago, Illinois 60616
Telephone: (312) CAlumet 5-5533
Medical director: Stanley Berlow, M.D.
Area served: Chicago area and surrounding communities, as well as entire State of Illinois, where feasible.
Ages accepted: Birth to 8 years.

ILLINOIS STATE PEDIATRIC INSTITUTE
1640 West Roosevelt Road
Chicago, Illinois 60608
Telephone: (312) 341-8000
Director: Herbert J. Grossman, M.D.
Area served: State of Illinois.
Ages accepted: Birth to 21 years.

MENTAL DEVELOPMENT CLINIC
Silvain and Arma Wyler Children's
Hospital
University of Chicago Hospitals and
Clinics
950 East 59th Street
Chicago, Illinois 60637
Telephone: (312) MU 4-6100, Ext. 5741
Clinic director: Arthur O. Stein, M.D.
Area served: Not limited, but particularly Greater Chicago.
Ages accepted: Birth to 15 years.

OUT-PATIENT DIAGNOSTIC CENTER
Dixon State School
2600 North Brinton Avenue
Dixon, Illinois 61021
Telephone: (815) 284-3311, extensions
498, 213, 673, 676
Clinic coordinator: Mrs. Lenore Hodapp,
ACSW.
Area served: Northern Illinois.
Ages accepted: Birth to 21 years.

INDIANA

*RILEY MEMORIAL CLINIC FOR
INTELLECTUALLY HANDICAPPED
CHILDREN
Indiana University School of Medicine
1100 West Michigan Street
Indianapolis, Indiana 46207
Telephone: (317) 639-8747
Clinic director: Arthur L. Drew, M.D.
Area served: State of Indiana.
Ages accepted: Birth to 16 years.

*ACHIEVEMENT CENTER FOR
CHILDREN
Purdue University
Room 101, Stanley Coulter Annex
West Lafayette, Indiana 47907
Telephone: (317) 447-1135
Executive director: N. C. Kephart, Ph.D.
Area served: Indiana and limited service
nationally.
Ages accepted: Birth to 12 years.

IOWA

CHILD EVALUATION CLINIC
643 10th Street SE.
Cedar Rapids, Iowa 52403
Telephone: (319) 366-4607
Medical director: Walter M. Block, M.D.
Area served: Cedar Rapids and Linn
County.
Ages accepted: Children below 17 years.

*THE CENTER FOR MENTALLY
RETARDED CHILDREN
Des Moines-Polk County Department of
Health
Argonne Armory Building
East First and Des Moines Streets
Des Moines, Iowa 50309
Telephone: (515) 283-2611
Medical director: Julius S. Connor, M.D.
Area served: Des Moines and Polk
County.
Ages accepted: Birth to 18 years.

GLENWOOD STATE HOSPITAL
SCHOOL
Out-Patient Department
Glenwood, Iowa 51534
Telephone: (712) 527-4811
Director: Leonard W. Lavis, M.S.W.
Area served: 51 counties primarily in the
southern half of Iowa.
Age accepted: All ages.

*CHILD DEVELOPMENT CLINIC
Department of Pediatrics
University of Iowa College of Medicine
Iowa City, Iowa 52240
Telephone: (319) 353-4825
Clinic director: Gerald Solomons, M.D.
Area served: State.
Ages accepted: Birth through 16 years.

WOODWARD STATE HOSPITAL SCHOOL
Diagnostic and Evaluation Clinic
Woodward, Iowa 50276
Telephone: (515) 438-2600
Director: W. C. Wildberger, M.D.
Area served: 48 counties primarily in the northern half of Iowa.
Age accepted: All ages.

KANSAS

*CHILDREN'S REHABILITATION UNIT
University of Kansas Medical Center
39th Street and Rainbow Boulevard
Kansas City, Kansas 66103
Telephone: (913) AD 6-5252, Ext. 725
Director: Herbert Miller, M.D.
Area served: Metropolitan Kansas City, plus regional consultation.
Ages accepted: Nursery school to vocational training.

CHILD STUDY UNIT
Kansas Neurological Institute
3107 West 21st Street
Topeka, Kansas 66604
Telephone: (913) FL 4-8581
Clinic director: M. Evangelakis, M.D.
Area served: State of Kansas.
Ages accepted: Birth through 21 years.

KENTUCKY

*MENTAL RETARDATION PROGRAM
Division of Maternal and Child Health
275 East Main Street
Frankfort, Kentucky 40601
Telephone: (502) 564-4830
Clinic director: Joanne Sexton, M.D.
Area served: Kentucky.
Ages accepted: Birth to 21 years.

DEPARTMENT OF NEUROLOGY
University of Kentucky Medical Center
Lexington, Kentucky 40506
Telephone: (606) 233-5000, Ext. 5375

Clinic director: David B. Clark, M.D.
Area served: State of Kentucky; out-of-State patients seen by special arrangement.
Ages accepted: All ages.

*DEVELOPMENTAL CLINIC
Department of Pediatrics
University Hospital
Lexington, Kentucky 40506
Telephone: (606) 255-3600, Ext. 5523
Clinic director: Vernon L. James, M.D., F.A.A.P.
Area served: Entire State of Kentucky.
Ages accepted: Up to age 16.

*CHILD EVALUATION CENTER
University of Louisville
School of Medicine
340 East Madison Street
Louisville, Kentucky 40202
Telephone: (502) 584-6197
Center director: Bernard Weisskopf, M.D.
Area served: Kentucky.
Ages accepted: Birth to 16 years.

LOUISIANA

NEW ORLEANS MENTAL HEALTH CENTER
3100 General De Gaulle Drive
New Orleans, Louisiana 70114
Telephone: (504) 367-3850
Clinic director: W. H. Shelton, M.D.
Area served: Parishes of Orleans, St. Bernard, and Palquemines.
Ages accepted: All ages.

MAINE

*MENTAL RETARDATION CLINIC
Central Maine General Hospital
Lewiston, Maine 04240
Telephone: (207) 784-4011
Clinic director: Russell Morissette, M.D.
Area served: Western and southern Maine.
Ages accepted: Birth to 6 years.

CHILD GUIDANCE CLINIC
Pineland Hospital and Training Center
Pownal, Maine 04069
Telephone: (207) 688-4811
Clinic director: Alfred E. Darby, Jr.,
M.D.
Area served: Towns of Cumberland,
Gray, New Gloucester, North Yar-
mouth, and Pownal.
Ages accepted: Up to 16 years of age.

*MENTAL RETARDATION CLINIC
Thayer Hospital
Waterville, Maine 04901
Telephone: (207) TR 2-2766
Clinic director: Edmund Ervin, M.D.
Area served: Northern and eastern part
of Maine.
Ages accepted: Birth to 6 years.

MARYLAND

ANNE ARUNDEL COUNTY MULTI-
PROBLEM CLINIC FOR CHILDREN
Annapolis, Maryland 21401
Telephone: (301) COlonial 7-8151
Clinic director: Julius Lobel, M.D.
Area served: Anne Arundel County.
Ages accepted: Birth to age 6 years.

CENTRAL EVALUATION CLINIC
FOR CHILDREN
University of Maryland Hospital
112 South Greene Street
Baltimore, Maryland 21201
Telephone: (301) 955-8950
Clinic director: Raymond L. Clemmens,
M.D.
Area served: State of Maryland.
Ages accepted: Birth to 21 years.

DIAGNOSTIC AND EVALUATION
CENTER FOR HANDICAPPED
CHILDREN
Department of Pediatrics
Children's Medical and Surgical Center
Johns Hopkins Hospital
Baltimore, Maryland 21205
Telephone: (301) 955-4000

Clinic director: Frederick Richardson,
M.D., M.R.C.P.
Area served: State of Maryland and
other areas.
Ages accepted: Birth to 21 years.

CHILDREN'S DIAGNOSTIC AND
STUDY BRANCH
National Naval Medical Center
Bethesda, Maryland 20014
Telephone: (301) 496-6914
Clinic director: Felix De La Cruz, M.D.
Area served: Limited to military depend-
ents who are normally eligible for care
at the National Naval Medical Center.
Ages accepted: Birth to 6 years.

SERVICE FOR RETARDED AND
HANDICAPPED CHILDREN
Prince George's County Health Depart-
ment
Cheverly, Maryland 20785
Telephone: (301) SPruce 3-1400
Clinic director: Hildegard Rothmund,
M.D.
Area served: Prince George's County.
Ages accepted: Birth to 18 years.

ROSEWOOD STATE HOSPITAL
CLINIC
Owings Mills, Maryland 21117
Telephone: (301) 363-0300, Ext. 210
Clinic director: Kurt Glaser, M.D.
Area served: State of Maryland.
Ages accepted: All ages.

MASSACHUSETTS

DEVELOPMENTAL EVALUATION
CLINIC
Mental Retardation Unit
Children's Hospital Medical Center
300 Longwood Avenue
Boston, Massachusetts 02115
Telephone: (617) REgent 4-6000
Unit director: Allen C. Crocker, M.D.
Area served: Primarily New England, but
no geographical limit.
Ages accepted: Birth to 18 years.

*CHILDREN'S DEVELOPMENTAL CLINIC
Cambridge Health Department
1530 Cambridge Street
Cambridge, Massachusetts 02139
Telephone: (617) TRowbridge 6-8621, Ext. 27 and 28
Director: Philip J. Porter, M.D.
Area served: Cambridge and surrounding communities.
Ages accepted: Birth to 16 years (primary focus on preschool age).

MENTAL RETARDATION CLINIC
Thorne Memorial Building
Barnstable County Hospital
Pocasset, Massachusetts 02559
Telephone: (617) 428-6034
Clinic director: Baruch Dodiuk, M.D.
Area served: Barnstable County (Cape Cod).
Ages accepted: Birth to 21 years.

MENTAL RETARDATION CLINIC
Paul A. Dever State School
Post Office Box 631
Taunton, Massachusetts 02780
Telephone: (617) 824-5881
Superintendent: Anne H. Lewis, M.D.
Area served: Southeastern Massachusetts.
Ages accepted: All ages.

*COMMUNITY EVALUATION AND REHABILITATION CENTER
Walter E. Fernald State School
Box C
Waverly, Massachusetts 02178
Telephone: (617) TW 4-3600
Director: Robert E. Flynn, M.D.
Area served: Middlesex County and part of Suffolk County.
Ages accepted: No restriction (infants and adults).

COMMUNITY EVALUATION AND REHABILITATION CLINIC
Wrentham State School
Wrentham, Massachusetts 02093
Telephone: (617) EV 4-3116
Clinic director: Spencer Ely Levin, M.D.
Area served: The Wrentham State School District.
Ages accepted: No specific age limits.

MICHIGAN

*TRAINING PROGRAM FOR PROFESSIONAL PERSONNEL REGARDING CARE OF MENTALLY RETARDED CHILDREN
University of Michigan (Mental Study Unit)
Ann Arbor, Michigan 48104
Telephone: (313) 764-5182
Clinic director: Richard J. Allen, M.D.
Area served: Mainly State of Michigan; with some patients from Ohio, Indiana and Illinois.
Ages accepted: Birth to 14 years.

*APPRAISAL CENTER FOR MULTIPLY HANDICAPPED CHILDREN
Children's Hospital of Michigan
5224 St. Antoine
Detroit, Michigan 48202
Telephone: (313) TE 3-1000
Clinic director: Charles G. Jennings, M.D.
Area served: State of Michigan.
Ages accepted: Birth to 8 years.

PLYMOUTH STATE HOME AND TRAINING SCHOOL
Northville, Michigan 48167
Telephone: (313) GL 3-1500
Clinic director: Jamil Kheder, M.D.
Area served: Wayne County.
Ages accepted: All ages.

MINNESOTA

*CHILD DEVELOPMENT SECTION
LAKELAND MENTAL HEALTH
CENTER, INC.
106 East Alcott Avenue
Fergus Falls, Minnesota 56537
Telephone: (218) 736-6981
Medical director: Rolf Daehlin, M.D.
Area served: Counties of Becker,
Douglas, Grant, Otter Tail, Pope,
Stevens, Traverse, and Wilkin.
Ages accepted: From birth on.

*CHILD STUDY CENTER
215 South Oak Street
Owatonna, Minnesota 55060
Telephone: (507) 451-6650
Medical director: Haddow Keith, M.D.
Area served: Dodge, Rice, Steele, and
Waseca Counties.
Ages accepted: Birth to 10 years.

CHILD EVALUATION CENTER
St. Paul-Ramsey Hospital
St. Paul, Minnesota 55102
Telephone: (612) 222-7341
Project director: Homer Venters, M.D.
Area served: Regional (primarily Ramsey
County).
Ages accepted: Children.

MISSISSIPPI

*CHILD DEVELOPMENT CLINIC
University Hospital
Jackson, Mississippi 39216
Telephone: (601) 362-4411
Clinic director: Margaret Batson, M.D.
Area served: State of Mississippi (Exception of 14 counties served by clinic in
Tupelo – Children from this area
must be referred by that clinic).
Ages accepted: Birth to 14 years.

*REGIONAL CHILD DEVELOPMENT
CLINIC REGIONAL REHABILITA-
TION CENTER, INC.
615 Pegram Drive
Tupelo, Mississippi 38802

Telephone: (601) 842-1891
Medical director: Luther L. McDougal,
Jr., M.D.
Area served: Twenty northeastern Mississippi counties.
Ages accepted: Up to age 16.

MISSOURI

ALBANY REGIONAL DIAGNOSTIC
AND EVALUATION CLINIC –
MENTAL RETARDATION
Box D
Albany, Missouri 64402
Telephone: (816) 726-5246
Medical director: Troy O. Morgan, M.D.
Region served: Area 1, northwestern, 12
counties.
Age served: All.

*MULTIPLE HANDICAP CLINIC
University of Missouri School of
Medicine
Medical Center
Columbia, Missouri 65202
Telephone: (314) GI 2-5111, Ext. 296
Medical coordinator: Clement E.
Brooke, M.D.
Area served: State of Missouri.
Ages accepted: Birth to 21 years.

HANNIBAL REGIONAL DIAGNOSTIC
CLINIC – MENTAL RETARDA-
TION
805 Old 61 Highway
Hannibal, Missouri 63401
Telephone: (314) 221-6002
Clinic administrator: Mr. J. D. Walker.
Region served: Area 3, 11 counties,
Middle East.
Age served: All.

JOPLIN REGIONAL DIAGNOSTIC
CLINIC – MENTAL RETARDATION
Post Office Box 1209
3600 East Newman Road
Joplin, Missouri 64801
Telephone: (417) 624-7004
Clinic administrator: Milton Sneddon.
Region served: Area 5, Southwestern, 12
counties.
Ages served: All.

*CHILD DEVELOPMENT CENTER
Children's Mercy Hospital
1710 Independence Avenue
Kansas City, Missouri 64106
Telephone: (816) GRand 1-0626
Clinic director: Ned W. Smull, M.D.
Area served: Kansas City area and western part of Missouri.
Ages accepted: Birth to 14 years.

KIRKSVILLE REGIONAL DIAGNOSTIC CLINIC – MENTAL RETARDATION
1702 East LaHarpe Street
Kirksville, Missouri 63501
Telephone: (816) 665-2801
Clinic administrator: Mr. Charles Brewer.
Region served: Area 2, 13 counties, Northeastern.
Age served: All.

POPULAR BLUFF REGIONAL DIAGNOSTIC CLINIC – MENTAL RETARDATION
1203 South Sunset Drive, Rural Route No. 2
Popular Bluff, Missouri 63901
Telephone: (314) 785-0101
Medical director: Charles A. Raper, M.D.
Clinic administrator: Mr. Moody Bryles.
Region served: Area 8, 11 counties, Southeastern.
Ages served: All.

ROLLA REGIONAL DIAGNOSTIC CLINIC – MENTAL RETARDATION
105 Fairgrounds Road
Rolla, Missouri 65401
Telephone: (314) 364-5687
Medical director: Barbara Russell, M.D.
Clinic administrator: Mr. Malcolm Jasper.
Region served: Area 7, 14 counties, South Central.
Ages served: All.

*CHILD DEVELOPMENT CLINIC
Cardinal Glennon Memorial Hospital for Children
1465 South Grand Boulevard
Saint Louis, Missouri 63104
Telephone: (314) PRospect 2-7990
Clinic director: Austin R. Sharp, M.D.
Area served: State of Missouri.
Ages accepted: Birth to 14 years (priority to infants and preschool children).

CHILD GUIDANCE AND CHILD EVALUATION CLINIC
Washington University School of Medicine
369 North Taylor
Saint Louis, Missouri 63108
Telephone: (314) FO 1-6884
Clinic director: Thomas Brugger, M.D.
Area served: Mainly Greater St. Louis (St. Louis City and County, East St. Louis, and other cities in western Illinois).
Ages accepted: All ages.

SIKESTON REGIONAL DIAGNOSTIC CLINIC – MENTAL RETARDATION
213 Malone, Post Office Box 752
Sikeston, Missouri 63801
Telephone: (314) 471-9455
Clinic administrator: Mr. A. David Ragan.
Region served: Area 9, 8 counties, Southeastern.
Ages served: All.

SPRINGFIELD REGIONAL DIAGNOSTIC CLINIC – MENTAL RETARDATION
Main Post Office Box 824
1515 East Pythian
Springfield, Missouri 65801
Telephone: (417) 869-0574, 0575, 0576
Clinic administrator: William Harrison, M. Ed.
Region served: Area 6, Southwestern, 14 counties.
Ages served: All.

MONTANA

***MONTANA CENTER FOR HANDI-
CAPPED CHILDREN**
c/o Eastern Montana College
Billings, Montana 59101
Telephone: (406) 252-9316
Clinic director: Allen P. Hartman, M.D.
Area served: Primarily the eastern half of
the State of Montana.
Ages accepted: Birth to 5 years, 8
months for initial referral. Exceptions
are sometimes made to this age limit.

**WESTERN MONTANA CHILD DEVEL-
OPMENT CENTER**
Missoula City-County Health Depart-
ment
New Annex to Courthouse
Missoula, Montana 59801
Telephone: (406) 549-6413
Clinic director: Kenneth J. Lampert,
M.D., M.P.H.
Area served: Primarily 7 western coun-
ties, but entire State of Montana
where feasible.
Ages accepted: All ages.

NEBRASKA

***HANDICAPPED CHILDREN'S
CLINIC**
The University of Nebraska College of
Medicine
444 South 44th Avenue
Omaha, Nebraska 68131
Telephone: (402) 551-0669, Ext. 201
Clinic director: Paul H. Pearson, M.D.
Area served: Nebraska and region
(limited as to number of people who
may be accepted from surrounding
States).
Ages accepted: Infancy through 16
years.

NEVADA

*SPECIAL CHILDREN'S CLINIC
Nevada State Division of Health

1941 Jefferson Street
North Las Vegas, Nevada 89030
Telephone: (702) 385-2111, Ext. 223
Clinic director: Kermit J. Ryan, M.D.
Area served: Nye, Esmeralds, Lincoln,
and Clark Counties.
Ages accepted: Birth to 6 years.

**BUREAU OF MENTAL RETARDA-
TION**
Box 2460
Reno, Nevada 89502
Telephone: (702) 322-6961
Clinic director: Thomas F. Linde, Ph. D.
Area served: State of Nevada.
Ages accepted: All ages.

*SPECIAL CHILDREN'S CLINIC
790 Sutro Street
Reno, Nevada 89502
Telephone: (702) 784-6321 and 6322
Clinic medical director: Emanuel Berger,
M.D.
Area served: Northern Nevada.
Ages accepted: Birth to 6 years. In
special instances up to age 9.

NEW HAMPSHIRE

**OUT-PATIENT CLINIC FOR RE-
TARDED CHILDREN**
Laconia State School
Laconia, New Hampshire 03246
Telephone: (603) 524-5373
Clinic director: Joseph Schlesinger, M.D.
Area served: State of New Hampshire.
Ages accepted: All ages.

NEW JERSEY

CLINIC FOR THE RETARDED
62 North Walnut Street
East Orange, New Jersey 07017
Telephone: (201) OR 6-8070
Clinic coordinator: Ada A. Abramson,
ACSW.
Area served: Essex and West Hudson
Counties, primarily.
Ages accepted: Children and adults.

*THE CHILD EVALUATION CENTER
Hunterdon Medical Center
Route 31
Flemington, New Jersey 08822
Telephone: (201) ST 2-2121
Clinic director: Avrum Labe Katcher, M.D.
Area served: State of New Jersey.
Ages accepted: Birth to age 19.

*CHILD EVALUATION CENTER
Hackensack Hospital
243 Atlantic Street
Hackensack, New Jersey 07601
Telephone: (201) HU 7-4000, Ext. 783, 784
Clinic director: Phoebe Hudson, M.D., F.A.A.P., and Evelyn Dresner, M.D., F.A.A.P.
Area served: All New Jersey.
Ages accepted: Birth to age 14 (stress on preschool child).

*CHILD EVALUATION CENTER
The Bancroft School
Hopkins Lane
Haddonfield, New Jersey 08033
Telephone: (609) HA 9-0961
Clinic director: W. H. Grover, M.D.
Area served: Camden, Gloucester, Burlington, and Mercer Counties.
Ages accepted: Birth to age 21.

*CHILD EVALUATION CENTER
Morristown Memorial Hospital
100 Madison Avenue
Morristown, New Jersey 07960
Telephone: (201) JEfferson 8-4500
Clinic director: Catherine E. Spears, M.D.
Area served: Morris, Sussex, Middlesex, Union, Somerset, Passaic, and Warren Counties.
Ages accepted: Birth through 20 years.

*CHILD EVALUATION CENTER
Jersey Shore Medical Center
1945 Corlies Avenue
Neptune, New Jersey 07753
Telephone: (201) 775-5500

Clinic director: Anthony P. DeSpirito, M.D.
Area served: Monmouth and Ocean Counties.
Ages accepted: Birth to age 14 (stress on preschool child).

*CHILD EVALUATION CENTER
United Hospitals of Newark
Babies' Unit Hospital
15-19 Roseville Avenue
Newark, New Jersey 07107
Telephone: (201) HU 2-6200
Clinic director: Mary Mazzarella, M.D.
Area served: Entire State of New Jersey, by referral.
Ages accepted: Birth to 21.

*CHILD EVALUATION UNIT
Barnert Memorial Hospital Center
535 E. 29th Street
Paterson, New Jersey 07514
Telephone: (201) 274-8215
Medical director: Harry Yolken, M.D.
Area served: Passaic and Bergen Counties.
Ages accepted: Any age.

EVALUATION CLINIC
Newark State College
Morris Avenue
Union, New Jersey 07083
Telephone: (201) 351-6850
Clinic director: Nellie D. Stone, D.S.W.
Area served: Union County and surrounding region.
Ages accepted: All ages.

NEW MEXICO

*CHILD STUDY CENTER FOR RETARDED CHILDREN
Bernalillo County Health Unit
605 Copper N.E.
Albuquerque, New Mexico 87101
Telephone: (505) 242-6694
Medical director: Eleanor L. Adler, M.D.
Area served: Bernalillo County (if feasible, counties of Valencia, Sandoval, and Torrance).
Ages accepted: Birth to 10 years.

*THE CHILD DEVELOPMENT CENTER
217 East Marcy Street
Santa Fe, New Mexico 87501
Telephone: (505) 827-2338
Medical director: Dina Bayer, M.D.
Area served: State of New Mexico.
Ages accepted: Birth to 10 years.

NEW YORK

*CHILDREN'S EVALUATION AND REHABILITATION CLINIC
Albert Einstein College of Medicine
Jacobi Hospital
Pelham Parkway South and Eastchester Road
Bronx, New York 10461
Telephone: (212) TY 2-6000, Ext. 369
Clinic director: Lawrence T. Taft, M.D.
Area served: Bronx, essentially, but some cases from other boroughs of New York City are accepted.
Ages accepted: No specific age limits.

THE SHIELD INSTITUTE FOR RETARDED CHILDREN
1800 Andrews Avenue
Bronx, New York 10453
Telephone: (212) CYpress 9-7600
Clinic director: Joseph Michaels, M.D.
Area served: Metropolitan New York.
Ages accepted: Birth to 12 years.

MORRIS J. SOLOMON CLINIC FOR RETARDED CHILDREN
The Jewish Hospital and Medical Center of Brooklyn
555 Prospect Place
Brooklyn, New York 11238
Telephone: (212) 857-8700, Ext. 584
Acting clinic director: John E. Allen, M.D.
Area served: The catchment area in the borough of Brooklyn designated by New York City Community Health Board.
Ages accepted: Birth to 14 years.

*BUFFALO DIAGNOSTIC AND COUNSELING STUDY CENTER FOR MENTALLY RETARDED CHILDREN
Children's Rehabilitation Center
A Unit of Children's Hospital
936 Delaware Avenue
Buffalo, New York 14209
Telephone: (716) 886-5100 or 883-5810
Clinic director: Robert Warner, M.D.
Area served: Buffalo and Erie County.
Ages accepted: Preschool children and emergency cases have priority.

PUTNAM COUNTY MENTAL HEALTH SERVICES
Putnam Community Hospital
Stoneleigh Avenue
Carmel, New York 10512
Telephone: (914) BR 9-8081
Clinic director: Gail A. Gaines, M.D., F.A.P.A.
Area served: Putnam County.
Ages accepted: No limits.

ASSOCIATION FOR HELP OF RETARDED CHILDREN
189 Wheatley Road
Brookville
Glen Head, New York 11545
Telephone: (516) 626-1000
Clinic administrator: Andrew Weickert, ACSW.
Area served: County of Nassau.
Ages accepted: All age groups.

KENNEDY CHILD STUDY CENTER
151 East 67th Street
New York, New York 10021
Telephone: (212) YU 8-9500
Clinic director: Mary T. Piana, M.D.
Area served: Those sections of New York City and the adjacent counties that are included in the Catholic Archdiocese of New York: Manhattan and Bronx.
Ages accepted: The developmental and training programs includes children from 3 to 8 years only, but for diagnostic evaluation, a wider age span is accepted.

*MENTAL RETARDATION CLINIC
Flower-Fifth Avenue Hospitals
New York Medical College
1 East 105th Street
New York, New York 10029
Telephone: (212) TRafalger 6-5500
Clinic director: Margaret J. Giannini,
M.D.
Area served: No geographical limitations;
all people are permitted to attend.
Ages accepted: Birth to 21 years.

CHILD EVALUATION AND TREAT-
MENT CENTER
St. Charles Hospital
Belle Terre Road
Port Jefferson, New York 11777
Telephone: (516) HR 3-2800
Medical director: Onedina Vega, M.D.
Area served: Suffolk County.
Ages accepted: Predominantly infancy
through 18.

DIAGNOSTIC CLINIC FOR DEVELOP-
MENTAL DISORDERS
Strong Memorial Hospital
260 Crittenden Boulevard
Rochester, New York 14620
Telephone: (716) 275-2986
Clinic director: Albert P. Scheiner, M.D.
Area served: Monroe County and sur-
rounding area.
Ages accepted: Birth to 18 years.

ROME STATE SCHOOL
South James Street
Rome, New York 13440
Telephone: (315) FF 6-2300
Medical director: Charles Greenberg,
M.D.
Area served: Counties of Albany,
Broome, Chenango, Cortland, Dela-
ware, Fulton, Herkimer, Jefferson,
Lewis, Madison, Montgomery, Oneida,
Onondaga, Oswego, Otsego, Rens-
salaer, Saratoga, Schenectady, Scho-
harie, Warren, and Washington.
Ages accepted: No limit.

CRAIG COLONY SCHOOL AND
HOSPITAL
Sonyea, New York 14556
Telephone: (716) 658-2221
Medical director: Vincent I. Bonafede,
M.D.
Area served: Livingston County.
Ages accepted: No limit.

WILLOWBROOK STATE SCHOOL
2760 Victory Boulevard
Staten Island, New York 10314
Telephone: (212) GI 8-1440
Medical director: Jack Hammond, M.D.
Area served: Richmond County and New
York City.
Ages accepted: No limit.

LETCHWORTH VILLAGE
Thiells, New York 10984
Telephone: (914) 947-1000
Medical director: Jacob Schneider, M.D.
Area served: Orange, Rockland, and
Sullivan Counties.
Ages accepted: No limit.

WEST SENECA STATE SCHOOL
1200 East and West Road
West Seneca, New York 14224
Telephone: (716) NR 4-6300
Medical director: Samuel Feinstein, M.D.
Area served: Erie, Niagara, Chautauqua,
Cattaraugus, Wyoming, Allegany,
Genesu, and Orleans Counties.
Ages accepted: No limit.

DEVELOPMENTAL EVALUATION
CLINIC
The Burke Rehabilitation Center
White Plains, New York 10605
Telephone: (914) White Plains 8-5144
Clinic director: Sidney A. Haber, M.D.
Area served: Westchester County, N.Y.
Ages accepted: Infancy to adulthood.

NORTH CAROLINA

*DEVELOPMENTAL EVALUATION CLINIC OF WESTERN NORTH CAROLINA, INC.
Post Office Box 5636
Asheville Orthopedic Hospital
Asheville, North Carolina 28803
Telephone: (704) 254-8876
Clinic director: Bernhard H. Hartman, M.D., F.A.A.P.
Area served: Western North Carolina.
Ages accepted: Birth to 21 years.

CHILDREN'S PSYCHIATRIC INSTITUTE OUT-PATIENT CLINIC
Murdoch Center
Butner, North Carolina 27509
Telephone: (704) 985-6581, Ext. 649, 651, and 745
Director: Christine McRee, M.D.
Area served: State of North Carolina.
Ages accepted: Children of all ages.

*DEVELOPMENTAL EVALUATION CLINIC
Department of Pediatrics
University of North Carolina School of Medicine
Chapel Hill, North Carolina 27515
Telephone: (919) 966-8417
Clinic director: Harrie R. Chamberlin, M.D.
Area served: State of North Carolina.
Ages accepted: Generally, under 4 years.

*DEVELOPMENTAL EVALUATION CLINIC
Mecklenburg County Health Department
1200 Blythe Boulevard
Charlotte, North Carolina 28203
Telephone: (704) 375-8861, Ext. 261
Clinic director: Laura Ross-Venning, M.D.
Area served: Mecklenburg and surrounding counties.
Ages accepted: Preschool, with exceptions.

*DEVELOPMENTAL EVALUATION CLINIC
Western Carolina University
Cullowhee, North Carolina 28723
Telephone: (704) 293-7340
Clinic director: Velta F. Briuks-Cannon, M.D.
Area served: 8 Westernmost counties.
Ages accepted: Children of all ages (birth to 21).

*DEVELOPMENTAL EVALUATION CLINIC
Department of Pediatrics
Duke University Medical Center
Durham, North Carolina 27706
Telephone: (919) 684-2354 or 684-3734
Clinic director: Marcel Kinsbourne, M.D., Ph. D.
Area served: North Carolina.
Ages accepted: Emphasis on preschool ages.

*DEVELOPMENTAL EVALUATION CLINIC
1661 Owen Drive
Fayetteville, North Carolina 28304
Telephone: (919) 485-6147
Clinic director: Josephine T. Melchior, M.D.
Area served: State of North Carolina.
Ages accepted: 3 to 12 years.

*DEVELOPMENTAL EVALUATION CLINIC OF EAST CAROLINA UNIVERSITY
513 East Eighth Street
Post Office Box 2711
Greenville, North Carolina 27835
Telephone: (919) PLaza 8-3426 or PLaza 2-5030
Clinic director: Malene Grant Irons, M.D.
Area served: State of North Carolina.
Ages accepted: Up to 21 years, but preferably from 3 to 16 years.
(Note — Branch Clinic: District Health Department, Elizabeth City 27909, Telephone: (919) 335-5429.)

*DEVELOPMENTAL EVALUATION CLINIC
Guilford County Health Department
936 Montlieu Avenue
High Point, North Carolina 27262
Telephone: (919) 883-9166, Ext. 27
Clinic director: John D. Bridgers, M.D.
Area served: Guilford and surrounding counties.
Ages accepted: Children of all ages.

DIAGNOSTIC CLINIC
Western Carolina Center
Morganton, North Carolina 28655
Telephone: (704) 437-8717
Director: J. Iverson Riddle, M.D.
Area served: Western North Carolina (30 Western counties).
Ages accepted: Children of all ages.

*DEVELOPMENTAL EVALUATION CLINIC
Granville County Health Department
Post Office Box 367
Oxford, North Carolina 27565
Telephone: (919) 693-7618
Clinic director: J. V. Weaver, M.D.
Area served: State of North Carolina, emphasis on Granville and Vance Counties.
Ages accepted: 3 to adolescence, emphasis on preschool.

*DEVELOPMENTAL EVALUATION CLINIC
Babies' Hospital
Wilmington, North Carolina 28401
Telephone: (919) 256-3783
Clinic director: Robert A. Melton, M.D.
Area served: Eastern North Carolina.
Ages accepted: Emphasis on preschool ages.

*DEVELOPMENTAL EVALUATION CLINIC
Graylyn Estates
Robinhood Road
Winston-Salem, North Carolina 27106
Telephone: (919) 723-8856
Clinic director: Alanson Hinman, M.D.

Area served: State of North Carolina.
Ages accepted: Birth to 21 years.

NORTH DAKOTA

*EVALUATION CENTER FOR EXCEPTIONAL CHILDREN
University of North Dakota
Grand Forks, North Dakota 58202
Telephone: (701) 772-3471
Medical director: Louis B. Silverman, M.D.
Area served: State of North Dakota.
Ages accepted: Under age 21 with priority to infants and younger children.

OHIO

*CLINIC FOR TREATMENT OF METABOLIC DISORDERS ASSOCIATED WITH MENTAL RETARDATION
Children's Hospital Research Foundation
Elland and Bethesda Avenues
Cincinnati, Ohio 45229
Telephone: (513) 281-6161, Ext. 288
Clinic director: Betty Sutherland, M.D.
Area served: Ohio and surrounding States.
Ages accepted: Birth to 16 years.

*HAMILTON COUNTY DIAGNOSTIC CLINIC FOR THE MENTALLY RETARDED
295 Erkenbrecher Avenue
Cincinnati, Ohio 45229
Telephone: (513) 212-8282, Ext. 45
Clinic director: Jack H. Rubinstein, M.D.
Area served: State of Ohio.
Ages accepted: Children and adults.

*COMPREHENSIVE CARE PROGRAM FOR CHILDREN WITH HANDICAPS
Case Western Reserve University, Department of Pediatrics
Cleveland Metropolitan General Hospital
Cleveland, Ohio 44109
Telephone: (216) 351-4820, Ext. 706
Medical director: Irwin A. Schafer, M.D.
Area served: Northeastern Ohio.
Ages accepted: Birth to 15 years.

MENTAL DEVELOPMENT CENTER
Hitchcock Hall
Case Western Reserve University
Cleveland, Ohio 44106
Telephone: (216) CEdar 1-7700, Ext. 763
Clinic director: Jane W. Kessler, Ph. D.
Area served: Northeastern Ohio.
Ages accepted: Birth to 16 years (priority to children of preschool age).

*CHILDREN'S HOSPITAL
Outpatient Department and Birth Defects Clinic
561 South 17th Street
Columbus, Ohio 43205
Telephone: (614) 253-8841
Birth defects director: Antoinette Parisi Eaton, M.D.
Area served: Central Ohio, but not restricted.
Ages accepted: Birth to 20 years.

CLINIC FOR THE MENTALLY RETARDED
Columbus State School
1601 West Broad Street
Columbus, Ohio 43223
Telephone: (614) 279-9471, Ext. 280 or 270
Clinic director: Gerhard E. Martin, M.D.
Area served: State of Ohio.
Ages accepted: Children and adults.

DIVISION OF CHILD DEVELOPMENT
561 South 17 Street
Columbus, Ohio 43205
Telephone: (614) 253-8841, Ext. 352 or 364
Clinic director: Robert A. Wehe, M.D.
Area served: State of Ohio predominantly, but not restricted.
Ages accepted: Birth to 6 years (new cases restricted to under 2 years at present).

*BARNEY CHILDREN'S MEDICAL CENTER
Evaluation and Diagnostic Clinic
1735 Chapel Street
Dayton, Ohio 45404
Telephone: (513) 461-3555
Clinic director: Meinhard Robinow, M.D.
Area served: Primarily Montgomery County and a surrounding six-county area.
Ages accepted: Birth to age 21.

*LUCAS COUNTY DIAGNOSTIC AND EVALUATION CLINIC FOR RETARDED CHILDREN
1155 Larc Lane
Toledo, Ohio 43614
Telephone: (419) 385-5771, -2, -3, or -4.
Clinic director: Ralph L. Zucker, M.D.
Area served: Northwestern Ohio.
Ages accepted: Children and adults.

OKLAHOMA

CHILD STUDY CENTER
Department of Pediatrics
University of Oklahoma Medical School
601 North East 18th Street
Oklahoma City, Oklahoma 73104
Telephone: (405) JA 4-4449
Clinic director: John A. Saunders, M.D.
Area served: Clinic and private cases on statewide basis.
Ages accepted: Birth to 14 years.

*CHILD STUDY CLINIC
Children's Medical Center
4818 South Lewis Street
Post Office Box 7352
Tulsa, Oklahoma 74105
Telephone: (918) RI 7-7542
Clinic director: James G. Coldwell, M.D.
Area served: Not restricted as to area.
Ages accepted: Birth to 9 years (emphasis on preschool children).

OREGON

*POLK COUNTY CHILD DEVELOP-MENT CLINIC
c/o Polk County Health Department
Post Office Box 34, County Court House
Dallas, Oregon 97338
Telephone: (503) 623-8171
Clinic director: Brace I. Knapp, M.D.
Area served: Polk County.
Ages accepted: Birth to 18 years.

*WASHINGTON COUNTY CHILD DEVELOPMENT PROGRAM
150 North Third Avenue
Hillsboro, Oregon 97123
Telephone: (503) 648-1111, Ext. 231
Clinic director: Edward L. Hendricks, M.D.
Area served: Washington County.
Ages accepted: Birth to 18 years.

*YAMHILL COUNTY CHILD DEVEL-OPMENT CLINIC
Yamhill County Health Department
Court House
McMinnville, Oregon 97128
Telephone: (503) 472-5161, Ext. 256
Clinic director: L. E. Ragan, M.D.
Area served: Yamhill County, Oreg.
Ages accepted: Birth to 18 years.

*CLACKAMAS COUNTY CHILD DEVELOPMENT CLINIC
Clackamas County Health Department
1425 South Kaen Road
Oregon City, Oregon 97045
Telephone: (503) 656-1991
Clinic director: James L. Schneller, M.D.
Area served: Clackamas County.
Ages accepted: All ages.

OUTPATIENT DEPARTMENT
Fairview Hospital and Training Center
2250 Strong Road, South East
Salem, Oregon 97310
Telephone: (503) 581-2531
Clinic director: R. H. Sinanan, M.D.
Area served: State of Oregon.
Ages accepted: All ages.

PENNSYLVANIA

ELWYN EVALUATION AND RE-SEARCH CENTER
Elwyn School
Elwyn, Pennsylvania 19063
Telephone: (215) LOwell 6-8800
Clinic directors: Gerald R. Clark, M.D., and David Baker, M.D.
Area served: Southeastern Pennsylvania and Philadelphia area.
Ages accepted: Birth to 21 years.

CHILD STUDY, TREATMENT AND RESEARCH CENTER
The Woods Schools
Langhorne, Pennsylvania 19047
Telephone: (215) SK 7-3731
Medical director: Jules E. Vassalluzzo, M.D.
Area served: Regional, national, and international.
Ages accepted: 3 years and up.

CHILD DEVELOPMENT CENTER
1605 West Main Street
Norristown, Pennsylvania 19401
Telephone: (215) 279-6100
Executive director: Frank W. Guthridge, P.T., M. Ed.
Area served: Montgomery County and surrounding areas.
Ages accepted: Birth to 18 years.

*DEPARTMENT OF REHABILITA-TION
Children's Hospital of Philadelphia
1740 Bainbridge Street
Philadelphia, Pennsylvania 19146
Telephone: (215) KIngsley 6-2700
Clinic director: Mary D. Ames, M.D.
Area served: Pennsylvania, Delaware, and New Jersey.
Ages accepted: Birth to 14 years.

*MENTAL RETARDATION UNIT
St. Christopher's Hospital for Children
Special Clinic Building
2603 North Fifth Street
Philadelphia, Pennsylvania 19133
Telephone: (215) GA 6-5600
Clinic director: John B. Bartram, M.D.
Area served: Philadelphia and surrounding counties.
Ages accepted: Birth through adolescence (primarily children of preschool age).

*DEVELOPMENTAL CLINIC
Children's Hospital of Pittsburgh
125 DeSoto Street
Pittsburgh, Pennsylvania 15213
Telephone: (412) 681-7700
Clinic director: Grace Gregg, M.D.
Area served: Mainly Tri-State (Pennsylvania, Ohio, and West Virginia) area, but will accept any child that we can help from anywhere.
Ages accepted: Birth through 16 years.

PUERTO RICO

*DIAGNOSTIC AND GUIDANCE CENTER – RETARDED CHILDREN
Ave. Universidad #55
Rio Piedras, Puerto Rico 00907
Telephone: 765-2349
Clinic director: Ana Navarro, M.D.
Area served: Commonwealth of Puerto Rico.
Ages accepted: 12 years and under.

RHODE ISLAND

*CHILD DEVELOPMENT CENTER
Rhode Island Hospital
593 Eddy Street
Providence, Rhode Island 02903
Telephone: (401) 331-4300
Clinic director: Paul H. LaMarche, M.D.
Area served: State of Rhode Island.
Ages accepted: Birth through age 21.

SOUTH CAROLINA

*CHILD EVALUATION CLINIC
1410 Blanding Street

Columbia, South Carolina 29201
Telephone: (803) 758-2191
Director: Charles A. James, M.D.
Area served: State of South Carolina.
Ages accepted: Birth to 8 years (older children may be accepted under special circumstances).

TENNESSEE

*TEAM EVALUATION CENTER
Baroness Erlanger Hospital
261 Wiehl Street
Chattanooga, Tennessee 34703
Telephone: (615) 266-4101 or 265-4261, Ext. 766
Executive director: Mrs. Charles A. Dobson.
Area served: Counties of Bledsoe, Bradley, Coffee, Franklin, Grundy, Hamilton, Marion, McMinn, Meigs, Polk, Rhea, Sequatchie, Van Buren, in Southeast Tennessee; and counties of Catoosa, Dade, Walker in North Georgia.
Ages accepted: Up to 21 (priority to preschool children).

DIAGNOSTIC AND OUT-PATIENT CLINIC FOR MENTALLY RETARDED CHILDREN
Clover Bottom Hospital and School
Donelson, Tennessee 37214
Telephone: (615) 741-4502
Director: Louise G. Patikas.
Area served: Middle Tennessee.
Ages accepted: All ages.

*CHILD DEVELOPMENT CENTER
4th Floor, 22 North Pauline Street
Memphis, Tennessee 38105
Telephone: (901) 278-5050
Medical director: Robert Jordan, M.D.
Area served: Diagnostic services to patients from Memphis and surrounding area, but no geographic limitation.
Ages accepted: Birth to 11 years, follow-up services through 21 years.

CHILD DEVELOPMENT CLINIC
George Hubbard Hospital
Meharry Medical College
1005 18th Avenue North
Nashville, Tennessee 37208
Telephone: (615) 256-3631, Ext.
348/464
Project officer: E. Perry Crump, M.D.
Area served: Metropolitan Nashville,
Davidson County, Middle Tennessee
area.
Ages served: No specific age limits.

TEXAS

*AUSTIN EVALUATION CENTER
2816 San Gabriel
Austin, Texas 78705
Telephone: (512) GR 7-9676
Clinic director: Gretchen Runge, M.D.
Area served: Travis County and other
adjacent counties (if caseload permits).
Ages accepted: Birth to 8 years.

*DIAGNOSTIC AND EVALUATION
CENTER FOR MENTALLY RE-
TARDED CHILDREN
Children's Medical Center
1935 Amelia
Dallas, Texas 75235
Telephone: (214) 637-3820, Ext. 431
Clinic director: Doman K. Keele, M.D.
Area served: Dallas County and areas
served by Dallas.
Ages accepted: Birth to 21 years (pri-
ority to those under 8 years).

*CHILD STUDY CENTER
1300 West Lancaster
Ft. Worth, Texas 76102
Telephone: (817) ED 6-5481
Clinic director: Thomas William Wilson,
M.D.
Area served: Ft. Worth and Tarrant
County.
Ages accepted: Birth to 14 years.

*CHILD DEVELOPMENT CLINIC
Department of Pediatrics
University of Texas Medical Branch

Galveston, Texas 77550
Telephone: (713) SO 5-1598
Clinic director: Arrnell Boelsche, M.D.
Area served: State of Texas.
Ages accepted: Birth through 14 years.

*CHILD DEVELOPMENT CLINIC
Texas Medical Center
Texas Children's Hospital
6621 Fannin Street
Houston, Texas 77025
Telephone: (713) JA 9-4451, Ext. 381
Medical director: Winston E. Cochran,
M.D.
Area served: Houston area primarily.
Ages accepted: Birth to 14 years (pri-
ority to those under 7 years).

*GULF BEND CLINIC
2806 Navarro
Victoria, Texas 77901
Telephone: (512) 575-0681
Clinic director: Eva Y. Seger, M.D.
Area served: Six counties: Calhoun, De
Witt, Goliad, Refugio, Jackson, and
Victoria.
Ages accepted: Birth to 17 years.

UTAH

*UTAH STATE HEALTH DEPART-
MENT CLINIC FOR THE MEN-
TALLY RETARDED AT LOGAN
Cache County Health Department
160 North Main
Logan, Utah 84321
Telephone: (801) 752-0521
Health director: Dr. Merrill C. Daines.
Area served: Cache, North Box Elder,
and Rich Counties.
Ages accepted: Birth to 21 years.

UTAH STATE DIVISION OF HEALTH
Crippled Children's Services
2570 Grant Avenue
Ogden, Utah 84401
Telephone: (801) 392-5962
Clinic director: Leon H. White, M.D.
Area served: North Davis, Weber, Mor-
gan, Cache, Box Elder, Rich Counties.
Ages accepted: Birth to 21 years.

*BUREAU OF SPECIAL HEALTH SERVICES
Utah State Division of Health
44 Medical Drive
Salt Lake City, Utah 84113
Telephone: (801) 328-6161
Clinic director: Joseph P. Kesler, M.D.
Area served: Summit, Daggett, Wasatch, Utah, Duchesne, Uintah, Juab, Sampete, Carbon, Millard, Sevier, Emery, Grand, Beaver, Piute, Wayne, San Juan, Iron, Garfield, Washington, and Kane Counties.
Ages accepted: Birth to 21 years.
(Note – The following itinerant clinics are held at certain predetermined times with personnel from the Utah State Division of Health at Salt Lake City: Provo, Vernal, Price, Moab, Richfield, and Cedar City.)

*CHILD DEVELOPMENT CLINIC
Primary Children's Hospital
320 12th Avenue
Salt Lake City, Utah 84103
Telephone: (801) 328-1611
Clinic director: Garth G. Myers, M.D.
Area served: Metropolitan Salt Lake City.
Ages accepted: Birth to 21 years.

VERMONT

*CHILD DEVELOPMENT CLINIC
Vermont State Department of Health
56 Colchester Avenue
Burlington, Vermont 05401
Telephone: (802) 863-6741 or 862-5701
Clinic director: Marion C. McKee, M.D.
Area served: State of Vermont.
Ages accepted: Birth to 21 years, emphasis on preschool age group.

VIRGINIA

*DIAGNOSTIC AND EVALUATION CLINIC
Arlington County Health Department
George Mason Center
1800 North Edison Street

Arlington, Virginia 22207
Telephone: (703) JA 7-4000, Ext. 101
Clinic director: Francis M. Mastrota, M.D.
Area served: State (except Fairfax County).
Ages accepted: Through school age.

*CHILD EVALUATION CLINIC
13 Midway Street
Bristol, Virginia 24201
Telephone: (703) 669-3031
Clinic director: Nellie Dorsey Wright, M.D.
Area served: State of Virginia, southwest area (Dickenson, Lee, Scott, Wise, Russell, Buchanan, Tazewell, Washington, Smyth, Grayson, Wythe, Bland, and Carroll Counties and the cities of Bristol and Galax).
Ages accepted: Children up to 10th birthday. Certain older children are accepted if already clients of other Bureau of Crippled Children's Clinics.
(Note – Application is made through the local health department in the area in which the patient resides.)

*CHILDREN'S MULTIPLE HANDICAPPED DIAGNOSTIC AND TREATMENT EVALUATION CENTER
Department of Pediatrics
University of Virginia School of Medicine
Charlottesville, Virginia 22903
Telephone: (703) 295-2121, Ext. 2218
Clinic director: Robert E. Merrill, M.D.
Area served: State of Virginia.
Ages accepted: Under 18 years.

*CHILD EVALUATION CLINIC
155 South Main Street
Danville, Virginia 24541
Telephone: (703) 797-1040
Clinic director: Frances Stoneburner, M.D.
Area served: State of Virginia (primarily Danville and surrounding counties).
Ages accepted: Pediatric age (through 12 years).

*CONSULTATION AND EVALUATION CLINIC
3750 Old Lee Highway
Fairfax, Virginia 22030
Telephone: (703) 273-2050
Clinic director: Pierre Lechaux, M.D.
Area served: All of Fairfax County.
Ages accepted: Birth through 12 years.

*TIDEWATER CHILD EVALUATION CLINIC
Norfolk Public Health Center
401 Colley Avenue
Norfolk, Virginia 23507
Telephone: (703) 625-6107
Clinic director: Nelson S. Payne, M.D.
Area served: Virginia State (tidewater area).
Ages accepted: Children of preschool age.

*CONSULTATION AND EVALUATION CLINIC
Medical College of Virginia
Box 152
Richmond, Virginia 23219
Telephone: (703) 770-4802
Clinic director: Ralph Ownby, Jr., M.D.
Area served: State of Virginia.
Ages accepted: Infancy through 8 years.

*ROANOKE CITY CONSULTATION AND EVALUATION CLINIC
Roanoke Health Center
515 Eighth Street, S.W.
Roanoke, Virginia 24016
Telephone: (703) DI 3-6911, Ext. 328
Clinic director: Douglas Pierce, M.D.
Area served: Approximately 14 counties in Southwest Virginia.
Ages accepted: Through age 12.

WASHINGTON

*CHILD STUDY SERVICE
Grays Harbor-Pacific Health District
223 Finch Building
Aberdeen, Washington 98520
Telephone: (206) 532-8631

Public health officer: Lauren H. Lucke, M.D.
Area served: Grays Harbor and Pacific Counties.
Ages accepted: Birth to 21 years.

*CHILD STUDY SERVICE
Whatcom-Bellingham Health District
509 Girard Street
Bellingham, Washington 98225
Telephone: (206) 733-9520
Medical director: Phillip H. Jones, M.D., M.P.H.
Area served: Whatcom County.
Ages accepted: Birth to 21 years.

*CHILD STUDY SERVICE
Kitsap-Bremerton Health District
Clare and Hebo Boulevard
Bremerton, Washington 98310
Telephone: (206) 377-4461
Clinic director: Shirley Benham, Jr., M.D., M.P.H.
Area served: Kitsap, Clallam and Jefferson Counties.
Ages accepted: Birth to 21 years.

*HANDICAPPED CHILDREN'S CENTER
Cowlitz-Wahkiakum Health District
County Court House
Kelso, Washington 98626
Telephone: (206) 393-2400
Health Officer: S. H. Gorton, M.D.
Area served: Cowlitz and Wahkiakum Counties.
Ages accepted: Birth to 21 years.

LAKELAND VILLAGE CHILD STUDY CENTER
Leslie F. Mason Memorial Hospital
Lakeland Village, Box 200
Medical Lake, Washington 99022
Telephone: (509) 299-3131
Superintendent: David Rosen.
Clinical director: Eugene Wyborney, M.D.
Area served: 19 counties of Eastern Washington.
Ages accepted: All ages.

*CHILD STUDY SERVICE
Skagit County Health Office
Court House
Mount Vernon, Washington 98273
Telephone: (206) 336-2106
Health officer: J. K. Neils, M.D.
Area served: Skagit County.
Ages accepted: Birth to 21 years.

*CHILD STUDY SERVICE
Thurston-Mason Health District
County Court House
Olympia, Washington 98501
Telephone: (206) 352-4851
Health officer: J. V. Deshaye, M.D.
Area served: Thurston and Mason
 Counties.
Ages accepted: Birth to 21 years.

*CHILD STUDY SERVICE
Benton-Franklin Health District
1218 North Fourth
Pasco, Washington 99301
Telephone: (509) 547-9737
Health officer: Vernon E. Michael, M.D.
Area served: Benton and Franklin
 Counties.
Ages accepted: Birth to 21 years.

*CHILD DEVELOPMENT AND MEN-
 TAL RETARDATION CENTER
Clinical Training Unit
University of Washington
Seattle, Washington 98105
Telephone: (206) 543-3375
Director: Robert W. Deisher, M.D.
Area served: State of Washington and
 Northwest area.
Ages accepted: Birth to 21 years.

*RETARDED CHILDREN'S CLINIC
Children's Orthopedic Hospital and
 Medical Center
4800 Sand Point Way N.E.
Seattle, Washington 98105
Telephone: (206) 524-4300
Clinic director: E. Franklin Stone, Jr.,
 M.D.
Area served: State of Washington.
Ages accepted: Birth through 16 years.

*CHILD STUDY SERVICE
Spokane County Health District
819 Jefferson Street North
Spokane, Washington 99201
Telephone: (509) 327-3331
Health officer: E. O. Ploeger, M.D.
Area served: Spokane County.
Ages accepted: Birth to 21 years.

*CHILD STUDY SERVICE
Tacoma-Pierce County Health Depart-
 ment
631 County City Building
Tacoma, Washington 98402
Telephone: (206) 383-3311
Health officer: Harlan McNutt, M.D.
Area served: Pierce County.
Ages accepted: Birth to 21 years.

*CHILD STUDY SERVICE
Clark Skamania Health District
2000 Fort Vancouver Way
Post Office Box 149
Vancouver, Washington 98663
Telephone: (206) 695-9215
Clinic director: Donald A. Champaign,
 M.D., M.P.H.
Area served: Clark, Skamania, and Klick-
 itat Counties.
Ages accepted: Birth to 21 years.

*CHILD STUDY SERVICE
Chelan-Douglas Health Department
316 Washington Street
Wenatchee, Washington 98801
Telephone: (206) 662-6167
Public health officer: Eleanor Snyder,
 M.D.
Area served: Chelan and Douglas
 Counties.
Ages accepted: Birth to 21 years.

*CHILD STUDY SERVICE
Yakima County Health District
City Hall
129 North Second
Yakima, Washington 98901
Telephone: (509) 543-0367
Health officer: Leland S. Harris, M.D.
Area served: Yakima County.
Ages accepted: Birth to 21 years.

WEST VIRGINIA

*MENTAL RETARDATION CLINIC
West Virginia University Hospital
Department of Pediatrics
Morgantown, West Virginia 26506
Telephone: (304) 542-6311
Clinic director: William G. Klingberg, M.D.
Area served: State – primarily Northern geographic area.
Ages accepted: Birth to 15 years.

*CONSULTATION AND EVALUATION CLINIC FOR MENTALLY RETARDED CHILDREN
151 Eleventh Avenue
South Charleston, West Virginia 25303
Telephone: (304) 348-3520
Clinic director: Mary S. Skinner, M.D.
Area served: State – primarily Southern geographic area.
Ages accepted: Birth through 16 years.

WISCONSIN

CHILD DEVELOPMENT CLINIC
Mental Retardation Center
Department of Pediatrics
University of Wisconsin Medical Center
1552 University Avenue
Madison, Wisconsin 53706
Telephone: (608) 262-1170
Clinic director: Harry A. Waisman, Ph. D., M.D., Professor of Pediatrics.
Area served: State.
Ages accepted: Birth to 16 years.

DEVELOPMENT EVALUATION CENTER
Central Wisconsin Colony and Training School
317 Knutson Drive
Madison, Wisconsin 53704
Telephone: (608) 249-2151, Ext. 312
Clinic director: John B. Toussaint, M.D.
Area served: State of Wisconsin.
Ages accepted: No age limits. Children and adults.

*SPECIAL DEVELOPMENTAL CLINIC
Milwaukee Children's Hospital
721 North 17th Street
Milwaukee, Wisconsin 53233
Telephone: (414) DI 4-7100
Clinic director: June Dobbs, M.D.
Area served: Milwaukee County and surrounding area.
Ages accepted: Birth to 16 years (with emphasis on the child up to 5 years).

WYOMING

*CHILD DEVELOPMENT CENTER
Wyoming State Department of Public Health
Cheyenne, Wyoming 82001
Telephone: (307) 777-7467, 777-7526
Clinic director: William K. Frankenburg, M.D.
Area served: State of Wyoming.
Ages accepted: Birth through 10 years.

The Directory for
Exceptional Children

D. R. Young (Ed.): *The Directory for Exceptional Children,* Sixth Edition. Boston, Porter Sargent, 1969, pp. 1150.

This current volume provides extensive information on the following types of services for the mentally retarded:
1. Private residential facilities for the mentally retarded. Included are over eighty pages of listings, by state, of private homes, schools, and other facilities of a private nature for the mentally retarded.
2. Private day care facilities for the mentally retarded. This extensive listing — over eighty pages — includes private schools, clinics, sheltered workshops, and training centers for mentally retarded children, which operate on a day basis only.
3. State and public facilities for the mentally retarded. Listed in this section are residential and day facilities for the mentally retarded provided by the state and various other public agencies.

This directory also lists residential facilities, schools and other facilities for children having other handicaps (e.g. psychiatric, orthopedic, sensory).

Audiovisual Materials

SELECTED FILMS DEALING WITH MENTAL RETARDATION

AIDS FOR TEACHING THE MENTALLY RETARDED   (38½ min.)   color
  Phase A (11 min.): Motor Training.
  Phase B (7½ min.): Initial Perceptual Training.
  Phase C (9 min.): Advanced Perceptual Training.
  Phase D (6 min.): Integrated Motor-Perceptual Training.
  Phase E (5 min.): Sheltered Workshop.
(Thorne Films, Inc., Boulder, Colorado)

ARTS AND CRAFTS FOR THE SLOW LEARNER   (27 min.)   color
  Craft activities suitable for six-year-old educable mentally retarded where the chronological age range from seven to thirteen are shown.

BEYOND THE SHADOWS   (26 min.)   color
  This film shows how a community can take steps to overcome its fears and prejudices and unite in a program to help its mentally handicapped. It focuses on a single city – Colorado Springs – and uncovers step-by-step action by which a few community members assisted mentally retarded children who were unable to benefit from local special education or state institutions.
  (Colorado State Department of Public Health.)

BUILDING CHILDREN'S PERSONALITIES WITH CREATIVE DANCING   (30 min.)
  color
  This award-winning film introduces basic principles of creative rhythms and motivates children to dance freely and creatively. It suggests ways of approaching creative rhythms with children and shows how to develop a sense of achievement and self-confidence on the part of children. (Baily Films)

CARE OF THE YOUNG RETARDED CHILD   (18 min.)   color
  Normal children from a few months to six years of age are shown in feeding situations. Mentally retarded children of the same ages are then shown and compared. Suggestions are given as to how equipment, treatment, and care can be adapted to help the retarded child develop. Children are shown being tested by Dr. Richard Koch, child psychologist, in Children's Hospital of Los Angeles. (International Film Bureau)

CHILDREN LIMITED (28 min.) color

Shows children in various stages of mental retardation and discusses briefly proper home treatment and care. Suggests that schools for the mentally retarded are best solution, and shows activities at Washington State School. Testing to determine the type of instruction to be given, academic and vocational training, and recreational activities. Emphasis is on what these children can do, not what they cannot. Suggests that state schools should be laboratories for studying causes of mental retardation, and emphasizes the need for more extensive programs for children limited. (Children's Benevolent Association) Colorado University Film Library.

A CHILD IS WAITING (60 min.)

Originally shown as a TV production on "Studio One," this is a drama enacted in a private school for retarded children. It tells the story of Reuben, who has been rejected by his mother and of Miss Horst, a would-be teacher who becomes emotionally involved and whose thinking is eventually clarified by the Director of the School, Dr. Clark. (National Association for Retarded Children)

CLASS FOR TOMMY (20 min.)

This is a story of a class established for the teaching of mentally retarded children in an effort to establish desirable behavioral patterns at an early age in order to allow these children more nearly normal happy lives. The picture centers around Tommy, a boy of six, and shows how classes and activities are especially devoted to aiding in overcoming both mental and physical handicaps. The film stresses the importance of teacher preparation, of teacher-parent planning, and of wholehearted cooperation between the parents and the school. (Bailey Films)

CLINICAL TYPES OF MENTAL DEFICIENCY (30 min.)

Summarizes brain conditions causing mental deficiency. Discusses classifications as to morons, imbeciles, and idiots. Suggests the magnitude of problems and social implication. Uses brain models and pneumoencephalograms to explain basic brain pathologies. Examples shown of physical and behavioral characteristics of these cases. Stresses need for institutional care and training. (Psychological Cinema Register)

EARLY DETECTION OF PKU IN THE HOSPITAL (20 min.) color

Excellent training film. Also excellent for general interest and education of the public. This film describes the Guthrie Test for PKU and techniques in its use. (Regional Offices of U.S. Children's Bureau)

EDUCABLE MENTALLY HANDICAPPED (29 min.) black & white

The characteristics and programs for handicapped children, especially the mentally retarded, are shown.

ETERNAL CHILDREN (30 min.)

Presents an intimate study of special problems of retarded children through heredity, brain injury, or various other causes, who are not equipped to keep pace in our competitive world. The film gives a frank and timely appraisal of the problem and shows care and training methods being evolved in special schools and institutions. Attention is focused on the urgent need to improve community facilities. (National Film Board of Canada)

THE FEEBLEMINDED   (44 min.)   sound
The various types of mental defectives found in an institution are shown, and also physiological and psychological differences between the clinical types described.

GIVE THEM A CHANCE   (12 min.)
Typical day in a special education class (chronological ages 7-13, mental ages 3-9), showing characteristic activities and teaching techniques. Filmed at a public school in Pennsylvania. (Audio-Visual Aids Library, Pennsylvania State University)

GROUP THERAPY FOR THE SEVERELY RETARDED   (15 min.)
Depicts an interesting experiment in therapy and demonstrates clearly the progress made by severely retarded children who were placed in an unstructured group situation.

HOME IS NO HIDING PLACE   (28 min.)
During the course of the film, the Occupation Day Center in New York City is visited as well as the Opportunity Center in Wilmington, Delaware, and St. Christopher's Hospital for Children. An introduction is made by Dr. Gunnar Dybwad.

INTRODUCING THE MENTALLY RETARDED   (30 min.)
Who are they and what are they like. Three classifications – educable (IQ 50-70), trainable (IQ 25-50), and custodial (cannot be taught anything). Two degrees of retardation: primary, which is of hereditary origin; and secondary, which has been caused by external forces. Serious mental retardation often accompanied by physical disability. Need for stimulating environment, wholesome play activities, attractive housing facilities for those who must be institutionalized, adequate hospital and laboratory accommodations, and job opportunities within their capabilities (1964). (Missouri Division of Health, Welfare)

JOURNEY FORWARD   (20 min.)   color
A visit to a center for training the retarded located in the city of Kingston-Upon-Hull, England. Shows youngsters of various degrees of retardation being trained through various directed experiences and appropriate active participation, as the film's narrator explains, beginning their "journey forward." The retarded are also shown in the vocational workshop, displaying their occupational skills which have been developed and for which, happily, they receive regular pay.

LEARNING IN SLOW MOTION   (30 min.)
Illustrates how the ability of the mentally retarded has been seriously underestimated. Both child and adult retardants shown in their normal hospital background and various stages of learning both laboratory and workshop tasks. It attempts to demonstrate the value of the experimental method in analyzing the learning problems of all types of mentally retarded and in devising training techniques to overcome their handicaps. (National Association for Retarded Children)

THE LEAST OF THESE   (20 min.)   color
Shows the operation of a residential facility program for severely mentally retarded children.

A LIGHT TO MY PATH   (15 min.)   color
Describes a community program of services for trainable mentally retarded children

from nursery school through workshops in the different grades.

MENTAL RETARDATION: Part I.   (30 min.)   color

Types of retardation; treatment and help for severely retarded physically handicapped children. There is much being learned about retardation: research and progress, assessment of chemical damage to the brain. Importance of early recognition, of retardation symptoms (1967). (Psychological Cinema Record)

MENTAL RETARDATION: Part II.

Special help and facilities for the home-bound retarded child. Classes for trainable and educable children so they can become eligible for special education classes. Vocational training in sheltered workshops. Tests for hidden abilities and work potential. New concepts in education for the trainable and educable child (1967). (Psychological Cinema Register)

MENTALLY HANDICAPPED CHILDREN GROWING UP   (30 min.)

This film, made in England, shows the difference that proper care can make in the development of the mentally retarded. Sixteen children living in the Fountain Hospital are paired according to sex, age, nonverbal intelligence, and clinical diagnosis, and one member of each pair is selected for care in a small residential unit. The marked improvement of the latter group illustrates the significance of the experiment. (National Association for Retarded Children)

MICHAEL – A MONGOLOID CHILD   (14 min.)

A fifteen-year-old mongoloid child is shown in his rural English family. He is able to do simple farm tasks. The acceptance of his handicap makes it impossible for him to leave the happy life in which he causes others a minimum of difficulty. (Psychological Cinema Register)

MODERATE RETARDATION IN YOUNG CHILDREN   (42 min.)

This film focuses on seven children five to seven years of age with mental age of four to five, or moderate retardation. It demonstrates their abilities and shows how various educational methods help them to progress. The film was produced by Western Reserve University, and a follow-up film, using the same children, is in process of development.

NEW EXPERIENCES FOR MENTALLY RETARDED CHILDREN   (36 min.)

This film depicts a program for in-service training of the moderately mentally retarded child at a residential summer camp. The relationship between school and camping program, and the training in self-care and social responsibility is clearly shown. (Virginia Department of Education)

NO LESS PRECIOUS   (14½ min.)

Walter Cronkite tells about what is being done in the field of mental retardation and presents film clips from meeting of Girl and Boy Scout troops for the retarded in Wyoming. The opening of the school for retarded in California, a year-round recreational activity for the retarded, the research currently being conducted, and many other newsworthy scenes. (National Association for Retarded Children)

ONE and TWO and THREE   (15 min.)   color

Mary, age six, who lives on a farm, tells her city cousin, Bill, age 12, all about her pets:

one horse, one lamb, two cats, three pigs, and three baby chicks. Pets are shown in groupings of one, two and three. Mary and Bill indicate "how many" with upraised fingers. The children then sing a song to the tune of "Mary had a little lamb," in which they repeat the number of animals they have observed. The film was especially made to provide the teacher of a class of mentally retarded children with a film on counting to demonstrate that two is more than one and three more than two, and that one and two make three. (Visual Aid Service, University of Illinois.)

PIONEERING DENTAL CARE OF THE RETARDED CHILD   (15 min.)   color
   Shows a special dental clinic in a hospital setting and demonstrates various techniques including the use of anesthetics. Not all retarded children need the specialized dental care described in this film, since most can attend a regular dentist.

PKU – PREVENTABLE MENTAL RETARDATION   (15 min.)   color
   Shows how mental retardation due to phenylketonuria, commonly called PKU, can be prevented by early examination and diagnosis of infants four to six weeks after birth. The series of actual cases emphasizes the need for universal checking of all children for PKU. A simple test that can be made at home is illustrated. (International Film Bureau)

THE PUBLIC HEALTH NURSE AND THE RETARDED CHILD   (24 min.)   color
   The aid which a public health nurse can provide to parents with retarded children is vividly portrayed as we observe the problems of a distraught mother greatly alleviated by the emotional support and counsel of a public health nurse, who detects that her child is retarded and marshals community facilities to provide help. Primarily designed for showing to nurses. (The University of Oklahoma and the Oklahoma State Department of Health)

RECREATIONAL ACTIVITIES FOR MENTALLY RETARDED CHILDREN (A COMMUNITY ENTERPRISE)   (28 min.)   color
   Summer recreation program for mentally retarded children. The activities include games, crafts, music, swimming, special outings, picnics and parties. Day camp program possible through cooperation of recreation department, parent group, Kiwanis and other groups. (Recreation Department, West Hartford, Conn.)

REPORT ON DOWNS' SYNDROME   (22 min.)   color
   Comprehensive statements on Downs' Syndrome, previously called Mongolism. General characteristics; treatment methods; latest findings in the area of genetics; information provided on the entire subject from first diagnosis through guidance and help offer by professional disciplines in the field of mental retardation (1964). (Psychological Cinema Register)

SELLING ONE GUY NAMED LARRY   (17 min.)
   The concise dramatic presentation of people at work. People very much like you and me – with one difference, they are mentally retarded. The film shows some of the two million mentally retarded persons presently employed on an equal basis with their co-workers, and who receive equal compensation. (National Association for Retarded Children)

SOMATIC ENDOCRINE TYPES OF NEUROPSYCHIATRIC DISORDERS   (19 min.)
   silent
   Different types of endocrinological malformations are shown, such as albinism,

hydrocephalus, cretinism, and mongolism.

TEACHING THE CHILD WHO IS RETARDED   (20 min.)   color

Classroom situations for retarded children at the University of South Dakota Summer School program. Various and detailed methods of teaching retarded children. (Visual Aids Dept., University of South Dakota, Vermillion, South Dakota)

TECHNIQUES OF NON-VERBAL PSYCHOLOGICAL TESTING   (20 min.)   color

The program of Dr. Richard Koch being conducted at the special diagnostic clinic at Children's Hospital, Los Angeles. Shows testing of children who have no speech or speech handicaps. This is an excellent film clearly demonstrating the techniques developed in this clinic. Carefully filmed close-ups of children and their performance during tests and testing procedures are highly educational. (International Film Bureau)

TESTING MULTIPLE HANDICAPPED CHILDREN   (30 min.)

Demonstrates a technique for evaluating children with multiple disabilities developed by Miss Elsa Haeussermann, Educational Consultant of Brooklyn Jewish Hospital. The testing procedure is demonstrated with three different children; one has a severe cerebral palsy condition with related speech problem, another presents severe visual and auditory impairment, and the third is hyperactive-distractible with mental retardation. (General Services Department, United Cerebral Palsy Assn.)

THERE WAS A DOOR   (35 min.)

Produced in England, this film deals with the care and treatment of the mentally retarded. It emphasizes the trend in Great Britain today for treatment, training, and social services within the general community rather than in large and remote institutions. The film is a sensitive document. It quietly presents a point of view, an overall solution, as shown by the dilemma of the family in the central situation. This dilemma concerns a mentally retarded son, now a young man, as an increasing burden to his parents. (British Information Services)

TIME IS FOR TAKING   (23 min.)   color

This film explores the world of Camp Kentan, a residential camp for educable and trainable mentally retarded children, operated by the Northern Virginia Association for Retarded Children. It is cheerfully filmed in very bright color, and accompanying music is quick tempo and gay. Camp situations, particularly the problems mentally retarded children and their counsellors face, are honestly shown.

TO SOLVE A HUMAN PUZZLE   (18 min.)

This film was produced for showing as part of the program of the International Awards Dinner of the Joseph P. Kennedy, Jr. Foundation, 1964. Scenes are shown of the award winners at work. The film then explores the problem of mental retardation from the view point of parents who tell of their personal experiences with their retarded children.

THE TOYMAKERS   (29½ min.)

Provides a compelling insight into the need for close ties between the community and the mentally retarded in institutions. The cast is composed of patients and staff of the Selinsgrove State School and Hospital in Pennsylvania, but the subject matter will be of interest to all localities. (Smith, Kline and French)

TRAINABLE MENTALLY HANDICAPPED   (29 min.)   black & white
Classrooms scenes are used to show the training methods used with mentally retarded children.

TUESDAY'S CHILD   (14 min.)   color
This film is exceptionally valuable as an introduction to the subject of mental retardation among children. Through a fictional story starring professional actors, the urgency of the problem is emphasized. Highly recommended for adult lay groups, teachers, school boards, business associations, service clubs and church groups. (National Association for Retarded Children)

THE WASSAIC STORY   (30 min.)
A visit to Wassaic State Training Schools where 4,000 patients suffering from varying degrees of mental retardation live. The film shows a habit training program for severely retarded children, a mother visiting her twenty-eight-year-old son, the disciplinary problems encountered, and other informative scenes. (National Council for Retarded Children)

WHO WILL TIE MY SHOE?   (53 min.)
Unrehearsed and candid discussion groups of both parents and retarded students are filmed, lending hitherto undisclosed insight into the sensitive area of mental retardation. The keynote is that of hope – for the parent who either did not know or would not admit that his child was afflicted and for the child himself who through specialized training can assume a useful role in his community. (National Association for Retarded Children)

SELECTED FILM STRIPS
DEALING WITH MENTAL DEFICIENCY

FILM STRIP #24 – THE FLAG AND OUR COUNTRY (Grade Level – Educable mentally retarded and primary)
Realizing the need for materials to aid the teacher in teaching democracy to the primary grades and to the educable mentally retarded, a set of four sound filmstrips are offered. They stress loyalty, love and admiration for our country.
   24-A How Our Flag is Made
   24-B Guarding Our Country
   24-C Our Country
   24-D Our Nation's Capital
Price: 4 filmstrips, 2 records and teacher's manual – $30.00

FILM STRIP #25 – OAKTREE 7 (Grade level – trainable mentally retarded and primary)
These four film strips are designed to help in teaching the mentally retarded habits of health, cleanliness, courtesy, fair play, cooperation, and safety.
   25-A Winter at Oaktree 7
   25-B Spring at Oaktree 7

25-C Summer at Oaktree 7
25-D Autumn at Oaktree 7
Price: 4 filmstrips, 2 records and teacher's manual – $30.00

FILM STRIP #26 – OCCUPATIONAL EDUCATION (Grade level – Junior and Senior High School)
These filmstrips are concerned with the unskilled and semi-skilled job areas in which the retarded and slow learner can function as adults. It offers an opportunity to bring the job and techniques into the classroom so that the pupils may realistically discuss their potential role in the working world.
117-A The Job Interview
117-B Stocker in a Super-Market
117-C The Waitress
117-D Fixing a Flat Tire
117-E How to Use Your Checkbook
117-F The Variety Store
117-G The School Cafeteria Worker
117-H The Nurses Aid
117-I The Gas Station Attendant
Price: Complete series of nine color filmstrips with teacher's manual – $35.00
Obtain from: Eye Gate House, Inc., 146-01 Archer Avenue, Jamaica 35, New York.

TRAINING THE MENTALLY RETARDED CHILD AT HOME
This film strip consists of forty-two frames and is accompanied by a regular long-play record. This program clearly and efficiently presents recommended procedures for the training of retarded children. Some of the subjects covered are the need for repetition, problems of dressing, importance of games, toilet training, the need for routine, feeding problems, and improving speech.
Obtain from: International Film Bureau, Inc., 332 S. Michigan, Chicago, Ill. 60604

SELECTED RECORDINGS
DEALING WITH MENTAL DEFICIENCY

COUNSELING WITH PARENTS AT TIME OF FIRST KNOWLEDGE OF RETARDATION
Speed: 33 1/3 r.p.m.; Running Time: 35 min.;
Rental cost: Shipping charges only.
A presentation by Reynold A. Jensen, M.D., Professor of Psychiatry and Pediatrics, University of Minnesota. Recommended highly. Can be borrowed with "Helping Parents in a Community Setting" or singly for group meetings, discussion sessions or meeting of any group interested in the problems of parents who have mentally handicapped children.

HELPING PARENTS IN A COMMUNITY SETTING
Speed: 33 1/3 r.p.m.; Rental cost: Shipping charges only.
Obtain from: The Woods School, Langhorne, Pennsylvania.
A presentation by Harriet E. Blodgett, Ph.D., Program Director at the Sheltering Arms Day School in Minneapolis, and Assistant Professor, Institute of Child Welfare, University of Minnesota.